Studies in Economic Ethics and Philosophy

Springer
Berlin
Heidelberg
New York
Barcelona
Hong Kong
London
Milan
Paris
Singapore
Tokyo

Bernard Hodgson

Economics
as Moral Science

 Springer

Prof. Bernard Hodgson
Trent University
Department of Philosophy
Peterborough, Ontario
Canada, K9J 7B8

ISSN 1431-8822
ISBN 3-540-41062-7 Springer-Verlag Berlin Heidelberg New York

Cataloging-in-Publication Data applied for
Die Deutsche Bibliothek – CIP-Einheitsaufnahme
Hodgson, Bernard: Economics as Moral Science / Bernard Hodgson. – Berlin;
Heidelberg; New York; Barcelona; Hong Kong; London; Milan; Paris; Singapore;
Tokyo: Springer, 2001
   (Studies in Economic Ethics and Philosophy)
   ISBN 3-540-41062-7

Springer-Verlag Berlin Heidelberg New York
a member of BertelsmannSpringer Science+Business Media GmbH

© Springer-Verlag Berlin · Heidelberg 2001
Printed in Germany

Hardcover Design: Erich Kirchner, Heidelberg

SPIN 10783692   42/2202-5 4 3 2 1 0 – Printed on acid-free paper

To Christine

"Hence choice is either reason motivated by desire or desire operating through reason, and such an origin of action is a human being."

Aristotle, *Nichomachean Ethics*, VI. 2.

Acknowledgements

It gives me considerable pleasure to take this opportunity to express my gratitude to those who have helped me bring this study to completion.

Among philosophers, I would especially like to register my appreciation for the assistance of the late Martin Hollis, James Leach, W. A. McMullen, and Alex Michalos. Their insightful criticisms of previous drafts of certain chapters and vigorous encouragement of the project have been invaluable. Other philosophers whose perceptive comments on earlier formulations of my ideas have enabled me to clarify central themes have included Tobias Chapman, Mary Hesse, Clifford Hooker, Isaac Levi, John McMurtry, Hugh Mellor, Wayne Norman, and Margaret Schabas.

As a philosopher, I have been particularly gratified with the enlightenment received from discussions with several economists on theoretical problems of mutual concern. Let me mention in particular the instructive observations of Avi Cohen, Jane Collier, Douglas Curtis, Torben Drewes, Shaun Hargreaves Heap, Michael Huberman, Tony Lawson, Andrew Muller, K.S.R. Murthy, Edward Nell, Ian Parker, Thomas Phillips, and Amartya Sen.

The mathematicians E. A. Maxwell and T. Noel Murphy have provided able tutelage on certain formal issues.

Of course, none of the above should be taken to agree with the views expressed in this work. Nor are they responsible for any of its possible errors.

Some of the chapters were written or rewritten while on research leaves at the University of Cambridge. For the generous hospitality and exceptionally stimulating environment in which to pursue my inquiries, I wish to thank the members of the Faculty of Philosophy, the Faculty of Economics, the Department of History and Philosophy of Science, and the Master and Fellows of St. Edmund's College. I am grateful to the British Council for the award of a Commonwealth Visiting Fellowship in support of one of the leaves.

I am obliged to Louis Taylor for his preparation of the manuscript for printing, and to Christine Hodgson and Kelly Liberty for their astute editing. Margaret Tully and Eldean Wills provided fine, patient word processing. Let me also acknowledge the wise, friendly guidance of Dr. Werner Müller and Marianne Bopp of Springer-Verlag in bringing the manuscript to publication.

Finally, to Christine, and to Matthew, Clare, and Nicholas, my deepest affection for being there with me.

A few of the sections draw, in revised form, on material in my "Economic Science and Ethical Neutrality I: The Problem of Teleology", *Journal of*

ACKNOWLEDGEMENTS

Business Ethics, 2 (1983), 237-253; "Economic Science and Ethical Neutrality II: The Intransigence of Evaluative Concepts", *Journal of Business Ethics*, 7, (1988), 321-335; and "Review of Shaun Hargreaves Heap's *Rationality in Economics*", in *Economics and Philosophy*, Vol. 8, No. 2, (1992), 290-298. I gratefully acknowledge permission to use the material mentioned.

Contents

CONTENTS

Chapter 6

Chapter 7

Chapter 8

Chapter 9

CONTENTS

Chapter 10

Chapter 11

Chapter 12

Chapter 13

CONTENTS

Chapter 14

Chapter 15

Chapter 16

Chapter 17

Chapter 1

Introduction

Since the inauguration of systematic studies in economics by the moral philosopher Adam Smith, philosophers and social scientists have engaged in an unflagging controversy regarding the proper method of inquiry to adopt in the construction of economic science. On the one hand, economic theory has been conceived as an essentially normative discipline which, by applying fundamental ethical concepts and principles, prescribes the canons according to which agents ought to engage in the production and exchange of material commodities. On the other hand, it has been argued that economics consists of a set of purely descriptive hypotheses explaining *de facto* regularities in the behaviour of producers and consumers, rather than a set of norms recommending justifiable forms of such activity. However, under the persistent influence of "positivist" doctrines of scientific method, in particular those advocating the disparate character of "values" in contrast to "facts", the latter interpretation has become the orthodoxy among economic methodologists. Hence the prevailing wisdom concludes that economic theory incorporates no categorical moral imperatives stating what an agent ought, on moral grounds, to do. Rather, to the extent that economics is concerned at all with ethical questions, only prudential imperatives are countenanced: such directives take ethical goals and values in the realm of economic action as given, and simply recommend optimal means for realizing these ends. But, somehow, economic theory itself comprises a body of "positive" knowledge, entirely "neutral" with respect to such external value considerations.

Although this old methodological warhorse has been flogged countless times, it continues to run aimlessly with undiminished energy. My concern in this essay will be with the present stage of its run, and it will be critical to begin by noting that both of the above groups, for all the polemic they direct against each other, do, by and large, *share* a basic philosophical doctrine – namely, a belief in the so-called "is-ought" dichotomy. That is, both sides uphold the thesis that normative and descriptive statements belong to different logical categories, that "values" are different in kind from "facts", that moral conclusions cannot be deduced from a set of non-moral factual premises, and other variants of the same theme. Consequently, it is understandable that if one party to the dispute were to affirm that explanations of economic behaviour demand a commitment to fundamental ethical principles, then it would conclude such explanations need to be of a different type than explanations of the motions of material bodies whose movements, in themselves, do not generate ethical questions; whereas, if the other party were especially concerned about subscribing to a cardinal tenet of logical empiricism, that of preserving a "unity of method" between the natural and social sciences, then it would be incumbent upon this party to continue arguing the irrelevance of moral imperatives to the explanatory force of economic theories, believing along with their opponents that the inclusion of such imperatives would entail a division of methods between natural and social science. And, of course, this is what has in fact taken place.

Moreover, as I see it, this adherence of both camps to the "is-ought" dichotomy is the main reason why our methodological warhorse has never reached its goal. In other words, both sides have been flogging the old horse with the same "fact-value" whip, albeit attempting to move it in opposite directions. Only by changing whips, in attempting to *bridge* the gap between the normative-descriptive bifurcation into which the interpretation of economic theory has fallen, will the flogging succeed. Such will be my ultimate strategy in this study. However, it is important to observe that I say *bridge* rather than *collapse* the gap; for, although the main burden of my argument will be to establish the essential inter-relatedness between economic values and facts, it will not be assumed, in the following discussion, that they are identical. In other words, a critical *synthesis* of the normative and descriptive dimensions of economic science will be my primary objective.

In order to provide a unified framework for conducting the inquiry, recourse will be made, for the most part, to a particular, but foundational case-study of contemporary economic theory – i.e., the neo-classical theory of individual consumer choice under conditions of certainty (to be called CCT). Now it is a considerable achievement that consumer theory has recently been developed to account for choices under less than certain conditions. However, our investigation will primarily focus on certainty situations. For most of the questions of the logical structure and moral presuppositions which we will pose in this enquiry can be adequately and more clearly handled by addressing the simplified case of choice under certainty.

Nevertheless, in order to avoid misunderstanding, it should be stressed at the outset that the fundamental theoretical views we shall argue for in this study are applicable to *both* choice under conditions of certainty and uncertainty. In other words, the basic results of our analyses are *not displaced* by a transition to a model of choice under uncertainty. Indeed, with respect to questions of the "logical structure" of CCT, we shall see that a move to uncertainty situations will only *ramify* the theses we shall defend.

It will be appropriate to introduce our investigations by anticipating the main theoretical paths that I shall follow. Although such a summation will unavoidably take on the air of a "manifesto", it is hoped that the arguments of the subsequent chapters will provide adequate support for the claims expressed.

In setting forth what has been received as the "orthodox" conception of scientific method in economics, neo-classical theorists have followed central tenets of empiricist philosophy. In particular, the orthodox view endorses two standard doctrines of the empiricist conception of scientific theory-construction:

1. The explanatory principles of scientific theories are comprised of contingent generalizations that are subject to empirical test.

2. The scientist *qua* scientist follows a prescription of "ethical neutrality" or "value freedom". Categorical moral judgments are not presupposed by the statements of the theories he constructs.

It is the primary intention of this study to philosophically discredit the application of the second doctrine to neo-classical economic theory.

Our inquiry begins by setting the problem of the ethical neutrality of CCT within the framework of certain problems of theory-construction in economics. It is found that explanations within CCT can be interpreted as special cases of action-theoretic explanations. But, in this light, it is argued that explanations within CCT do not, *at a first level of analysis*, meet our first empiricist requirement governing scientific method. For its basic explanatory principle is analysed as an a priori, empirically unfalsifiable generalization.

An action-theoretic understanding of CCT also elicits the fact that the explanatory system of CCT is intended to directly apply to a *rational* agent – rational economic man (*homo economicus*) in his consumer behaviour. But *homo economicus* is observed to be an idealized agent, endowed with certain cognitive and affective traits that can only be approximated by actual agents. Accordingly, CCT is interpreted as taking on the form of a *theoretical idealization*.

An appreciation of the preceding rationality assumption provides the key to identifying the precise kind of theory CCT articulates. In sum, it is argued that, *in its conceptually prior form*, CCT formulates a normative theory of rational behaviour. Such a normative theory, moreover, is argued, against the second empiricist doctrine, to presuppose moral values.

Within this perspective, a shift from conditions under which an agent has certain knowledge as to the consequences of his decisions to those wherein he is uncertain as to outcomes is found to have important political implications for the moral dimensions of CCT. Here we shall observe that the normative capstone of neo-classical economics is to be found in the subsumption of CCT within an overarching theory of social choice – more particularly, in the demonstration within "welfare economics" that a perfectly competitive economy will deliver a general equilibrium that is, in a well-defined sense, socially optimal. In this, the neo-classical synthesis aligns itself with the classical tradition wherein the "system of natural liberty" gives expression to the natural harmony of each with all. But against such a back-drop it is assumed that the individual agent-consumer is sovereign, and most critically, remains so across any evidential context with the general presupposition that the individual is the best judge of what is good for him. However, once an individual consumer is faced with uncertain situations, we shall argue that such an assumption of economic individualism is no longer reliable, and, hence, that the support it lends to the classical connection of individual liberty with the communally valuable is significantly undermined.

From the preceding "holistic" viewpoint, the theory of individual choice is best understood as part of a total theoretical system for both conceptualizing the economic phenomena it explains and recommending the order exhibited by such phenomena as conducive to our common good. Moreover, each of the original postulates or "axioms" of CCT are "essential" to the systemic integrity of the total neo-classical framework: we shall see that none of them can be infirmed without putting the explanatory *cum* normative import of the overall system at serious risk.

Of course, such a necessarily true, normative idealization that was not ethically neutral would be anathema to an empiricist understanding of scientific method. However, at a final level of analysis, this inquiry contends that CCT can satisfy "liberalized" empiricist canons for the explanation of actual behaviour and the validation of explanatory hypotheses.

Towards this end, a connection between normative and descriptive factors is first established for individual behaviour by arguing that normative principles demand a psychological vindication in the form of motivations to follow such principles. Such a requirement is then applied to CCT in its normative reading as recommending rules for rational choice.

Secondly, by viewing individual economic choice in its political environment, a mechanism is elucidated for *converting* an originally a priori, normative theory into a testable empirical science of actual behaviour. Such a mechanism is analysed as operating through the application of institutional constraints to economic motivations.

We shall find that such social constraints may be based on moral criteria governing the selection of economic goals. But if economics is, in this way, to become a moral science, and yet remain a rational form of inquiry, it must first be ascertained whether ethical principles are themselves rationally justifiable. Our final study takes up this classic philosophical problem in terms of its relation to the justification of CCT and the concept of human freedom presupposed by neo-clasical economics. However, the investigations end with scepticism that the moral principles presupposed by CCT *are* sound ones.

Chapter 2

Theory-Construction in Economic Science

An inquiry into the logic of theory-construction in economics portends considerably more than an exercise in logic. Formal perplexities in this science have had substantive effects. More specifically, confusion concerning the epistemic status of their explanatory hypotheses and the scientific method for validating such statements has frequently led economists to formulate and accept unsound theories. A critical examination of this methodological confusion among economists would appear, therefore, to be a prerequisite for an appreciation of the explanatory force of economic theories in general. Such an investigation is the intent of this chapter.

My analysis will revolve around the so-called "problem of verification" in economics – to what extent do, or need, economists subscribe to appropriate scientific canons of confirmation in accepting or rejecting their explanatory hypotheses? This general issue can be usefully discussed in the context of two inter-related sub-problems – a) the use of theoretical idealizations in economics, and b) the alleged "analyticity" or necessary truth of economic generalizations. However, all such inquiries into the logical structure of theoretical reasoning in economics will only be pursued insofar as they shed light on, give rise to, and provide the conceptual materials for examining the primary concern of this study – the entrenched normative-descriptive controversy concerning the nature of economic theories. But it is not to be supposed that this relation is not mutual. For, as will become evident, confusions with respect to the normative-descriptive status of economic theory are often at the source of errors concerning the manner of confirming economic laws.

In dealing with questions of the philosophical issues involved in the construction of an economic theory, it invariably promotes the plausibility of an analysis to have reference to an actual case-study. The theory of consumer choice will prove instructive, not only since it provides clear and serious problems concerning the role of moral judgments in micro-economics, but also because choice theory supplies the foundational concepts and postulates on which a good deal of "mainstream" economic theory rests.[1] The particular form of the theory of choice to which we will have recourse is the neo-classical one of individual choice under conditions of certainty, as typically represented by indifference curve analysis.[2] In this model, an individual consumer is confronted with a decision to choose between a set of alternative combinations of (at least) two commodities subject to a budget constraint determined by the size of his income. The criteria for certainty or complete knowledge are specified by the conditions that (1) the consumer knows all possible alternatives available to him in the decision-situation and (2) he can ascertain the unique outcome which will infallibly (rather than probably) follow each choice, in terms of which of the various combinations will yield equivalent utility or subjective satisfaction, and which ones will yield greater or less satisfaction relative to others. The consumer, furthermore, is *free* to buy whatever he can afford, in the sense that, within the range of his income, he is not subject to coercion or prevention in carrying out his purchases.

Consumer choice theory, of the indifference curve variety, is regularly systematized by beginning with a set of primitive axioms concerning the individual consumer, S, confronted with a choice between and comparison of alternative combinations (A,B,C, etc.) of various commodities (q,r,s, etc.). For example, A might represent a combination of 4 operas and 7 football games. The axioms of this version of consumer choice theory (hereafter labelled CCT) follow:

A_1 (comparability or completeness) Given any two alternatives to compare, say A and B, any consumer either prefers A to B, B to A, or is indifferent between A and B.

A_2 (non-satiation) No consumer is sated with any particular commodity. That is, he prefers to possess more of any available commodity.

A_3 (transitivity or consistency) For any three commodity combinations, say A, B and C, if S prefers A to B and B to C, then he prefers A to C. Likewise if S is indifferent between A and B and between B and C, then he is indifferent between A and C. In this sense, the consumer is *consistent* in his choices. Given A_1 and A_3, we can say that the consumer is able to rank, in ordinal manner, commodity-bundles in order of preference.

A_4 (diminishing marginal rate of substitution) Roughly, this postulate asserts that the amount of y the consumer is willing to give up to get an additional unity of x becomes progressively smaller as the quantity of y diminishes. Consumers are relatively stingy with relatively scarce goods.

7

Now, on the basis of these four postulates,[3] economists intend, in a purely "positive" vein, to explain and predict the behaviour of the individual "rational" consumer – the one who employs the optimal means in seeking to maximize his "utility" or subjective satisfaction from the possession of material commodities – given the constraints of his budget or income and complete knowledge or certainty as to outcomes. (The optimal means is one that cannot be bettered towards the realization of an objective although it might be equalled.) Such prediction and explanation would be claimed by the majority of neo-classical economists to be of the orthodox "deductive-nomological" variety. That is, the four axioms are set forth as contingent universal generalizations or causal "laws" which, in conjunction with singular statements expressing "antecedent conditions", logically entail a statement of the item of behaviour to be explained or predicted.[4] (Such explanation might, of course, take place through the deduction of lower-level generalizations or theorems which, in turn, imply the description of the event to be explained.) In now standard terminology, the conjoint statement of the explanatory laws and initial conditions is called the "explanans", whereas the description of the event to be explained is designated the "explanandum".

For example, employing our axioms as premises in conjunction with particular budget constraints, economists deduce the theorem that, for any consumer, the point of equilibrium, or allocation of income that maximizes his utility, will be the one at which he purchases that combination of commodities wherein the ratio of the marginal utilities of any two goods is equal to the ratio of their respective prices or, equivalently, the one at which the marginal rate of substitution of one good for another is equal to the ratio of their prices.[5]

In terms of the conventional geometrical representation:

Let x be one economic commodity – e.g., shirts.
Let y be another economic commodity – e.g., ties.

Points A, B, C, etc. represent particular commodity-bundles or combinations of x and y – e.g., (5 shirts, 4 ties).

Let I be the budget or disposable income of consumer S.

Let the price of x be Px.
Let the price of y be Py.

I/Py - I/Px represents the budget line formulating the income constraint and delimiting the set of attainable commodity-bundles for S. Its equation, then, will be: $PxX + PyY = I$.

MM, NN, OO, etc. are our indifference curves. Single indifference curves describe a locus of points which stand for commodity-bundles among which S is indifferent. Higher indifference curves represent higher levels of utility.

Our indifference map for consumer S follows:

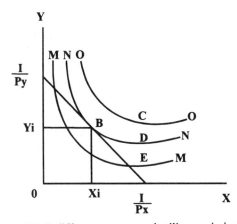

Figure 2.1: Indifference curves and utility maximization

At B, $\dfrac{MUx}{MUy} = \dfrac{Px}{Py} = MRSxy$, where MU = marginal utility and MRS = marginal rate of substitution. At this point, i.e., where the budget line is tangent to the highest attainable indifference curve, S is in equilibrium and is maximizing his utility.

1. Verification and Idealization

Although CCT, along with its extensions and subsumptions,[6] will offer an instructive case-study for the philosophical problems raised by economic theory that we will examine in this inquiry, we may return now to the specific issues we have claimed are generated by economic theory-construction.

In this particular context, the philosophical importance of the explanatory system formulated by CCT lies not in the validity of specific deductions, which are, in fact, valid and mathematically elegant; rather, philosophical discussion centres on the theory itself as it functions in explanation. One main issue arises with the frequent claim that economic theories belong to the class of scientific theories designated as "idealizations", which theories present unique difficulties with respect to confirming their truth. What then is the logical structure of scientific idealizations, how are they confirmed, and why are they employed? Do economic idealizations differ in important methodological respects from natural scientific ones? Indeed, as Rudner correctly points out,[7] a good deal of economic theory *is* idealization, and, hence, an inquiry into the "idealizing" that takes place in economics will go some way in appraising the current explanatory status of economic theory itself.

"Ideal" theories in natural science comprise general laws characterized by the fact that they are stated as universally valid under certain extreme or ideal conditions, which it is usually physically impossible for actual phenomena to fully exemplify. Consider, for instance, the law of the lever in physical mechanics. This statement is formulated for perfectly rigid and homogeneous bars, extreme values which are not completely realizable, but only approximated by actual bars. Likewise, the zero volumes and masses of molecules represent extreme values of the variables in the statement of the Boyle-Charles law for ideal gases.

In similar fashion, the ideal character of our theory of consumer behaviour, CCT, is indicated especially by the limiting condition of the consumer's *complete knowledge*: (a) his awareness of all the alternative choices available to him and (b) his certainty concerning the unique outcome of every possible choice in terms of its capacity to generate subjective satisfaction or utility. Such extreme information-gathering abilities on the part of the individual consumer is rarely, if ever, exemplified in concrete cases.

Sometimes, methodologists emphasize a *transitory* status for idealizations. That is, it is suggested that as scientific investigation advances, further "disturbing factors" are included among the antecedent conditions of "ideal" hypotheses rendering them more literally true, "realistic", or accurately descriptive of empirical phenomena. Related to this suggestion is the frequent claim that idealizations are simply *heuristic devices* rather than genuine theoretical systems. They are to be construed as techniques which, by "isolating" or abstracting a few prominent causal variables determining a complex event, and in ascertaining the extent to which these main variables fall short of being the sufficient cause of the event, assist the scientist in *discovering* the other causal variables; in this way, the scientist becomes capable of formulating a more exact, "realistic" general law which can then be subjected to empirical test.

For instance, the basic economic "law of demand" that "whenever the price of a commodity rises, less units are purchased at successively higher prices" has sometimes been interpreted as a *rule of procedure* to the effect that the economist should determine the market conditions which would falsify such a simplified statement of the law. Under the circumstances of the celebrated "snob appeal", for example, certain goods are purchased for the prestige that only their relatively higher prices provide; accordingly, if the price of a "prestige" commodity rises, one is just as likely to purchase the same quantity as held at the lower price. However, although this "heuristic-device" characterization is true of some uses of idealizations, it errs by over-emphasis, in not recognizing the alternative employment of idealizations as themselves full-fledged explanatory theories. Furthermore, it errs in failing to appreciate the methodological rationale behind the explanatory use of what have been called "theoretical idealizations". Why then are idealizations employed as explanatory systems rather than more "realistic" counterparts?

The wisdom behind this use lies in the fact that descriptive truth is not the only criterion of rational acceptability for scientific theories, and that sometimes such factual truth is increased only at the cost of other important "cognitive utilities". In particular, the incorporation of further boundary conditions within a theoretical idealization, in order to enhance the descriptive truth of the general hypotheses involved, might be attainable only at the expense of significantly diminishing the simplicity in the statement of these hypotheses. However, it often happens that it is just this simplicity which enormously facilitates the mathematical formulation of the hypotheses, which in turn is often the *sine qua non* for the deductive systematization of a theory – that is, the ordering of a theory into general laws and their implied consequences, whether deduced theorems or descriptions of specific events. Moreover, such deductive power well promotes the testing, predictive capacity, and applicability of a scientific theory. Hence, scientific wisdom prescribes that in weighing the cost of increasing descriptive truth against simplicity in statement, one sometimes must give greater weight to the latter. Otherwise, the construction of a particular theory might not be possible at all.

The use of theoretical idealizations in neo-classical economic theory, moreover, has invoked just such a consideration. In illustration, we might conveniently refer back to our theory of consumer behaviour, CCT. Here, we may observe that the postulates of CCT (A_1-A_4), if understood in their exact formulation, are in fact descriptively false statements. The most controversial, albeit crucial postulate, is transitivity axiom A_3 which characterizes the consumer as being able and, in fact, ordering his preferences amongst any

11

three commodity-bundles in a fully determinate way such that there is a single best option. Again, such an ordering provides the interpretation for the consistency of consumer behaviour. But such normal experience as indulging in the pleasure of random variability in consumption is at odds with the universal truth which the completely general, non-statistical formulation of the transitivity axiom claims.[8] An even more critical difficulty, impinging on the universal truth of the transitivity axiom, is provided by situations in which utility is a multi-dimensional concept.[9] Consider the case in which an individual consumer, John, prefers choice A to B and B to C based on one factor of subjective satisfaction, but C to A based on a different factor; hence, John might prefer (A) a Ferrari, to (B) a Mercedes, on grounds of superior elegance, and (B) to (C) a Buick, for the same reason, but C to A on the different basis of durability. Such an empirical finding, however, would refute the universal factual truth-claim of the transitivity axiom, since John prefers A to B, and B to C, but not A to C. (See Paul Anand[10] for some contexts where such multi-dimensionality ensures intransitivities.)

Nevertheless, as illustrated in Figure 2.1 above, axioms A_1-A_4, in their completely general formulation, can be represented geometrically by a set of non-intersecting, negatively sloping, convex indifference curves, while the consumer's income constraint can be represented by a linear function defining a straight line. However, if we were to attempt to increase the descriptive "realism" of CCT by adding further "boundary conditions" to any of the axioms, we would radically alter the shape of the curves. For instance, if in intending to increase the factual accuracy of postulate 3, we were to permit intransitive preferences under the special conditions of "multi-dimensionality", we could no longer count on the curves not intersecting. But without such a property, the prediction of the purchase which would lead to consumer equilibrium or maximization of utility could no longer be determined as the point at which the budget line is tangent to the highest indifference curve, as there would no longer be any guarantee of a uniquely highest curve.[11] Hence, neo-classical economists have insisted that the gain in the use of a mathematically precise concept of equilibrium, in simplifying and systematizing both descriptive and normative uses of the theory of choice, outweighs the loss in "realism" due to the descriptive inaccuracy of the axioms. Moreover, they have pointed out that descriptions of real economic events can always be compared as to the degree to which they approximate the realization of equilibrium states.[12] Manifestly, the admonition that economic theories be made "mathematically tractable" has been more than a plea by mathematicians for employment.[13]

However, it must be admitted that the scientific status of idealizations in economic theory has not been highly regarded by many philosophers of science, some of whom have denied them any explanatory power.[14] In this context, one persistent charge levelled against economic idealizations or "ideal types" has been that the fundamental technical terms of such theories lack an adequate empirical interpretation. Such an interpretation would provide observable, experiential conditions for the application of these terms to particular entities. But, in the absence of such interpretation, it is claimed that the scope of application of idealized economic theories has remained vague, and has thus barred their hypotheses from fulfilling a fundamental empiricist condition of adequacy for the constituents of scientific explanation – viz., they are capable, at least in principle, of observational test.[15]

It seems to me, however, that the preceding criticism is entirely misdirected in the case of neo-classical economics. Indeed, as we shall argue in Chapter 4, neo-classical theorists have been *excessively* concerned to provide an empirical interpretation or "operational clarity" for their technical terms. And, ironically, as we shall further argue, such an over-scrupulous scientific conscience has actually impoverished the explanatory power of economic theory.

Nevertheless, let us reconstruct an empirical interpretation of the basic concepts of our idealized theory of consumer choice, CCT, that, although not explicitly provided by neo-classical economists, would give expression to their intent.

Within the neo-classical framework, the most important technical term of CCT is that of "preference". Utility or subjective satisfaction is not considered a basic concept of CCT but is itself defined in terms of preference. Thus, the central notion of the combinations of goods which yield equal "utility" is defined as those combinations between which the consumer is indifferent:

A has equal utility to B (for consumer S)
= df. S is indifferent between A and B.

It is this fact which has led some "ordinalists" to contend that their theories, such as CCT, permit the economist to dispense with the concept of utility altogether in the explanation of consumer behaviour. In any case, the operative concept for ordinalists to define becomes that of "preference" (and thereby its negative correlate "indifference").[16] Now, preference belongs to that class of terms which are most suitably construed as dispositional ones, designating, roughly, an internal "standing" state of an individual, characterized by a tendency to certain overt behaviour (response) under certain observable circumstances (stimuli). Moreover, the other basic technical terms of CCT, those of "wanting" and "believing", are likewise most appropriately interpreted as dispositional in character.[17] But the obstacles to supplying explicit definitions in terms of observables for disposition terms are well-known. Explicit definitions provide necessary and sufficient criteria for the application of a term in any context; however, one fundamental difficulty with disposition terms is that no overt response or symptom of a disposition is a necessary condition for its presence. A scowl might be a symptom of anger, but a person can be angry without scowling.

A requisite alternative means, proposed by Carnap,[18] for introducing disposition terms into a scientific theory is that of (a chain of) reduction sentences. A (bilateral) reduction sentence for a particular disposition term, D, is of the logical form, $Cx \supset (Dx \equiv Rx)$, where, if object x meets test conditions C, then D is true of x if and only if x manifests response R. It is evident that reduction sentences generally can furnish only a partial, conditional determination of the criteria of application of a technical predicate on the basis of observables, in particular for those objects which satisfy certain test conditions (i.e., C).

Consider, then, that we introduce the dispositional concept "preference" into theory CCT by a reduction sentence. Let 'D' then represent "preference", 'C' and 'R' the specific test conditions and manifest reactions respectively for preference, both 'C' and 'R' being expressible in observational vocabulary. Hence, the determination of meaning for D is partial in that for objects not meeting test conditions C, whether or not they possess dispositional property D remains "open" or unspecified. Now economists constructing CCT have generally stipulated that overt choice behaviour, that is, the actual purchasing of a commodity-bundle,[19] is to be considered as determining the observable response 'R'. The observable test conditions, 'C', invoked are twofold and quite demanding:

1) Consumer freedom – S's behaviour must not be subject to

a) external coercion, like threat, or

b) prevention of (i) the external kind as exemplified, for example, by the strict governmental rationing of a particular commodity or (ii) the "internal" variety due to psychological impediments such as "abnormal" phobias towards the purchasing of certain kinds of commodities.

In sum, if a consumer's behaviour satisfies the condition of freedom, then any action (i.e., purchase) in which he wants to engage is both physically and psychologically possible for him to perform.

2)   Consumer information – S must be "adequately informed" with respect to the available commodity-bundles at the time of choice. Let us take this condition as being met by directly presenting S with A and B, but no other bundles, and mentioning he may choose either one.

Accordingly, an expanded schema of a reduction sentence, $Cx \supset (Dx \equiv Rx)$, introducing the "preference" of any consumer, S, might be roughly:

(s) (t) {(S is both free and adequately informed at time t) $\supset$ [(S prefers A to B at t) $\equiv$ (S purchases (chooses) A and S does not purchase B at t)]}.

or verbally: if any consumer, S, acts freely and is aware of the fact that A and B are his only alternatives at time t, then S prefers commodity-bundle A to B at t, if and only if he chooses (i.e., purchases) A but not B at t.

Notice, then, that the test conditions and response behaviour expressed by reduction sentences can be formulated exclusively in terms of observational data. Such sentences, then, provide an empirical interpretation for the dispositional property expressed by D. Hence, although such an interpretation is, as explained, only partial, nevertheless, *given* the presence of the test conditions for an object x, the occurrence of the response furnishes conclusive experiential evidence, solely on the basis of observational findings, that x has property D. But the axioms of our paradigm economic theory, CCT, incorporate only such dispositional terms as its theoretical vocabulary. Hence, in explicit rebuttal of the familiar objection, we may observe that the postulates of a foundational theoretical idealization in economics *are* amenable to empirical test. Economic idealizations need not lack explanatory power on these grounds.

2. Explanation and Necessary Truth

We argued above that the basic technical concepts of the theory of consumer choice (CCT) could be given an empirical interpretation and that, thereby, the individual axioms of this theoretical idealization are rendered testable. However, we may not rest on empiricist laurels. For we shall see that the fundamental generalization actually employed by CCT in the explanation of consumer choice requires the axioms of CCT *to be used in combination.*

And, in this context, we shall find that the problem of the imperviousness of economic idealizations to empirical test returns with a vengeance. In addressing this problem, furthermore, we shall observe that the principles of a *positivistic* empiricism must be left behind if we are to understand the logic of explanation provided by CCT.

The grounds for such major findings are to be found in the real source of the difficulty concerning the testability of theoretical idealizations in economics. I refer here to the controversy concerning the "analyticity" versus the "empirical content" of basic economic laws and theories. It is often alleged by empiricist methodologists that the ideal economic generalizations deployed in putative explanations are logically necessary or analytic, not subject to empirical test, in the sense that their assertions are true by definition or by the meanings of the terms used. Accordingly, it is further claimed that such a priori truths possess no explanatory or predictive power for actual empirical phenomena. In reference to social scientific hypotheses in general, Rudner, for example, comments ... "confusing the statements constitutive of contingent idealizations with analytic statements has perhaps been one of the main sources of the mix-up concerning idealizations in the social sciences".[20]

On a straightforward level, it must be admitted that Rudner's charge is justified in the use which many economists make of their ideal hypotheses and theories. As Hutchison notices,[21] it has frequently been an irresistible move for economists, in attempting to secure their ideal hypotheses from falsification, or preserve their universality, to turn them into tautologous assertions.[22] But the cost of such a move has, of course, been to simultaneously secure these generalizations from explanatory power. For instance, consider that an economist conventionally *defines*, as some do, the concept of demand as ... "the increase (decrease) in consumption at successively lower (higher) prices". Then, obviously, the assertion that ... "Whenever the price of a commodity decreases, then demand increases" is analytically true, entailed by the definition of demand. But such a tautologous statement cannot furnish a scientific explanation for changes in price phenomena.

The preceding complaint against the analyticity of some ideal economic hypotheses and theories, though important and well-taken, is, nevertheless, a familiar and obvious one. A more perplexing and deeper question concerning the "analyticity" of economic theories may be directed toward the entire "conceptual system" underlying foundational but idealized economic theories, particularly our theory of consumer behaviour, CCT. Our elucidation of this question will reveal the fundamental conceptual connection of consumer choice theory with general action-theory. It will prove useful, therefore, to introduce the problem at its origin in action-theory.

The task, then, can be described as one of determining the logical character and scientific adequacy of the explanation of human actions in terms of a conceptual system involving the "ordinary concepts" of wants, beliefs and preferences. Now, it has been a fundamental empiricist tenet that the logical status of the relation between the antecedent and consequent of a law-like generalization cannot take the form of a logically necessary connection, but must be a contingent one. In other words, falsification of empirical laws by observational findings must be at least conceivable. *A fortiori*, since the empiricist tradition generally maintains that scientific explanation takes place by subsuming the event to the explained under empirical "covering-laws", it insists that the explanatory principles of adequate explanations be accessible to disconfirming experiential evidence. But the nomological explanation of human actions in terms of wants and beliefs presents puzzling difficulties for this criterion of acceptable scientific explanation. Basically, the problem can be stated in the form of a dilemma – either our explanatory laws for human action are empirically false and therefore unacceptable, or, in the attempt to make them true, they become empirically unfalsifiable and again unacceptable. Perhaps a simple illustration will best explicate this point.

Suppose, then, that the action to be explained is John's taking, while driving, a detour through an out-of-the-way, albeit picturesque village called Petersville. We might proffer a putative explanation of this action by claiming that John wanted to satisfy his aesthetic sensibilities and believed the indirect route through Petersville to be conducive to satisfying this want. Consider further that the proposed explanation is admittedly incomplete, in the sense of being elliptic, for it tacitly presupposes but does not mention a universal law, call it G, concerning human action, to the effect that roughly:

> G: Whenever any person, S, wants ϕ and believes p – that doing A is a means of attaining ϕ – then S will do A.

Accordingly, G, in conjunction with singular statements affirming antecedent conditions supplying particular values of S, ϕ and p, might be claimed as logically implying and thereby explaining the taking of the detour through Petersville.

(In this case, S = John who:

(1) wants ϕ = aesthetic enjoyment

17

(2) believes p = the detour to be conducive to achieving ϕ

(3) does A = takes detour).

However, in correct criticism, someone might immediately point out that G is not universally true, as it is claimed to be, and therefore unacceptable as an explanatory principle.[23] Various kinds of empirical falsehood to which G might be subject could be mentioned. Some of the most important of them would be those (i) wherein S wants ψ more than ϕ (i.e., S prefers ψ to ϕ), (ii) wherein performing A is physically or psychologically impossible for a particular S, and (iii) wherein S believes that doing B is a better means of achieving ϕ than doing A. Consider, for instance, that the following facts are actually true of John in our illustration. He did in fact desire aesthetic enjoyment, but believed that the original route *not taken* was more conducive to such pleasure than the indirect detour. But in any case he preferred to visit a friend in Petersville more than enjoy the scenery on the original, direct route and this was his operative reason for making the detour. (Indeed, it might have been the case that he wanted above all to take the direct route but the road was blocked off due to construction, thereby making it physically impossible to do so.)

Suppose, therefore, that in the light of these various kinds of counter-examples to our putative explanatory generalization, G, we reformulate G to eliminate such exceptions to its truth. Is there a general law available to serve as an explanatory premise in explanations of human actions that is in fact universally true? Let us consider the following schematic statement (G') as an appropriate candidate:

> G': Whenever any person S (1) wants ϕ, (2) does not possess any preferred want ψ, (3) believes p – that performing A is a means of attaining ϕ, (4) does not believe that any other action is a better or equally efficient means of attaining ϕ than doing A, (5) A is not physically or psychologically impossible for S, then (6) S will do A.[24]

Now, suppose we grant that the antecedent conditions of G' are sufficiently numerous to establish its universal truth or applicability. Nevertheless, we are then confronted with the new problem that our strengthened hypothesis, G', appears to be logically, or better, analytically true in that it is difficult, if not impossible, to conceive of an observational finding which could disconfirm it.[25] But, if G' is such an analytic principle, how can it function as an explanatory or predictive premise in a scientific argument?

This dilemma, furthermore, is directly relevant to the explanatory status of fundamental economic theories, especially our theory of consumer choice, CCT. For as we shall establish below, CCT can be readily construed as a special case of general action-theory, namely the case wherein the values of ϕ, the desires or wants of an agent, are restricted to economic goals, that is the subjective satisfaction derived from the use of material commodities. And, not surprisingly, a more precise examination of the manner in which CCT actually functions as a special case of general action-theory will reveal that the analyticity difficulty remains just as serious in CCT. Such an investigation will, moreover, help us to locate the precise source of the analyticity problem for economic theories, especially the theory of choice.[26]

More specifically, consider that the particular action to be explained is a piece of consumer choice behaviour. (As mentioned above,[27] in contemporary economic theory, consumer choices are identified with actual commodity purchases.) We find then that such an (external) choice could be explained by subsumption under a generalization, G", comprised of an antecedent consisting of a conjunction of the axioms and constraints of CCT, and an item of consumer choice as the implied consequent. (G" will be schematized below.) But by imposing a suitable restriction on G', G" can be seen to be simply a special case of G'; consequently, the charge that G' is analytically true recurs for G". The qualification consists, as mentioned above, in confining the human wants mentioned in G' to the economic ones of desiring satisfaction from the possession and use of material commodities. But such a restriction does not alter the apparent analyticity or necessary truth of G'; it simply limits the range of values of ϕ in the antecedent condition (1), S wants ϕ. (And given this restriction, the kind of action specified in the consequent of G' will, of course, also be limited in G" to the economic action of a consumer choosing, that is actually purchasing, a commodity-bundle to satisfy his wants.) Accordingly, let $A_1 \ldots A_4$ represent the axioms of CCT, C the conjunction of constraints (income, freedom, complete knowledge), S any consumer, and B an economic choice consisting of a consumer purchase. Economic generalization, G", then, might be schematized as:

$$G": (S)\,(B)\,[(A_1 \,\&\, A_2 \,\&\, A_3 \,\&\, A_4)\,\&\,C] \;\rightarrow\; B$$

or, verbally, if any consumer, S, satisfies axioms A_1-A_4 and is acting under constraints C, then he will perform actions of kind B.

The fact that G" is merely a special case of G', and in this sense that the theory of consumer behaviour, CCT, only a special case of general action-theory, can now be more fully disclosed by the following factors:

19

a) Axiom 2 of CCT (A_2 of G"), specifying that the consumer is not sated, provides an equivalent counterpart[28] for condition (1) (S wants ϕ) in G'. That is, given Axiom 2, it is true that S, now a particular consumer, at least wants some K, a sub-class of the possible values of ϕ, K representing the satisfaction anticipated from the use of a commodity-bundle containing a greater quantity, than currently consumed, of at least one of the goods in the bundle.

b) Axiom 3, affirming transitivity of preference, furnishes the counterpart of condition (2) in G'. For Axiom 3 entails that, at any particular moment, the consumer will possess some particular economic want, K_i, to which there exists no other, K_j, that he prefers. Moreover, it should be noted that Axiom 1 simply provides a necessary condition, so to speak, for Axiom 3. For Axiom 1 expresses the fact that the consumer *can* compare any two alternative commodity-bundles in order of preference.

c) The knowledge constraint of CCT (included in C of G"), entailing that the consumer knows the available action-choices (purchases of commodity-bundles) that will lead to the fulfilment of his wants, and the comparative efficiency of different choosings in achieving this fulfilment, parallels belief conditions (3) and (4) of G'. (Note, however, that since we have assumed choice under conditions of certainty, our agent, S, not only *believes*, as in G', that a particular action best attains his ends, he *knows* this. However, this stronger epistemic state can only reinforce the analyticity claim.)

d) The constraints in CCT that the consumer chooses freely and within the resources of a certain income completes a counterpart for the ability conditions (5) of G'.[29]

In other words, an examination of the axioms and constraints of CCT establishes, with one qualification to be mentioned presently, that the antecedent conditions of economic generalization G" can be included within the scope of the antecedent conditions of action-theory generalization G'. Hence, we might verbally reformulate G", indicating more clearly its status as a special case of G', along the following lines:

> G": Whenever any consumer S, (1) wants K, the satisfaction derived from the use of some larger commodity-bundle, X, than currently consumed, (2) has no preferred want $\psi*$, (3) knows p, that action B, the choosing or purchasing of X, to be a means of realizing K, (4) knows that no other action is a better or equally efficient means of achieving K than B, and (5) is psychologically

and physically able (i.e., has the freedom and income) to do B, then S performs action B (purchases X).

(*Note our qualification – in condition (2), ψ is to range over any kind of human want, not just economic ones, whereas strictly speaking, transitivity axiom 3 of CCT entails only that there will be a most preferred *economic* want. However, without extending ψ to any kind of want, G" would simply be false. For a consumer might fail to purchase X (do B), not only due to a preferred economic want like the greater satisfaction anticipated in purchasing Y, but also on account of an overriding *non*-economic want – for example, a moral desire to distribute his income to someone else rather than employ it in personal consumption.)

However, in league with G', generalization G" appears doomed as a possible explanatory principle for economic action, since it again seems that G" is analytically true, not accessible to empirical falsification. Intuitively, at least, this charge appears potent – if one wants to enjoy the use of material goods, has no overriding want, believes the most efficient fulfilment of this want contingent upon performing a certain action (purchasing X), and is able to perform the action, then what conceivably *could* count as rendering the subsequent performance of the action false? Surely the analyticity here is grounded in the very meaning of having wants and beliefs in such circumstances. In other words, can it not be argued that the conditions (1-5) constituting the antecedent of G" *logically entail* the performance of the action specified in the consequent?

Many economists themselves have been cognizant of the criticism that the theory of individual choice, perhaps the foundation of economic science, is analytically or necessarily true. Some of them even emphasize the non-contingency inherent in the theory, but consider this no cause for dismay or grounds for denying scientific explanatory power to the axiom-set. Von Mises is perhaps the foremost exponent of this group; in fact, he welcomes the necessary a priori character of the truth of the fundamental theorems of economics such as those of CCT:

> What assigns economics its peculiar and unique position in the orbit of pure knowledge and of the practical utilization of knowledge is the fact that its particular theorems are not open to any verification of falsification on the grounds of experience ... The ultimate yardstick of an economic theorem's correctness or incorrectness is solely reason unaided by experience.[30]

Nevertheless, for von Mises, such a priori truths are not, as a positivistic empiricist must conclude, mere analytical tautologies. Rather, they are to be classified as *synthetic a priori* propositions on the grounds that they provide information concerning the categorical structure of everyday social phenomena.[31]

Indeed, a survey of the understanding of economists as to the logical structure of the basic "laws" of economic theories, including CCT, reveals a remarkable variety of interpretations. Hutchison, for instance, would agree with Von Mises that fundamental economic theorems are necessarily true, but insists that they remain solely of an *analytic a priori* species. Consequently, according to Hutchison, they are not empirically falsifiable, do not exclude any conceivable occurrence, and are, therefore, "devoid of empirical content".[32] Hutchison's reason for this conclusion is that such "propositions of pure theory" are no more than conventional definitions relating the meaning of key economic terms like preference and choice.[33] Robbins claims that basic economic generalizations are indubitable,[34] but that their certainty can even be established *a posteriori*; for he maintains that such laws refer solely to the incontrovertible contents of private, inner experience, the given data of immediate, subjective awareness.[35] Still differently, Lange[36] expresses the orthodox belief that the laws of economic choice are no different in logical status than the laws of natural science, that is, synthetic *a posteriori* statements, generalizations descriptive of empirical reality, but also subject to refutation by experiential findings. Indeed, Rosenberg[37] has recently traversed the epistemological spectrum, moving from a traditional view of economic generalizations as contingent, empirically testable hypotheses to one reconceiving the principles of neo-classical economics as comprising an a priori unfalsifiable branch of applied mathematics. And yet, even more disparately, these debates concerning the character of the truth-conditions of economic laws have been curiously circumvented in what has become the dominant view among economists: endorsing a thesis promulgated by Milton Friedman,[38] it is contended that the so-called "realism of the assumptions" or, more accurately, the truth of the fundamental laws of economic theories, is not to be considered a necessary criterion for the acceptance of such theories.

Interestingly, the diversity of interpretations of the logical status of basic economic laws reminds one of a similar controversy with respect to the postulates of Newtonian mechanics, especially the first one. Alternative construals of the logical status of this postulate have likewise run the gamut from conventional definition, synthetic a priori statement, to a general empirical hypothesis requiring experimental confirmation. It might be expected, therefore, that a proposed resolution to the problem of the "analyticity" of the theory of economic choice, CCT, would display a parallel to an understanding of the logical status of Newton's first axiom. Such a parallel will be evidenced below. But, first, it is to an answer to the analyticity problem in economics that I now turn.

Since, as shown above, the question of the analyticity of economic choice theory is parasitic on the problem of the analyticity of general action-theory, it will be wise to reply to the latter difficulty first. In this regard, it is noteworthy that, upon investigation of actual cases, one observes that *particular* action-explanations do not *explicitly* mention our action-theory generalization, G'. Rather, we find that individual actions are explained in terms of *specific* wants, preferences and beliefs in contrast to the completely *indeterminate* mention of these states in G'. For instance, to return to our previous illustration, we accounted for John's making a detour on the grounds that he possessed a determinate want, namely to visit a friend in particular preference to enjoying the scenery, and had the specific belief that the fulfilment of this want was contingent upon the action taken. Moreover, besides such common sense explanations, particular social scientific explanations likewise refer to the inter-relation of *specific* wants, preferences and beliefs in their explanatory premises. For instance, an individual senator's engagement in the role provided by a political career might be explained in terms of his actual want or desire for public adulation and his specific belief that this desire would be best satisfied by the social status or prestige surrounding the politician – however deluded the belief!

The critical logical point to notice in the preceding explanations, however, is that their empirical testability is no longer as troublesome. Analyticity is not as ineradicably entrenched. For although in any particular action-explanation, a reference to a structure of *some* wants and beliefs invariably persists, one can readily conceive of the empirical falsehood of the *explanation* in that any individual action could have been performed on account of *some other* or *different* particular wants and/or beliefs than the ones which were operative. Thus, John might have made the detour, not, as suggested, to visit a friend but because he wanted to replenish his gas tank and there was no station on the direct route. Or, we might grant the truth of the politician's desire for approbation but highlight the proffered explanation's empirical falsifiability by considering the alternative possibility that he believed employment as a professional athlete a better means to social approval than the political life. In sum, actual explanations of human actions infer (*via* an implicit use of general principle G') a specific action from a specific set of wants and beliefs. The basis of the *explanatory argument's* contingency, then, is found in the fact that, in general, particular human actions might have been caused by a variety of different sets of wants and beliefs than the specific ones which were actually responsible.[39]

Actual explanations of consumer behaviour follow a similar pattern (as would be expected, given that economic choice theory is a special case of action-theory). Suppose that an economist is asked why John, when confronted with the opportunity to buy either commodity-bundle A (10 opera tickets, 20 shirts) or B (15 opera tickets, 15 shirts) or C (20 opera tickets, 10 shirts), and possessing sufficient income for each purchase, in fact buys combination C. Our economist proffers an explanation in terms of bundle C being the preferred want in comparison to B or A. But such an account is amenable to empirical test for the reason (among others) that John might have had a different specific preference, say A over C. (In effect, John need not have found such comparatively greater satisfaction in the use of opera tickets rather than shirts.) Once economic wants (beliefs, preferences) have been specialized to refer to determinate wants for particular commodities, one can conceive of falsifying instances for *explanatory arguments* in the economic theory of consumer behaviour.

It is important to avoid misunderstanding here of our discussion of the relation between generalizations G' and G" and action-theoretic explanations. We do not intend to imply that whereas G' and G" are to be interpreted as a priori true, their *instances* are empirically testable. For even when G' (or G") *are* instantiated by assigning determinate wants, beliefs, etc. to a particular person, the resulting proposition remains impervious to experiential falsification. To return to our previous illustration, consider the following instantiation of G':

> If John (1) wants to visit his friend, (2) does not have any overriding want, (3) believes that making a detour is a means of visiting him, (4) does not believe that any other action is a better or equally efficient means of visiting him, (5) making the detour is not physically or psychologically impossible for John, then (6) John will visit his friend.

On our analysis, the relation between antecedent conditions (1-5) and the action reported in (6) is, again, *not* empirically falsifiable. If (1-5) are true of John, their conjunction logically entails (6) – that John will visit his friend. But, on the other hand, we *are* claiming that a significant element of empirical testability can be preserved for the explanatory arguments provided by action theory (and CCT), even though such testability is not to be located in generalizations G' (or G") serving as major premises in such arguments.

Rather it is to be found in the consideration discussed above that the same action might have been caused by different wants and/or beliefs than the particular ones which were operative.

3. Necessary Generalizations and Corrigibility

But what then *is* the empirical significance of action-theory generalization G' and its economic counterpart G"? In the light of the above argument, it appears that only the more determinate specification of wants and beliefs in a particular action-theoretic explanans can be judged as true or false on the basis of empirical evidence. Consequently, do we need to include G' and G" as explanatory principles in action-theory and economic theory at all? Perhaps these general statements are merely "disguised definitions", without empirical content, simply stipulating the way the meanings of the concepts of preference, belief, wants and actions are to be related. This interpretation would be given by many economists. Hutchison certainly would regard G" as a "proposition of pure theory" whose use is confined solely to terminological questions, to ... "implications of our definitions which might otherwise have escaped our attention and reveal unexpected relations between our definitions which are thus explained and clarified."[40]

Of course, for Hutchison, such propositions would lack any explanatory or predictive power, or, in his terms they would "have no prognostic value or 'causal significance'".[41] However, surely Hutchison overstates the case. For, in some sense, G' and G" seem to be somehow synthetic, rather than "merely analytic" or tautological. In particular, G' and G" affirm that every human action is caused by *some* set of beliefs and preferred wants. But surely to say only this is to provide some information, however indeterminate, about extra-linguistic fact, namely, information concerning the *kind* of events which cause human action – more specifically, that actions are caused by a set of "private" mental events, that is occurrent wants and beliefs. However, such information strikes one as necessarily true, in the sense of being experientially unfalsifiable. If we were to deny that a certain action was caused by some structure of preferences, wants and beliefs, could we any longer be said to be talking about the sort of thing called actions? Granted we could put this point in a "quasi-analytic" way. Thus, we might say that the truth of G' and G" is guaranteed "by virtue of the meanings of the terms involved". For if we were to deny G' and G", what could we possibly mean by performing actions or having wants and beliefs? However, so under-standing G' and G" does not succeed in removing synthetic or descriptive

25

content from these principles, as they continue to report the categorical structure of human action in the everyday world. And yet, if our analysis of G' and G" is correct, it weighs hard on an empiricist conscience. For have we not raised the spectre of synthetic a priori propositions, in the sense of propositions with descriptive empirical content that are nevertheless non-contingent, not subject to experiential falsification?

Can we arrive at a clearer understanding of the logical status of G' and G"? Admittedly, intense philosophical controversy concerning the analysis of "necessary truth" still continues; some indeed have challenged the usefulness of the analytic-synthetic distinction itself.[42] Nevertheless, as I see it, the most helpful and persuasive insight into the logical status of statements like G' and G" is to be found in a conception of what might be called a *relativized* synthetic a priori principle.[43] Such generalizations are logically synthetic, providing information concerning extra-linguistic reality. Moreover, such statements are empirically unfalsifiable, but only *relative* to a particular "conceptual scheme" or rule-governed "language structure".[44] Most importantly, the basic empiricist tenet prescribing the *corrigibility* of all scientific statement is here sustained in that such synthetic a priori statements can be revised or abandoned in adopting a different, alternative conceptual structure. Accordingly, any instance of *this kind* of synthetic a priori generalization does not, so to speak, possess absolute or *permanent* necessity; on the contrary, it remains subject to the empiricist dictum of "permanent control". Furthermore, no such "conceptual truth",[45] however entrenched its truth, is of any use for scientific explanation and prediction unless it at least facilitates the formulation of *explanatory arguments* which *are*, even within a particular conceptual structure, amenable to disconfirmation by observational findings.

An illustration of this type of synthetic a priori principle is provided by the law of the conservation of energy which, in one formulation, asserts that "the total quantity of energy in any closed physical system remains constant". Within the conceptual framework of classical mechanics, it is arguable that this law takes on the status of a non-contingent truth, implicitly defining, say, the expression "closed physical system". Accordingly, we may conclude that the "law" of the conservation of energy is not subject to refutation or revision *via* empirical test within the conceptual structure of classical mechanics. However, not only could the law of conservation of energy be rejected or modified by adopting an alternative framework, but it indeed has been so revised in accepting the new conceptual framework of relativistic physics.

This conception of a non-absolute synthetic a priori principle sheds significant light on the question of the logical status of generalizations G' and

G" of action-theory and our economic theory of choice, CCT. The conceptual scheme in terms of which we interpret human behaviour as action includes the "convention", albeit a peculiarly synthetic convention, as explained above, that actions are to be conceived as events caused by some set of wants and beliefs; such a presupposition is (part of) what we mean by the concept of an "action". But G' simply expresses such a "meaning convention" or principle for interpreting human behaviour in a more complete form taking into consideration competing wants, alternative actions, etc. Hence, within *one* conceptual structure enabling our understanding of human behaviour, G' is true *ex vi terminorum*, not capable of empirical falsification. In effect, G' functions as a convention implicitly defining the concept of an action. *A fortiori*, G", formulating this principle for the special case of economic actions, exhibits the same logical character, it being a "conceptual truth" that the purchasing of commodities is caused by some set of preferred (economic) wants and beliefs. But G' and G" can be of use for scientific explanation and prediction for, as seen above, when supplemented with more determinant specifications of particular wants and beliefs, they do make possible the framing of explanatory arguments that are subject to observational test.

Nevertheless, it remains important to stress that G' and G" might yet be scientifically rejected by adopting an alternative conceptual scheme for analyzing human behaviour; for G' and G" are instances of what we have called a *relativized* synthetic a priori principle. In particular, the social scientist might find it preferable, for methodological reasons, to abandon the commitment to the existence of inter-subjectively unobservable mental events like those designated by the expressions "wants" and "beliefs" as the cause of behaviour, a commitment presupposed by the conceptual scheme interpreting human behaviour as action.[46] With this rejection would go the need for G'. Consequently, the economic theorist, wedded as he now is in CCT to an action-theoretic account of economic behaviour, in adopting an alternative scheme, would no longer be obliged to employ G". Indeed, economists who have endorsed radical behaviourist principles by following the "revealed preference approach" to the theory of consumer behaviour have already made such a methodological break – although ill-advisedly, as we shall argue in Chapter 4. Or, alternatively, the explanation of all human behaviour (including the economic) by means of a neurophysiological model, without an ontological commitment to private mental events like wants, is not entirely fanciful, as recent scientific and philosophical debate testifies.[47]

As suggested above, the analogy of G' and G" with Newton's laws of motion, particularly the first, is illuminating. In Newton's formulation the

27

first law asserts: "Every body perseveres in its state of rest, or of uniform motion in a straight line, unless it is compelled to change that state by forces impressed thereon".[48] To my mind, the most perspicacious way of interpreting the logical status of the first law is again that of a relativised synthetic a priori principle. Under this reading, this axiom is to be understood as a principle which helps specify a conceptual scheme for analyzing or interpreting the motion of material bodies. Without some such scheme, physical motion would be unintelligible and no lower-level experimental laws concerning such motion would be possible to formulate. Such a statement is synthetic in that it informs us of the categorial structure of physical reality: the motion of a physical body is to be conceived as the kind of event which is caused by the impact of an *external* physical force, rather than by some "entelechy" or internal force within the body. However, there is also a quasi-analytic character to the axiom in that it so instructs us about extra-linguistic reality *via* its very role as a "meaning convention", in its formulating and relating the meanings of such notions as "absence of force", "uniform motion", and "equal time intervals".[49] But under this reading of its logical character, empirical findings could not disconfirm Newton's first law: a denial of the axiom would simply indicate that one did not understand the way the concepts "motion", "force", etc. were being used in Newton's theory. (Once again, our analysis leads us to see that meanings and facts are not, as conventional empiricism would have it, disparate notions, but, rather, integrated ones.)

However, even on this interpretation, Newton's axioms do possess an explanatory role, since they enable the formulation of *explanatory arguments* which are empirically testable. And significantly, at least one important manner in which these postulates, so interpreted, give rise to falsifiable explanations is *the same as* the way in which G' and G" do so. Thus, it is not possible, within Newtonian mechanics, to conceive a falsifying instance for the first axiom in terms of a body altering its acceleration without being induced to do so by some external force; however, by supplementing the first axiom by a more determinate description of the operative force-function we do obtain an explanatory argument that is accessible to experiential refutation. (The axiom itself, it will be remembered, refers indeterminately to simply *some* unspecified (external) force affecting uniform motion.) For instance, the deceleration in velocity of a small iron object might be accounted for in terms of a frictional force exerted by the surface over which it moves. However, an alteration in the velocity of a certain body does not logically entail which particular *kind* of force (among several possible ones) is causally responsible, and, in this sense, the proposed *explanation* is capable of experimental rejection – thus, the deceleration might have been due, not to friction, as claimed, but to a magnetic force applied behind the moving body, or to the impact of another body, etc.

Again, moreover, if Newtonian mechanics is interpreted as a conceptual scheme for moving bodies, it should be remembered that it is only one among alternative possible schemes, and its postulates can have only a *relativized* synthetic a priori status in that they are subject to revision by utilizing another scheme. Indeed, this conclusion is strikingly borne out in the light of the significant modifications which the Newtonian axioms have undergone in the new conceptual framework for motion generated by general relativity theory.

Chapter 3

Rationality, Values, and Economic Theory

We argued in the preceding chapter that explanations furnished by the neo-classical theory of individual choice (CCT) need not be analytically trivial in that they are, in the sense outlined, capable of falsification by means of observational evidence. Nevertheless, it has remained an occupational trait among many economists to resist, at all costs, the empirical refutation of proposed explanatory arguments.[1] To this end, one celebrated stratagem has been to claim that neo-classical economic theory assumes the activities of a *rational* agent. Hence, to take the case of CCT, all instances of consumer choice which at first sight cannot be accounted for by the axioms of this theory are apparently rendered logically innocuous, not involving evidential counterexamples to the theory, by designating them "irrational" behaviour.

A full scale treatment of the use of the concept of "rationality" in the neo-classical theory of choice will underlie much of what is to follow in this inquiry. But we shall introduce our analysis of this pivotal concept in this chapter.

1. Rationality and Means

We might usefully begin with the following critical note on the employment of the concept of rationality in a *descriptive-explanatory* context. I refer to the fact that it is necessary to appreciate a basic twofold aspect of the notion of rationality. It would not suffice to describe "rational" economic behaviour as simply behaviour wherein an economic agent seeks to maximize some value. Lange, for instance, states ... "A unit of economic decision is said to act rationally when its objective is the maximization of a magnitude."[2] Suppose, then, a neo-classical theorist were to formulate a rationality assumption, R, for CCT, along Lange's line as: "all consumers seek to maximize their utility or satisfaction derived from the use of commodities."[3] But, as neo-classical theorists would understand such maximization as acting on one's strongest preferences, our analysis of G' and G" in the last chapter would indicate that R is a universal a priori truth functioning as a synthetic "meaning convention" relating the meaning or use of the concepts of seeking (wanting) and satisfaction. Given our conception of the structure of the causation of action, if one did not intend to act on one's strongest preference, one would not be performing actions at all. However, it would then follow that R's conception of economic rationality, specified solely in terms of the *ends* or goals of economic agents, is methodologically vacuous: interpreted according to R, the concept of rationality would not furnish the economist with a principle enabling him to discriminate rational from irrational consumer actions. For all such actions would count as rational for the simple reason that, as the conceptual vocabulary of neo-classical economics implies, no consumer could seek *not* to maximize his utility. Hence, an appeal to the absence of this kind of rationality on the part of the consumer, for the purpose of preventing an instance of his behaviour from providing a falsifying counterexample to the axioms of CCT, would be futile. It is imperative, then, that in order to play an explanatory role, a rationality assumption must include, not only a reference to the consumer's objective, but also a reference to the *means* he employs in enacting his decisions – specifically, that the "rational" consumer choice exhibits the utilization of the best or optimal means available for attaining the goal of maximum satisfaction from the use of commodities.[4] From this point of view, but *not* all,[5] the theoretical significance of the rationality assumption turns on its use as a measure of the *efficiency* of actions chosen.

To be fair, most economists have realized the need to stress this dimension of rationality. Baumol, for one, in analysing the geometrical representation of choice-theory, asserts ... "in this way, the indifference map together with the price line permit us to predict the demand pattern of the "rational" consumer – the consumer who spends his money efficiently in the pursuit of his needs and interests."[6] And understood in this way, the use of the rationality assumption in CCT does possess explanatory relevance in the desired sense of accounting for apparent counterexamples, on the grounds that this assumption, implicitly included in the statement of the theory, has not been satisfied. For there are numerous possible ways in which consumers might employ non-optimal means in the pursuit of maximum satisfaction. A consumer might, for example, choose an inferior course of action due to a mistaken belief generated by (irrationally) basing the belief on insufficient empirical evidence. For instance, consider that I continually purchase a red wine in preference to a white wine for a meal of fish, believing that the former will satisfy my appetite more completely than the latter, even though I have never had the previous experience of combining fish with white wine. Rather my belief rested on a distaste found for white wine consumed with red meats. When, on a future occasion, I find to my regret that the use of white wine with fish is, in fact, more conducive to my satisfaction than that of red, I would be wise to conclude that my original erroneous belief was unreasonably predicated on such sparse experiential evidence. It can be argued, furthermore, that lack of behavioural compliance with axiom A_3 of CCT, characterizing transitivity of preference, may issue in "irrational" choice patterns in our defined sense; for, in cases of intransitive orderings, for a single choice occasion, no optimal choice leading to the maximization of utility is (or even can be) made. This is due to the fact that when preferences are intransitive for such an occasion, no single alternative, to which none other is preferred, can be identified – although the convention of uniformly characterizing intransitivities as irrational has not gone without its recent critics.[7]

2. Rationality and Value-Ascriptions

In the preceding section, the concept of rationality was introduced in its descriptive/explanatory sense, as characterizing economic agents who do in fact make the most efficient use of resources in the pursuit of maximum satisfaction. But the concept of rationality exhibits an even more significant dualistic nature than the means-end distinction discussed above. For it is to be observed that the assumption of rationality conveys a further connotation of a *normative* kind, as prescribing what action-choices a consumer *ought* to make. It will be appropriate then to begin our examination of this most critical dimension of economic theory-construction – namely, the interpretation of economic theory, particularly the theory of consumer choice, not as a set of descriptive empirical hypotheses used to explain why actual consumers behave as they do, but as a normative system directed towards *recommending* the ideal pattern of choices to be made by the rational consumer who is seeking to maximize his material utility.

Understood in this manner, the axioms of consumer choice supply foundational *prescriptions* for economic policy. Friedman and Savage, in analysing the rationality assumption of the theory of choice under conditions of risk, give expression to the need for such an alternative interpretation of choice-theory:

> The maximization of such an expected value may also be regarded as a maxim for behaviour ... Success of the maxim ... depends not on its empirical verification for the economic behaviour of men at large, but on its acceptability to people who are particularly concerned with such decisions, as a rule guiding "wise" behaviour.[8]

However, it is of the first importance to note the "orthodox view" among neo-classical economists as to the relationship between the descriptive/explanatory and the normative/prescriptive roles of the theory of choice (CCT). Encouraged by recent positivist principles insisting that value judgments and factual statements are different in kind, it remains the consensus of "mainstream" economists that a) the normative and descriptive functions of CCT belong to mutually exclusive categories and b) the normative deployment of the axioms of the theory is parasitic on their *primary* function as descriptive hypotheses explaining actual economic behaviour.[9] Given an understanding *via* the theory of choice why individuals exhibit the patterns of consumer behaviour they do, we can then utilize such "positive" science in instructing them as to how they might behave more efficiently in allocating their income to receive maximum satisfaction from their purchases.

Now, it will be the main burden of this study to take issue with this orthodox assertion of the *heterogeneity* of the normative and descriptive dimensions of CCT in elucidating how the orthodoxy undermines an appreciation of the essential inter-relatedness or conceptual connection between the normative and descriptive aspects of theory-construction in economics. Towards this end, we will have recourse, in this section, to general value theory as our first plank in bridging the normative-descriptive chasm created by the received interpretation of economic theory. Again, the theory of consumer behaviour, CCT, will provide a foundational case-study.

It is evident, first of all, that when, by means of axiom 1 of CCT, we affirm that an individual consumer, say John, wants (commodity-bundle) X, we imply that John values X. For, as outlined above, a consumer wants a commodity-bundle because he values the end of subjective satisfaction he believes its use will generate. Or, in other words, the consumer extrinsically values a commodity-bundle since its use leads to the subjective satisfaction which he intrinsically values. In short, then, we will simply say that a consumer values the commodity-bundle itself when he wants it. But what is the meaning of such a value-imputation? More precisely, under what conditions would we consider this imputation of valuing to John to be a correct one; or, in other words, what conditions would indicate that John does or does not subscribe, as claimed, to valuing X?[10]

In reply, it is clear that, on the one hand, we regard value-imputations as, in general, groundless if the agent did not appeal to the ascribed value in justifying or recommending a decision as to a particular course of action. The structure of an agent's values provides him with data on the basis of which he can decide what *ought to be done* in certain circumstances. In particular, thus, if John not only wants, that is values a commodity-bundle X, but prefers X to another valued bundle Y, we legitimately expect that John would *justify* a choice of X, given the availability of both X and Y, by claiming that he valued X more highly than Y and that, therefore, his actual choice was the best "thing to do" in the circumstances. Similarly, of course, knowing John's value-structure, an external observer, like the economic theorist, can recommend or prescribe choice X to John. In upshot, since its axioms incorporate value-ascriptions (given S wants A, S prefers A to B, etc.), the normative aspect of the theory of consumer behaviour, its provision of standards for appraising and guiding rational choice, is firmly established.

On the other hand, however, a factual, descriptive factor is also included as a necessary condition for correctly imputing a value to someone. Briefly, if we claim that a person S holds a particular value X, we thereby imply that S will actually display a tendency or *disposition* to behave, given certain circumstances, in the kind of ways that manifest subscription to X. For instance, if the assertion that a particular soldier values courage is to be regarded as a true predication, then one would thereby legitimately expect the soldier not to desert under enemy fire. Ascribing values to someone, then, implies the attribution of a behavioural disposition. The disposition is, of course, more accurately described as a complex disposition or perhaps a unique bundle of dispositions for the reason that a certain value-subscription can be manifested in several ways. Our soldier, for example, might alternatively have displayed his valuing of courage by aggressively attacking the enemy. Moreover, as will be outlined below, it is this descriptive-dispositional aspect which supplies the explanatory force of value-imputations.

Consider, then, axioms 1 and 2 of CCT implying that a consumer, S, wants a commodity-bundle X and, therefore, that S values X. If such an assertion is true, then under certain conditions, S would exhibit the distinctive manifestation-behaviour of the characteristic disposition of a person who values a material commodity – for instance, that under conditions of a specific kind, S would actually purchase X. In sum, our initial bridge between the normative and descriptive dimension of the economic theory of choice is to be found in the following factors:

a)   the axioms of consumer choice incorporate the imputation of the holding of a value to an individual (the consumer); and

b)   the necessary criteria for correctly imputing a value-subscription to an individual include *both* i) a presupposition that the individual will have recourse to the ascribed value in the context of deciding and justifying how he *ought to act* and ii) a presupposition that the individual display a disposition to *act* in ways which exhibit the actual holding of the ascribed value.

In effect, one cannot legitimately affirm one aspect of value-ascriptions (the normative-prescriptive) without *ipso facto* implying the other (descriptive-explanatory).

Indeed, one may offer an even more direct (though related) link between the normative and empirical aspects of choice-theory *via* a connecting principle. First, consider that, in general, at the very least, to affirm of S that he actually values X, entails that S accepts that he ought to perform certain actions that lead to the realization of X. The connecting principle, call it P, would be: "Whenever anyone accepts that something ought to be done in particular circumstances implies *ceteris paribus* that he actually performs the action in those circumstances". Now, irrespective of the important question concerning the a priori versus empirical truth of P, I think it would at least be conceded that P *is* true. But, if true, then whenever one is confronted with an instance of someone consenting to an imperative prescribing a particular action under certain circumstances, one is by virtue of P thereby given sufficient grounds for believing that the action, other conditions being equal, will be performed if the circumstances arise. But, as noted, the axioms of consumer-choice theory, in ascribing values to someone, entail the acceptance of action-imperatives, which in turn, by virtue of our general connecting principle, P, implies the (*ceteris paribus*) performances of the relevant actions, which performances are expressible in purely descriptive terms.

Of course, the bridge provided between the normative and descriptive aspects of CCT by means of the covering principle, P, is qualified by the limiting condition expressed by the *ceteris paribus* phrase asserting "other conditions remaining equal (or constant)". Thus, we find that, in P, consent to an imperative to an action only entails the performance of the action, *ceteris paribus*. But such a qualification reminds us that CCT is an idealization, predicting and explaining consumer behaviour under extreme or "ideal" conditions that are normally only approximated by empirical phenomena. Let us focus more closely on this feature in examining the manner in which the descriptive aspect of value-imputations provides explanatory power for CCT.

We saw above, then, that the postulates of CCT, in attributing wants to some consumer, S, thereby imputed valuations of the form "S values X". It was further observed that the descriptive significance of value-imputations implies the attribution of a disposition, normally a complex bundle of dispositions, to exhibit certain behavioural "responses" (R_1, R_2, etc.) under various specified "stimulus" conditions (S_1, S_2, etc.). Now, the peculiar consequence of the extreme kind of idealization characterizing the axioms of CCT, ascribing values to consumers under ideal circumstances of complete freedom and knowledge, is that such idealization enables the economic theorist to narrow the complex set of dispositions normally implied by valuations to a single, unique disposition. Furthermore, such idealization permits the formulation of a disposition to behave uniformly (rather than probably) in a certain manner under specific conditions. More particularly, suppose it is the case that a consumer values commodity-bundles X, Y, Z in that (transitive) order of preference. By implication, then, the consumer will possess a behavioural disposition which, and this is the critical point, would most appropriately be interpreted by the following, roughly formulated, generalization. We will label this disposition-characterizing generalization, D.

> D: Any consumer who transitively values a set of commodity-bundles will, in a situation wherein he possesses complete knowledge and freedom, invariably purchase the commodity-bundle representing the most preferred value.[11]

Consider, further, that S subsequently purchases X when confronted with the opportunity to buy X or Y or Z, and that an explanation is offered for this event by claiming that S wanted or valued X, and did so more than Y or Z. In the light of the preceding analysis, we can see that such an explanation is incomplete as it stands; most importantly, a more complete explanation would take place by subsuming S's purchase under, or deducing it from, a disposition-characterizing generalization such as D. (In effect, D can be understood as an abbreviated variant of G"[12] in the specific context of viewing CCT as formulating *a system of valuations*. Hence, in accord with G", D exhibits the logical status of a necessary, a priori truth: it is not subject to refutation by observational findings. Nevertheless, in the manner of G", it would still provide for *explanations* that were empirically falsifiable. Similarly, D would only command a *relativized* (synthetic) a priori truth status: it could be abandoned by adopting an alternative "conceptual scheme" for interpreting human behaviour.)

Chapter 4

The Intransigence of Evaluative Concepts

We have noted that the majority of neo-classical economists prefer to construe economics as an ethically neutral, purely "positive", empirical theory of behaviour. However, we have just observed that the neo-classical theory of choice ascribes a pattern of evaluations to consumers, and that value-imputations link empirical with normative factors. Might we not, then, proceed directly to argue further that the "orthodox" commitment to the ethical neutrality of economics is a misguided one. Not immediately. For we must first address certain forceful attempts by members of the "orthodox group" to short-circuit any argument that would seek to infer moral commitments from certain uses of evaluative discourse. In particular, we need to examine strategies that have sought to excise from economic theory the "mentalistic" vocabulary required to describe valuations *per se*. More precisely, I refer to recent efforts by some neo-classical economists to dissociate the theory of consumer choice (CCT) from ethical presuppositions by either (i) *re-interpreting* such *prima facie* evaluative concepts as "indifference", "preference", "rationality", "maximizing utility", etc. as in reality non-valuational, or (ii) by taking the further step and arguing that such evaluative concepts can be *eliminated* from CCT without loss of explanatory power and, therefore, should be, in the interests of an unambiguously "positive" science.

However, it will be my position in this chapter that such re-interpretations and theoretical parings both 1) needlessly truncate the explanatory power of CCT, and 2) preclude the effective normative application of the theory in the construction of prescriptions for economic policy. Hence, a critical examination of the manoeuvres of these methodologists will serve to further elucidate the ineradicable role of values in economic theory-construction. (For ease of reference, we shall call advocates of tactics i) and ii) "neutralists"; of course, not all value-neutralists concerning CCT would invoke such measures.)

1. Excising Evaluative Concepts

Let me first clarify procedure i) of re-interpretation. This neutralist tactic concentrates on the basic concept of "utility" which, as traditionally interpreted, refers to some consequential property of the action of choosing a commodity-bundle, which property the agent finds desirable and is seeking to maximize. Along indifference curves, distinct combinations of goods are conceived as yielding an equal amount of such utility and it is *for this reason* that an agent is indifferent between such combinations. Similarly, any consumer prefers one bundle A to another bundle B *on the grounds* that more of this property is generated by choosing A than choosing B. The traditional use of the term "utility", then, can be understood as providing a concept to stand for the *evaluative basis* of any consumer choice. In motivational terms, there is some property of the anticipated consumption of goods which moves agents to purchase them.

However, it is contended by many who reject this traditional conception of utility in economic theory that it is *superfluous* for the scientific explanation and prediction of consumer choice. Rather, according to one group of such theorists,[1] utility is better understood as a purely *structural* feature of the theory of choice. The philosopher, David Braybrooke, summarizes such interpretations in claiming that the neo-classical concept of utility refers to "nothing more than a quantitative metaphor for speaking of orders of preference."[2] In a similar vein, the economist, Jack Hirshleifer, comments "What modern economists call 'utility' reflects nothing more than rank ordering of preference."[3] Utility, according to this view, should be construed as merely a *choice-indicator*, where the phrase "more utility" simply marks off the fact that "one collection of goods is preferred to another"; likewise, the phrase "equal utility" signifies that an agent is indifferent between several collections; but "preference" and "indifference" in turn are translated, respectively, as "choosing A rather than B" and "choosing A and B with equal frequency"; finally, "choice" itself is identified with the overt purchasing of commodity-bundles when alternatives are available.

Accordingly, the axioms of CCT are understood to represent entirely structural elements concerning ordered relation between preferences; but as preferences themselves receive a behaviourist translation into observable purchasings, proponents of the structuralist view believe themselves entitled to eschew the ordinary understanding that orders of preference for objects are determined by one's reasons or evaluative grounds for the preferences. Moreover, such ordering is claimed to bring about the maximization of utility, construed purely "formally": in effect, the originally normative principle characterizing the "rational" consumer as the one who chooses that combination of goods which maximizes his utility is to be re-conceived in purely descriptive fashion as meaning that, assuming constant tastes, prices and income, any consumer will choose that combination A rather than any other available ones B, C, D, etc., given that A has been chosen rather than B, C, D, etc. in his past behaviour.[4]

In sum, the apparently evaluative concepts of CCT are to be re-interpreted in a non-valuational "structural" manner as simply "logical constructs" or "definitional shorthands" for concepts referring to *observable choice behaviour*. Jerome Rothenberg[5] endorses and describes this viewpoint most clearly when he remarks that the principle of utility maximization in the theory of choice makes no reference to the substantive grounds for choice, which restraint, he believes, entails that the theory is without normative presuppositions and that it is beholden to no empirical theory of psychology as to the nature of the actual wants which motivate economic agents. (That the rejection of both of these factors is not unrelated will be made clear in Chapter 9.)

I turn now to the second procedure (ii) employed by certain neutralists – that of seeking to eliminate concepts with *prima facie* evaluative meanings. Here, we find attempts to construct a theory of choice whose axioms need include no mention of all such problematic concepts as "indifference" or "utility".

One such purified choice theory which remains very prominent is that introduced by Samuelson[6] under the title "Revealed Preference Theory". As in procedure (i), the approach is predicated on a behaviouristic construal of choice. But the behaviourist methodology is more radical. For an attempt is made to explain purchasing patterns by a set of empirical axioms explicitly mentioning only publicly observable, overt market behaviour. The essential content of the axioms follows:

B_1 From any set of obtainable commodity-bundles, the consumer will be induced to choose (i.e., purchase) one.

B_2 (Formulating consumer consistency) If commodity-bundle A has been chosen when B is also obtainable and B is no more expensive than A, then B will not be chosen, if A is also obtainable.

The preceding hypotheses, then, reveal Samuelson's avowed intention to "develop the theory of consumer behaviour freed from any vestigial traces of the utility concept."[7] Moreover, as the economist Stanley Wong correctly observes,

> Outside the theory of consumer behaviour, the major impact of the Samuelson Programme is on methodology ... The importance of Samuelson's methodology is indisputable. A vast majority of economists have adopted Samuelson's methodology to the point of regarding it as the scientific methodology appropriate to economics.[8]

It is important to identify the precise manner in which the preceding (i) re-interpretations or translations and (ii) suggested eliminations of the *prima facie* valuational concepts of CCT do seek to realize the intention of neutralists to conceive of the axioms of CCT as value-free. Towards this end, suppose we make the critical demarcation of cases wherein an economist in constructing CCT:

a) restricts himself to a description of the value systems held by the agents whose behaviour he is explaining, rather than

b) includes *his own* value-judgments concerning the moral worth of certain consumption patterns as part of the content of the theory.

Of course, only b) would remove the "value-freedom" of CCT, would entail that CCT incorporates (allegedly illicit) moral presuppositions. Nevertheless, it is plain that tactics (i) and (ii) of our neutralists fit hand-in-glove with their intention to conceive of the axioms of CCT as value-free. For if (i) and (ii) *are* defensible, they lead to the conclusion that these axioms do not report the content of *evaluations at all, even of the consumers whose behaviour is to be explained.* A fortiori, the axioms of CCT would not include the value-judgments of the neo-classical economists who have constructed or use the theory. Put another way, by excising evaluative concepts *in toto* from the system of concepts deployed to describe and explain choices, it is presumed that the neo-classical theorist would thereby insulate CCT from his own backsliding – viz., from introducing his own evaluative commitments into the theory. For either through the behaviourist translation or elimination of value terms we have described, the theory would be deprived of a language to express anyone's value-judgments. In this light, it is not surprising to find Samuelson bluntly remarking that the basic maximizing principle of the theory of choice ... "does not imply that consumers behave rationally in any normative sense."[9]

Such conceptual austerity, furthermore, finds re-inforcement in the theory of scientific method preferred by most neutralists within neo-classical economics. For it is clear that this orthodoxy remains wedded to a primitive "operationalist" philosophy of science,[10] introduced over seventy years ago, and to whose first formulation even its original proponents have long ceased to adhere. Basically, operationalist methods insisted that no technical concepts should be introduced into a scientific theory that could not be explicitly defined in terms of vocabulary referring to the publicly observable operations of exact measurement. And, not surprisingly, such an (extremist) conception of scientific method has promoted and grounded the eviction of evaluative language from economic theory-construction. For, as we have seen in CCT, the description of the evaluative bases for action makes at least *prima facie* reference to such publicly unobservable, introspective, mentalistic entities as "reasons", "states of desire and preference", "subjective satisfaction (utility)", etc. Accordingly, one of the motives for and alleged benefits of foregoing such valuational elements in behaviourist re-constructions of CCT has been that such an abstinence would enable the theory to be based on "objectively observable data"; only in this way, it is argued, do the hypotheses of choice theories become testable and hence scientifically respectable.

2. Explanatory Impoverishment

Despite their entrenchment within mainstream methodology, it can now be shown that such re-interpretations and eliminations of the *prima facie* evaluative concepts of the theory of choice unnecessarily reduce its explanatory power. In the first place, it is important to notice that the meaning of the description of the item of consumer behaviour to be explained, namely that of the "choice of a particular collection of commodities" carries certain significant implications. For the concept of the "choice" of an action does not refer to the action-event *simpliciter*, but to an action performed *in a certain manner*. And the qualifying phrase designates the fact that the action was performed deliberately, *for a reason*. If one chooses to purchase one commodity-bundle *rather than* other available ones, then there must be some *grounds* for the choice – otherwise, one hasn't "chosen" at all.[11] Of course, our value-neutralist of behaviourist persuasion might therefore simply reply *tant pis*, and gladly admit that economists are simply explaining the "mere taking", rather than the choosing of commodities. And, as the related concepts of reasons, bases, or grounds for choosing inevitably convey the suggestions of normative standards which determine such grounds, such a neutralist, once informed of the meaning of "choice", would be even more eager to eliminate the concept of choice from

41

his theoretical vocabulary. But, we shall argue, only at the cost of thereby impoverishing the explanatory scope of economic theory.

In particular, such a theorist would be precluded, in principle, from accounting for behaviour wherein an agent is confronted with *conflicts* of reasons or motives in his purchasing strategies. Such conflicts can arise once we move beyond relatively *simple* types of choice situations wherein an agent orders his preferences on the basis of *the same reason*.

To see that this is so, consider the consumer who chooses to buy certain economic goods for *divers* reasons, and that the reasons come into conflict by generating non-transitive preferences. To take a simplified example, suppose John prefers choice A to B and B to C based on one reason, but C to A based on a different ground. To re-introduce our illustration of Chapter 2, suppose John prefers (A) a Ferrari to (B) a Mercedes on grounds of superior elegance and (B) to (C) a Buick, for the same reason, but C to A on the basis of durability. Of course, such an empirical finding would be inconsistent with transitivity axiom (A_3) of CCT, since John prefers A to B and B to C, but not A to C. However, no revised theory of choice, which remained subject to neutralist re-constructions of types i) and ii), could ever explain or predict an instance of consumer behaviour following upon such a non-transitive preference ordering. For appeal to the reasons, let alone the conflicting reasons, which might motivate such behaviour, would be blocked by these neutralists' own behaviourist tactics. *Why* John behaves as he does must remain indeterminate for their theories of choice. Admittedly, if John were to choose from amongst the automobiles for the same reason, a non-transitive preference would not have occurred. But, of course, we find, as a matter of empirical fact, that consumers do carry out purchasing plans resting on varying, frequently conflicting, grounds. Consequently, the explanatory scope of the theory of choice would suffer serious diminution under such neutralist constructions as a result of not being able to account for behaviour arising out of such preference-structures.[12]

The reaction of many economic neutralists to such facts has been confused. Some, believing that intransitivities are not troublesome as long as preferences or tastes remain stable, simply proceed on the assumption that the consumer does not change his tastes, and maintain that the theory of choice at least has explanatory force for any choice-situation where the assumption is true.[13] But, as we have seen, such a belief is erroneous – conflicting grounds for purchases can generate non-transitive orderings irrespective of whether tastes are changing or not; indeed, they can generate them on a single choice occasion. Other economists, arguing from the point of view that the theory of choice is intended to explain the behaviour of "rational" consumers, contend that non-transitive preferences are evidence of irrationality. Rothenberg,[14] for example, claims that when preferences are not transitive the individual "acts as if he did not know what he wanted," which trait Rothenberg describes as "the essential quality of irrationality", because it prevents the adaptation of means to realize ends which is a hallmark of rational behaviour.

Well, although Rothenberg's conception of irrationality is (in part) appropriate,[15] it supports a conclusion the exact opposite of the one he advances. For, consider that the evaluative bases of the preferences for economic goods, such as the elegance and durability of the automobiles in the above example, are just those characteristics of the commodities which the consumer wants. This is so, for, in general, any object x is wanted only if there is some property of x for which it is wanted. Consequently, contrary to Rothenberg, if conflicting reasons or "desirability-characteristics"[16] necessitate non-transitive preferences, one can only "act like one knows what one wants" by following, not eschewing such preferences. By not doing so, one thereby would act irrationally on Rothenberg's own definition of irrational behaviour. The concept of "utility", furthermore, has been traditionally employed in economic theory to designate whatever property is believed present in the use of a commodity, which property the agent wants, and for which reason, therefore, he purchases the good. We can conclude, therefore, that the effort of neutralists to expel a substantive concept of utility from the corpus of economic theory will succeed only at the unacceptable cost of a severe impoverishment of the explanatory scope of the theory of choice, even when it is understood as dealing only with "rational" economic actions.

It is significant that this conclusion follows, even if, on a deeper analysis, we were to classify at least some non-transitive preferences as irrational. For, as mentioned in Chapter 3,[17] if, at a particular point in time, a consumer's preferences are not transitive, then there is no choice to which none other is preferred at that moment. And, on these grounds, we might argue that, for this moment of choice, such preferences are irrational. Presumably, however, the source of such irrationality would reside in the fact that the particular consumer was unable to assess the comparative significance or worth of the conflicting reasons for his choices. If he could effect such a comparative appraisal of his reasons or values, then the spectre of non-transitive preferences might be removed. For one reason might be sufficiently strong to override a competing one. A more rational agent than John, for instance, might find the durability of the automobiles of sufficient merit to outweigh considerations of their elegance, when these values come into conflict. However, it is plain that this very explication of the irrationality of non-transitive preferences would require that theories of rational choice take closer cognizance of the reasons or evaluative bases guiding choice. But neutralist theories of types i) and ii) seek to abandon such scrutiny altogether.

We mentioned above that normative standards determine the reasons for choice. Now it is especially significant that the standards themselves are various, and that sometimes one standard might conflict with another. An illustration is in order.

Suppose, then, that a particular consumer prefers commodity-bundle A to B, and B to C, on the basis of an egotistical hedonistic standard prescribing that he ought to maximize his personal pleasure; nevertheless, he prefers C to A for the reason that buying C is believed to contribute to the amelioration of an unjust distribution of income to the labourers who produce A, which prospect is in accord with a Kantian moral standard the consumer tries to follow of never treating another person only as a means to the realization of his personal satisfaction.[18] Those consumers who are now deliberating whether or not to purchase California grapes in preference to other varieties provides a topical example of such a choice-situation. In any case, in order to adequately explain or predict which purchase our consumer actually makes, an economic theorist would need to be able to determine not only the manner in which a value standard permits the ranking of preferences according to the standard, but in those most critical cases where standards conflict, he must also ascertain the order in which the particular agent *ranks the standards themselves*. Not only should a perspicacious economics incorporate value concepts in its theoretical framework; it should also leave theoretical room for reference to a *hierarchy of values*.

3. Loss of Normative Applicability

The preceding illustration draws our attention to the other aspect of the theory of choice within which *prima facie* value concepts like utility have a controversial status – namely, the normative dimension. Now, both value-neutralists and anti-neutralists are agreed that the theory of choice is to be adapted to play the significant normative role of *recommending* the optimal pattern of choices to be made by the rational consumer seeking to maximize his satisfaction derived from the use of material goods. As indicated above,[19] however, they differ in their interpretation of the relation between the descriptive/explanatory and the normative roles of the theory. Before elaborating an anti-neutralist perspective in subsequent chapters, it will be instructive to examine an important type of argument set forth by neutralists concerning the normative dimension of CCT. The thesis of Kelvin Lancaster provides an important representative case.

Lancaster,[20] after commenting favourably on the behaviouristic means offered by Revealed Preference Theory of expelling the problematic concepts of utility, preference, indifference, etc., from "positive" aspects of consumer behaviour, proceeds to argue that these concepts are similarly unnecessary for the discussion of normative or "welfare" aspects of such behaviour. Instead of the old Utilitarian criterion of welfare constructed on the standard that a prudent agent ought to choose actions that maximize his utility, Lancaster proffers, as a normative counter-part of Revealed Preference Theory, a new welfare criterion in terms of "expanded choice", viz:

> An individual's welfare has unambiguously increased from situation I to situation II if his choice is expanded as a result of the change, that is, if in Situation II he can have
> a) what he chose in Situation I and
> b) at least one choice not available to him in Situation I.[21]

Now, this move to a choice-criterion of consumer welfare is not merely an intellectual exercise without methodological underpinning. For it should be observed that this is the natural, indeed *only* standard accessible once utility has been removed from the set of primitive theoretical concepts of the theory of choice, a procedure outlined above as tactic ii), which Lancaster as a behaviourist *cum* neutralist endorses. For consider that an economic agent purchases that commodity-bundle represented at the point of "equilibrium" on his highest attainable "indifference curve": if such a representation does *not* mean that the agent is maximizing his utility or subjective satisfaction, which interpretation would have provided a natural translation into Utilitarian prescription, then the theorist must begin searching for some other manner in which to employ the hypotheses of the theory of choice for normative purposes. Well, what our neutralist *does* interpret the purchase of a commodity-bundle to mean is that the consumer is buying that combination of goods which he simply has historically chosen to buy. In this context, the most obvious normative step is seductive – namely, to conclude that what the agent *ought* to choose is what he *does* choose. And it would therefore follow, as Lancaster puts it, that his welfare increases or he is "better off" in position B than in position A as long as he has more choices available in position B.

But the move, although alluring within a behaviourist *cum* neutralist context, is nevertheless fatal, and for the very reason that it is carried out *within such a context*. In an opposed anti-neutralist interpretation, the accepted claim that the choice of A would maximize utility *ipso facto* carries Utilitarian prescriptive force for the agent. But the behaviourist-naturalist is precluded from the assertion of such a connection as part of the cognitive content of the theory of choice. Indeed, on his interpretation, "the choice of A" entails no assertion that A was chosen for any reason or on any evaluative basis at all, as the description refers merely to the consumer's actual, overt purchases of A when alternatives were available. But such "takings", even if they can be correctly called "choices", not being actions performed for certain reasons, would have at most an undetermined contingent connection with normative grounds for action like utility maximization. And, in the light of this predicament, it would be arbitrary and spurious, à la Lancaster, to claim, at least by implication, that the expansion of such "choices" *per se* constitutes a legitimate normative criterion, that a policy of expanding choices *ought* to be adopted. For choices are desirable only if they *do* realize some value or conform to some norm which the agent prizes, and such a normative presupposition is just what the behaviourist-neutralist denies. In sum, such a neutralist backs himself into a methodological dilemma. Having construed choices in the context of an explanatory theory of consumer behaviour as without an evaluative meaning, he yet wants in welfare economics to construe those very same "choices" as "good", but we have seen that he can meet his aims only at the price of inconsistency. And yet if he interprets the theory of choice consistently, he rules out the desired applicability of the theory of choice to normative questions of economic policy.[22]

Of course, we may expect that logical positivist orientations in neo-classical economics will not go gently into the methodological night.[23] For, it will still be objected, from the perspective of an operationalist behaviourism outlined above, that anti-neutralist theory-constructions violate correct principles of scientific method since they engender untestable scientific theories.

Such a methodological scruple is, however, a needless and debilitating one. The original advocates of operationalism abandoned its initial formulation for good reason. Confronted with the fact that the model science of physics itself contained terms apparently referring to imperceptible entities for which no operationalist definition in terms of observables could be provided, it came to be realized that the requisite methodological prescription was not to demand the *translatability* of all theoretical terms into observational ones; rather, it was sufficient that any scientific hypothesis incorporating terms purporting to denote unobservable entities be capable of *confirmation* or validation on the basis of observable data, and that this was possible without the prior realization of the translatability thesis.[24] For some reason, the majority of neo-classical economists reflecting on methodological issues have remained with the early positivists in refusing to distinguish questions of meaning and reference from those of confirmation – if an economic hypothesis contains terms apparently referring to unobservable entities, it is concluded that either such terms can be defined by means of the observation language or the hypothesis is scientifically spurious. The point, however, is that such a stringency is not necessary to permit the testability of a theory. As long as statements incorporating mentalistic *cum* value concepts can be confirmed (or disconfirmed) by publicly observable data, they comply with correct principles of scientific method. But the evaluative mental states referred to by these concepts do find public expression in the observable choice behaviour they systemically cause; hence, such confirmation is tractable.

A further objection should also be considered at this point. I refer to the claim that the anti-neutralist standard of utility maximization is unacceptably wedded to psychological and ethical hedonism.

In response to this objection, it must be admitted that the concept of utility involved in the purchase of economic commodities was traditionally interpreted in a hedonistic fashion as referring to expected pleasurable states of consciousness which would accompany the use of material goods. And in line with classical Utilitarian ethical theory such enjoyable mental states were considered not only the ultimate ethical justification for action but also its sole motivation – pleasure was both the standard of the desirable and the only object desired. However, such a "hedonistic bias", although historically under-standable, should not be considered a necessary element in an anti-neutralist interpretation of the theory of choice. For, the anti-neutralist can leave open the important questions of the legitimate moral justifications and actual psychological motivations for action. But what he refuses to accept is that questions of the moral and psychological bases for action (whatever they may be) are entirely inessential to the explanatory forces or normative applicability of a theory of choice. And, although tainted by its historical association with hedonistic ethical theory, he might still retain the concept of utility to do double duty in using it to refer to both the moral guide and the psychological goad to economic conduct. (The rationale for requiring it to do double duty will be explained in Chapter 9.) Of course, at this level or stage of inquiry, with the notion of utility being thus noncommittal with respect to the *specific content* of moral reasons and psychological motivations, the capacity of economic theory to recommend or explain concrete choices must be held in abeyance until the content is supplied.

Although the substantive issues involved will be pursued later in this study,[25] we might put the preceding considerations in another way by observing that the integration of an adequate psychology of choice into CCT must also be capable of serving as an appropriate ethics of choice. More precisely, insofar as CCT includes a specification of certain mental causes in the explanation of consumer behaviour, such causes must also suffice in the identification of the reasons or evaluative grounds for *rational* economic conduct. From its inception, economic science has been charged with the dual task of constructing theories of human behaviour that possess both explanatory power and normative force. Not surprisingly, such a symbiosis has been notoriously difficult to sustain without impugning the scientific integrity of economics. And, in the contemporary context, we have observed attempts by certain value-neutralists to secure such integrity with radical surgery – by entirely removing evaluative concepts from a foundational theory (CCT). More particularly, such efforts were found to deploy "operationalist" interpretations of theoretical vocabulary *via* behaviourist reductions of the mentalistic language required to formulate valuations to terms referring only to publicly observable phenomena. The enactment of their surgery, however, has been to undermine the symbiosis in both its dimensions: not only has the explanatory power of economic theory been needlessly circumscribed, but the normative applicability of such theory has been seriously obstructed.

In sum, the analysis of this chapter has revealed that the alliance of value-neutrality with operationalist *cum* behaviourist programmes is a degenerative one.[26] Such neutralist efforts are, therefore, ill-founded.

Chapter 5

The Ethical Content of "Formal" Structures

So far our examination of the normative dimension of economic theory-construction has been restricted to a peculiarly "amoral" variety. In particular, we have investigated that feature of the theory of rational choice (CCT) in which it is shown as prescribing the best or optimal means for a consumer to attain his end of maximum satisfaction from the use of material goods, irrespective of whether or not such maximizing behaviour would be in conformity with ethical principles. Indeed, formulating another principle of what we have called the "orthodoxy" in contemporary methodology, neo-classical economists have generally argued that economic theory implies no *categorical* (moral) imperatives prescribing actions that all agents ought, unconditionally, to perform. Rather, endorsing principles of scientific method urged by logical empiricists, such "mainstream" economists have insisted that their theories only underwrite *hypothetical* or prudential imperatives which take final (economic) ends as given, and merely prescribe efficient means for attaining these goals. Following the positivist lead, this situation has frequently been characterized as the compliance of economic theory-construction with the alleged "ethical neutrality" of all genuine scientific methods.[1]

Nevertheless, there still remains a persistent source of disagreement with this "official view" of economic methodology; a minority of economists and philosophers of science would yet maintain that important sectors of economic theory incorporate a stronger normative element in a recourse to distinctly moral judgments in the formulation or justification of their hypotheses. It is sometimes alleged, for example, that the entire neo-classical micro-economic theories of the rational consumer and entrepreneur involve a commitment to the traditional ethical theories of Utilitarianism and political liberalism. Historically, some members of this dissident group have gone so far as to claim that economics in general is primarily a normative theory, recommending *bona fide* moral ideals for the production, distribution and consumption of material goods, whereas any descriptive/explanatory role that economic principles possess is at best a by-product of the application of its ethical norms.[2] And there are recent signs that the minority voice is increasing in volume and significance.[3]

Moreover, it seems to me that the minority rejection of "value-free" economic science is in fact a more accurate understanding of economic method. In an initial defence of this maverick point of view, it will be useful to anticipate a possible reply to our conclusion of the preceding chapter. In particular, it might be rejoined that strategies i) and ii) of that chapter *do* (illicitly) realize their original objective. For, the reply might continue, the behaviourist translation or elimination of the evaluative concepts of CCT has at least enabled economists to abstain from introducing their own value judgments into the construction of a scientific theory. And on our own understanding above, only such subjective intrusions would compromise the value-neutrality of the economic scientist *qua* scientist.

We may agree that, given certain *aims* for theory-construction and precautions in realizing those aims, an economist *may* avoid compromising his value-neutrality in the construction of his theories. He may, no doubt, limit himself to reporting the values of the subjects he is studying without appraising such values. Nevertheless, it is not at all clear that the neutralist tactics discussed in the last chapter deliver the value-neutrality they promise. Indeed, it will prove instructive to notice that, even under conditions when neutralists abstain from referring to the values of the agents under investigation, they do not *ipso facto* abstain from importing (perhaps unwittingly) their own value presuppositions into the content of their theories. Although, in principle, strategies to exclude evaluative concepts from the description and explanation of consumer choice need not have camouflaged the persistence of ethical commitments in CCT, we shall observe that economic practice bespeaks just such methodological double-speak.[4]

To see that this is the case, we might approach the theme of the last chapter from, so to speak, the opposite direction. Suppose we *were* to grant the acceptability of a purely "formal" or structural interpretation of CCT. Even under this (unnecessary) concession, we shall argue in this chapter that certain so-called structural principles of CCT are not, in any case, ethically neutral. The austerity of their vocabulary has yet tolerated the covert presupposition of moral commitments. In support of this conclusion, we shall examine (i) the allegedly "given" end of consumer behaviour – i.e., the "maximization of utility" and (ii) transitivity axiom A_3. (For the purposes of this chapter, a "formal" or "structural" interpretation of a choice principle may be under-stood as one that remains noncommittal as to the qualitative content of what satisfies any consumer, since it makes no reference to the substantive evaluative bases or reasons for preference orderings.)[5]

1. Maximizing and Moral Options

What presuppositions of moral value, then, are contained in the meaning of the concept of maximization of utility, even when limited to a "formal" construal of this concept. Admittedly, it is true, as Boulding points out,[6] that the employment of the utility calculus of CCT, if interpreted structurally, does not logically entail a commitment to conceiving the choices of any consumer as motivated by a "selfish" form of self-interest. Granted the maximization principle formulates a version of psychological egoism, since the agent is described as seeking the greatest possible satisfaction *for himself* from the use of consumer goods; nevertheless, it is yet possible that he achieves maximal satisfaction through intermediate altruistic acts, such as finding personal satisfaction in "philanthropic" measures of distributing the goods he has been able to purchase to others who cannot afford them. (Nor, of course, does a formalistic construal of the "maximization of utility" preclude the possibility that an agent be motivated by considerations of self-interest of a completely selfish type – that, for instance, the consumer seek his maximal subjective satisfaction solely through his private consumption of the commodities he buys.)

Nevertheless, the implicit value-ladenness of the consumer's goal of maximum utility, understood structurally or formally, is to be discovered in an analysis of the meaning of the concept of *maximizing simpliciter*, as employed in CCT, rather than the utility maximized. Generally speaking, neo-classical economists have accepted an interpretation of the concept of maximizing as it was defined within the framework of the type of classical Utilitarian ethic formulated by Bentham. Now, within Benthamite Utilitarianism, an agent's maximizing his utility is to be understood in an exclusively "expansionist" sense – that is, an agent is able to augment his total utility only if he increases the quantity of his satisfied desires.[7] Accordingly, in applying this Benthamite explication of rational decision-making neo-classical economists conceive a consumer as maximizing the utility he derives from the use of commodities only if he expands as far as possible the quantity of satisfied desires for available goods. Such an interpretation of the *form* of maximization is clearly manifest in the postulation of non-satiation axiom (A_2) where a consumer is described as preferring to possess additional units of any available commodity, rather than resting content with his already attained level of consumption.[8] And, hence, he would increase his satisfied desires, and thereby maximize his utility, only if he purchased increasingly more material goods when they became obtainable.[9]

Such a method of maximizing subjective satisfaction does, however, presuppose the acceptance of an (unavowed) value-judgment rejecting the preferability of *alternative* means of *maximizing* satisfaction. For increasing satisfied desires is not the *only* accessible method of maximizing utility. Such a disposition is not logically or empirically necessary. One need only return to an elucidation of a formula defining satisfaction in Stoic moral philosophy[10] to recognize that there are moral options within maximizing behaviour.

We find, then, that the Stoic school understood that an individual's personal satisfaction was a matter of the ratio of his satisfied to unsatisfied desires. Hence, such satisfaction might be represented by equation, Q,

$$Q: \text{satisfaction} = \frac{\text{fulfilled desires}}{\text{unfulfilled desires,}}$$

where the higher the ratio, the greater the satisfaction. Hence, and most importantly, it is clear that, under such a schema, an agent can increase his satisfaction by *either* increasing the numerator or decreasing the denominator, or both. *A fortiori*, it is *not* the case, contrary to the policy of Benthamite Utilitarianism and the axioms of CCT tacitly aligned with this viewpoint, that the agent can only maximize his satisfaction by adding to the numerator, that is, by increasing his satisfied desires. Rather, his greatest possible satisfaction would be achieved, in line with the Stoic formula, by maximizing the satisfaction ratio – that is, by *both* augmenting his satisfied desires and lowering his unsatisfied ones.

Moreover, it seems to me that formulating prudential decisions in accord with the preceding equation is a more rational, because better informed, policy for an agent to endorse than one conforming to Benthamite Utilitarian policy. In light of the vicissitudes of the "human condition", especially due to the all too common unintended consequences of action-choices, it is surely an unenlightened agent who fails to take into consideration that a frequent source of *dissatisfaction* is found in acting on desires that fail to realize their anticipated satisfactions.

Furthermore, for the neo-classical consumer who subscribes to the "expansionist" rule of utility maximization recommended by Benthamite Utilitarianism, a psychological mechanism is operative which augurs further sources of dissatisfaction. Now, whereas it is true that the fulfilment of a desire brings about a state of satisfaction, contrariwise, the arousal of a new desire engenders a dissatisfied state until that desire is fulfilled. But we have observed that the neo-classical Benthamite seeks to maximize his subjective satisfaction from the consumption of material goods solely by increasing the quantity of his satisfied desires for such goods. Consequently, for such an agent, the consumption of commodities will be "cumulative" – the securing of one desired commodity-bundle will only prompt a desire for more goods in an unending cycle. Hence, no matter what degree of material satisfaction he realizes, he will be prey to perpetual dissatisfaction. And, thus, the attaining of any *final* equilibrium state at which the neo-classical consumer, being completely satisfied or "sated" with his attained accumulation of commodities, will have no motivation to alter his purchasing, is empirically impossible.

In sum, the preceding observations serve to establish two conclusions:

a) The claim by many neo-classical economists that, if CCT is interpreted structurally, it can be seen to be value-neutral cannot be sustained. For a structurally interpreted CCT includes the formulation of an expansionist Utilitarian norm for *maximizing* utility even when "utility" is emptied of descriptive content.[11]

b) On the basis of an assessment of two kinds of liabilities in the Utilitarian "expansionist" rule for maximizing satisfaction, it is manifest that a more rational policy for an enlightened consumer would take advantage of a Stoic desideratum. That is, a truly rational consumer would sometimes *contract* his desires, thereby diminishing the chance of frustrating them due to the unintended consequences of choices, and also rendering possible the realization of a final equilibrium state. Such an agent would not, therefore, proceed on the assumption of CCT that "more is better", and, thus, would not act on the (false) basis that preferring more of any obtainable commodity will uniformly yield greater satisfaction.

With respect to b) it should not be overlooked, however, that we have recommended only the inclusion of the Stoic element as a desideratum for the maximization of subjective satisfaction, not the wholesale replacement of the Benthamite Utilitarian policy by the Stoic one. For it must be admitted that Stoic moral philosophers erred at the opposite extreme to Benthamites, by their almost exclusive advocacy of the value imperative suggested by the denominator of equation Q – that a rational agent should seek to maximize his satisfaction by curbing his desires. Hence Epictetus advises:

> He who is entering on a state of improvement, having learnt from the philosophers that the object of desire is good, of aversion evil, and having

> learnt too, that prosperity and ease are not otherwise attainable by man, than in not being disappointed of his desire, nor incurring his aversion, such a one removes totally from himself and postpones desire.[12]

But the absurdity of Epictetus' advice, if adopted as a *sole* policy for rational choice, is clearly evident. Since, as Epictetus himself affirms, all personal satisfaction occurs through securing objects of desire, if one uniformly and consistently suppressed all desire, then one could attain no satisfaction at all.

The normative upshot of our criticism of the rule for *maximizing* (utility) implicit in CCT would be the following. Any rational agent should attempt to maximize his satisfaction from the consumption of commodities by integrating into a single policy *both* the numerator and denominator of equation Q – that is, by simultaneously seeking to increase fulfilled desire and reduce unfulfilled ones. Translated into concrete terms, although it would take us too far afield to go into detail here, such a policy would, not surprisingly, recommend the ancient Aristotelian injunction to be *moderate* in attempting to satisfy oneself from the use of material goods. Although the possession of a certain quantity of commodities is necessary to reach this goal, the interminable pursuit of continually more such satisfaction in trying to maximize it is self-defeating.

Needless to say, the madness in the neo-classical subscription to an expansionist criterion for maximizing consumer satisfaction has not been without method. For the inclusion within CCT of a less than expansionist maximizing rule for a rational consumer would contravene such an entrenched moral imperative of historical liberalism as the "growth ethic", the desirability of aggrandizing the appropriation of personal material goods. And neo-classical economists have presupposed the validity of this ideal in constructing their theories of the behaviour of rational consumers and entrepreneurs; indeed, the norm of acquisitive aggrandizement or "possessive individualism"[13] has in part defined the meaning of rational economic behaviour in neo-classical theory.

2. Liberal or Illiberal Growth Ethic

It is significant that concrete economic activity in our times has resulted in a paradoxical status for the "liberal growth ethic." Put summarily, as Mishan for one has perceptively argued,[14] certain common features of contemporary productive processes threaten to transform this normative principle into an illiberal growth ethic. Why?

Suppose, for the sake of argument, we were to adapt Lancaster's criterion, presented in Chapter 4, section 3, and agree that a consumer's welfare or personal good increases as his "effective" range of choices increases. By effective we shall understand that the consumer is capable of enacting the additional choices. Clearly such a criterion is reinforced by classical conceptions of political liberalism wherein it is deemed conducive to the common good that an individual be free to act as he chooses, as long as his choices do not harm others or interfere with the capabilities for free choice of other agents.[15] In any event, it would follow from the criterion that an individual consumer's effective choice and thus welfare would increase if:

i)   his real income increased such that he had greater purchasing power for the goods currently produced, or

ii)   more consumption goods were produced increasing the range of commodities over which he could dispose his given income, or both i) and ii).

Aggregating over different individuals, social welfare would increase insofar as these conditions were applicable to such consumers. Not surprisingly, as Mishan explains,[16] advocates of economic growth have used just such a criterion to urge the expansion of the production of consumer goods on the grounds that, in increasing effective choice, such growth in output directly increases social welfare.

Such an understanding of an economic "growth ethic" is reinforced in neo-classical economics by non-satiation axiom A_2 of CCT, implying, as we have seen, that the rational consumer would prefer to have more goods, if possible. However, the growth in production which serves such insatiability can significantly undermine the liberal dimension of the liberal growth ethic.

In initial support of this claim, we may remember our observation, in criticism of Lancaster, that an appeal to expanded choice does not, in itself, have positive normative force. Rather, some value must be realized by the further choice: for present concerns, let us say the choice secures some end the agent finds desirable. With respect to the consistency of the free-market economy's espousal of individual liberty, the critical point here is that market processes themselves, particularly those of the producer, should not create consumer desires, but satisfy the desires "given" to productive processes by individual participants in the economy. Clearly a "management of consumer demand" by producers would violate the classical constraint on individual liberty that one party's free practices (here that of the producer) do not obstruct the opportunities to exercise free choice on the part of others (the consumers). But such practices as the "synthesis" of consumer wants by industrial advertising, in order to absorb the growth in productive capacity fostered by advances in technology, stand accused of just such a violation. (We shall return to a more extensive discussion of the relation between the "manipulation" of consumer desire and individual autonomy in Chap. 13.)

There is, furthermore, an important link between economic growth and environmental consequences that bears on the capacity of the growth ethic to remain compatible with principles of liberalism. I refer to the topical problem of the generation of "external diseconomies" or "negative spillovers" as a by-product of the expansion of certain types of production in contemporary society. A familiar example is that of the traffic congestion and pollution caused by the growth of automobile production. As those on the receiving end of such disutility are not compensated by the offending producers, there are social costs of production not expressed in the price system of a free-market economy. It is evident that such externalities contravene both exceptive conditions of political liberalism: the choices of certain producers directly bring about dissatisfaction or loss of welfare for others, and limit the capability of others to freely choose certain activities. Moreover, the public's understandable resistance to being victimized by such spillovers has led to an increasing degree of governmental control of the productive activities of firms responsible for the social costs. Ironically, prescriptions for growth within a free-market economy, promoted jointly by technological developments in production and insatiable consumption, augur nothing less than the attenuation of both the entrepreneurial and consumer choice definitive of a market system. There are other reasons for economic growth, such as sustaining an adequate level of employment. But arguments that such growth expands individual freedom of choice are often less than compelling ones.

3. Consumer "Consistency" and its Value

The second, allegedly purely structural element of CCT that, upon analysis, can be shown to possess (covert) evaluative content is the transitivity of preferences as formulated by "consistency" axiom A_3.

Now it is especially crucial to the theoretical adequacy of CCT that A_3 should survive criticism of its coherence and general truth. For a bedrock feature of the explanatory framework of CCT is the conception of consumers as attempting to maximize their utility derived from the purchasing of commodities, on the basis of their preferences for combinations of these

56

commodities. However, as we pointed out in Chapter 3, if the preferences of a particular consumer do not satisfy the transitivity postulate, then he will not possess an uniquely determined preference ordering. Hence, his intransitive set of preferences will express the fact that there will be no commodity-bundle which is unambiguously highest on his scale of preference.[17] But, under these circumstances, no consistent utility function can be assigned to such a consumer, and, therefore, his behaviour will be outside the range of the theoretical competency of CCT. That is, his behaviour can be neither adequately explained nor predicted within CCT.

Empirical observations have confirmed, furthermore, that such intransitive preference structures *are* sometimes exhibited in the behaviour of consumers.[18] An important question, therefore, arises. Under which additional factual assumptions regarding consumer tastes, other than the assumptions explicitly stated in simplified codifications of CCT, is A_3 true of consumers, and of whom, consequently, CCT would be competent to explain or predict their behaviour? In reply, we find that the common assumption appealed to by neo-classical economic theorists is that of "constancy of tastes".[19] Thus, the "consistency" of consumers, which neo-classicists claim to be implied by A_3, refers, roughly, to the fact that if S prefers A to B on one occasion, he will, given the same prices and income, exhibit the same ordering on other occasions.[20] And, of course, if such consistency were absent, transitivity of preference would no longer be guaranteed across the relevant period of time. Accordingly, CCT is claimed to account for the behaviour of consumers who do not significantly *change* their comparative likes or dislikes for available commodities, at least for the time span between (1) the period for which economists have identified an individual's preference structures and (2) the time at which the event to be explained occurred or the predicted event will occur. Conversely, if a consumer's taste or preference orderings were continually in a state of flux, then CCT would be incapable of explaining or predicting his choices.

It might be objected here that we are placing an unreasonably heavy explanatory burden on neo-classical theory. For CCT, it might be argued, does not intend to account for consumer choice *across time*. Rather, the axioms of CCT, in particular transitivity axiom A_3, are true of the preference-structure of any consumer only for a particular instant. But, in order to explain actual consumer choices over a period of time, the axioms of CCT would admittedly need to be supplemented by hypotheses describing the transformation of preference-structures over time.

Such an objection is, however, misdirected and of no avail to neo-classical theorists. For, even though CCT is employed as a statical theory, it is, nevertheless, used, without the supplementation of transformation principles, as a theory of *comparative* statics. That is, given a consumer's utility function, the theory seeks to identify, for changes in prices and income, *successive* consumer equilibria, or shifts from an original point of optimal allocation of income amongst commodities to a subsequent one – even though no account of the elapsed time or psychological processes occurring during the readjustment is provided. But the agent's preference-structure as represented by his utility-function must remain constant or no determinate identification of the series of equilibria is possible. And it is just such stable preferences which are presupposed in the affirmation of transitivity axiom A_3. Clearly, then, in *comparing* successive equilibria, the neo-classical theory of choice (CCT) must not only be applied over time, but A_3 is the *sina qua non* of such applicability.

Of course, if CCT were conjoined with a theory explaining the evolution of consumer wants and their propensity to change, as "Institutionalists" and Marxist economists have strongly urged,[21] then CCT would not be so incapacitated when confronted with choices determined by volatile preference-patterns. Neo-classical economists have, however, resisted such advice.

But why? Surely sound recommendations as to methods for enlarging the explanatory scope of a theory are to be welcomed by serious scientists, and taken into consideration in reconstructing their theory. Thus, given an understanding of the law-governed processes responsible for altering consumer tastes, a neo-classical economist might abandon the unqualified form of his transitivity axiom A_3, adding an explicit *proviso* in the form of an antecedent condition to A_3 that consumer tastes are stable, while also appending further postulates to his original set to cover those cases where the agent's preference pattern undergoes significant change. And yet, this kind of theory revision has been resisted.

Moreover, in my opinion, such revision has been avoided because of the covert *normative* content of the transitivity axiom, *even* as structurally interpreted. Again, as so interpreted, A_3 is concerned with a complete, transitive ordering of alternatives irrespective of the evaluative grounds or reasons for such rankings. Nevertheless, even when thus limited to such "formal" considerations, the empirical applicability of A_3 demands a high degree of stability in a consumer's wants. How then have neo-classical economists sought to interpret the not uncommon existence of unstable wants? Would they not simply agree to a straightforward interpretation from a methodological point of view, that such phenomena are beyond the explanatory scope of their theory of consumer behaviour (CCT) and, therefore, evidence of an important limitation of the theory?

The typical response of neo-classical economists has, however, been significantly different. Recourse has been taken to *criticizing* unstable wants from the *normative* perspective of the neo-classical concept of "rational economic man". The transitivity axiom's presupposition of enduring tastes is to be understood as indicating that CCT takes as its subject matter *only* the behaviour of *rational* economic agents. And, at the centre of the meaning of the proposed ideal development of human nature encompassed by the concept "rational economic man" is that of a severed "calculatedness". By definition, rational economic man or *homo economicus*[22] formulates *deliberate* choices from amongst alternative actions. Such an attitude, neo-classicists believe, requires that the rational man repress the spontaneous satisfaction of his immediate impulses, thus introducing a significant degree of stability in his wants, which, in technical terms, permits a complete, transitive ordering of his preferences, which, in turn, renders possible (the neo-classical theory's concept of) the maximization of his utility.[23]

(A qualifying remark is appropriate here. We may observe that, at a moment in time, even when motivated by random spontaneity of desire, it remains logically and empirically possible for an agent to exhibit transitive preferences in accord with A_3 – although less probable. Nevertheless, if his motivations are of this characteristic pattern across time it is highly likely that he will be subject to changes of taste or preference reversal in the extended period and thus frustrate the applicability of A_3 for that period.)

When challenged, then, some neo-classical theorists would grant that A_3 of CCT is not true of consumers whose purchasing exhibits spontaneity or random variability in their preference-structures, or the persistent flux in wants such a structure expresses. Nevertheless, these theorists continue, it is their intention in the employment of CCT to explain *rational* economic action, whereas the "erratic" purchasing patterns following upon intransitive preferences are, by neo-classical definition, essentially *irrational*. Or, put another way, the transitivity axiom (A_3) of CCT formulates a principle of *consistency* for economic agents, and is to be understood as describing regularities in the behaviour of *homo economicus* who behaves thus consistently, not as describing the behaviour of impulsive, inconsistent consumers. As Robbins characterizes the position of neo-classical economics:

> And thus in the last analysis Economics does depend if not for its significance at least for its existence, on an ultimate valuation – the affirmation that rationality and the ability to choose with knowledge is desirable. If irrationality, if the surrender to the blind force of external stimuli and uncoordinated impulse at every moment is a good to be preferred above all others, then it is *true* that the *raison d'être* of Economics disappears.[24]

We find, then, that in defining the value of "rationality" within the corpus of CCT, economic theorists have proposed the behaviour of an ideal economic man, one who subscribes to a norm of methodical, self-controlled deliberation in economic choice-situations. Hence, the transitivity postulate A_3 would be misinterpreted as purely "formal" or "structural", without the presupposition of any normative aspect of choice-processes. For neo-classical economists have *limited* the truth conditions of A_3 to the behaviour of agents whose purchasing patterns manifest their adherence to this norm of "calculatedness" expressed in the ideal of "rational economic man" (*homo economicus*).

Now, at this juncture, we need not identify and establish the distinctly moral commitments embedded in the "orderly personality" presupposed by A_3. This will be reserved for the next section. Rather, suppose, for the sake of argument, we were to accept the neo-classical conception of utility maximization as an ultimate goal or intrinsic moral value. Is it, nevertheless, possible to show that transitivity axiom A_3 of CCT has deficient *instrumental* value? Would an agent whose choices regularly satisfy A_3, nevertheless, contrary to the claims of neo-classical theorists, *fail* to uniformly maximize the utility he derives from the activity of consuming material goods?

The history of critical commentary on neo-classical economic theory testifies to the fundamental importance of this question. Now, we have seen that, in order to introduce the proper stability in his desires, it is incumbent upon the rational economic man to adopt a disciplined, planned approach to decision-making. As Alfred Marshall expresses this attitude in the *locus classicus* of neo-classical economics, his *Principles of Economics*:

> The side of life with which economics is specially concerned is that in which man's conduct is most deliberate, and in which he most often reckons up the advantages and disadvantages of any particular action before he enters on it. And further it is that side of his life in which, when he does follow habit and custom and proceeds for the moment without calculation, the habits and customs themselves are most nearly sure to have risen from a close and careful watching of the advantages and disadvantages of different courses of conduct.[25]

Most importantly, such calculatedness of the economic man, whether as producer or consumer, implies that certain psychological dispositions or character traits are to be eschewed. The rational consumer, as characterized by Marshall, never buys on impulse, constantly repressing any spontaneous urge to indulge himself in the purchase of "transient enjoyment" in preference to a "lasting source of pleasure".[26] He is, moreover, ever vigilant of the need to exert self-control by patiently postponing present satisfaction in order to save his income for future use.[27] And, as a general practice, the neo-classical consumer prefers a pattern of "wholesome" consumption consisting in the purchase of durable goods providing continuing sources of satisfaction, rather than the capricious consumption of "ephemeral luxuries".[28] In fact, in Marshall's view, ... "It is deliberateness, and not selfishness, that is characteristic of the modern age".[29]

Beginning with Weber, critical reaction to the preceding picture of rational economic man and the evaluative attitudes he encapsulates have been vehement and persistent. Weber,[30] for instance, saw in *homo economicus* a personification of the capitalist spirit of "worldly asceticism". For Weber, the deliberate, self-controlled calculations of the ideal economic man of neo-classical price theory were underwritten by what he called the "rationalistic economic ethic"[31] of capitalistic economic systems, which ethic commanded the repression of personal enjoyment in order to maximize material wealth. As Weber put it ... "The *summum bonum* of this ethic [is] the earning of more and more money, combined with the strict avoidance of all spontaneous enjoyment of life."[32] According to Weber, this systematization or rationalization of economic conduct was morally supported, indeed commanded, by the religious ethic of Protestant Calvinism.

More contemporary writers have further elucidated and criticized what they take to be the underlying moral basis of the capitalist economic system described by neo-classical theory. Schumpeter, for instance, characterized the repressive notion of rational economic action outlined in Marshall as due to "mid-Victorian morality, seasoned by Benthamism".[33] Similarly, Weisskopf in his *Economics and Alienation*[34] argues that the scheme of economic rationality for the ideal agent formulated by Marshall, although set forth under the pretence of an empirical hypothesis intended to describe and explain *de facto* economic behaviour, was actually grounded, perhaps unconsciously, in Marshall's adherence to, and promulgation of, the austere morality of Victorian bourgeois society. Moreover, according to Weisskopf and other critics,[35] the systematic impulse-control characteristic of neo-classical economic rationality is *not* conducive to the general well-being of the individual, nor to the long run survival of particular societies. Building on recent psychoanalytic theories,[36] they claim that the methodical, regular repression of random or spontaneous impulse demanded of rational economic man, only induces mental disorder or anguish for the individual and eventual anarchic rebellion for the societies whose institutions foster such repression.

Of course, even if these ominous predictions of the fate of *homo economicus* and the capitalist societies he populates are sound, nevertheless, it would be premature to conclude that the question we posed concerning the instrumental value of the transitivity postulate A_3 had been answered in the negative. For the question at issue was whether or not the "consistency" or stability in an individual's preference-structure would maximize his *material* satisfaction brought about by commodity consumption; but the personal misery mentioned by the above critics as following upon the behaviour of *homo economicus* is best understood as referring to the overall well-being of an individual, not just the material utility to which our question confines itself. And it is possible that even though the disposition cluster of self-restrained calculatedness did yield maximum long-run material satisfaction, such a gain might be overridden by the dissatisfaction present in the psychic disorder induced by the repression of immediate impulse demanded by the calculatedness. In any case, the relevant question, in the more limited context of our analysis, is whether the constant calculatedness of the ideal economic man of CCT does, in fact, even bring about maximum material satisfaction for the consumer.

Although this question can be straightforwardly posed, it is exceedingly difficult to provide an unambiguous answer. No doubt, if the "consistency" of the consumer presupposed by transitivity axiom (A_3) were that of strictly logical consistency, no rational agent would demur from behaving thus consistently. However, the "consistency" described by A_3 is clearly not logical consistency as an agent would not be deliberating in a self-contradictory manner in *revising his tastes*, however abruptly, from one choice-occasion to the next. But under these circumstances A_3 would often be false of the preference-structure of an agent whose practical reasoning, nevertheless, obeys the rules of logic. If not a strictly logical notion, then, perhaps the consistency of the rational consumer can be interpreted as a justifiable "pragmatic" claim on his rationality.

Under this interpretation, from the point of view of one type of value-theoretic framework, the claim that a rational agent would be consistent in his choices in the manner implied by A_3 is entirely defensible. For within the classical Utilitarian framework for prudential decision-making, which is essentially that employed by CCT,[37] the justification of an action depends on the desirability of its expected consequences. But, from such a viewpoint, prior to making a choice from amongst alternative courses of action, a rational agent would take into consideration the long run, rather than merely the immediate consequences of the available actions. Such an enlightened agent, appreciating that satisfying experiences accrue over the time-span of his entire life, and recognizing that the prospect of being thwarted in the pursuit of such satisfaction will depend in part on the occurrence of avoidable future contingencies, will construct an overarching strategy for decision-making. Such a strategy requires that he sometimes be willing to forego the gratification of immediate impulse in order that future dissatisfactions be avoided and attainable satisfactions increased. In the context of selecting a rational strategy for consumption, moreover, there is the all too familiar prospect of the occurrence of a future contingency which would disastrously truncate the degree of satisfaction attainable from buying material goods, if a consumer indulged himself primarily in gratifying his immediate economic impulses. His resource for securing any satisfaction from consumption, i.e., his income, is limited; hence, if he spends all or most of it on immediate consumption, he will be left in the unenviable position of lacking the means for even a minimal, let alone maximal, fulfilment of future consumption desires. One need not fear the spectre of becoming a joyless, repressed *homo economicus* in order to see the familiar wisdom of deliberately planning for future consumption needs by not squandering one's income on immediate consumption.

Moreover, a close reading of Marshall's *Principles* testifies to the fact that, within neo-classical theory, the prescription, presupposed by A_3, that a rational consumer ought to avoid momentary impulses for particular commodities in favour of an enduring, stable set of wants and preference rankings, can, *in part*, be understood as simply applying the Utilitarian norm enjoining a rational agent to gauge the justifiability of an action on the basis of a comprehensive overview of the value of both proximate and remote consequences. As a result, he will be disposed to defer immediate satisfaction if the greater value of more distant satisfactions warrants such a measure. And it is to the merit of neo-classical economists to have introduced a formal refinement of this prescription. Let us see how.

We have noted that the axioms of CCT imply that, at a particular moment in time, the rational consumer maximizes his satisfaction when his behaviour accords with the equimarginal principle, that is, when he distributes his income amongst alternative commodity-bundles such that the marginal utility per dollars worth of each commodity is the same. *A fortiori*, neo-classicists argue, if goods are to be bought at different moments in time, the rational agent will maximize his utility by equating the marginal utilities for the commodities purchased at different times. Hence, the *ideally rational agent* will display no *temporal preference*, that is, no ranking of present over future consumption solely on the grounds of temporal priority. In other words, he will not favour the *immediate* gratification promised by present purchases. Thus, Marshall cautions ... "A prudent person will endeavour to distribute his means [income] between all their several uses [alternative purchases], present and future, in such a way that they will have in each the same marginal utility."[38] The fact, furthermore, that the equimarginal principle, as applied to inter-temporal consumption, is being used within neo-classical theory, in the first instance, as a norm recommending rational consumption, rather than as an empirical hypothesis describing actual consumer practices, is revealed by the fact that Marshall himself does *not* believe that, in inter-temporal circumstances, the equimarginal principle truly describes even probable consumer behaviour. For, as Marshall sees it, such rationality succumbs to all too human nature:

> If people regarded future benefits as equally desirable with similar benefits at the present time, they would probably endeavour to distribute their pleasures and other satisfactions equally throughout their lives. They would generally be willing to give up a present pleasure for the sake of an equal pleasure in the future, provided they could be certain of having it. But in fact, human nature is so constituted that in estimating the "present value" of a future benefit most people generally make a second deduction from its future value, in the form of what we may call a "discount" that increases with the period for which the benefit is deferred. One will reckon a distant benefit at nearly the same value which it would have for him if it were present; while another who has less power of realizing the future, less patience and self-control, will care comparatively little for any benefit that is not near at hand.[39]

In general, current neo-classical theory follows Marshall in claiming that a rational agent should not be *generally disposed* to follow immediate, transitory impulses in consumption, as such an attitude would undermine his ability to satisfy future desires. But the avoidance of such a disabling condition is, of course, facilitated by the inculcation of the opposite condition – viz., to be generally prone to act on more constant, lasting tastes or desires.

These considerations are reinforced by the fact that if the consumer is to distribute his limited financial resources efficiently over present and future wants, it will be incumbent upon him to possess adequate prior *knowledge* of not only the likely content of his future desires for commodities, but also his probable order of preferences for future goods. However, if his preference orderings are in a state of continual flux, this situation decreases the likelihood that he will be in a position to be equipped with such knowledge. In sum, the recommendations of "consistency", implicit in the meaning of transitivity axiom A_3 of CCT, can be understood as a special case of a general Utilitarian policy for prudential decision-making recommending a pattern of stability in personal desires and preference rankings.

It must be admitted, moreover, that, irrespective of any application to economic behaviour, this policy can be defended in its own right. If the opportunity for satisfying experiences is likely to extend over time for some individual, it is an incontrovertible maxim for his rational choice that if he is aiming to maximize his utility or satisfaction, he should take into consideration temporally remote as well as more immediate possibilities for having such experiences. But the Utilitarian policy enjoining stable desires has been observed to follow from this maxim when an individual is maximizing utility subject to a constraint of limited resources. And on one reading of the intent of neo-classical theorists, the initially questionable presupposition of A_3, recommending stable tastes and preferences, has been shown to be a special case of such Utilitarian policy for the constraint of limited consumer income. But that presupposition posed the most serious threat to agreeing that behaviour in conformity to A_3 lead to the realization of the rational consumer's goal of maximum material utility. Accordingly, *under this reading*, our question concerning whether or not A_3 actually does possess sound instrumental value, that is, whether constructing transitive preference orderings does contribute to the maximization of the agent's material satisfaction, can now be answered in the affirmative.

Nevertheless, as is made evident in Marshall's *Principles*, the prescription of stable wants and preference orderings assumed by A_3 is not *only* to be interpreted, in a fully accurate analysis of the theory of consumer behaviour, as an endorsement and application of Utilitarian principles to the field of consumer choice. For a deeper reading of Marshall indicates the stability prescription is also to be understood, within neo-classical theories such as CCT, in a manner not only of dubious instrumental value for a prudent Utilitarian consumer, but also in a manner which presents a serious dilemma for the preservation of consistency in the use of fundamental tenets of neo-classical economics.

The clue to the need for a second interpretation of the stability imperative of CCT is to be found in the extreme, *indefeasible* character with which it is maintained by neo-classical theorists, even in the presence of circumstances which indicate that continued application of the imperative is unsuitable. For, suppose the constraint on a consumer's maximizing his utility is minimal, almost to the vanishing point – viz., let us assume that an individual's income is so abundant that persistent indulgence in the satisfaction of immediate, random desires for consumer goods would be of negligible consequence for his ability to meet future wants. In this situation, it would appear that any prescription of stability in wants and preferences, for the purpose of avoiding the deleterious effects of submitting to impulsive buying, would be without point. And yet, these implications of the presence of circumstances of considerable affluence rather than scarcity in personal financial resources are not taken into consideration in CCT. Indeed, Marshall can be observed castigating the rich as well as the poor when their consumption manifests that they are yielding to the desire for "transient luxuries".[40]

Moreover, in so far as maximizing consumer satisfaction is at issue, it is evident that a calculated policy of self-restrained steadfastness and long-run stability in wants and preferences can be carried too far. As a matter of empirical fact, most persons do find substantial satisfaction in a degree of spontaneity and random variability in their consumption activity. And as long as they are prudent in the distribution of their financial means to allot sufficient funds for the accommodation of future consumption needs, it would surely be self-defeating, given a goal of maximizing their utility or subjective satisfaction, to repress all measure of consumption arising out of immediate impulses, if they found such spontaneous consumption satisfying. Again, however, neo-classical theory ignores the occurrence of particular circumstances wherein maximizing utility is compatible with a degree of random impulsiveness or spontaneity in consumer choices, indeed where maximization of utility is *incompatible* with the suppression of all degree of such spontaneity. Marshall, for instance, simply recommends a blanket policy of the patient, unimpulsive purchasing of durable goods which will be lasting sources of enjoyment. As he remarks:

> The true interest of a country is generally advanced by the subordinating of the desire for transient luxuries to the attainment of those more solid and lasting resources which will assist industry in its future work, and will in various ways tend to make life larger.[41]

But is not the neo-classical espousal of an ideal of economic man *qua* dispassionate, self-restrained calculator in circumstances where spontaneity *is* satisfying and innocuous, an espousal of irrational economic man?

Most importantly, the uniform and persistent rejection of spontaneous consumption, even under conditions where this kind of consumption would be in the interest of the consumer, appears to run counter to a cardinal tenet of neo-classical economics – the doctrine of Consumer Sovereignty. This doctrine asserts two central beliefs: a) the individual consumer himself, rather than some "external authority", is in the best position to judge the sources of his own material satisfaction, and b) the final end or goal which ultimately justifies all economic activity, including production, is that of the maximal satisfaction of the given desires of individual consumers. Are neo-classical economists, then, not being inconsistent in continuing to affirm a) and b), and yet refusing to endorse spontaneous consumption when an agent, who has sufficient income such that he is not acting out of neglect of longrun consequences, finds a measure of such spontaneity personally satisfying? Why then have neo-classical economists continued to run this risk of inconsistency?

Again, we can do no better than return to a reading of Marshall's *Principles* to detect the primary reason behind the continuing neo-classical intransigence to including randomness and spontaneity within their theoretical framework for consumer behaviour. But the reason will provide an anomaly for neo-classical theory.

Now, it is an essential characteristic of such theory to conceive of consumer intentions as functioning *independently* of productive processes within the economic system. More precisely, the theory assumes that producers determine what to produce by aligning their decisions with data concerning consumer tastes which is *given* them through, for instance, surveys of consumer attitudes. Hence, if the economic processes of competitive capitalism are to be proven optimal within neo-classical theory, they are to be shown so by their tendency to most efficiently allocate resources to satisfy given consumer wants.[42] However, if we re-examine our last quotation from Marshall as representative of neo-classical theory, spontaneity in consumer practices springing from desires for immediate, "transient" satisfactions are not to be simply "taken as given". Rather they are considered outside the *normative* limits of neo-classical theory – as Marshall puts it, they don't "serve the interests of the country". What does he mean?

It seems to me that Marshall, albeit begrudgingly, is committing the neo-classical theory of consumer behaviour to a methodological dilemma which it has yet to escape. On the one hand, he claims that "consumption is the end of production",[43] and that "all wholesome enjoyments, whether luxurious or not, are legitimate ends of action, both public and private".[44] In other words, Marshall wants to accept the now orthodox doctrine that consumers are sovereign – the final purpose of productive processes is and should be the maximal satisfaction of *de facto* consumer wants. And yet, on the other hand, Marshall is disinclined to take consumer tastes as given. Rather he exhibits an inclination, however reluctant, to *evaluate* the worth of given tastes from the point of view of whether or not the purchasing patterns to which they give rise contribute to the efficiency of the *productive processes* in the consumer's society. It is on this basis that Marshall rather ambivalently agrees to the usefulness of the concept, central to classical economic theory,[45] of *productive* consumption, which he defines as "the use of wealth in the production of further wealth, and it should properly include not all the consumption of productive workers, but only that which is necessary for their efficiency."[46] And when Marshall spells out the kind of consumption which is to be classified as efficient, it is seen to exclude none other than the buying of "superfluous luxuries",[47] or goods affording "immediate and transitory enjoyment",[48] and other kindred sorts of spontaneous purchasing. For Marshall, such practices display a lack of "wisdom, forethought and unselfishness"[49] on the part of an uneconomic man.

Although not explicitly mentioned by Marshall, the reasons why erratic, spontaneous consumption would be detrimental to industrial efficiency are not hard to find. For if consumption *per se* does not demand systematic planning, successful industrial *production* does. Furthermore, the rational planning of productive processes is, in part, *dependent upon* a lack of capriciousness, and the presence of regularity and stability in the pattern of consumption itself. For consider that, within a particular market, consumer attitude tests reveal a pattern of marked instability in wants, as consumers exhibit spontaneous variability rather then deliberate "calculatedness" in their purchasing. Well, if such general instability was the rule rather than the exception in consumer wants, it would be well-nigh impossible for entrepreneurs to determine exactly which kind of goods consumers preferred, in order to be in a position to allocate resources toward the efficient production of such goods. Or, if entrepreneurs did decide to manufacture a certain type of product, the variability of consumer desires would remove any guarantee that actual industrial production would be capable of serving consumer sovereignty, of satisfying individual wants.

This last prospect, furthermore, makes a final, clear-cut answer to our question concerning the instrumental value of the "consistency" postulates A_3 difficult to come by. For the dilemma which troubled Marshall is ineradicable within the boundaries of a neo-classical economic system. On the one hand, individual consumers are held to be sovereign or autonomous – in Kantian terms, they are to be taken as "self-legislating" in their consumption practices. Accordingly, they are to be left free to follow their own tastes, to construct their own preference scales, while productive processes are to be efficiently organized with the aim of supplying commodities that will provide optimal satisfaction of such given desires of individual consumers. And it is possible that consumers have a general tendency towards a randomly variable, inherently unstable pattern of wants, generated by spontaneous desires for immediate gratification. And such gratification is not necessarily in contravention of the rational consumer's goal of maximizing his utility.[50] On the other hand, however, it is not possible to organize productive processes toward the goal of maximum satisfaction of consumer wants if those wants are constantly in a state of flux. And, of course, goods must be produced before they have any capacity to satisfy any wants, stable or unstable.

As I see it, the only escape from this dilemma is for neo-classical theorists to admit the *interdependence* of the two main divisions of economic forces – consumer wants and productive processes. Profits will not be maximized unless entrepreneurs cater successfully to consumer demands, but consumer utility will likewise not be maximized unless consumers develop a pattern of wants that are accessible to rational entrepreneurial planning. Granted such an admission would force neo-classical economists to concede one of the main objections from Institutionalist and Marxist perspectives to neo-classical economic models in general – that such models do not take sufficient cognizance of the interdependencies between the functions of different sectors of the economic system. But such a concession is surely a lesser price to pay than continuing to promulgate a radical incoherency with respect to consumer sovereignty as the ultimate arbiter of economic activity.

4. Marshall: Rationality and Virtue

Despite the dilemma just reviewed, it might yet be objected that the qualities of character displayed by *homo economicus* in forming preferences in accordance with transitivity axiom A_3 are not promulgated by neo-classical economists as genuine ethical ideals, that is as qualities that ought to be desired for their own sake. Rather, it might be argued, such (alleged) virtues of human temperament as deliberateness and self-control exhibited by *homo economicus* have *only* an instrumental value and, therefore, "factual" status, which status fails to signify the use of (suppressed) moral judgments on the part of neo-classical theorists. The sole ultimate end posited by CCT, the objection might continue, is that of the maximum satisfaction of given wants, whatever they might happen to be for any particular consumer. But the theory countenances no value-judgments as to the ethical desirability of alternative kinds of wants. If an agent prefers body-rubs to opera, CCT must and does preserve its "neutrality" with respect to the moral value of such a preference-ordering.

Of course, it is true, the argument claims, that even a consumer whom moralists might denounce as being motivated by a corrupt preference-ordering must satisfy A_3 if he is to maximize the satisfaction of the wants so ordered. And, if he is to behave consistently with A_3, then he needs to manifest the "orderly personality" typical of rational economic man. But this last requirement merely records an instrumental empirical truth concerning a means-end relationship. As a matter of verifiable fact, unless a consumer is disposed to suppress immediate impulses in favour of considered, calculated tastes, then he will not develop that pattern of stability in his wants which in turn makes it empirically possible for him to choose in accordance with A_3. And empirical predictions concerning the comparative efficiency of means – in this case dispositional traits of human character – for attaining given ends, do not transgress the scope of a value-neutral, "positive" science.

In short, it would be argued that a claim of ethical presuppositions for A_3 is the reverse of the truth. The rational consumer does not, by ordering his preferences in a consistent or transitive manner (i.e., satisfying A_3), intend to avow an intrinsic value-commitment in the form of exhibiting his allegiance to moral virtues of methodicalness and self-restraint; rather, by developing such "firmness of character" he is able to satisfy A_3 with great uniformity. Put another way, rational economic man as defined by CCT represents an ideal type in a normative, but *amoral* sense – the actions of *homo economicus* provide the standard for rational choice, but only in the sense of economic *efficiency*, that is, in specifying the optimal courses of action for satisfying given wants. But whether these wants are *worthy* of satisfaction is deemed to be beyond the economic universe of discourse.

The substance of the preceding objection is a familiar enough refrain and, no doubt, still records the "official view" of contemporary economists and methodologists. Nevertheless, it seems to me that the objection can only be sustained at too high a cost.

In order to elucidate my rejoinder, once again it will be instructive to notice that the contemporary viewpoint belies the status of neo-classical consumption theory as articulated in its classical source, the *Principles* of Alfred Marshall. For it is plain that, as Marshall saw it, it is not sufficient for the economist to take consumer wants as *given* "data", upon which to construct his theories of rational *qua efficient* processes for maximizing the satisfaction of such wants. On the contrary, according to Marshall, the problem of want satisfaction is of secondary and derivative importance within the scope of economics in comparison with an inquiry into the development of what he calls "activities"[51] ... "It is not true therefore that the theory of consumption is the scientific basis of economics. For much that is of chief interest in the science of wants, is borrowed from the science of efforts and activities."[52] Now "activities" are understood by Marshall to refer to the distinct kinds of efforts or practices which are demanded of agents in their participation in the processes of different types of economic systems. And of primary concern in the study of "activities" are the comparative qualities of human character which are expressed in different forms of these activities.

With respect to the type of activities involved in the sphere of consumer behaviour, Marshall is intent on identifying the qualities of character manifest in the systematic deliberative processes in which *homo economicus* engages prior to the selection of a commodity-bundle. And, consistently with the traits mentioned in the previous section, Marshall concludes that rational economic man would exhibit a methodical, frugal, self-controlled character in his consumer choices.

Most importantly, it is also plain that for Marshall such qualities are undeniable *moral* virtues, that is, *categorically* desirable dispositional traits of human character. The value or "welfare" of an economic process is not, from the highest point of view, to be judged according to the "efficiency" with which it satisfies given desires, but rather by the degree of moral excellence in the character traits required of agents taking part in the process. Accordingly, the economic activities in which these virtues find their expression are also and primarily to be considered intrinsically desirable, that is, worth pursuing for their own sake, not merely as means to the realization of some further end. Thus, because they express the virtues of orderliness and self-restraint, the deliberative processes of the rational consumer outlined in Marshall's demand theory are, above all, to be desired as ends-in-themselves, and only secondarily as instrumental to maximizing the satisfaction of an agent's desires for material commodities.

We might usefully compare Marshall's claim here with a recent distinction. In terms of current philosophical discussion, neo-classical economists would be disposed to classify the deliberative processes issuing in maximizing choices as exhibiting instrumental, but not "expressive" rationality.[53] For Marshall, however, such a classification would express a distinction without a real difference in the case of the neo-classical agent – that is to say, the qualities of character exhibited by economic man in his methodical deliberations as to which action-choices would most efficiently attain his material ends *give expression* to his self-identity as a moral agent.

Of course, it is open to contemporary followers of the general outline of Marshall's economics, who nevertheless disagree with his viewpoint concerning the "highest good" of economic processes, to appeal to the wisdom of historical perspective. Marshall, it might be claimed, was writing at a time when the logical grounds for separating "scientific" factual statements from pseudo-scientific value-judgments were, as yet, ill-understood; consequently, the inclusion of moral attitudes in the construction of his economic science was only to be expected. We may grant that Marshall's economic theory embraces categorical moral imperatives of the form "everyone ought to do A", recommending that certain kinds of actions are worth performing for their own sake, as well as hypothetical imperatives of the form "if anyone has (economic) want W, then he ought to do A to satisfy W". But, the criticism continues, we now more clearly realize that only the latter kind of imperative is acceptable to proponents of an "objective" or value-free social science.

However, certain aspects of economic processes which were evident to Marshall himself, but which appear to have escaped his disciples, discredit this appeal to contemporary enlightenment. Indeed, our discussion here may be understood as providing a case-study which clearly confirms Lakatos's claim that "philosophy of science without the history of science is empty, and history of science without the philosophy of science is blind".[54]

To begin with, we might further develop the theme introduced towards the end of the last section. Insofar as the neo-classical economist is occupied with constructing theories of rational choice, it is not only the practical reasoning of *homo economicus* as a consumer that he is concerned to specify, but also the structure of the deliberations of this agent in his role as entrepreneur or producer. Accordingly, within neo-classical economics, the same general conceptual scheme employed in the theory of consumption, that of individualistic constrained maximization, is applied *mutatis mutandis*, to the theory of the entrepreneur or firm. As the individual consumer or household is conceived as maximizing his utility subject to the constraint of his purchasing power, so the individual entrepreneur is understood as maximizing his profits under the constraint of his costs of production. Moreover, although it is useful for purposes of theoretical analysis to consider the rational consumer and the rational entrepreneur as separate entities, in the "real world" of concrete economic affairs they are often the same agent. It is the same person who, if he were rational, would equate marginal cost and marginal revenue in order to maximize profits, who, as consumer, would equate the ratio of marginal utilities to the ratio of prices in order to maximize utility. (And sometimes vice-versa – i.e., under those conditions when the consumer is also a decision-maker with respect to productive processes.)

The significant upshot of the possible identity of the rational agent *qua* consumer and producer is that the character traits which would impugn his rationality in the former role would also do so in the latter. Let me explain this parallel.

Less contentiously than when forming optimal consumer choices, it can be argued that *homo economicus* must, as entrepreneur, be deliberate, firm, and calculating if he is to adopt courses of action that will maximize profit. His decision-making must not, at least typically, be determined by habitual reaction or random, spontaneous impulse. But suppose that as a consumer he acts irrationally – that is, he exhibits erratic choices, due to being moved by random, immediate desires that are the expression of an impulsive, capricious temperament. Since such a temperament is tantamount to a standing disposition to engage in unrestrained, erratic behaviour, whatever the situational context, it is highly probable that an irrational pattern of consumption will be matched by a similar irrationality in entrepreneurial behaviour.

However consider further that,

a) in attempting to remain "value-neutral", a contemporary neo-classicist endorses the orthodox criterion of "consumer sovereignty" – that the desirability of an economic system is to be judged by the efficiency with which the processes within the system lead to the satisfaction of individual consumer wants, *taken as given*, but that

b) the preponderant majority of the "data" provided for economic analysis is constituted by variable, spontaneous consumer wants.

In this case, the unwelcome paradox would arise that any theory that might possibly be constructed to specify the manner in which a rational consumer could most efficiently satisfy such random, immediate wants would clash with the neo-classical theory of production; for the latter theory requires that the rational entrepreneur repress any propensity to act on spontaneous impulse in order that he might most efficiently secure the object of *his* desire – i.e., maximum profits. Furthermore, given the uniformity of the dispositional traits of "personality-types", there is little empirical likelihood that any real-life agent would be inclined to simultaneously fulfill the rationality conditions for both spontaneous and self-restrained contexts. For the circumstance described in b) therefore, our economist would be formulating diverse theories of rational consumption and production that could not both be empirically instantiated by the same person. Hence, the neo-classical theorist is faced with a dilemma. He must either (1) develop an implausibly bifurcated theory of rational economic behaviour or else (2) rescind the criterion of consumer sovereignty along with whatever support for value-neutrality it affords.

In actual fact, contemporary neo-classical economists have sought to do neither. The principle of consumer sovereignty remains the avowed final standard for measuring the "welfare" produced by an economic system, and neo-classical theory continues to describe the actions of a single rational economic man who is claimed to be deliberate and calculating in both consumption and production. But this is a sleight of hand. In effect, neo-classical economics only gives lip service to consumer sovereignty, at least as a universal criterion of economic welfare. For it becomes clear that the hypotheses of rational choice formulated in neo-classical economics take only stable, ordered desires as values, the maximal satisfaction of which is of theoretical concern. Hence, random, spontaneous desires are *ipso facto* classified as irrational, or designated "uneconomic" and barred from neo-classical theory's universe of discourse.[55] But some consumers do exhibit a disposition to spontaneous wants, and it is arguable that CCT is thwarting, not respecting, the sovereignty of such agents in implying they are irrationally motivated. In effect, with respect to the class of spontaneous desires, and contrary to the claims of the "orthodox" interpretation, CCT does not keep to a value-neutral imperative of the form "if you want B, you ought to do A", but tacitly affirms a categorical value-judgment of the type "you ought not to *want* the kind of wants exemplified by B".

Faced with this charge, the neo-classical theorist does, nevertheless, have a last methodological resort. He can admit that random "impulses" are excluded from the scope of CCT, but remind proponents of the preceding objection that

74

CCT, as a model of *rational* choice, intends to delineate the most efficient processes for maximizing utility; however, under those circumstances when a set of wants is random and unstable, it is well-nigh impossible to identify a procedure for maximizing the utility to be obtained from satisfying such wants. For, as observed in Chapter 3, unless "consistency" axiom A_3 is fulfilled, an adequate utility function would not exist, since there would be no action-choice to which no alternative was preferred.[56] But in circumstances where wants are random and transient, it is highly probable that A_3 would not obtain. In brief, on the assumption that rationality entails maximizing, it is an intractable task to construct a theory of rational choice for unsystematic, unstable wants. And given the unreasonable, because unrealizable, demand that only a completely general theory of rational choice, governing both (i) ordered, enduring, and (ii) random, transient desires, should be constructed, then, surely second-best – a theory limited to completely ordered desires – is preferable. For some theory, however circumscribed the range of phenomena it covers, is better than no theory at all.

The preceding reply is not without force. However, even if, for the sake of argument, we were to grant that it is sound, its conclusion does not accomplish what it was designed to secure – namely, a preservation of the ethical neutrality of neo-classical economics, particularly CCT. In the first place, by arguing that it is even conceptually impossible to accommodate given wants characterized by randomness, spontaneity and kindred properties within a theory of *rational* choice, it entrenches, rather than removes, the need to include categorical value-judgments in CCT – i.e., that the spontaneous wants of immediate impulse ought to be repressed.

Moreover, there is a more severe, but also more subtle reason why the conceptual structure of CCT cannot sustain value-neutrality in this context. And although Marshall failed to clearly recognize its philosophical implications concerning the value-freedom of economic science, the following quotation (call it J) reveals that the original codifier of neo-classical economics was at least cognizant of the substantive grounds for these implications:

> J: Speaking broadly, therefore, although it is man's wants in the earliest stages of his development that give rise to his activities, yet afterwards each new step upwards is to be regarded as the development of new activities giving rise to new wants rather than new wants giving rise to new activities.[57]

75

We might begin to see the import of Marshall's comment by noting the circumstances under which the use of hypothetical, rather than categorical, imperatives would support a claim to value-neutrality of a social scientific theory. This would be the case if (i) the desires of the subjects under study are "given" or taken as "data" for scientific investigation, without the theorist himself passing any value-judgment on the intrinsic worth of the desires, and (ii) the description of the "means" or courses of action asserted by the theory as necessary to securing the subjects' ends, that is, to satisfying the given desires, must themselves be purely "factual" or empirical judgments, rather than "value-laden". The futility of keeping to condition (i) in CCT, when wants are unstable, has already been discussed. But condition (ii) fares no better. For the validation of (ii) requires, amongst other factors, that the subjects' wants are not themselves a product of the courses of action which the social scientist designates as means to the fulfilment of the wants. If they are, then the assumption that these wants are *given* as data for investigation is a logically incoherent one. In effect, under such conditions it would not be possible to satisfy (ii) without violating (i). But the fact that CCT is liable to just such a dilemma is a direct implication of Marshall's proposition, J, the empirical truth of which proposition, furthermore, is well-attested. It is critical then to gain an understanding of what Marshall means by "activities giving rise to wants".

We may proceed here by way of illustration. For our purposes, the most useful example is provided by the economic "activities" consisting in the choices and prior deliberations of consumers. Suppose, for instance, that we are accounting for the consumer behaviour of what Marshall calls the historical "savage" or "uncivilized" contemporary man, those whom he classifies as "having no pride or delight in the growth of their faculties".[58] The character of such men is, for Marshall, comprised of such un-Victorian qualities as idleness, capriciousness, incontinence, self-indulgence and extravagance. Consequently, their consumption preferences will express a pattern of impulsive, unsystematic desires issuing in the purchase of "transient luxuries" or leading to the indulgence of "sensuous craving".[59] Not surprisingly, Marshall identifies such "unwholesome" commodities as alcohol, tobacco and "fashionable dress" as typifying the purchases of these men of inferior virtue. As a case in point, he suggests we look at ... "that part of the English working classes who have no ambition and no pride or delight in the growth of their faculties and activities, and spend on drink whatever surplus their wages afford over the bare necessities of a squalid life".[60]

In marked contrast, Marshall also categorized the buying patterns of the rational economic man of CCT, whose firm, "active-minded"[61] character disposed him to methodical deliberation resulting in well-ordered, consistent wants. But the critical point lies in the response to the question whether such wants have as their objects a distinctive class of commodities. For we find that Marshall maintains that the high-grade mental activities involved in the careful deliberation of the rational consumer *determine what kinds of goods he will desire*. In general, the rational agent will want commodity-bundles which exercise and develop the higher faculties and activities. As examples of such commodities Marshall mentions "artistic and professional services, expansive house room, and distinguished clothing".[62] Or from the opposite perspective, Marshall cautions that the rational consumer will avoid "food and drink that gratify the appetite and afford no strength, and of ways of living that are unwholesome physically and morally".[63]

Although the suitability of Marshall's examples might well be questioned, it seems to me that historical observation bears out the empirical truth of his main point concerning "new activities giving rise to new wants". Economic processes, including the deliberative cogitations of the rational consumer, are a *cause* of economic wants in the form of desires for certain *kinds* of consumption. But the normative implications of this relationship are of the first order of importance. Once again the neo-classical "welfare" criterion of "consumer sovereignty" with its attendant claim to ethical neutrality has been rendered incoherent. The neo-classical economic system cannot be vindicated on value-free "hypothetical" grounds – that whatever be the wants of individual consumers that are given, the activities of the system will be maximally conducive to their satisfaction. *For these very activities systematically determine the nature of the wants.*

It is significant that Marshall himself would probably not have been perturbed by the revelation of this theoretical anomaly. Again, as far as he was concerned, the ultimate justification of an economic system was not, as his followers have maintained, provided by the efficiency with which its characteristic processes led to the satisfaction of given consumer wants. Rather, in the final analysis, economic processes were to be appraised by their contribution to the development of the moral virtues of that ideal human character which we sketched above in the person of *homo economicus*. Insofar as the activities in both the demand and supply sectors of the economic system demanded the individual acquisitiveness, the calculatedness, the self-restraint, etc. – in short, the rationality – of *homo economicus* – to that extent the system was vindicated.[64] Admittedly, in violation of the contemporary doctrine of consumer sovereignty, a progression in the alliance of economic processes with the appropriate character virtues brings about re-orderings of preferences and new types of consumer wants. But, appealing to a sanguine conviction in moral evolution, Marshall contends that such a consequence is to be considered a "new stage upwards" in mankind's "development".[65] As far as the patriarch of neo-classical economics is concerned, far from believing, in company with his present day followers, that *de facto* consumer tastes are to be held "sovereign", to be taken "as data" in determining the "welfare" produced by an economic system, we find him recommending that such systems take on the capacity for radically *modifying* prevailing consumer wants – otherwise, their potential contribution to higher levels of human good would be seriously curtailed.[66]

It will come as no surprise that Marshall concludes that the kind of economic system which best expresses the virtues of *homo economicus* is the capitalist free enterprise variety. Herein, whether labourer, entrepreneur, or consumer, we encounter one rational type exhibiting the moral excellences of "possessive individualism", self-control, and deliberateness distinctive of *homo economicus*. It appears that, for Marshall, with the advent of the free enterprise economy, an eminently desirable juncture has been reached – the congruence of maximally efficient economic processes with the behaviour of ideally virtuous agents. Nor should this connection be viewed as one of accidental coincidence. For these very economic processes are *constituted* by the action-choices of rational economic men.

Chapter 6

Teleology and Utilitarian Economics

> Yet still in an explosively changing world, we have a fragmented economics
> ... One reason for this goes deep. It is the lack of a philosophical basis for
> economic theory. Economic life is looked upon as deliberative action, and
> again it is looked upon as action determined by the combination of tastes and
> circumstances. Which is it? Can it be both? Nobody asks, and such
> problems being unrecognized, the diversity of hidden assumptions creates a
> babel of conflicting languages.[1]

The preceding quotation from G. L. S. Shackle well articulates one of the
most severe sources of confusion besetting methodologists in their attempt to
resolve questions concerning the normative/descriptive status of economic
theory, especially the theory of choice (CCT). On the one hand, constituting
the prevailing "orthodoxy" among economic methodologists are those
economists and philosophers of science who once again have endorsed
principles of scientific method urged by logical positivists, a cardinal tenet of
whom has been has been that of the "unity of method" between the natural
and social sciences.[2] Hence, in conformity to what are taken to be
"mechanistic models" of the natural sciences, it is argued that economic
events such as consumer choices are explained by invoking causes comprised
of "antecedent conditions" or events logically "external" and temporally prior
to these events (effects). Or, more precisely, economic events are explained
by deducing such items of behaviour from "ordinary" causal laws representing
uniformities in such mechanistic sequences. In particular, thus, a mechanistic
model of explanation would avoid any mention of the family of intentional
entities consisting of the reasons, motives, goals, purposes, social conventions,
moral principles, etc. for the sake of which, or in compliance with, the
economic agent might be claimed to undertake his activity. As Jevons
succinctly put this viewpoint in the last century, economic theory in general is
to be conceived as a "mechanics of utility and self-interest."[3]

On the other hand, economic theory has also been construed as a
"teleological" rather than "mechanistic" model of explanation, accounting for
an economic action, not merely by adducing its antecedent, external causes,
but by citing the agent's goals or objectives for the sake of which he

deliberately undertakes the action. Under this interpretation, it is argued that since economic behaviour belongs to the category of human action, it is *purposive*, and, as such, cannot be adequately explained by its subsumption under standard causal laws, of the same form as employed in the natural sciences, but only by deduction from laws of a special type. Or, even more disparately, eschewing any appeal to explanatory laws, it is contended that such purposive explanation takes place, not by specifying causes, but by ascertaining the suitable reasons or grounds for the action, as determined by the appropriate social norms or moral principles to which the "rule-following" agent subscribes in seeking to realize his ends. Given this perspective, explanatory principles of the type of G" of CCT are to be understood, not as empirical generalizations, but as "rationalizations" for certain types of action.[4]

As the preceding characterization of the mechanism-teleology controversy suggests a host of interrelated problems in the philosophy of the social sciences, it will serve the purposes of clarity to sort out some of the primary ones in the specific context of an examination of the moral presuppositions of CCT. In this regard, it will be useful to introduce some issues of ethical import by placing them in the context of the historical foundations of CCT. And to use the phrase "historical foundations" is not to suggest that the problems are of only antiquarian interest. The contemporary theory of consumer behaviour is heir to its original construction, and has yet to escape many of the conceptual confusions which beset the initial nineteenth-century formulation. Moreover, the sources of the confusions are often most clearly detected in the first versions of CCT, when many of its technical refinements were yet to be developed.

1. Utilitarianism and the "Reduction" of Purposive Explanations

We might instructively begin by observing that perplexities concerning the ethical implications of deciding whether CCT is better understood as describing and explaining mechanistic processes or purposive actions are not of recent vintage. Indeed, one can go some way in unravelling these issues by observing their historical sources in the connection between the development of the neo-classical theory of rational choice and the framework of nineteenth century Utilitarian ethics. Of course, this affinity is not simply a surprising historical accident. The groundwork for the construction of the theory of consumer choice was laid by theorists who, for the most part, endorsed some version of Utilitarianism as an ethical system – Jevons and

Edgeworth are perhaps the most notable examples among English economists.[5] The kinship between classical Utilitarianism and CCT, furthermore, is not merely that they share common concepts and principles. For they also share the central methodological difficulty under investigation in this study. That is, Utilitarianism itself has been a most significant integration and conflation of factual and normative elements from the moment Bentham began his *Introduction to the Principles of Morals and Legislation* with the assertion:

> Nature has placed mankind under the governance of two sovereign masters, *pain* and *pleasure*. It is for them alone to point out what we ought to do, as well as to determine what we shall do. On the one hand the standard of right and wrong, and on the other the chain of causes and effects, are fastened to their throne.[6]

Indeed, it should become clear in the course of this study that, from one point of view, CCT can be usefully construed as simply a refinement of the classical Utilitarian explication of prudential decision-making, and the application of the normative theory thus developed to prescribing, for an enlightened agent, the best "thing to do" in trying to maximize his satisfaction from the purchase of material commodities.[7] Nor by "prudential" decision-making is it intended, as is common in philosophical analysis, to differentiate prudential values from fully moral ones. For, to anticipate our discussion in Chapters 11 to 13, the neo-classical theories of rational choice (of both the consumer and the firm) are "prudential" in the sense of conceiving an agent as concerned to promote his own interest rather than be concerned with the interests of others, on the basis of a *moral point of view itself.* For neo-classical theories continue the ethical tradition of the "invisible hand"[8] or "system of natural liberty" stemming from Adam Smith. That is, they assume that if an agent is left free to act in a solely self-regarding fashion to maximize his own interests within a perfectly competitive market economy, then, as an empirical consequence, the common good or welfare of society itself will be maximized. Any other policy is alleged to lead to a lesser common good.[9]

The ramifications of the Utilitarian perspective will continue to occupy us at later points in our analysis of CCT. In the present context, I should like to examine the implications of viewing CCT within the framework of Utilitarian moral philosophy to the extent that they illuminate the mechanism/teleology controversy concerning the structure of economic theory in general.

First, some terminological house-cleaning. By a teleological form of explanation, I shall mean one wherein the initial or antecedent conditions of the action to be explained require a reference to the end or goal for the sake of which action was performed. And a purposive explanation will be a teleological one which also includes the "intentional" properties that (i) the goal of the action is the end as conceived and desired *by the agent himself* and (ii) where the action is believed *by the agent* to be a necessary means to the attainment of that end. Contrariwise, a mechanistic explanation of human action will include, in the antecedent conditions, either no reference to the "goal" of the action, or no mention of intentional properties concerning the agent's desires and beliefs about his end-in-view and its requisite means.

Philosophical arguments abound concerning the relationship between purposive and mechanistic explanation of human behaviour. Our particular concern in this chapter will not require that we join issue on the general controversy whether explanations by purpose can always, in principle, be "reduced to", or translated into, mechanistic ones. Rather our interest will centre on a case study of the explanatory adequacy of one such reduction – that provided by certain interpretations of the economic theory of rational choice (CCT). But our investigation will be double-edged. For an examination of CCT *qua* Utilitarian system, insofar as it issues in mechanistic and/or purposive explanations, will help to further our primary aim of clarifying the fact-value problems of economics.

In this regard, we might first note that the content of purposive explanations contains a normative underpinning. For, to reformulate a claim made in Chapter 3, the assertion that an agent S performed an action A in order to realize a particular end E, or to satisfy his desire for E, can be understood as implying that S values E, or that E possesses some "desirability-characteristic" for S. (Of course, in limiting cases, S might perform A because A possesses intrinsic value – in other words, A is an end-in-itself or desirable-in-itself.) The basis or source of the value of E for S might refer to some desirable consequence brought about by the action, the conformity of the action to a social rule or moral principle endorsed by S, and so on.

At first sight, moreover, the account of consumer behaviour provided by CCT seems to be most appropriately placed within the category of such teleological explanation. For, as outlined in Chapter 2, the explanation of the purchasing of commodity-bundles subsumes the explanandum-event B, under general law, G", which could apparently be characterized as a teleological law, for its antecedent conditions include a reference to the end (K), for the sake of which the purchasing is carried out, namely, the "satisfaction" derived from the use of commodity-bundles. Teleological explanation within CCT, moreover, seems to fit our definition of the sub-class of purposive ones, since the end desired (K), and the action (B) believed necessary for the (efficient) realization of K, describe a decision-theoretic "situation" as perceived by the agent himself.

Furthermore, it seems that the value-basis of actions governed by G" is ready at hand – the agent, S, can be seen as following the traditional Utilitarian rules for "prudential" decision-making. For in his performance of B, manifesting a purchasing strategy consisting of the choice of a commodity-bundle fulfilling the condition of equalization at the margin, S is *ipso facto* maximizing his utility or subjective satisfaction. May we not, then, straightforwardly conclude that the explanation of behaviour furnished by CCT, is of the purposive rather than mechanistic type, and that its normative basis is to be understood as the obvious application of the rules of Utilitarian decision-theory to consumer choices?

Such a conclusion would be misleading and premature. In the first place, the history of the integration of the neo-classical theory of choice within the framework of a Utilitarian model of practical reasoning attests to a persistent muddle concerning whether or not CCT is more plausibly interpreted as a purposive or mechanistic explanatory system. This state of affairs might strike one as puzzling; for, in the first instance, classical Utilitarianism appears as a paradigm moral theory stipulating a hedonistic standard for the justification of practical decisions – that actions are right insofar as they produce pleasurable consequences.[10] And, surely the applicability of an ethical theory is not, primarily, *ex post facto*, to determine whether actions already performed have been wise or foolish, right or wrong. Rather its fundamental application is *ex ante*, in the context of moral reasoning *qua deliberation*, in deciding, on the basis of the appropriate rule, what one ought to do – in the case of the classical Utilitarian standard that one ought to choose that action whose end is one of maximum pleasure. Seen in this context, an ethical theory such as Utilitarianism would, evidently, be best suited to integration within purposive explanation where moral standards would govern the positing of desirable goals in pursuance of which an agent would undertake actions.

Nevertheless, for the most part, the inclusion of Utilitarian moral philosophy within the economic theory of choice has, from the beginning, taken a different direction – that of being deployed to construct a mechanistic theory. The pioneers in the construction of the neo-classical theories of entrepreneurial and consumer behaviour – Jevons, Edgeworth, Walras and Pareto – all conceptualized market behaviour in Utilitarian *cum mechanistic* terms – as the mechanics of pleasure and pain.[11] In fact, as Pikler points out,[12] Edgeworth and Pareto went so far as to model the theory of consumer behaviour on the field theory of the motion of a physical object in classical mechanics. Edgeworth's understanding of the person as a "pleasure-machine" provided a vigorous, albeit strange, general conceptual framework for such modelling:

> A system of such charioteers and chariots is what constitutes the object of Social Science. The attractions between the charioteer forces, the collisions and compacts between the chariots, present an appearance of quantitative regularity in the midst of bewildering complexity resembling in its general characteristics the field of electricity and magnetism ... at least the *conception of Man as a pleasure machine* may justify and facilitate the employment of mechanical terms and mathematical reasoning in social science.[13]

Although the distinction between purposive and mechanistic behaviour is not clearly formulated by these early theorists, the general import and rationale behind their conception of consumer behaviour as the mechanics of pleasure and pain is clear enough. In conscious analogy to the motion of a material object whose movements are causally necessitated by the antecedent physical forces, such as gravity and magnetism, to which it is subject, the behaviour of any economic agent, like consumer S, is considered to be the causally necessitated effect of the antecedent psychic forces to which he is subject – in the case of S his sensations of pleasure and pain. The causal process might be represented, in simplified fashion, something like this:

a) The initial use of diverse combinations of commodities induces in S different degrees of sensations of pleasure and pain.

b) In the tradition of associationist empiricist psychology, on the occasion of conscious reflection, these sensations, or "primary impressions", induce secondary impressions consisting of desires for such commodity-bundles, varying in intensity in proportion to the strength of the original impressions.

c) The desires or standing wants, on the occasion of their realizability in a future price-income situation, in turn induce S to purchase that set of commodities whose initial consumption had caused stronger impressions than the alternative bundles now available to him. Translated into terms of CCT, S will not be at his point of equilibrium wherein his "utility" (in traditional terms his psychic pleasure) is the maximum possible.

Now, it is critical to note that the preceding explanation-sketch which we have attributed to these nineteenth century theorists is not a purposive one. For the final state (E) of the process, the occurrence of consumer equilibrium, cannot be adequately interpreted as *goal of human action*. The fundamental reason that E cannot be so categorized is that it is a defining feature of action-goals that they constitute "ends-in-view" at which an agent *consciously aims* and, hence, that the reflective deliberations or directed reasonings of agents *make an essential difference* with respect to whether or not the realization of the goal occurs. However, the manner in which our nineteenth century theorists used the concept "equilibrium state E" indicates that they understood this concept as designating *merely* the terminating point of a natural process, that is, an "end-state" uniformly following upon the consumer's behaviour, and which would regularly obtain *independently* of the rationality or irrationality of any practical reasoning on the part of the consumer. In other words, the correlation between an economic agent's behaviour and its consequences, in the "field of his desires", was conceptualized as a "blind" contingency, that is, as unconditioned by his conscious deliberation. It was empirically guaranteed by the "laws of motion" of psychic processes that consumer behaviour, irrespective of the conscious intent of the agent, would regularly be equilibrating by affecting a terminal state of maximal subjective pleasure, in the same manner as the effects of the movement of an inorganic object, in a field of physical force, were guaranteed by the laws of physical motion.

2. Mechanistic Confusions

The preceding construal of consumer behaviour is, however, a defective one. Even if, in general, teleological descriptions can be "reduced to" a mechanistic counterpart, the nineteenth century analysis of economic choice initiated an espousal of a mechanistic concept of economic behaviour in a *specious* sense that still persists to confound contemporary theorizing. Since consumer activity in accord with CCT was (wrongly) conceptualized as a mechanism not significantly different from inanimate natural processes in the *level of complexity* of its antecedent determinants, it was typically concluded that such behaviour *must* occur, in the sense that it was *unavoidable*. And this condition was underwritten by an uncritical, over-simplified assimilation of the laws of economics to those of physics. Because the consumer's "situation", antecedent to his choices, was not (correctly) understood as being accessible to his conscious revision, the laws correlating such antecedent states with his subsequent behaviour and its outcome were considered to be as permanently or timelessly *applicable* as the laws of physics; hence, these laws were understood to govern behaviour which could be deemed inevitable or *unalterable*. Seen in this light, it is no wonder that consumer behaviour conforming to the implications of neo-classical theory was often characterized as subject to "impersonal market forces", while the equilibrating tendencies of such behaviour were classified as "automatic". The continuance of such discourse in recent economic analysis, moreover, attests to the fact that this kind of defective mechanistic view of consumer activity remains a prevalent one among neo-classical economists.[14]

But why is such a view to be labelled a defective one? Two related implications of this kind of mechanistic interpretation of CCT bear out our negative assessment. First, such an interpretation covertly tends to underplay, and, in an important way, misrepresents the very real and significant role of *cognitive* processes such as a consumer's deliberative reasoning in determining how to maximize his utility from the consumption of material goods. Somehow, as long as he is free from external "perturbating factors" like governmental control, the consumer is conceived, irrespective of his practical reasoning, to be moved by "natural" market forces to his maximum satisfaction. We shall return to an analysis of the error of this implication, along with its ethical ramifications, at different stages of the remaining part of this inquiry.[15]

Secondly, such a crudely mechanistic analysis of rational choice has led to an unwarranted moral perspective on CCT – indeed, on "mainstream" economic theory in general. For, suppose that it is true that CCT *does* have a particular ethical system embedded within it. Then it will be the case that this neo-classical reading of CCT *qua* mechanistic processes will suggest no need, indeed will preclude the possibility of an *alternative* moral basis for consumer behaviour to the one already (albeit unadmittedly) present in neo-classical theory. For there would be no point to prescribing a different form of behaviour, as the (empirical) possibility of such behaviour is precluded by the (implied) claim of the mechanistic view that the scientific laws constituting CCT are applicable to *any* antecedent setting of consumer behaviour.

3. Ethical and Psychological Hedonism

A more explicit discussion of my contention that a mechanistic misreading of the structure of CCT is responsible for undermining recognition of alternative moral foundations for this theory will be deferred until other related issues have been introduced in Chapter 8. However, for the purposes of this chapter, it will prove instructive to anticipate our analysis of this issue in terms of its historical ancestry. And we might first remark that the presence of a problem here should not be unexpected, given the historical integration of Utilitarian moral philosophy in the original formulations of the economic theory of choice. For the defence of Utilitarianism has itself been party to a parallel form of argument to the one involved in the mechanistic preclusion of different ethical foundations for CCT. I refer here to attempts to validate Utilitarianism, in its classical form as a version of ethical hedonism, by a doctrine of psychological hedonism.

We find, then, classical Utilitarianism prescribing pleasure as the sole moral end, the only desirable consequence of action, that end which is worthy of choice. But, as encapsulated in Mill's notorious "proof" of the greatest happiness principle,[16] the *justification* for such an ethical doctrine was in terms of the *empirical* theory of psychological hedonism – viz., that the only end that agents actually do desire, the sole motivation to perform any action, is the expected pleasure the performance of the action promises as a consequence. This attempt to justify ethical hedonism has been under continual attack from empiricist philosophers, usually on the grounds that such a deduction of a moral conclusion concerning what *ought* to be desired from purely factual premises concerning what *is* desired commits the naturalistic fallacy.

Such an objection, however, overlooks at least Mill's insistence that the justification is not deductive in form. Moreover, since an agent's being under an obligation presupposes his ability to fulfill it, if psychological hedonism *were* true, it would certainly, in some sense, support and indeed entrench the claims made for ethical hedonism by classical Utilitarianism. For it would be *pointless* to prescribe, in opposition to ethical hedonism, that anyone ought to forego the pursuit of pleasure and choose a different moral end, if it was empirically necessary, according to psychological law, that he be motivated to seek pleasure alone.

The inclusion of psychological hedonism by Utilitarian economists in the original nineteenth century construction of CCT was simply a matter of applying a theory believed to apply universally to all areas of human motivation to the special case of economic motives. Accordingly, any consumer is considered to desire a commodity for the sole motive that he expects its purchase will be conducive to his subjective pleasure, or that he prefers one commodity-bundle A to another B only for the motive that he believes A's purchase will bring him more pleasure than B would. In consequence, any consumer is understood as purchasing a commodity-bundle by being motivated only by the expectation that its consumption will generate more conscious pleasure than any available alternative.

Most importantly, the integration of psychological hedonism into the construction of CCT had, and often continues to have, significant implications for questions concerning the moral presuppositions of CCT. In the first place, it forestalls criticism that CCT is only and merely a moral theory *recommending* courses of action as those which maximize subjective utility or pleasure.[17] For unlike ethical hedonism, psychological hedonism does intend, on the basis of putative laws of human motivation, to formulate predictions of the actual behaviour of agents. But secondly, and more critically, such integration serves the purpose of arresting criticism, from a *moral* point of view, of whatever moral foundation CCT might (covertly) comprise. For, on the one hand, economic theorists can disclaim any involvement in normative issues, alleging to be concerned only to conjecture and confirm descriptive hypotheses accounting for economic action as an effect of hedonistic motivation. But, on the other hand, even if they *were* to endorse an ethical foundation for a social scientific theory like CCT, they can still, as it were, have their moral cake and eat it. For, as we have seen, the *only* moral theory that the truth of psychological hedonism would *permit* or render possible at all is the Utilitarian version of ethical hedonism. As long as we are working within a teleological conception of ethics, it would be empirically impossible for an agent to choose to follow the moral principles of any other ethical system. In sum, as far as the prospects for synthesizing normative and empirical dimensions of a science of human behaviour is concerned, a classical Utilitarian framework stacks the cards in favour of itself. (Of course, one needs to observe that any theory of human motivation that explains human behaviour in terms of a single, universally operative type of desire may play the same game.)

However, an important ambiguity in the application of psychological hedonism to consumer choice by early neo-classical theorists should be noted. In particular the inductive role of pleasure within CCT is unclear. Is the occurrence of a pleasant sensation in consuming a commodity to be interpreted as the *original cause* which induced the present desire for the commodity, or should pleasure be understood as the *intended goal* of the future consumption of the good, providing the ground or *reason* for the present desire for it? In the light of our depiction of the mechanistic account of consumer choice presented above, we may conclude that our early neo-classicists would have to reply that pleasure functions primarily as the past or original cause inducing present consumer desire. Insofar as the consumer anticipates future consumption, his pleasurable experiences are best understood as established antecedent conditions which causally necessitate future commodity-bundle choices. Hence, strictly speaking, his "utility" or conscious pleasure does not play the role of a full-fledged goal or end-in-view whose realization would turn on the rationality of the agent's deliberations.

But it is just such an interpretation of the concept of pleasure that has been exploited by contemporary philosophers to attack the doctrine of psychological hedonism, and, thereby, to discredit an important historical defence of ethical hedonism. Thus, Broad[18] (correctly) cautions that psychological hedonism is a theory about the reasons, ends, or motives of desire, not about the causes of desire. If past pleasurable experiences alone cause present desires, this empirical fact does not entail that such desires have as their only goals future pleasurable experiences, or that we are only motivated by the desire for such anticipated pleasures. Most importantly, the argument of Broad and others continues, we do desire *other* ends, have different motives or reasons for action than expected pleasure – such as social esteem, self-realization, moral excellence, etc. Consequently, it is concluded that psychological hedonism is simply a false empirical theory of motivation.

We might expand and more clearly identify the normative implications of the preceding criticism of psychological hedonism. Now, mention of the objects or ends of desire brings with it the concepts of ethical norms, reasons, social conventions, etc. which define and prescribe the content of such ends. For example, Jones might intend to change jobs in order to secure employment that provides greater opportunity for his personal development. And he is pursuing such an end because he has "internalized" the moral rule: "everyone ought to take advantage of opportunities for self-realization". But suppose we were to further assume that Jones has no "ulterior motive" than to pursue such self-expression – irrespective of whether the effect were to bring him pleasure. However, if psychological hedonism is interpreted correctly and assumed to be true, such an assumption must be false; for the sole (final) end that agents such as a consumer (empirically) could desire would be expected pleasure. Consequently, the only practicable moral system which could serve as an ethical foundation for a social scientific theory of human behaviour, such as CCT, would be that of ethical hedonism as expressed, for instance, by classical Utilitarianism. But, if arguments along the lines of Broad are sound, psychological hedonism is an ambiguous and false theory of human motivation and would not, therefore, support such normative implications.

It seems to me that the critical distinction concerning pleasure as cause or end is a sound one, and it is clear that our Utilitarian economists conflated the concepts distinguished. Nevertheless, recognition of these points does not, as some philosophers appear to believe, *immediately* issue in an air-tight and final refutation of psychological hedonism, and thus remove the type of ground such a theory would give to ethical hedonism. In the next section, I will attempt to support my reservations in the form of a useful "thought-experiment".

4. Psychological Hedonism and Radical Behaviourism: A Thought Experiment

Suppose we attempt to conceptually marry two important mechanistic frameworks: traditional hedonistic psychology and contemporary behaviouristic psychology of the stimulus-response (S-R) reinforcement type. In fact, if our "thought-experiment" can effect such a union, we will have witnessed a successful endeavour to reduce a teleological form of explanation to a mechanistic one.

We may begin by pointing out that recourse to S-R behaviourism can be argued to be an available ploy for a contemporary psychological hedonist who wished to resolve a methodological difficulty in the role played by "desire" in the mechanistic system proposed by his nineteenth century forebears. The rationale for traditional hedonism's introduction of such a mentalistic element into its explanation of human behaviour is not surprising. For although it might be empirically true that a pleasant experience accompanying an activity induces the agent to prolong the activity, a law-like connection must still be established between pleasure and *future* actions. Accordingly, it was found necessary to affirm the existence of, in Humean terms, a "secondary impression", or "passion", a reflective "idea" of the pleasure associated with the original action, furnishing a motivation in the form of a "desire" to repeat the action when the opportunity arises, and thereby re-experience the pleasure following upon such an action. However, as Charles Taylor queries in another context,[19] does not this introduction of the proposed state of desire in effect illicitly transform a purportedly mechanistic explanatory system into a teleological one? Are not agents performing actions in order to attain a *desired goal* of pleasure and, therefore, are we not explaining behaviour by the end the agent consciously seeks? And, as talk of ends introduces the concept of reasons specifying the content of ends, it is understandable why philosophers like Broad would contend that psychological hedonism is basically a theory about the reasons or objects of desire.

However, it is germane to our present concerns how S-R reinforcement theory would deal with the threat presented by traditional psychological hedonism's apparent reintroduction of teleology into a mechanistic theory. B. F. Skinner boldly outlines the behaviourist strategy in his *Science and Human Behaviour*:

> Instead of saying that a man behaves because of the consequences which *are* to follow his behaviour we simply say that he behaves because of the consequences which *have* followed similar behaviour in the past. This is, of course, the Law of Effect or operant conditioning.[20]

In line with its general methodological prescription of eliminating reference to conscious inner processes or internal mental events in accounting for human action, radical behaviourism eschews recourse to hedonism's postulation, in its explanatory framework, of psychic desires for expected pleasure. Rather, present behaviour is explained by subsumption under the Law of Effect describing the process of "operant conditioning". In such a process "pleasure" is transferred from a teleological motivating role as the anticipated future object of present desire to a mechanistic motivating role as a reinforcing consequence of past behaviour. Thus, we find, roughly, that in the presence of a particular environmental stimulus-situation, S, a piece of behaviour (response R) has certain "pleasurable" consequences which function so as to "reinforce" the S-R connection, that is, to increase the probability that S will be followed by R in the future. But any particular "action" or behavioural res-ponse is therefore interpreted as an effect of an efficient cause provided by the antecedent stimulus-situation irrespective of consequences following *this* response. And the particular empirical correlation is itself to be explained in terms of the past learning history of the agent.

It will be noticed that the appropriation of the pleasurable states of traditional hedonistic psychology by S-R theory, and the transformation of their role into the "reinforcers" of S-R explanations, needs qualification, as indicated above by the use of quotation marks for "pleasure" when this term was used in explicating S-R theory. For pleasure *qua* quality of a private mental state would be as subject to excision from radical behaviourism as the internal desire for anticipated pleasure. Accordingly, within S-R theory, the concept of a "pleasurable" consequence, if used at all, would be used to denote a publicly observable "reinforcing" consequence of behaviour whose criterion of identification, again, is simply that of being an (external) event resulting from behaviour whose occurrence increases the frequency with which that kind of behaviour will be elicited by a recurrence of the antecedent stimulus. Nevertheless, regardless of the physicalistic "purity" of behaviouristic explanations, S-R theory, if sound, can be seen as effectively averting the suspicion directed towards traditional hedonism of re-introducing a teleological or purposive type of explanation since, in S-R accounts, "pleasure" no longer constitutes a *future* goal for the sake of which action is undertaken, but merely a contingent consequence of *past* action.

The original formulation of CCT would be, moreover, an apparently paradigm candidate for re-interpretation in terms of S-R reinforcement theory. All that would be required would be the removal, as an essential element in the explanation of a present consumer choice, of the intermediate "secondary impression", i.e., the mentalistic *desire* for the pleasure expected to follow upon consumption, and the relocation of "pleasure" from an object of desire to a reinforcing consequence of past choices. Thus, a consumer's equilibrating behaviour in a particular price-income situation would be explained as taking place not *in order* that he might realize an intended end-in-view of maximizing the expected subjective pleasure to be attained by his purchases, but as a function of the fact that equilibrating behaviour[21] emitted in such a price-income situation in the past has resulted in "rewarding"[22] or reinforcing states of affairs that increased the likelihood such behaviour would recur, given a similar (stimulus) situation.

How, then, might such a behaviouristic re-interpretation of CCT revitalize psychological hedonism in accounting for consumer behaviour, and entrench the normative import of such an account?

We might first remind ourselves of the standard criticism of psychological hedonism: since it is not a theory concerning the causal origin of present desires, then any appeals to states of pleasure as that which *produced* present wants or desires are irrelevant to confirming the truth of psychological hedonism, which is essentially a theory attempting to explain behaviour in terms of the motivational efficacy of an antecedent desire for expected pleasure. However, if S-R reinforcement theory is sound, then accounting for behaviour by the motivational efficacy of purposive desires for *future* ends of that behaviour is spurious in the first place; rather, it is only reinforcing "rewards", consequent upon *past* behaviour which can function as motivators of present actions.

Suppose, futhermore, that we *were* to accept S-R theory's mechanistic re-location of motivation, but preserve a mentalistic concept of pleasure. That is, suppose we were to agree that only past consequences of behaviour have present motivational capacity but conceive of such consequences as pleasurable states of mind. In that case, a re-constituted version of psychological hedonism would gain a foothold as an all-inclusive theory of human motivation. Thus, we would now find psychological hedonism claiming that any agent would perform an action in a given situation only if he is motivated to do so by the previous pleasurable consequences of performing that kind of action in a similar situation. Indeed, I suggest this *is* the mechanistic principle intended, but ambiguously delivered, in the original constructions of CCT.

Furthermore, if pleasure is the one and only motivation for action, then the only practicable moral underpinning for a social scientific theory such as CCT would be one which defined the intrinsically good or desirable in terms of pleasure – that is, ethical hedonism. Indeed, we have observed above that Utilitarian economists already affirmed the existence of pleasurable consequences of past actions as the sole cause of intermediate desires for anticipated pleasures, which desires caused current behaviour. Hence, strictly speaking, no relocation of pleasure *qua* motivator, only the expulsion of the intermediate link of desire, is required in order to embed CCT within a mechanistic framework of S-R behaviourism, liberalized to accommodate psychic pleasures, and thus for CCT to presuppose our revised form of psychological hedonism along with its (implicit) support of the (hedonistic) Utilitarian ethical dimensions of CCT. In short, such a liberalized S-R theory, if sound, would provide an exceptionally strong conceptual foundation for CCT. Not only would the mechanistic construal of the original formulation of CCT receive the fashionable dress of the theoretical vocabulary of an important contemporary science, but the (covert) support such a science furnishes for an (uncriticizable) moral theory would also be available.

And yet, in the final analysis, would such a collusion of S-R behaviourism, psychological hedonism, and Utilitarian economics win the day? I think not. For one of the parties to the union cannot play the theoretical role demanded of it – i.e., S-R behaviourism. What then is the relevant shortcoming of the mechanistic-*cum*-behaviourist explanations provided by S-R theory (including its liberalized variety).

The failing of concern is that, although such theories offer plausible explanations at the general level of accounting the *directedness* of behaviour, at the more particular (lower) level, they do not offer appropriate explanations of why a person performed a certain action on a particular occasion. Hence, as R.S. Peters puts it,[23] we might countenance such behaviourist theories of motivation as logically appropriate to answering genetic questions of why agents have developed an interest in pursuing certain goals, and some goals rather than others. And, in this light, we may agree that our S-R version of psychological hedonism might possibly be a correct account of the *acquisition* of different varieties of purposive behaviour. Nevertheless, it is an explanatory theory of the wrong logical type to provide an adequate alternative account of a particular action which has already been explained purposively in terms of the end towards which an agent directs it. For instance, we may have explained John's paying his bills by specifying the end he seeks to realize – say, his staying out of debt. But we do not explain this action by citing, in accord with the Law of Effect, the "rewarding" consequences that followed such behaviour in the past, even though we might grant that there is nothing logically out of place in claiming that John's goal of staying out of debt would not have been acquired and entrenched if such a process of "operant conditioning" had not occurred. In short, even if *some* mechanistic reductions of purposive explanations of particular events should be found to be defensible, S-R reductions will not be among them.

In the context of present inquiry, moreover, it is significant that this criticism of the explanatory capacity of S-R behaviourism has normative consequences that complement the ethical implications of the traditional philosophical attack on psychological hedonism of which Broad was an exponent. For, as we pointed out above, it is to the category of moral standards, social norms, etc. that we must make appeal in order to identify the content of the ends or goals at the basis of purposive explanations. Consequently, if in the fashion of behaviourist methodology, appeal to such ends were abandoned in the construction of social scientific theories, there would be a genuine threat both of undermining recognition of the precise role which moral rules and social conventions play in determining human behaviour, and of ignoring the usefulness of including reference to such norms in theoretical explanations of behaviour.

With this in mind, consider our contention that S-R theory is, at best, an account of the genesis of the ends or goals at which agents consciously aim, which type of account leaves intact a purposive explanation of a particular action in terms of an agent's desire for a goal thus acquired. It is plain that it is only the latter category of explanation that could have a bearing on moral issues concerning which ends are intrinsically good or desirable. Even if it were empirically true that we are causally determined to acquire goals by the conditioning of only one kind of reinforcing consequence of past behaviour, this fact would not entail that we pursue only one kind of goal, *let alone one that it is identical in empirical content to that of the reinforcer.* For it is conceivable that a single kind of reinforcing consequence generates sequences of behaviour directed towards a host of different goals defined and governed by diverse moral standards.

We may apply this conclusion to the classical Utilitarian understanding of CCT. In this context, we can maintain that although we may have been causally conditioned to acquire the goal-directed behaviour of purchasing commodities by the reinforcing consequence of pleasure alone, the goals or reasons for such purchases need not be comprehended by the *single* end of expected pleasure, but may comprise various ends governed by different ethical principles and social rules, some of which might very well be non-Utilitarian. For instance, a consumer may be buying commodities in order to support his dependents out of a motive of moral duty, even if the action is expected to lead to his personal displeasure.[24] And explanation of any particular instance of consumer choice would still require a specification of the particular end for the sake of which the consumer purchased the commodity. For, in general, as in the case of other forms of purposive behaviour, although the acquisition of a pattern of consumer behaviour might be amendable to a mechanistic explanation in terms of S-R reinforcement theory, the initiation or activation of a particular instance of such behaviour is not so amenable.

In sum, our "thought experiment" has an important lesson to tell us. For we have sought to reinforce the mechanistic understanding of CCT, supplied by earlier Utilitarian economists, by embedding this theory of choice within the contemporary framework of S-R behaviourism. But the failings of such an attempt attest to the general threat furnished by behaviourist-*cum*-mechanistic frameworks of distorting and camouflaging the moral presuppositions of theories of human behaviour.

And yet, to be fair, we must not leave the interpretations provided by S-R behaviourism painted entirely black. For we must not underestimate the importance of the acquisition of motives to engage in "goal-directed" or "rule-following" behaviour as exemplified by moral conduct. Further discussion of this issue will be set aside until Chapter 9 wherein we will argue for a general conceptual relationship, of paramount importance, between moral obligation and psychological motivation. Nevertheless, we might anticipate the main import of this investigation by remarking that appeal to empirical motivations will supply the ultimate vindication of moral rules themselves.

Chapter 7

Functionalism and the "Systems Approach"

One aspect of the critical problem concerning competing mechanistic and teleological interpretations of the structure of social scientific theories in general, and CCT in particular, which raises especially important questions about normative presuppositions, is that of the "functional" structure of certain theories. Significantly, the implications of the use of functional terms in everyday discourse has also played an important role in arguments defending and attacking the affirmation of a "fact-value" or "is-ought" separation in ethical theory itself. This chapter will begin, therefore, with an attempt to show that the analysis of functionalist language within ethical theory helps to clarify the issue of the "value-impregnation" of functionalist theories of human behaviour. Following upon this task will be an elucidation of the functionalist structure of explanations of consumer behaviour provided by CCT, and an appraisal of the explanatory and normative adequacy of placing such a structure within a general systems theory.

1. Functions and Moral Judgments

First let us review the logic of functional language within moral reasoning itself. Now, it is probably still accurate to say that it remains the consensus in contemporary moral philosophy that the meaning of any value-judgment cannot be equated with that of any factual judgment. Upon further logical considerations, it is maintained that no ethical conclusions can be validly deduced from a set of premises all of which are non-ethical. Nevertheless, the validity of this doctrine has not gone without persistent criticism. For instance, one type of objection has proceeded along the following lines.

First, it is granted, in conformity to the "non-naturalist" consensus, that there is no factual property that is common and peculiar to all uses of "good" in the making of value-judgments. Nevertheless, it is argued,[1] if we confine our attention to value-judgments that are uttered with respect to a particular *class* of objects, then one *can* isolate an empirical property or set of such properties which any member of that class of objects must possess in order to be (correctly) called "good". For example, although good knives and good raincoats need share no common "good-making" characteristics, unless a particular knife is sharp and a particular raincoat is waterproof neither thing is a good instance of its respective *kind* of object. Accordingly, it is concluded that once we realize that the term "good" is essentially an attributive adjective which is properly applied in the form "X is a good A", where A stands for a specific class of objects, rather than in the predicative form "X is good" *simpliciter*, then, *ex hypothesi*, the naturalistic thesis that we *can* define goodness in terms of factual properties, and, consequently, infer prescriptive statements from purely descriptive ones, is sound.

A standard non-naturalist rejoinder[2] to this sort of objection is to grant their opponents the premise that goodness is an attributive property, but to deny that this entails the general thesis that within *any* particular class of objects the meaning of a good member of that class can be specified in terms of empirical properties. For such a specification is legitimate only in those special cases where the term "good" qualifies as a *functional* word, and where understanding the meaning of a functional word requires a knowledge of the use to which the object it denotes is typically put, or the end which that object serves. Hence, the terms "knife" and "raincoat" are straightforwardly functional words, being defined by the ends their referents fulfil – namely, cutting objects and repelling water, respectively. Thus, dull knives and leaky raincoats, being objects which fail to fulfil their function or end, would be classifiable as poor or bad instances of their kind; contrariwise, they would be classified as good knives or raincoats to the extent that they fulfilled the end for which they were designed in an *efficient* manner. Furthermore, the non-naturalist rejoinder continues, the normative presuppositions of the use of functional terms is not an indication of a unique, purely descriptive meaning of "good" when used to qualify functional terms, but is a product of the fact that functional words themselves are not employed in a purely descriptive fashion – rather their meaning entails a specification of the good-making characteristics of the objects to which they refer.

In any case, according to the non-naturalist, the critical point to observe in the analysis of moral concepts is that not *all* objects which are called good (or bad) are properly characterized as functional ones in the first place – that is, as objects primarily defined by an end which they serve. Most importantly, it is not the case that such terms as "man" and "action", which are especially significant in contexts of moral judgments, are functional ones. Hence, the use of "man" and "action" does not logically entail a fixed set of empirical properties which constitute the defining properties of a good man and a good action.

It is not necessary, given the aim of the present discussion, to join the general controversy over the status of functional terms in the analysis of moral judgments. But it will be instructive to bear in mind two points concerning value judgments within functional contexts for our investigation of the functional character of the theory of consumer choice.

In the first place, it is noteworthy that the evaluation of functional entities has a basic conceptual connection with questions of *choice in general*. For, we have mentioned that a functional entity is one designed to be used for attaining an end envisaged for that kind of object. Hence, if we had the desire for the relevant end, and were given the opportunity to choose a member of this class of objects from several alternatives, it follows that, *ceteris paribus*, we would choose the best possible member – that is the one which most efficiently attains the sought-after end. Moreover, in order to understand the end which a functional object – an A – fulfils, and consequently, in order to be in a position to identify good A's or the standard of merit for A's, it is necessary that we learn the preferred properties when people are choosing some A's in preference to others.

Secondly, and most significantly, neither side to the naturalist/non-naturalist controversy disputes the fact that the introduction of functional concepts or the affirmation of functions carries with them evaluative implications – they differ rather on whether this normative context is to be interpreted as supporting a naturalistic analysis of moral concepts. Accordingly, we may expect that if functional concepts are employed in the construction of explanatory theories of human behaviour, they would *ipso facto* introduce a normative element into these theories. And the economic theory of choice (CCT) is no exception to this rule. However, we shall also see that such a claim can be sustained only by rejecting certain endeavours of economic methodologists to make CCT just such an exception.

2. Functional Explanations and Value-Laden Theories

It will be helpful to begin by clarifying the basic concepts to be found in social scientific theories characterized as "functional".[3] Although the meaning given to certain key functionalist concepts has not been entirely consistent, by and large functionalist theories attempt to account for human behaviour along the following lines.

FUNCTIONALISM AND THE "SYSTEMS APPROACH"

First, functional explanation appears, at least *prima facie*, as a version of teleological explanation, that is, as outlined in the preceding chapter, one which employs an essential reference to the end or goal for the sake of which the phenomenon to be explained occurs. Basically, functional varieties of teleological patterns of explanation can be distinguished by a special feature of the end towards which the explanandum-event is directed. Briefly, the end of a functionalist account can be classified as a "need" or "functional requirement" of some system. A "system", for present purposes, can be identified with an individual organism or human agent. And a "need" is to be interpreted as a necessary condition for some generally desired end-state, which state is typically construed biologically as "continued existence" or "survival". Strictly speaking, then, a need is best interpreted not as the final end of the system but as an "intermediate" end or means which is required to bring about the ultimate end, say survival. Hence, schematically, a functional explanation of the existence of some institution or action A, would cite some "function" or causal consequence of the existence of A, which consequence could be identified as the fulfilment of a need or necessary condition of the survival or other desired condition G of some system S. An oft-cited biological illustration is that the beating of the heart (A) fulfils the "functional requirement" of circulating the blood (N) which is necessary to maintain a "healthy state" (G) of the human organism, S.

The normative element of a functional analysis enters at two levels, with increasing degrees of "value-impregnation". The first level, more obviously innocuous to positivist epistemology, could be given the familiar label of instrumental value, wherein the social scientist takes *as given* the goals actually desired by the agents under scrutiny and formulates directives on how to optimally secure those ends – in the case of functionalist theories these ends might be either the intermediate ones we have called "needs", or the ultimate ones for which these needs are necessary conditions. But the imperatives thereby constructed are only hypothetical in form, neither demanding nor soliciting the theorist's own value-judgments in supplying the content of the ends. Rather, in these imperatives of the general form, "If a person wants E, then he ought to do A", the antecedent is an observational given for the theorist, whereas the consequent affirms no more than the empirical claim that B is causally efficacious for E (or more efficacious than available alternatives to A). Of course, the performance of A might describe the behaviour of few (if any) agents since it could be empirically true that most of the agents under study behave "irrationally", in the sense of adopting inefficient courses of action in pursuit of their goals. However, such circumstances do nothing to alter the empirical status of the claim that "A is (maximally) conducive to E", to be confirmed by observational evidence. In any case, if such aberrant circumstances do hold, the social scientist can still formulate an "idealized" model, describing the behaviour of the "rational" agent who *does* adopt the optimal means to the realization of the given ends, and then compare the extent to which actual behaviour conforms to the rational model.

In terms of the logic of functional concepts in moral reasoning presented above, we might say that once human action is to be explained in terms of needs and actions undertaken for the sake of consequences that fulfil such needs, then the content of such a functional explanation is (partly) normative. For the meaning of the ultimate end (e.g., the "healthy state" of an organism), for whose realization satisfaction of the needs is necessary, entails standards for evaluating the actions undertaken in terms of their degree of instrumental value in attaining the end. Nevertheless, such a functional context would generate idealized "rational" models of human action, since there is no empirical guarantee that agents will choose to perform those actions with the "functions", i.e., the actual consequences, of satisfying the relevant needs. However, so the positivist argument runs, there is no requirement that the social scientist, in constructing rational models for functionalist explanation, be ethically committed to the realization of the defined final ends or intermediate needs. For, presumably in describing these goals, he is simply observing and reporting the evaluations of the actors under investigation.

Insofar as functional theories employ hypothetical imperatives, the philosophical implications are familiar and relatively uncontroversial. However, at the second level of the "value-ladenness" of functionalist explanations, a conflict between "value-free" methodologists and their opponents is unavoidable. It is this level, furthermore, that involves a genuine challenge to the "objectivity" of social scientific inquiry. For, at this second level, we find that primarily in defining a system's ultimate goal, but even in selecting one particular type of action from among possible *alternative* types that have the effect of meeting the system's needs, the theorist introduces his own moral standards. (Our discussion in Chapter 5 of a Benthamite rule for utility maximization in CCT rather than a Stoic "contractionist" one, provides an illustration of the second level of value-ladenness.) Of course, if by happy coincidence the theorist's standards correspond to those of the agents being studied, his hypotheses would turn out to be "objectively" true, but such an eventuality is improbable given the variety in moral standards accepted by different people. In any case, it remains the orthodox doctrine of methodologists that when a theorist does project his own value-judgments into the construction of his theoretical statements, he thereby prevents such statements from functioning as publicly testable empirical hypotheses and thus renders them impotent of explanatory power. In the interest of the appropriate aims of science, therefore, it is officially prescribed that such "subjective" evaluations be abandoned in theoretical enquiry.

It will be within the final intentions of this study to undermine the preceding methodological directive. At this point, however, it is necessary that we outline the logical structure of CCT insofar as it can be construed as a type of functional theory.

3. Functionalist Accounts of Economic Choice: Mechanism and Systems Theory

As far as historical precedence is concerned, the theory of economic choice supplied a "functional analysis" of consumer behaviour long before this phrase became a technical concept of social scientific inquiry. In any case, we find that the structure of CCT employs the central concepts of, and well fits the explanatory pattern of a functionalist approach. For consider the following factors:

i)   The "system", S, under investigation refers to an individual economic agent., i.e., the consumer, the elements or "parts" of S being, in classical empiricist fashion, the set of interrelated psychic states constituting S, primarily his interacting beliefs and desires.

ii) The final end-state or ultimate "goal", G, of S consists in the maximization of S's utility or subjective satisfaction.

iii) The "functional requirement" or "need", N, of S can be understood as the state of equilibrium defined by the marginality conditions. "N", therefore, affirms a necessary condition (indeed for CCT both a necessary and sufficient condition) for the occurrence or maintenance of G for S.

iv) The entity or event to be explained by a functionalist account is an action, A, of S, namely the choice of a combination of commodities. A, then, could be described as having the "function", that is, the causal consequence of inducing or preserving equilibrium state N which, in turn, guarantees maximum utility G for S.

Briefly, then, a functionalist interpretation of the explanation of consumer choice in CCT would understand the choice in terms of the contribution it makes to the acquisition or maintenance of the maximum utility of the consumer by means of the choice's fulfilment of the conditions of the consumer's equilibrium. The questions of paramount importance in the context of our present inquiry concern the nature of the explanatory and normative dimensions of this functionalist interpretation of CCT.

To begin with, we might ask whether or not the economic processes described as the realization of equilibrium and thereby the maximization of utility are intended by functionalist construals to denote the outcomes of evaluation, at least in the weaker sense of those of the consumer, not the economist. We might expect that a positive answer to this question would be unavoidable given the fact that what is to be explained, namely the choices of agents, suggests that their evaluations determine the desirability of available objects of choice. We shall find, however, that such an expectation will be frustrated by functionalist models of consumer choice.

Our functionalist construction of CCT appears, moreover, to be suitably classifiable as a teleological, indeed purposive explanatory model. For is not the explanandum-event, A, representing an equilibrium-choice, to be explained in terms of A being an action believed by the agent to bring about a goal, G, which he consciously values and seeks?

Not surprisingly, however, the general disposition of contemporary economists has been to follow the mechanistic lead of their nineteenth century Utilitarian forebears by devising non-purposive formulations of functionalist theories of rational choice. One such construction which is currently in vogue is the attempt to provide a mechanistic version of a functionalist analysis of CCT by considering this theory a special case of a general *systems theory*. Let me explain.

Of course, system theorists[4] are themselves divided as to whether all "system approaches" to the explanation of social phenomena are solely mechanistic in form. Within economics,[5] however, the prevailing tendency has been to deliberately base their interpretation of CCT *qua* system on an analogy with *mechanical* systems, and our attention, therefore, will be centred on the tenability of such a mechanical model for CCT.

Unfortunately, there is not a precisely uniform specification of the meaning of "system" amongst system theorists. We will, however, define a system along Bertalanffy lines[6] as a set of elements (sometimes labelled the "parts") standing in interaction (i.e., in causal relations). As in our general conception of CCT as a functional theory, the "system" under investigation in CCT is to be understood as the individual consumer, the "parts" of this system as his internal psychological states, in particular his beliefs and desires.

The underlying *modus operandi* in the "system approach" to the construction of a social scientific theory is for the theorist to be guided by formal identities or "structural analogies" between various "levels" of phenomena. Methodologically, the most fruitful interpretation of the meaning of "structural analogy" as employed in general systems theory would be that of an isomorphism of the laws accounting for the phenomena of different levels. Within the context of our analysis of a theory of individual choice, we may limit our attention to three levels of phenomena corresponding to three types of entity or system – an inanimate physical object, an individual human *qua* biological organism and an individual agent (the consumer). For the purposes of this chapter, we may concentrate on the latter two categories.

The basic structural analogy which is claimed by system-theoretic economists to hold between the behaviour of a person *qua* living entity and *qua* agent-consumer is that both exhibit the pattern of "homeostatic" processes. And the fundamental idea of a homeostatic explanation is to understand the behaviour of a system in terms of its regular tendency to maintain some *equilibrium state*. The stock example cited is the biological one of the preservation of an equilibrium consisting of a constant body temperature in particular kinds of organisms.

If we take the case of the human body, considered as a system S, we observe that under the causal influence of changes in the temperature of the external environment I of S, the "parts" or physiological processes, P, within S, such as blood pressure, perspiration and the contraction of muscles, undergo alteration so as to maintain S in an equilibrium or "steady state" E, that is, within a restricted range of temperatures. Of course, as in functional analyses generally, strictly speaking, E is not the final "end-state" realized by such processes but is itself a necessary causal condition of the final "end", G, the survival of S, since temperatures beyond the range of E will terminate S's existence.

Similarly, a systems-oriented economist would claim, the axioms of CCT lend themselves to a functional *cum* system-theoretic analysis. For the behaviour of the system, now the consumer, call him S', is explained in terms of the behaviour's regular tendency to maintain equilibrium state E' – that of "equalization at the margin". The environment, I', comprises the relative prices of the available commodities along with the consumer's income. Changes in I' cause the processes constituting S', that is, his beliefs, desires, preferences, and choices, P', to change so as to induce S' to buy commodity-bundles that keep him at the point of equilibrium, E'. And E', as we have seen, is intermediate to S''s final "end-state", G' – that of maximum utility or subjective satisfaction.

The preceding comparative sketch of the "systems behaviour" of the human body and the individual consumer already exhibits the similarity in formal or structural relations into which the set of external and internal states affecting S and the set affecting S' enter (i.e., I, E, P and G on the one hand, and I', E', P' and G' on the other). More explicitly, if the general laws covering the two classes of phenomena were explicitly stated, and to the degree that the structural analogy is exact, there would be an isomorphism between the laws explaining the physiological phenomena and those explaining the economic – that is, there would be an identify of syntactical structure between these laws.

The consequence of such a "systems analysis", if successful, in furnishing CCT with a mechanistic or non-teleological pattern of explanation can also be made evident. First, on the basis of the above schema, it is to be observed that we can identify the antecedent conditions, I, of the homeostatic bodily processes, P, where I = the temperature of the external environment, and confirm the regular effects that changes in I cause in P *independently* of referring to any goal of heat equilibrium, E, *for the sake of which* P occurs. In short, we are epistemically equipped to explain P-processes mechanistically (as defined on page 82 above) by subsumption under laws connecting an "efficient" cause with its contingent effects. But, likewise, a system-theoretic economist would argue, we can identify the antecedent "environmental conditions", I', of consumer beliefs, preferences and choices, P', where I' = the price-income situation, and note the uniform effects which alterations in I' induce in P', independently of referring to a (consciously intended) goal of marginal utility equilibrium E' (and ultimately maximum utility G'). Hence, the functionalist *cum* system-theorist would conclude that we are also in a position to provide a mechanistic explanation of P' events. Or, if a teleological explanation T of a consumer choice has already been formulated in terms of the choice being required, given initial conditions I', in order to attain a goal of equilibrium E' (or thereby G'), then a mechanistic translation of T along such functional, system-theoretic lines is constructible.

As it stands, however, there would be ground for doubting the "purity" of such a system-theoretic reduction of purposive concepts. For the retention of such mentalistic concepts as consumer desires and preferences would, as we noted in the last chapter, apparently preserve purposive elements. In order to meet this difficulty, system-theoretic accounts of consumer behaviour are typically buttressed by a behaviouristic interpretation of the consumer's psychological states (P') – in particular, his desires, preferences, choices, and utility. That is, in a manner we first encountered in Chapter 4 and that will be extended below, the P' states are defined in terms of overt purchasings. But with such an elimination through translation of mentalistic concepts from CCT has gone a theoretical vocabulary committed to the expression of purposive notions – of conscious desires for particular ends, and beliefs about action-choices conducive to the ends. Upon such a conceptual paring, G', representing the "end-state" of maximum utility, would not be understood as an "end-in-view" or goal at which an economic agent consciously aims, but merely as the (non-intentional) terminating point of a "natural process" comprised of a pattern of consumer purchases. It would, for instance, be interpreted along Little's lines[7] as referring to the commodity purchase which will, in fact, be made.

Moreover, the abandonment of teleology *via* a behaviourist systems analysis again arrests recognition of any value-ladenness in CCT, even in the weaker sense of reporting the evaluations of the consumer himself. For once preferences are identified with publicly observable purchases, the theorist believes himself entitled to bypass commitment to the ordinary understanding that orders of preference for objects are determined by the subject's "internal" evaluation of the comparative worth of the objects. On such grounds, we noted in Chapter 4, certain economists claim a very strong sense of "value-freedom" for CCT – viz., that *no one's* value-judgments were being reported by the theory of choice, let alone those of the neo-classical economist employing the theory. We may expect economic behaviourists to appeal to similar arguments to defend the ethical neutrality of system-theoretic understandings of CCT. But we also argued in Chapter 4 that behaviourist appropriations of innocence were purchased with the loss of explanatory and normative solvency for theories of choice. The analysis of the present chapter will show that the alliance of behaviourism with system-mechanism fares no better.

Of course, in the light of our earlier discussion in Chapter 6 of the "field theoretic" constructions of choice theory introduced by nineteenth century Utilitarian economists, it is sobering to remind ourselves that mechanistic reductions of CCT, however fashionable, merely rehearse an entrenched tradition. To my mind, however, no matter how sovereign the tradition, it has not earned the allegiance given it. I would like, therefore, to direct some critical comments to the latest offspring of this lineage – that is, to the presentation of CCT *qua* functional *cum* system-theoretic framework. Our investigation will centre on the explanatory adequacy and the normative fecundity of the pivotal concept of equilibrium as it is used within such a framework. (Additional issues raised by the type of "systems analysis" which some economists have applied to CCT will be discussed in Chapters 8 and 16.)

4. The Concept of Equilibrium: Explanatory Adequacy

In the first place, it is crucial that the concept of equilibrium be employed with caution in system-theoretical explanations. In particular, it is imperative in any construction of CCT that this concept be embedded in hypotheses with *empirical content or meaning*, rather than be used tautologously. For only in the former case can "equilibrium" contribute to the explanatory capacity of the theory. The meaning and danger of a tautological employment is connected with a similar problem concerning the meaning of the concept of utility understood as "satisfaction". For just as "satisfaction" can refer merely to the realization of any desire as expressed by the phrase "to satisfy a desire", so also the occurrence of any desire, say in the form of the activation of a latent dispositional state, can and has been understood by economists[8] as equivalent in meaning to the initiation of a *disequilibrating* state. This sense parallels the one in which the exertion of any "force" on a physical body is disequilibrating with respect to the body's initial state. But, under this interpretation of desire in CCT, the occurrence of an equilibrium state will mean no more than that some occurrent desire has been realized – that is, some disequilibrating state has been "equilibrated". In this case, however, a state of equilibrium is not some end-state, extrinsic to the realizing of the desire, and separately identifiable from it. Hence, if the concept of equilibrium is understood in this sense, functionalist *cum* system theoretic analyses of CCT which claim that the end-state of the realization of a consumer's desires consists in the occurrence of an equilibrium state, are empirically empty, asserting no more than that the realization of a consumer's desire is the realization of his desire. And the explanatory force of such an empirically empty assertion is, of course, *nil*.

Differently interpreted, however, the concept of equilibrium can possess empirical content and thus be available for explanatory purposes. When so employed, an "equilibrium state" has the general designation of a "rest state" or, more specifically, a state wherein the values of all the variables asserted to be in causal interaction by the postulates of the theory are such that there is "no tendency to change" in the system composed of those variables.[9] By "no tendency to change" is meant that some empirically determinable outcome induced by the system's processes remains constant. For instance, the physiological processes that are causally relevant for determining the internal temperature of a human organism will, in equilibrium, generate a temperature that does not vary beyond a narrow range of 97° to 99° F.

One important qualification should be added to this definition of equilibrium. It is common to describe equilibrating processes with reference to an external environment, the defining variables of which may or may not be considered constant in value. (Environmental variables held constant for a selected period of time can be labelled the "parameters" of the system.) Two types of equilibrium of increasing strengths follow upon the difference between systems operating within constant or changing environmental conditions. If an equilibrium state is preserved within a system, given constant environmental conditions, such a state can be classified as one of *static* equilibrium. If, however, an equilibrium is maintained even when the environment of a system is seen as varying, then the equilibrium state can be classified as the stronger one of *dynamic* equilibrium. To take our example, if we were to hold constant the environmental element of the temperature of the surrounding air, it would be evident that the temperature of the human body constitutes at least a static equilibrium; and as long as the external temperature did not undergo an extreme variation, body temperature would also exhibit a dynamic equilibrium.

What, then is the precise character of the concept of equilibrium employed in CCT? Technically, as briefly indicated in Chapter 5, CCT is standardly characterized as a theory of "comparative statics". Such a theory formulates an essentially statical notion of equilibrium, although of a somewhat hybrid variety. For, by comparative statics is meant a theoretical analysis which compares two equilibrium states of a system under two different sets of values for the environmental or "exogenous" parameters. We find, then, that under one set of values, which are held constant, the mechanisms of the system, S', induce a static equilibrium. But, the "exogenous" parameters (such as prices and income) are then conceived as changing to a new set of values, held constant at this juncture, and the mechanisms of S' determine a new static equilibrium. In brief, in comparative statics the economist studies static equilibrium conditions for different environmental conditions, but without describing the character of the processes causing changes in the environmental states.

Unfortunately, however, a hybrid answer must also be given to the question whether or not the concept of "static" equilibrium as used in CCT is theoretically tenable. Once again, the problem at issue is whether CCT can avoid the charge of employing this concept tautologically and, therefore, with no explanatory capacity to account for consumer behaviour. To deal with this question, we must first take a closer look at the determinate content of the concept of consumer equilibrium.

It will be remembered that at the point of consumer equilibrium in CCT, E', the ratios of the marginal utilities of the available commodities is equal to the ratios of their respective prices:

$$\text{i.e., } \underline{MUx} = \underline{Px} \text{ etc.}$$
$$MUy = Py$$

But what exactly is the factual meaning, if any, of this criterion of equilibrium?

At a first level of analysis, the equilibrium criterion of CCT implies that the marginal utilities of the final dollar spent on each commodity are equal, that is that the increments in the total utility for the last dollar are equal. Marginal considerations are, therefore, only meaningful in reference to *totalist* factors. To what empirical facts, therefore, does total utility refer? Indeed, this question can be seen as even more pressing since the consumer is understood to be in equilibrium at precisely E' for the very reason that commodity purchases at E', and at no other point, lead to maximum total utility for the consumer. Hence, if "equilibrium", as formulated by system-theoretic constructions of CCT, is to be useful for explanatory purposes some definite empirical meaning must be given to the concept of *utility per se*, and one which does not lead to a tautologous or empirically vacuous status for the content of mechanistic hypotheses describing the processes resulting in the maintenance of consumer equilibrium.

Nineteenth century Utilitarian economics, we observed in the last chapter, identified utility with a quality of a mental state (i.e., pleasure) expected to follow certain activities. Given this meaning for utility, the consumer was understood as being in equilibrium when the increments of conscious pleasure he experienced, from an additional dollar spent on each commodity, were equal. However, the difficulty of identifying the pleasurable state in separation from the action presumed to precede it, and, therefore, its ineptness for explaining that action, provides a serious difficulty for such a construal of utility.[10]

In any case, contemporary economists aligned with a mechanistic systems approach have generally abandoned the attempt to interpret utility mentalistically as a conscious state of pleasure. Rather, in order to secure a mechanistic account of choice behaviour in the manner discussed above, we have seen that the concept of utility incorporated within a system-theoretic understanding of CCT has been given an increasingly behaviouristic interpretation. And yet, remnants of the old Utilitarian conception of utility keep intruding themselves into this brave new theoretical framework. A review of the indifference curve representation of utility in CCT well illustrates this ambivalent situation.

The question of the empirical meaning of an indifference curve itself is a case in point. On the one hand, conventional textbook analyses often do preserve (perhaps unconsciously) the classical Utilitarian tradition. Hence, a particular indifference curve is frequently construed as an "iso-utility" curve in the sense that combinations of goods located along an indifference curve yield equal amounts of utility *qua* subjective satisfaction or conscious pleasure.[11] In this light, the consumer is understood to be indifferent between these combinations *because* he believes their consumption to generate equal pleasure. A higher indifference curve represents a locus of commodity-bundles giving rise to equal pleasure, but these bundles are preferred to the bundles on a lower curve since the former yield more pleasure than the latter. Now, economists have rightly appreciated that such a theoretical framework only invokes an ordinal measurement of utility rather than a stronger cardinal one – that is, as long as any two levels of utility, a and b, can be measured (ordinally) as to whether a > b, then there is no need to measure (cardinally) the degree of difference between a and b. However, recourse to the weaker, ordinal form of measurement does not, as the writings of some theorists suggest,[12] *ipso facto* eliminate reference to utility *qua* subjective pleasure *in toto*. Ascending indifference curves may still represent increasing levels of equal quantities of pleasure, granted that there is no measure of the quantity of pleasure by which the bundles on any curve surpass or fall below those on other curves.

Nevertheless, other system-oriented theorists, who still work within the indifference curve model, have preferred to make a clean break with the classical Utilitarian origins of CCT and its concept of pleasure as a quality of a conscious mental state. Again, the general drift has been to eschew teleological *cum* mentalistic theory-construction by translating the basic concept of utility and its implications into behaviourist language referring to publicly observable phenomena.[13] In effect, such translations express a view that we examined in Chapter 4 – that utility should be re-interpreted as a purely *structural* property of choice theory. To the extent that the term "utility" represents a unique entity at all, it should be understood as a "logical construct" or "convenient fiction", operating as a shorthand device for *indicating overt choices*. Thus, to re-introduce the translation schema set forth in Chapter 4, the phrase "more utility" merely refers to the fact that "one collection of goods is preferred to another". Likewise the phrase "equal utility" signifies that an agent is indifferent between several commodity-bundles. "Preference" and "indifference" in turn are translated, respectively, as "choosing A rather than B" and "choosing A and B with equal frequency". Finally, "choosing A" is defined in terms of "external events", as "purchasing A when alternatives are available".

Of course, once utility is so interpreted, the concept of consumer equilibrium in CCT must and does receive a similar behaviourist translation. Since utility is interpreted in terms of overt choices or actual purchases, the location of equilibrium, previously specified in terms of marginal utilities, likewise demands translation into the language of observable choices. Economists have sought to fulfill this task by replacing "marginal utility" by "marginal rate of substitution". Thus, at the point of consumer equilibrium, E', the consumer is now described as equating the marginal rate of substitution of the last dollar spent on the obtainable goods – that is, at equilibrium:

$$MRSxy = \frac{Px}{Py}$$

Roughly, this condition states that a consumer reaches equilibrium point E' when and only when the number of units of one commodity he forgoes in purchasing an additional unit of another commodity is equal to the ratio of their respective prices.

But why does such a position constitute an *equilibrium* for the consumer? A characteristic reply, given by Baumol, is that if the consumer is purchasing a commodity-bundle at that point, he "has no motivation to revise his purchasing plan."[14] And if he is not so purchasing, he does have such a motivation.

So far, however, Baumol has done no more than speak tautologously. For, given no motivation, an equilibrium or steady state of human activity would exist since it is an analytic truth that the presence of any motivation to perform an action is, *ceteris paribus,* a *disequilibrating* state. Nevertheless, Baumol does proceed in an attempt to furnish a substantive empirical sense for the equilibrium condition by offering an account of why there would be a lack of motivation under the equilibrium conditions. In the context of his behaviourist framework for economic choice, the account, however, is a sleight of hand. For, in effect, he reverts to retranslating the condition in terms of equality of marginal rates of substitution back into terms of marginal utility, arguing that the consumer can increase his utility by moving toward the equilibrium point, E', and, therefore, would be motivated to do so; on the other hand, moving from E' would decrease his utility and therefore he would not be motivated to so move.[15] But the speciousness of Baumol's manoeuvre is transparent. If, as an economic behaviourist would have it, utility is only a "logical construct" upon overt choices, bereft of ontological reference to any subjective motivating states such as desired pleasure, then no substantive account is given of a consumer's motivation by merely citing alterations in his utility resulting from the exhibition of new purchasing behaviour. For *ex hypothesi*, the empirical meaning of such changes in utility would only amount to an abbreviated way of referring to a revision of overt choices, that is, to the exhibition of new purchasing behaviour.

Nevertheless, although Baumol is not alone in this sort of fainthearted behavourism, others[16] have tough-mindedly kept to a behaviourist analysis of consumer equilibrium. Thus, remaining with the description of equilibrium in terms of marginal rates of substitution, they conclude that purchases under these conditions would lead to stability or equilibrium – viz., a position from which the consumer would not be motivated to move – for the reason that by buying the combination of goods at this point, he would be securing his *most preferred* combination from those available.

Now, although such an analysis is not, like Baumol's, self-defeating from a behaviourist point of view, it is not, however, without its own conceptual difficulties. For, insofar as the *modus operandi* of behavourism is concerned, the notion of preference itself cannot refer to a (relational) *mental state* of preference which the consumer introspects as holding between commodities, but must itself be interpreted in terms of observable behaviour – that is, to repeat, where preference is defined as "choosing (i.e., purchasing) A more often than B" and indifference as "choosing A and B with equal frequency". However, even though such a translation has the virtue of remaining consistent with the canons of behaviourist concept formation, the question again arises as to why point E', now interpreted as representing the equality of marginal rates of substitution to price ratios, would constitute a position of consumer stability or equilibrium. *Ex hypothesi* the behavioural theorist is precluded from claiming that choices at E' would maximize a quantity of mentalistic pleasure and, in this way, utilize implications of psychological hedonism to the effect that an agent's activity would terminate if he were to reach a point of maximally attainable pleasure as there would be no motivation to move from such a position.

No doubt, equilibrium choices at E' may be *publicly identified* in a coherent behaviourist fashion: they would refer to purchases which the consumer shows no tendency to revise, as evidenced by the observable fact that they are continually repeated in the same price-income situation. But an *explanation* of the stability observed at E' would apparently require recourse to non-behaviourist laws of motivation linking mental states (immediately) causing and effected by such equilibrium choices. However, neo-classical economists have been generally loathe to incorporate *any* type of hypotheses of empirical psychology in their explanation of consumer behaviour,[17] being under the impression that economic principles alone should suffice to account for economic behaviour. Such an impression is, however, a misguided one, as an appraisal of the explanatory force of system-behaviourist formulations of CCT, which make no recourse to psychological laws, will serve to indicate.

Curiously, such formulations usually begin on the right track. Along with other presentations of CCT, they commence by describing the consumer as faced with deciding between accessible action-choices on the basis of the order of his preferences for the *consequences* of the various possible actions. It is then affirmed that, at equilibrium point E', the consumer selects that action whose consequence or outcome is the highest in his order of preference. So far, the behaviourist analysis shows no divergence from the traditional hedonistic interpretation of consumer behaviour. The break with the traditional analysis enters with the system-behaviourist understanding of the meaning of the "consequence" or "outcome" of an equilibrium choice. A behavioral economist, of course, refuses to accept the hedonist's identification of the consequences of purchases with pleasurable mental states of the consumer. With what then *does* he identify the consequences of equilibrium choices?

It is at this juncture that the system-behaviourist runs into conceptual difficulty. For one might expect that he at least identifies the outcome with some substantive event, albeit, in contrast to traditional hedonism, with some publicly observable aspect of bodily behaviour. Such a procedure is not, however, carried out.[18] Rather, in that strange convolution of reasoning we first observed in Chapter 4, the outcome or "utility" of a choice is reduced by behaviourist translation to a purely "formal" utility; accordingly, a choice that maximizes utility is conceived as one which the consumer would choose rather than any obtainable alternative,[19] and, hence, a maximizing choice is deemed to be an equilibrating one. But in what way an appeal to such an interpretation of a maximized utility amounts to more than an empirically empty, indeed viciously circular explanation of equilibrating behaviour escapes this writer. For surely the factual content of such an account is no more than the claim that, in any particular price-income situation, any consumer would choose that collection of goods from among the available options which he would choose.

By moving to this kind of behaviourist reading of consumer equilibrium in order to abandon an admittedly dubious hedonistic psychology underlying the classical Utilitarian interpretation of CCT, the system-theoretic economist has thrown out the baby with his bathwater. For, if the explanatory and predictive force of CCT is to be preserved, the concept of utility must continue to be interpreted as denoting *some* kind of substantive consequence of the purchase of commodities, even if the specific factual content of such an effect is more varied in kind than the uniform, single consequence of a "feeling of conscious pleasure" introduced in the original, Utilitarian rendering of CCT. Plainly, any possibility of putting CCT to empirical use in explaining actual consumer behaviour demands that economic theorists have recourse to the findings of empirical psychologists as to what kind of "internal" motivations are regularly operative with consumers in the formation of their purchasing strategies.

5. The Concept of Equilibrium: Normative Adequacy

We have seen that neo-classical economists prefer non-purposive interpretations of "functionalist" analyses of choice. And towards this end they have had recourse to system-theoretic *cum* behaviourist explanations of consumer practices. But we have argued that there are serious failings in such accounts from the point of view of CCT as a descriptive/explanatory science. However, the collusion of behaviourism and systems-theory also mangles the normative dimension of theories of rational choice. We shall now proceed to sustain this charge.

Now we saw earlier[20] that those economists who belong to the orthodox group which espouses ethical neutrality, would not wish to disavow the normative *applicability* of CCT. For, along with their opponents, they intend to put the theory of choice to normative use as a policy science prescribing rules for the optimal decisions to be undertaken by the rational consumer. But system-behaviourist versions of mechanistic reductions of CCT *bar its normative deployment*. Let me expand on this claim.

The transition from descriptive to policy science presented, as we pointed out in Chapter 6, no barrier to the traditional Utilitarian formulation of CCT. Indeed, within that framework, the descriptive and normative uses were two sides of the same theoretical coin. For consumer behaviour was described and explained in terms of an agent being motivated to choose maximum anticipated happiness, and happiness constituted the agent's ultimate good. But once this Utilitarian knot between positive and normative aspects of behaviour is severed, either on grounds of its moral or empirical inadequacy, the amenability of descriptive theories of choice to normative employment becomes problematic. Most behaviourists, of course, have claimed to reject Utilitarian economic theories for empirical rather than ethical reasons, insisting, for instance, that a Utilitarian rendering of CCT fails to adequately explain actual consumer behaviour. However, in tackling the policy side of the theory of choice, their analyses suggest that they have not perceived that the normative-descriptive gap, once closed by Utilitarian definition, requires careful bridging when the Utilitarian link is abandoned.

Suppose, then, the system-behaviourist is asked why the consumer *ought* to allocate his income to purchasing that combination of commodities at the equilibrium point, E'. In economic parlance, why would the "welfare" of the consumer be at its maximum if he made such a purchase? May such equilibria also be reasonably construed as optima? Now, it will be recalled that system-behaviourists do continue to use their version of a "utility function" for individual consumers. However, their behaviourist concept of utility has been employed strictly within the limits of a descriptive theory intending only to explain or predict actual choices, and where "utility" has been scrupulously shorn of value connotations. Accordingly, ascending degrees of the "utility function" are taken to number successively higher levels of "preference" for sets of commodity-bundles (between which the consumer is indifferent), but where "set A is preferred to set B" has been given the behavioural meaning "A has been chosen rather than B, even though B could have been chosen". Consequently, we have observed that the maximization principle affirming that a consumer will choose that combination of goods which maximizes his utility is to be interpreted as meaning that, assuming constant tastes, prices and income, he will choose that combination A rather than any other available ones B, C, D, etc., given that A has been chosen rather than B, C, D, etc., in his past behaviour. Or, in epistemic terms, within CCT an agent is (implicitly) defined as maximizing his utility, if and only if he chooses that object which, on the basis of historical evidence, he has indicated he has an overriding propensity to choose.

But the question remains as to whether what Little[21] advocates as a translation of a (descriptive) utility theory into choice theory permits a tenable normative application in prescribing what choice a "rational" consumer ought to make in seeking to maximize what is "good" for him. Suppose, for instance, we were to construct a "welfare" function for an individual consumer, where individual points described by this "W-function" represented consumer choice ordered *normatively*, according to whether any choice was "better", "equally good", or "worse" than any other choice. And let us call the utility function of CCT defined by economic behaviourists the U-function. We might then put our question as to the normative usefulness of the system-behaviourist construction of CCT by adapting a succinct formula of Kenneth Boulding – viz., Is the U-function identical with any defensible W-function?[22]

The answer to this question, moreover, is not as automatic and straightforward as many treatises in economic theory suggest. That is, it is not the case that we can unproblematically simply rechristen CCT, construed behaviouristically as a "positive" model explaining actual choices, as a normative model adequately prescribing *worthwhile* choices. This rechristening would indeed be possible if there were some kind of necessary connection between economic choices conforming to the equilibrium point, E', and the good of the individual. But even if we were, for the sake of argument, to permit the consumer's good to be equated with his own maximum happiness, a behaviouristic interpretation of CCT precludes the affirmation of such a necessary connection. As presented above, under a system-behaviourist analysis, the equilibrium point is taken to refer to a maximally preferred purchase only in the sense that the consumer has uniformly chosen that bundle rather than the other available possibilities. But, surely, the proposition "S purchases what he has regularly chosen rather than available alternatives" does not, in itself, logically entail "S secures maximum personal satisfaction". Only if background assumptions are (implicitly) included in the content of the proposition "S chooses A" specifying the reasons or motives for the choice, or the standards of evaluation used by S in making choices in terms of some kind of desirability of ends, would there possibly be an entailment relation between "S chooses A rather than B" and "S secures more satisfaction from A than B". But inclusion of reasons, motives and value-standards for choosing has been deliberately and systematically renounced in the system-behaviourist interpretation of CCT. (Behaviourists employ a concept of choice which might be called "choice *simpliciter*", referring to the overt act of selecting an object in the context of obtainable alternatives, irrespective of questions concerning what reasons or evaluations, if any, might be determining the choices.) Of course, the economic behaviourist is free to covertly rely on mentalistic concepts such as reasons, which he has formerly repudiated as inadmissible in the construction of scientific theories – but inconsistency is a more obvious scientific vice than the mentalism he professedly abjures.

Admittedly, some behaviourally inclined economists have persevered in consistently rejecting mentalistic theory-constructions, and yet continued to seek a means of providing a normative application for CCT. Little, for one, appreciates that in the context of a behaviourist analysis of CCT, it remains logically possible for a consumer to attain a situation A where he is "in a chosen position" as compared with situation B, but where he is less satisfied in A than he would have been in B. Nevertheless, Little contends[23] the behaviourist might still make appeal to an *empirical* connection between choice *simpliciter* and personal satisfaction or happiness. That is, he might argue that there is good empirical evidence that if, in buying A rather than B a consumer receives the "object of his choice", his "welfare" is greater, or that he has more happiness from such a purchase than he would have had if he had bought B.

But *is* the accumulated factual evidence sufficient to warrant such a conclusion concerning the agent's welfare? In general, is it uniformly or even probably true that as long as an agent is able to select, from all the possibilities open to him, that action which he would choose for himself, then he secures for himself the maximum possible satisfaction? Or, more particularly, is such a hypothesis at least true in those cases of the purchase and consumption of economic goods?

Manifestly, the preceding question is a meaningful and important one. (We shall address its political implications in Chapter 12.) And yet the further significant question arises as to how it is to be answered. Why *would* receiving the commodity-bundle of one's choice lead, as a matter of empirical fact, to more satisfaction than buying a bundle one would not have chosen for oneself?

Indeed, Little[24] himself suggests some reasons why such an empirical relationship would *not* be universally true. One type of counter-example occurs in those cases where an individual's happiness, consequent upon the buying of material commodities, is, in part, a function of the pattern of consumption of other individuals.[25] Little cites the example[26] of a man who, due to a rise in income, has an expanded range of possible choices available to him, and from this range *does* select the bundle "of his choice". However, during the same period of the increase in his purchasing power, there has been a disproportionately higher increase in the income or purchasing power of the members of his economic class. In these circumstances, if a significant element in his reasons or motivations for buying commodities is the ostentatious prestige provided by luxury expenditure, then it is highly dubious that the satisfaction of the individual has increased, even though he

117

has moved from one position of technical "equilibrium" to a "higher" one, and in so doing has purchased the commodity-bundle "of his choice".[27]

As I see it, the preceding example amplifies our earlier denial of a logical entailment between choice and satisfaction. For, in order to answer the question concerning the presence of an empirical relation between personal choice and satisfaction, once again it would be necessary for the system-behaviourist to determine what precisely were the evaluative standards, reasons, or purposes for an individual's pattern of consumption in the first place. He must, that is, find out what "reason-giving" considerations motivate what kind of consumer to make what kind of purchases. In other words, in order to put CCT to normative use, an economic behaviourist must return to identify exactly those factors which one might, broadly speaking, call the "psychological causes" of behaviour. However, he has previously rejected just such mentalistic determinants as inadmissible to the corpus of a scientific theory like CCT when pursuing the "positive" aims of the explanation and prediction of human behaviour. But, if it can be shown that his methodological scruples over the incorporation of psychological predicates in the language of a "descriptive" science are ill-founded, surely it would unify and simplify economic reasoning to include them, considering that the crucial adaptation of the "positive" theory for normative purposes will eventually demand recourse to such psychological predicates anyway. Moreover, we have already argued in Chapter 4[28] that the methodological scruples of behavioural theorists generally *are* misguided in empirical theory-construction itself.

In raising the question of the reasons which operate as the "psychological causes" of behaviour, we have broached a major dispute in contemporary philosophy – the so-called reasons/causes controversy. Indeed our brief comments here have already given evidence of a particular stance which we will take on this issue. It is plain, therefore, that a more full-scale examination of this debate is incumbent upon us. Such will be the topic of the next chapter.

Chapter 8

Reasons, Causes, and Economic Methodology

In recent philosophy, the traditional teleology versus mechanism dispute has received new life and illumination in the form of a vigorous controversy concerning "reasons and causes". Although some of the philosophical matters dealt with under the title of the reasons/causes argument have already been discussed in our above analyses of the teleological dimension of CCT, other issues at the heart of the controversy crystallize very effectively some of the central problems pervading the greater part of this study. In this chapter, therefore, I proceed to inquire into the relevance of the reasons/causes issue to the methodology of CCT.

1. Rational and Causal Explanation

What, in the first place, is philosophically at stake in the controversy can be identified by recognizing that the argument has its origin in the recon-struction of ordinary, commonsense explanations of human action. It is noted that such explanations can be understood as providing the reasons *why* agents perform the actions that they do. When asked, for instance, why John is pouring water into his car's radiator, someone might seek to explain this action in replying that John is doing so *in order to* cool the car's overheated motor, that such is *his reason* for pouring the water. More explicitly, John's reason for his action can be analyzed into two components:

a) a certain ultimate or intermediate end desired by the agent and towards which, therefore, he has some kind of "pro-attitude", or which end he in some way *values*.

b) a belief that a certain action (or set of actions) is necessary to bring about the desired end.

In the case under discussion then, an explanation of John's action in terms of *his reason* can be construed as comprising (i) his purpose, or goal of cooling the motor and (ii) his belief that pouring water into the radiator was necessary to attain his end-in-view. Hence, it can be observed that such a "his-reasons" account for human behaviour constitutes a teleological, indeed purposive form of explanation since the antecedent conditions of the action to be explained include reference to some end conceived and desired by the agent, and action believed by him to be required to bring about the envisaged end.

So far our elucidation of what has been called a "rational explanation" of an action has been straightforward and familiar enough. One sort of philosophical perplexity arises with the question of whether or not "reasons can be considered causes" or, more precisely, whether rational explanation is a version of, or at least compatible with causal explanations of human behaviour. The topic is a large one, and some of its critical areas must be left beyond the scope of this inquiry. Nevertheless, it will be profitable to examine three aspects of the reasons/causes dispute which are of especial import in understanding the methodology of CCT. These aspects can be initially indicated in noting three important objections to the thesis that rational explanation is a type of causal explanation:

A) As observed earlier, the primary explanans-statement of a causal explanation is a general law describing an empirical regularity. The antecedent and consequent clauses of such laws refer to kinds of events, the so-called cause and effect, which events are deemed in the empiricist tradition to be only *contingently* related. (Premise 1) However, the major premise in the explanans of a rational explanation, for instance as represented by G' formulated in Chapter 2, designates a non-contingent, necessary relation between reasons (desires and beliefs) and the actions they explain. (Premise 2) Accordingly, it is concluded by some philosophers[1] that "reasons cannot be causes" or, more specifically, that rational explanation is not a type of causal explanation, but is in fact incompatible with such explanations.

B) Rational explanation, as the title suggests, makes at least implicit reference to the deliberative, problem-solving, cognitive capacities of human beings. Herein an agent is conceived not merely as an unreflective object, *being moved* passively and "automatically" by external stimuli. Rather a person is conceived as a *self-moving* agent, capable of correctly understanding his environmental "situation", preliminary to forming intelligent choices from amongst alternative courses of action in order to most efficiently attain the end to which he himself imputes a value. It is argued, however, that causal explanations would be capable of by-passing any recourse to mentioning such "intentional" phenomena as reasoning, deliberating, choosing, and valuing in accounting for human behaviour. Consequently, the conclusion set forth in A) that rational explanation constitutes a *rival* explanation to causal explanation is asserted again by certain philosophers.[2]

C) Adducing the reasons for an action in order to explain it can be seen as including an essential *normative* element since, from the agent's point of view, his desires and beliefs play a crucial role of *justifying* the action he performs. For, as outlined above, the agent believes his action will bring about some end he finds worthwhile, desirable, or valuable in some respect. However, on recognizing that manifestly non-purposive causal explanations, invoking no appeal to anyone's reasons, do not exhibit any attempt in the explanans to furnish justifications for the explanandum event, some philosophers have again concluded that rational and causal explanations are incompatible.

If we remind ourselves that generalization G", set forth in Chapter 2, section 2, furnishes the major explanatory premise of CCT, it is evident that neo-classical explanations of consumer behaviour themselves form a particular subset of "rational explanations" – that is, those cases where the agent's reasons for doing what he does are limited by economic wants and beliefs, i.e., a desire for the subjective satisfaction or "utility" obtainable from the use of material commodities, and the belief that purchasing a certain set of goods will maximize that utility.

We have had occasion to see, moreover, that the three objections to interpreting rational explanation as a species of causal explanation are especially pressing in coming to an understanding of the methodology of CCT. For:

1) We saw the severe conceptual difficulties,[3] confronted with the apparently "analytic" truth status of G", of specifying the type of empirical significance available for this explanatory postulate.

2) We remarked in the last two chapters that, historically, influential economic theorists have sought to base their understanding of CCT on an oversimplified analogy with physical models drawn directly from classical mechanics; consequently, the critical function of rational thought processes involved in deliberation, calculation, problem-solving, etc. in the determination of consumer choices has been ignored or underestimated. (This consequence will be further explored in this chapter.)

121

3) We have noted that variance among economic methodologists in their interpretation of general economic principles, such as G" of CCT, some construing them as empirical laws describing invariable sequences of causes and effects, while others view them as rationalizations prescribing justifications for anticipated actions.

Let us begin our examination of the implications of the reasons/causes dispute for the appropriate interpretation of CCT by dealing first with the problems raised by objection A above.

2. Necessary Connections, Causality, and Action

An immediate difficulty, obstructing any explication of the problems generated by objection A, arises from the bewildering variation in meanings employed by philosophers in talking about the family of concepts comprising analyticity, necessity, contingency, empirical versus logical relations, *a priori* versus *a posteriori* truth, etc. In this context, one is faced with empiricist dictums such as "causal laws express contingent regularities", and "the antecedent and consequent clauses of causal laws must be logically distinct", without being given any clear analysis of the meaning of such key concepts as "contingent regularity", "logically distinct", or the relation between these concepts. Nevertheless, as these technical terms have traditional significance we will continue to employ them, while attempting to provide a clearer, if somewhat stipulative, specification of their meaning.

What then is meant by the first premise of objection A – that the statement of a causal law expresses a contingent proposition, or, in terms of the invariable sequences of cause and effects to which lawlike propositions refer, that, as Melden puts it, the cause "must be logically distinct from the alleged effect"?[4]

This premise is best understood as giving expression to the Humean axiom of traditional empiricism that there are "no necessary connections between matters of fact". More specifically, for any actual, particular event in the universe – ϕ – it is logically possible that:

a) ϕ be other than it actually is – that is, that it not have existed or have a different set of properties than those that actually are true of it, independently of any change in the existence or properties of any other event, and

b) ϕ be exactly as it is, that it have and continue to have the same properties true of it, independently of the existence or properties of any other event.

Although, in the first instance, the preceding empiricist axiom is set forth as an ontological principle characterizing extra-linguistic events, it has traditionally spawned two *epistemic* corollaries concerning our *conceptualization* of the contingently related events:

(i) any law-like statement describing invariable sequences or constant conjunctions of types of events is only contingently true, and always remains subject to refutation by the contents of future experience; for it remains logically possible for the properties of the kind of event designated by the antecedent clause (the cause) to change, even though those designated by the consequent clause (the effect) continue the same (or vice-versa).

(ii) each particular event, including causally related ones, must be conceivable separately from any other event, or in more recent terminology, must be identifiable independently of the identification of any other event. In linguistic terms, it must be possible to describe any discrete event without including the description of any other event. If, for example, the frictional force exerted by the surface of a table causes the deceleration in the velocity of a ball moving across its surface, it must be possible to identify the frictional force independently of the identifications of the deceleration, and vice-versa.

However, the second premise of objection A affirms the existence of a non-contingent or necessary relation between a reason (consisting of a desire and belief) and the action explained by adducing such a reason. In particular, as pointed out in our elucidation of G' and G",[5] by a necessary relation between a reason and an action we mean that, given a *ceteris paribus* clause indicating the absence of countervailing factors, it is "analytically true" that if a person desires a certain goal (G) and believes an action (A) necessary to attain that goal, he will perform A. For it is part of the meaning of desiring G and believing A necessary for G, that the desire and belief issue in doing A. Consequently, if, in the absence of interfering factors, A is not performed, the agent cannot correctly be said to possess the particular reason – i.e., the specified desire and belief – for performing the action.

But if both premises of objection A are true, the conclusion is soundly reached that reasons are not causes, and hence that rational explanations are not a species of causal explanations.

Needless to say, various ploys have been taken to discredit the truth of the first and/or the second premise. An influential line of attack is that exemplified by Donald Davidson in his article "Action, Reasons, and Causes".[6]

Basically, we can interpret Davidson as arguing that one can render innocuous the threat of a logical or non-contingent connection between cause and effect by discriminating between *ontic* and *epistemic* levels when talking about causality. For causality, Davidson implies, is *in re*. That is, a causal relation exists between events in the extra-linguistic world, irrespective of our conceptualization of this relation in coming to know it, or, relatedly, of our description of it in language. Thus, Davidson claims that "to describe an event in terms of its cause is not to confuse the event with its cause",[7] and that "the truth of a causal statement depends on *what* events are described; its status as analytic or synthetic depends on *how* the events are described".[8] For instance, "the cause of B caused B" would be a necessary, analytically true statement, there being a connection of meaning between the subject and predicate. Nevertheless, if "B" = "the deceleration of the sphere" and "the cause of B" = the frictional force exerted by the table", then, upon substitution, we would have the true statement "The frictional force exerted by the surface of the table caused the deceleration of the sphere" which is, however, a contingent, synthetic statement, there being no connection of meaning between the subject and predicate. Hence, alternative *descriptions* of the same causal relation have provided, on the one hand, a non-contingent, analytic statement of the relation, and, on the other hand, a contingent, synthetic one.

Davidson and other philosophers with similar views[9] can be best understood, therefore, as committed to the philosophical thesis that it is only at the epistemic or linguistic level that questions as to the contingency versus necessity of the relation between causes and effects can be meaningfully asked, whereas, the existence (or non-existence) of a particular causal relation is a fact (or not) at the ontic level, a feature of the extra-linguistic world (logically) prior to the conceptualization or linguistic description of this relation.

However, even leaving aside the general metaphysical question of whether it makes sense to talk about causal relations between events at some type of "noumenal" or preconceptual level prior to the linguistic description of these events or, with Kant, we conceive of causality as a principle to be *limited* to the categorial or conceptual level, as a relationship holding between events only *as described*, significant criticism can yet be directed to such a reply to objection A.

In the first place, suppose the philosophers endorsing this reply are working – as many are – within the empiricist tradition. In this context, it is not at all clear that they would want to be adamant in relegating questions of necessity or contingency to matters concerning "how the events are described" or the determination of the logical status of alternative descriptions of the causally related events. Rather, they should insist that the concept of contingency be applied not only, or even primarily, to statements or propositions, but also to extra-linguistic reality. Since Hume, it has been an irrevocable postulate of those wishing to call themselves empiricists that the observed causal relation between actual events in the world, *denoted* by causal statements, is a contingent one, in the sense that is logically possible that an event cited as a cause occur and its expected effect not occur. However, if contingency and necessity are to be predicated only of linguistic entities such as statements, as is implied in the Davidsonian reply to objection A, then the affirmation of this fundamental empiricist postulate is rendered a category-mistake.

We might articulate the preceding comment from the opposite direction. In particular, those philosophers who defend the position that, generally speaking, the occurrence of logical or necessary connections at the conceptual level between descriptions of causes and descriptions of effects does not entail a necessary relation between the events referred to by those descriptions, must still provide some convincing *positive* reasons of their own why the denoted events *are* only contingently connected. That is, reasons must be given for concluding that, in the context of the putative causal relations under consideration, it is conceivable that someone's wanting ϕ and believing doing A a means of attaining ϕ obtain, but, in the absence of countervailing factors, such a cause not be followed by the occurrence of its presumed effect – the doing of A. But it is at this point that the force of Davidson's manoeuvre in securing the contingency demanded of genuinely causal relations dissipates.

To show this outcome, we might begin by reminding ourselves of the logical status of G'. Hence, G' was observed in Chapter 2 to be best interpreted as a quasi-analytic "meaning convention" implicitly defining the concept of an action as an event caused by some set of wants and beliefs. G', furthermore, was seen as spelling out in a determinate manner the complete structure of interrelated wants and beliefs to be employed in interpreting human behaviour, when such behaviour is conceived as action. Included in the meaning of the concept of an action, therefore, is the implication that an action is caused by a structure of beliefs and wants, as specified in the antecedent of G'. (Or, correlatively, it is (part of) the meaning of the description of the structure of wants and beliefs constituting the antecedent conditions of G', that the occurrence of such conditions logically necessitates the performance of the action mentioned in the consequent.)

125

But if this interpretation of G' is sound, it establishes that Davidson's move to preserve the contingency of particular causal relations between reasons (wants and beliefs) and actions is spurious. For, as mentioned above, if the claim that the events denoted by reasons and the actions they rationalize are contingently connected, it must be logically possible that the former events occur but not the latter. However, our analysis of G' has confirmed that such a state of affairs is not logically possible. For, in any particular case, as long as the conditions specified in the "countervailing factor" clause of G' are satisfied, it is logically impossible, if an agent wants ϕ and believes action A is a necessary means of attaining ϕ, that he not perform A. This is so, we have seen, because the *meaning* of having wants and beliefs in such circumstances logically necessitates the performance of the action.

We may put the preceding point in a more general way. Although the underlying principle in Davidson's argument, that of distinguishing the conceptual or descriptive order from the ontological order, is a sound, and frequently fruitful one in philosophical analysis, he errs in overlooking the *relationship* between these orders, particularly with respect to our understanding of human action. For, in general, extra-linguistic entities are *identified* or described as certain *kinds* of entities by classifying them in terms of a concept. Of course, the concepts employed for such purposes exhibit various levels of abstraction. Some of the most general levels are the familiar classifications of entities as material objects, organic things, persons, physical events, human actions, etc. However, the critical point in the context of the present discussion is that upon identifying an entity by subsuming it under the concept of an action, we thereby implicitly attribute to that entity the defining characteristics of the class of actions. But as we have seen,[10] *amongst these defining characteristics* is the consideration, call it C, that actions are to be conceived (and therefore described) as events that are *caused* by some set of wants and beliefs, the explicit structure of which causality is set out in G'. Consequently, insofar as our particular theoretical task is to determine the cause of a slice of extra-linguistic reality which has been identified *as an action*, the relationship between the selected cause and the action will inescapably be a non-contingent one. For defining characteristic, C, of the concept (i.e., "action") used in identifying or classifying this segment of reality commits one, as a matter of logic, to a specification of the appropriate antecedent causal conditions.

In other words, one can grant Davidson the following point. In general, extra-linguistic entities have no logical relations such as contingency, necessity, etc. with other entities until such entities are conceived or identified and thus described. And if their causal relations are *not* among the defining characteristics of the concepts used in identifying these entities, then, under one set of descriptions such entities might exhibit non-contingent causal relations, and contingent ones under another. But, again, we have argued that among the defining features of the concept of an action *is* an action's cause (wants, beliefs). Hence, contrary to Davidson, one cannot *describe* an item of extra-linguistic reality *as an action* without, *ipso facto*, being committed to the non-contingent relation between that item *as described* and its cause.

Nevertheless, it has been premature of those other philosophers who have stressed the logically necessary connection between reasons and actions to employ such a consideration as a premise in inferring the conclusions that reasons are not causes or that explanation by reasons is different in kind from explanation by causes. Now, such philosophers argue that, given their non-contingency, general principles like G', under which actions are subsumed, do not have the status of causal generalizations as do the generalizations under which physical events are subsumed. Two comments might be made to elucidate the fallacy in such an inference.

1) Admittedly, an action-theoretic conceptual scheme countenances non-contingent causal relations. For we have argued that in defining human actions in terms of the kind of events (i.e., reasons) which cause them, we *ipso facto* commit ourselves to a non-contingent causal relation between reasons and actions. But are we compelled to conclude, therefore, that the *definition* is illegitimate on the grounds of the general principle of empiricist epistemology that all causal relations are contingent? Not necessarily – we have the option to conclude that this principle does not merit the universal validity empiricists claim for it. There are, moreover, pragmatic grounds for taking up such an option. Consider, for instance, the extensive explanatory utility which the action-theoretic scheme has exhibited in providing the underlying conceptual framework both for everyday commonsense explanations and for explanations within the economic theory of choice. Presently, furthermore, we shall elucidate the unique and effective manner in which this scheme lends itself to normative use. Given these utilities, it seems to me that the option of denying universal scope to the empiricist principle would be preferable *as long as* the basic generalization of action-theory (G'), and the explanations it governs, are not removed from the dictum of "empiricist control". That is, G', like any legitimate scientific statement, must remain *corrigible* in the process of scientific inquiry, and the

explanatory arguments covered by G' must, in some significant sense, be amenable to observational refutation.

But arguments presented in Chapter 2 show that this requirement concerning empiricist control can be met. It will be useful, then, to summarize, and amplify, some of the main points of those arguments. In the first place, we might take note again of the extreme generality of G', that it comprises an *indeterminate* mention of beliefs, wants and actions without mentioning the specific type of beliefs, wants and actions occurring on a particular occasion. And it is just this generality which permits the empirical testability of *explanations* of particular human actions. For all such explanations affirm the performance of a specific action as caused by a *determinate* set of wants and beliefs. And any such explanation is subject to experiential falsification on the general grounds that particular actions might have been caused by *different* kinds of beliefs and desires than the particular ones which *were* causally responsible.

We might complement this reminder of Chapter 2 with the following observation. It is to be granted that no such "conceptual truth" as G' is of any final use for scientific explanation and prediction unless it at least facilitates the derivation of generalizations which *are*, even within a particular conceptual scheme, amenable to disconfirmation by observational evidence. But G' fulfils this condition. Once the indeterminate wants, beliefs and actions of G' have been specialized to refer to various kinds of determinate counterparts, lower level generalizations, connecting more particular kinds of reasons and actions, can be derived. And, most importantly, such generalizations *do* express a contingent connection. Our lower-level principles would belong to empirical psychology and would report causal, but contingent, connections between specific types of dominant desires and the particular sorts of actions believed to be the optimal means for satisfying such desires. Thus, a particular causal law might describe a regular connection, in suitable circumstances, between any agent's overriding desire for personal power and an action consisting of the choice of a political career.[11] Or another law might articulate a uniform connection, given appropriate circumstances, between a dominant desire for security and the choice of a civil service occupation. But even if universally true, such causal connections would only be contingently so. For instance, it is logically possible, that the operative (rather than the self-delusory) reason why someone chooses a political career be an altruistic desire for public service – the charge of factual naiveté to such a suggestion does not preclude its conceivability.

We observed in Chapter 2, furthermore, that G" remained scientifically corrigible for the reason that the conceptual scheme to which G' belongs, namely that which conceives human behaviour as action, might be revised or abandoned by adopting a different conceptual scheme for interpreting human behaviour such as those embedded in behaviourist and neurophysiological theories of behaviour.[12] However, it is worth adding here mention of some methodological consequences of any attempt to abandon an action-theoretic conceptual scheme for understanding economic behaviour in favour of a neurophysiological one. (We have already examined the serious failings of using behaviourist schemes in Chapters 4, 6 and 7.)

Now, we may agree, with Hume, that in conceiving (and thus describing) an extra-linguistic entity as (merely) a *physical* event, rather than an action, one affirms only a contingent relation between that event and its cause. Consequently, we may also agree that the antecedent and consequent conditions of generalizations describing regular causal sequences between (mere) physical events are contingently connected. Accordingly, such generalizations can be understood as formulating empirical laws subject to experiential falsification. It is the case, moreover, that the conceptual framework of neurophysiological theories does conceive or identify (extra-linguistic) *phenomena under the description of physical events, not actions.* Hence, a neural theory of human behaviour could, unlike its action-theoretic competitor, be comprised, at even the highest explanatory level, of contingent, empirically falsifiable generalizations.[13] In upshot, if we were to replace our action-theoretic framework for explaining consumer behaviour with a neural one, we would be able to replace non-contingent explanatory generalization (G") with contingent ones. Should the economic theorist seek to do so?

Although it would take us too far afield to consider all the myriad philosophical issues raised by this important question,[14] it strikes me that it can only be answered on pragmatic grounds. Which framework most effectively meets the theoretical *aims* involved in attempting to understand economic behaviour?

Seen in this light, it seems to me that one central aim of such an enterprise gives the nod in favour of an action-theoretic framework. We have emphasized that the economic theorist seeks to devise an explanatory system that can be *conveniently adapted for normative uses.* But an action-theoretic system, with its inclusion of goals, desires, beliefs – in short, the reasons – of behaviour, already wears its normative applicability on its theoretical sleeve. On the other hand, a neurophysiological system, making no recourse to an agent's justificatory reason for his behaviour, cannot be so directly put to normative employment – if it can be at all.[15]

2) It needs to be remembered, nevertheless, that the admission of a non-contingent causal connection at the level of the most basic generalization (G') of action-theory does not necessarily demarcate the epistemological foundations of action-theory from those of natural scientific theories. For, to return to our analysis in Chapter 2, Section 3 of the epistemic status of Newton's first axiom of motion, we observed that one defensible manner of interpreting this most basic scientific principle was that of a logically necessary, experientially unfalsifiable "meaning convention" which stipulated the meaning, say, of "the absence of external forces acting upon a body".

Moreover, this comparison between action-theory and classical mechanics may be usefully extended. For, in a wider metaphysical sense, Newton's first axiom might also be understood in a manner which parallels G''s definition of the concept of an action. Hence, the first axiom might be interpreted as supplying a (partial) definition of the concept of physical or *mechanical* motion itself, *qua* movement of a material body which is caused by the impact of an *external* force rather than by some "entelechy" or internal force within the body. Upon this interpretation, a re-formulation of the first axiom as the general proposition that "no body alters its motion unless caused to do so by some external force affecting it" would, as before, be necessarily true by virtue of the meaning of its constituent terms and, hence, not accessible to refutation by observational findings. Accordingly, analogous to the case of action-theory, causal generalizations at the most primitive level of physical science, permit interpretation as asserting non-contingent truths. Nevertheless, in concert with the situation of action-theory, to the extent that the specific kind of external force which is acting upon a moving body is made explicit, two consequences follow. First, particular *explanatory arguments* can be constructed which are capable of observational disconfirmation. Secondly, falsifiable empirical laws can be derived. The first consequence has already been illustrated on pages 28-29. An example of the second is furnished by any physical law, wherein the change in the momentum of a body is causally induced by the operation of some *specific* external force, as with the inverse square law describing accelerations in the momentum of a body as caused by its coming under the gravitational attraction of other physical bodies. Such a law describes a contingent regularity since it is logically possible that the alternation in the momentum of a body be caused by the exertion of an external force of a different character (as indeed happens if subjected, say, to an electro-magnetic force).

To sum up. We have supplied the content of the concept of someone's "reason for an action" in terms of the antecedent considerations of beliefs and (overriding) desires for which the agent performs an action. And we argued that it is part of the *meaning* of the concept of an action that an action is to be conceived as *caused* by the type of entities constituted by desires and beliefs. Hence, our analysis is committed in a very strong sense to countenancing the causal status of reasons, for, otherwise, we would not preserve consistency in our definition of action. Moreover, we have already replied to one objection (A) to the identification of reasons with causes from the point of view of the "necessary" character of the relation between reasons (desires, beliefs) and actions.

3. Rational Causality, Deliberation and Intentional Systems

We have yet to answer objections (B) and (C) above. In the case of B it is argued that, unlike accounts in terms of mechanistic causes, rational explanation necessarily includes a presupposition of the deliberate exercise of the cognitive or ratiocinative capacities of the agent, his ability to intelligently assess a situation in order to identify an effective course of action to achieve the goals he posits. And again, with respect to C, it is contended, in contrast to causal explanations, that explanations by reasons imply a *justification* for the action performed. Although we will argue that neither objection precludes the causal role of reasons, they do nevertheless bring to light important inadequacies in some prevailing understandings of action-theoretic explanations, especially those provided by CCT. We shall consider objection B first, although, as will become clear later in this study, neither objection can be successfully tackled in isolation from the other. (Objection C will be examined in the next chapter.)

In order to gain a critical perspective on the methodological implications of the deliberative dimension of rational explanations, it will be fruitful to examine certain features of the "purely mechanistic" explanations of "merely physical" phenomena, that is, those wherein questions of the exercise of rational thought-processes are not at issue, even though such explanations bear important structural similarities to the rational explanation of purposive human behaviour. I refer again to system-theoretic explanations of physical phenomena that employ the notion of the movement of a physical system towards some type of *equilibrium*. Consider, for example, the case of the progress of a system towards a position of "stable equilibrium", where "stable equilibrium" designates, roughly, a state such that, whenever the external environment remains constant, and any other initial condition undergoes change, the system exhibits a tendency to return to its original state. To take an oft-cited example,[16] suppose a spherical object has moved to a position of rest at the base of a semi-circular container. If the sphere is displaced from this position, then, within a certain range of displacement, it will return to its original "steady-state" at the base.

Again, we find the concept of a stable equilibrium found in the explanation of certain physiological processes of the human organism, often in the form of an explanation of the preservation of a "steady state" or "homeostasis" of certain properties of the organism. We might remember, for instance, the case described in Chapter 7 of the maintenance of the temperature of the human body within a certain life-sustaining range by particular physiological processes. That such processes induce a stable equilibrium is exhibited by the fact that if the temperature of the external environment is held constant, whereas the internal temperature of the body rises due, say, to strenuous exercise, an increase in perspiration and the respiration rate will cause the body to return to its original temperature.

We further observed in the preceding chapter that the concept of equilibrium played a significant role in functional forms of explanation, particularly that of CCT. In the light of the present discussion, it is now clear that the position of an individual consumer's equilibrium formulated by CCT may also be characterized as one of *stable* equilibrium. For CCT defined an equilibrium state as one towards which consumer buying tends, and at which, once realized, there would be no tendency for a consumer to alter his pattern of purchases. Of course, if an external "exogenous" causal variable were to change – e.g., a reduction in a commodity price – CCT describes the consumer as induced to move from the original equilibrium point. Nevertheless, upon the increase of this price to its original amount, the consumer will return to the original position.

In general, then, we find that certain kinds of natural events and human activities, i.e., those to which "equilibrating" or homeostatic properties can be significantly ascribed, display a similarity of logical structure. However, it is of the first importance for present purposes to realize that whether or not any sequence of events, natural or human, exhibit a tendency to establish a steady state or (stable) equilibrium is entirely an *empirical* question – there is no necessary, *a priori* reason why any kind of actual events, in the natural or human domain, would exhibit equilibrating tendencies. But once this point is appreciated, it makes all the difference with respect to the question of whether purposive or rational explanation can be assimilated to explanations of the "ordinary" causal variety. Or, since we have concluded above that reasons are causes, this point has a direct bearing on the question of what *kind* of causal processes reasons can be identified with. Let me explain.

Consider, then, that by an "ordinary" causal explanation we understand a "purely mechanistic" one as characterized above. As instances of such explanations we can take our accounts of the movement of the physical sphere in its container and the variations in body temperature. Now it is clear that the explanations provided for both these phenomena *are* factually sound. It is empirically true that gravitational phenomena, in the former case, and physiological processes, in the latter, *do* regularly occur as described. More precisely, the general laws covering such events have been empirically validated. Furthermore, the cause-effect sequences referred to by these laws are, in a crucial sense, "unintentional" or "automatic". Briefly, in a sense to be explicated more fully below, by an *automatic* causal process we shall understand one which is not dependent on deliberate control – that is, conscious, intentional human decision. Hence, both natural gravitational processes and the human organism's temperature mechanisms can be classified as automatic – they both occur independently of human intention.

Again, the preceding have been two cases of ordinary or "purely mechanistic" causal explanation. Consider, however, a member of the class of purposive explanations. In particular, let us examine a purposive reading of the explanatory model provided by CCT. Seen in this light, we are better able to appreciate that the proffered explanations of CCT are factually true *only* for the ideal case of the actions of the *rational* economic man and (generally) false if claimed to describe the behaviour of other agents. Moreover, to the extent that a consumer's behaviour *fails* to agree with the predictions of the axioms of CCT, although directing his behaviour towards the equilibrium end affirmed in CCT, i.e., the maximization of his utility, then such behaviour can be *criticized* as not being the product of the appropriate deliberative procedures embedded in CCT as the means towards utility maximization. In short, according to the explanatory model, the consumer has acted irrationally. Nevertheless, his unsuccessful behaviour is *rectifiable*, on condition that he consciously subjects it to revised practical reasoning or intentional control by adopting the means encapsulated by the axioms.[17] For instance, his original foundering might have been due to transgressing axiom 3, by not ordering his preferences in a transitive manner. Such a mistake is, however, *avoidable* through a renewed deliberation that recognizes the necessity of a transitive ordering for attaining the equilibrium providing for maximum utility.[18] In sum, the equilibrating processes described by CCT are not, in league with gravitational phenomena and the body's homeostatic temperature mechanisms, species of the "ordinary" causal variety as adumbrated above. That is, the causal sequences referred to by CCT are not "automatic", they can and do vary (succeed or fail) in reaching their equilibrium state in proportion to the rationality or irrationality of intentional human deliberation and decision.

Furthermore, it is in this sense of rational consumers being able to *correct for* irrational activity by means of reflective deliberation, that an understandable and genuine sense can be given to the concept of a consumer as a self-determining and responsible agent. For their behaviour, unlike moving spheres and automatic physiological processes, is not the inevitable "blind" effect of *unavoidable* external causal conditions. For, insofar as the consumer can critically appraise his end-in-view, and assess his past purchasing behaviour in attaining that end, the *knowledge* thus acquired can itself function as a new causal condition permitting and indeed inducing different, more rational purchasing behaviour in the future. In this sense, then, the consumer-agent has "liberated" himself from the constraint of *ignorance* implicit in the previous set of causal antecedents, which ignorance brought about irrational behaviour.[19] Moreover, since his purchasing is corrigible by means of his own practical deliberation, he can be legitimately considered responsible for his consumption practices.

Nevertheless, it should be noted that this conception of the consumer's agency or self-determination does not commit us to an acceptance of a libertarian doctrine of "contra-causal" freedom.[20] For we are not denying that there might be antecedent conditions, say factors of his learning experience, which are necessary and jointly sufficient causal conditions for the rational consumer's acquisition of the requisite knowledge – and such learning is as subject to the governance of deterministic causal laws as other phenomena. In general, the processes referred to by "S's having a reason" belong to the general class of causal sequences, but also to the sub-class of those causal processes which are *corrigible* upon submission of such processes to S's deliberative assessment. And, thus, such "rational man" explanations can be placed in the class of causal explanations, but *not* of the "ordinary" or purely mechanistic kind.

Further light can be shed on the distinction between automatic equilibrating systems and those involving intentional control by examining the differences in the nature of the equilibrium "end-states" of each. Of course, in an important sense, the equilibrium states of automatic and deliberative equilibrating systems are similar, since such end-states, if they *are* realized by either type of system are consequences or *effects* of prior causal processes – in the former case of non-purposive mechanisms, in the latter case, of purposive decision-making. However, the effects themselves can be instructively discriminated. It is empirically true that automatic end-states occur irrespective of the excellence of deliberative processes, whereas intentional end-states obtain only on condition that the events of the equilibrating system can be correctly described as rational deliberative processes. Put another way, *defective deliberative* states constitute *interfering conditions* for intentional equilibrating systems, but not for automatic ones. It is not unexpected, therefore, that it is less generally true that equilibrium states obtain for intentional systems than for automatic ones – for the simple reason that the "irrational" interfering conditions to which the former are subject are not rare, but all too frequent human phenomena.

It should be stressed, furthermore, that the practical reason we have claimed for the enlightened consumer comprehends his critical appraisal of both his final ends and the means he enacts to attain these ends. His practical knowledge, in other words, can extend beyond that of merely instrumental values, beyond that of the identification of the efficiency of alternative means to secure given ends. We are, in short, conceiving economic rationality to extend to full-fledged *moral* knowledge. Of course, we may grant that such a robust view is incompatible with both the orthodox scepticism concerning moral beliefs of "positive" economics and the "noncognitive" ethics buttressing this orthodoxy – a canon among contemporary economists extensively documented by Subroto Roy.[21] However, we shall later[22] adduce considerations to be sceptical of the general non-cognitivist dogma barring the rational criticism of final ends, and the received limit to economic rationality which the dogma underwrites.

4. Deliberation and Ethical Conservativism

Not surprisingly, writers on economic methodology in the neo-classical tradition have typically underplayed or misrepresented the deliberative aspect of the equilibrating processes of economic choices, and have thereby distorted the ethical implications of CCT. Some, in failing to observe the role that deliberate control can play in the actual occurrence of equilibrium, seem to simply assimilate the kind of equilibrating mechanisms appropriate to a theory of rational choice such as CCT to those of automatic physical systems, in viewing the entire economy as a system of "natural" or "impersonal market forces". Blaug,[23] for instance, suggests that Adam Smith's "invisible hand", which allegedly functions to ensure that the pursuit of self-interest will promote the common good,[24] be identified with the "automatic equilibrating mechanisms" postulated by neo-classical theories of producer and consumer behaviour.

The sort of confusion exemplified by Blaug is often compounded in neo-classical discussions of economic methodology through a misconception of the meaning of the "necessity" or "unalterability" of the regularities described by deterministic scientific laws. Admittedly, a universal law of nature does assert a causal necessity between the antecedent and consequent conditions formulated by the law. That is, if the antecedent conditions are realized, the occurrence of such a state of affairs is always a sufficient condition for the occurrence of the event mentioned in the consequent. Even if the regularity referred to by the law is one of human behaviour, the uniform conjunction of antecedent and consequent events is not alterable by human control or decision. Nevertheless, it is to be remembered that the conditional supported by a universal law is a *counterfactual* one asserting that if certain initial conditions *were* satisfied, then certain events *would* regularly follow. But the central consideration with respect to laws of human behaviour is that, although the regular sequence between antecedent and consequent events is not amenable to human choice, it frequently *is* accessible to an agent's conscious decision as to whether or not *the antecedent conditions will be satisfied*. In this way, the behaviour characterized by the consequent conditions, which behaviour is necessitated *if* the antecedent conditions were to occur, is rendered *avoidable* for rational agents. (And, of course, if the antecedent conditions of an empirical law are not satisfied, the fact that the consequent event does not take place offers no refutation of the law.)

It is just this failure to appreciate the precise role which deliberative processes or practical reasoning play in the manner in which human behaviour validates social scientific laws which has led to the endorsement of an ill-founded ethical standpoint towards CCT in particular, and, in fact, towards "mainstream" economics in general. For economists of neo-classical persuasion, in conflating the meaning of the *deterministic* status of laws governing human behaviour with that of the *avoidability* or *unavoidability* of the behaviour predicted by such laws, have often illicitly argued for a doctrine of ethical conservativism with regard to economic behaviour. In simplified form the epistemic phase of their argument (call it D) can be presented thus:

D:

P1   If economic behaviour is predicted by deterministic laws then all such behaviour is causally necessitated.

P2   X-type behaviour is predicted in the consequence of a (deterministic) economic law.

C: ∴ X-type behaviour is (causally) necessitated – i.e., it will occur and cannot be avoided.

Now consider that it *is* true that X-type behaviour – say a pattern of consumer choice – gives expression to certain moral principles. And let us assume that such behaviour does, as a matter of observable fact, occur. Finally, suppose we define ethico-economic conservativism in terms of a disposition to endorse *de facto* economic behaviour as morally desirable, and, therefore, not to be altered.

But if the preceding assumptions did obtain, and argument D *were* sound, then our neo-classical conservative *would* have adequately defended his supportive attitude toward the morality of actual economic behaviour. For he would be a bearer of a happy coincidence. Not only would *de facto* economic behaviour be in accord with his moral principles, but no *other* behaviour prescribed by *different* moral principles would be empirically possible, since only the behaviour actually occurring would be compatible with scientific law. Consequently, recommending that the actions of economic agents exhibit conformity to an alternative set of moral principles than the one with which they already do agree would be *pointless* – after all, "ought implies can" and the moral principles recommended by our economic conservative would be the only ones with which economic behaviour *could* comply. Moreover, the conservative could also plausibly contend that he could have it both ways – viz., that he could adopt an attitude of moral approval towards the prevailing pattern of economic behaviour while still preserving this ethical neutrality as a scientist. For, as a responsible theorist, he might continue to disclaim any commitment to normative claims, being concerned only to conjecture and confirm descriptive hypotheses. Nevertheless, as a responsible "citizen", he might claim to be fully justified in morally commending given behaviour which accords with the axioms of his covering theory – and in an unimpeachable, because "scientific" sense. For, again, it just so happened that it was empirically necessary, according to scientific law, that economic subjects exhibit the behaviour predicted by his theory; *a fortiori* the only practicable moral principles for guiding consumer activity would be the ones already expressed by actual consumer practices.[25]

However, in the light of our analysis of the import of cognitive processes on equilibrating models involving the selection of reasons for action, we can see the fallacy in the neo-classical, "conservative" argument. Basically, the conservative errs because he equivocates with respect to the meaning of the phrase "behaviour which is compatible with scientific laws of human behaviour". As we have seen, it is true that if the antecedent conditions of an economic (or any other) law are satisfied, then the behaviour predicted in the consequent is causally necessitated – no alternative behaviour is possible, such behaviour being incompatible with the implications of the law. Nevertheless, it *is* possible, by means of the practical deliberations of economic agents, that the satisfaction of the antecedent conditions *be avoided*, and thus, the behaviour which otherwise would have been necessitated, *had* such conditions been fulfilled, need not take place.[26] And if alternative behaviour does occur, it might very well be in conformity to *different* moral principles than those espoused in the conservative's allegiance to the moral principles being followed in the economic *status quo*. (However, it is also important to realize that if such novel behaviour does occur, it does not thereby constitute a phenomenon which is incompatible with the scientific (economic) law at issue, since, *ex hypothesi* such behaviour is outside the scope of the antecedent conditions formulated in the law.)

5. Marx, Mill and "Eternal" Laws

The kind of misunderstanding of economic theorists with respect to the logic of validating social scientific laws, argued above, is well illustrated by Marx's critique of methodological aspects of Mill's theory of production. Mill, in his *Principles of Political Economy*, had argued that ...

> the laws and conditions of the production of wealth, partake of the character of physical truths. There is nothing optional, or arbitrary in them ... these are ultimate laws, which we did not make, which we cannot alter, *and to which we can only conform*.[27]

To these constraining laws of production Mill contrasted the "rules" for the distribution of wealth which were constructed entirely on the basis of social customs that were a matter for voluntary human choice. Accordingly, such rules could vary directly with intentional variance in choice. Marx, however, attacked Mill's analysis, charging that Mill had represented production ...

as distinct from distribution, etc. as encased in eternal natural laws independent of history, at which opportunity *bourgeois* relations are then quietly smuggled in as the inviolable natural laws on which society in the abstract is founded. This is the more or less conscious purpose of the whole proceeding. In distribution, by contrast, humanity has allegedly permitted itself to be considerably more arbitrary.[28]

Marx's point, then, is that, in order to covertly defend and entrench what are in fact *alterable* "bourgeois" social relations in the sphere of production – that is, institutional norms within a capitalist form of society prescribing such conventions as entitlements to the ownership of private property – economists like Mill have fallaciously re-classified such transient, corrigible conventions as "inviolable" empirical laws, to which an economic subject *must* conform. According to Marx, such methods make it ... "possible to confound or to extinguish all historical differences under *general human* laws",[29] where such historical conditions refer to specific forms of production correlated with a particular type of society's institutional arrangements – such as legal conditions on property ownership in activities of capitalist production.

It seems to me that one can describe the accuracy of Marx's critique of Mill as right in its spirit, although confusedly expressed in its letter. For it is true that Mill and the neo-classical economists who have followed Mill have been guilty of misrepresenting the meaning of "ultimate laws ... to which we can only conform". In effect, these theorists are under the mistaken impression, analysed in the previous section, that the presence of a universal law governing a type of human behaviour entails the inevitability or *unavoidability* of the occurrence and recurrence of that kind of behaviour. And, seemingly, by a fortunate but allegedly undesigned coincidence, this behaviour also conformed to the neo-classical evaluative standard of "rational economic man". However, as Marx noticed, the behavioural satisfaction of such laws was not, contrary to the implicit beliefs of Mill and later neo-classicists, "independent of history". In other words, as I see it, Marx obliquely appreciated the *conditional* aspect of the validation of empirical laws. That is, only if certain initial conditions were satisfied, which sometimes required the fulfilment of "historical conditions", would the behaviour predicted in the consequent of such a law be causally necessitated. But historical conditions vary with changes in the type of production processes prevailing in a particular historical period. Accordingly, when such historical conditions as a particular kind of production process, along with the legal conventions promoting the preservation of this process, do not exist, the antecedent clause of the social scientific law will not be true, and, therefore, the behaviour described in its consequent will not have been necessitated. In this sense, then, economic laws are not *eternal* laws which are "independent of history", since historical conditions are included in the very formulation of the antecedent conditions of these laws.

As mentioned, however, Marx, although vaguely recognizing the conditionality restriction of nomological necessitation, fails to get his analysis entirely straight. For he misidentifies the implications of his analysis with respect to the truth conditions of general laws. Thus, we find Marx suggesting in the quoted passage that economic laws themselves have only a transient, temporary validity, being true for certain forms of production and their presupposed social or institutional setting – e.g., capitalistic processes and the institution of private property – and false when such historical contingencies change. Such a conclusion is, however, confused and unnecessary. The relevance of "historical differences" to the causation of economic or other human behaviour can be preserved without impugning the permanent status of the truth of social scientific laws; we need only realize that the truth of any empirical law is *applicable* only when the causal conditions specified in its antecedent have been satisfied.

The preceding observations of Marx's critique of Mill took place within the context of theories of production. However, as our argument in the previous section attests, the conclusions here also apply, *mutatis mutandis*, to a correct understanding of the theory of consumer choice (CCT). Indeed, an assumption of (spurious) grounds for political passivity brought about by a mistaken understanding of the type of necessity implied by social scientific laws has a long history in the application of economic theory in general. Such was the case, for example, in the acceptance of Adam Smith's generalizations invoking economic "naturalism". As Eric Roll describes the impact of Smith's economic theory ... "this theory gave to the conduct of the prospective leaders of economic life (i.e., the industrial capitalists) an impact of inevitability";[30] and, as Roll also remarks ... "among the forces which freed English foreign trade from regulations, which removed prohibitions ... Adam Smith's work occupies a prominent place."[31]

Chapter 9

Justification, Obligation, and Consumer Motivation

Insofar as the equilibrating events referred to in CCT incorporate cognitive, deliberative processes, the actions following upon such decision-making are susceptible to *normative* criticism as to their *justifiability*. For we have observed that the underlying practical reasoning can be viewed as an attempt by the agent-consumer to select an appropriate purchasing strategy on the basis of his ranked desires for commodity-combinations, and his beliefs as to the availability and comparative capacity of sets of commodities to satisfy his desires. In other words, the consumer, if challenged, can give *his reasons* for his particular action-choices in attempt to *justify* them. But his practical deliberation is not necessarily foolproof; his beliefs, for instance, might be ill-founded, or, although as we shall see this is a much more contentious issue,[1] his goals or desires might be rationally indefensible. Consequently his behaviour, or the practical reasoning leading to it, is also liable to the assessment of a more enlightened external observer.

Of course, a presupposition of the meaningfulness of the critical appraisal of consumer choices is that the equilibrating framework in which they take place not be classifiable as what we have called an automatic one. That is, the securing of equilibrium must not be empirically necessitated, independently of the success or failure of the rational thought-processes of economic agents. Or put the other way around, only instances of deliberative equilibrating activities are meaningfully defended or criticized on the grounds that it is possible to fail to repeat rational deliberation leading to successful action-choices that attain the equilibrium goal, and possible to avoid irrational deliberation engendering inept choices that do not attain equilibrium. In other words, it would be pointless and fruitless to *appraise* consumer behaviour unless it was *alterable* through the adoption of more rational/irrational deliberative procedures.

If we return to an examination of our economic generalization, G", set forth in Chapter 2, it can be seen that this principle lends itself naturally to an interpretation as a *rationalization*: for its consequent reports an action, the buying of a particular commodity-bundle, for which its antecedent provides reasons for performing – the consumer's desire for maximal material satisfaction and his belief that the particular purchase will meet this desire.[2] And the formation of such reasons on the part of the economic agent demands his rational deliberation, which practical reasoning can be performed well or poorly. Hence, such reasoning is subject to critical appraisal either to defend it in order to reinforce it, or to assail it in the hope of reforming it. In short, the *reason-giving* explanations furnished by the theory of consumer choice (CCT) take place within a *normative* context, as indicated by the fact that the antecedent of its general explanatory principle (G") proffers a justification for the intentional action described by its consequent.

Such a consideration, however, places the explanatory framework of CCT squarely at the centre of the foremost dimension of the reasons/causes dispute. For the most significant criticism of the side in the controversy who claim that "reasons cannot be causes" was the one we summarized in the last chapter as objection C which concerns the normative aspect of reason-giving explanations. The heart of the argument expressing this objection can be plainly stated. Thus, we find premises being set forth that:

a) Causes do not *justify* the effects they necessitate, or that causal explanations provide no assessment of the event to be explained,[3] whereas

b) Rational explanations necessarily include a delineation of the justification for an intentional action in the deliberations of the agent.

Therefore, given a) and b) it is concluded that "reasons are not causes" or, more precisely, that explanations citing the agent's reasons for his behaviour are different in kind from explanations which adduce the causes of such behaviour.

However, although the core of this type of argument of those who wish to deny that rational explanation is a form of causal explanation can be badly put, it is not, I wish to argue, convincing. Now, most philosophical attempts to defuse the kind of criticism under consideration have concentrated on similarities in logical structure between reason-giving explanations and the general class of causal explanations. In particular, it has been argued[4] that there is nothing in principle preventing one from interpreting such an assertion as an agent's "having a reason" for his action due to some property of it which he values as, in context, constituting a sufficient set of conditions for the action, or as related to his action in such a way as can be understood as an instance of an empirical law, and that such interpretations coincide with the scientific concept of cause. Although not denying the importance of such inquiries, I think further light can be shed on the notion of reasons as causes by proceeding to another level of analysis in examining the substantive content of the reasons or evaluative grounds for action. Such an analysis, moreover, is best suited for bringing to the surface the specific manner in which normative/prescriptive elements are integrated with explanatory/descriptive ones in CCT. The ensuing discussion brings one to the intersection of economics, moral philosophy and moral psychology, a crossroads too many economists hesitate to approach.

1. Reasons, Norms and Motivations

In recent moral philosophy the affirmation of the "is-ought" distinction has been based on arguments concerning the definition or *meaning* of moral concepts and judgments. Perhaps the most forceful contemporary proponent of the distinction has been R. M. Hare[5] who divides the total meaning of moral and other value judgments into descriptive and prescriptive components. Briefly, according to Hare, one could take the descriptive meaning of a value-judgment such as "honesty is good" as referring to the factual basis of the judgment, that, for instance, honesty engenders communal trust, permits interpersonal communication, prevents enmity, etc. On the other hand, the prescriptive meaning concerns the speaker's acceptance of practical imperatives or commitment to courses of action following upon sincere assertion of moral judgments – hence, to take the honesty example, he would, where possible, tell the truth, admonish those who do not, support laws punishing deliberate deception, etc. Most importantly, it is only *via* their prescriptive meaning that moral judgments perform their essential function of guiding our conduct. Hare's "anti-naturalist" type of analysis, moreover, is behind his acceptance of "Hume's Law", that one cannot deduce an "ought" or moral conclusion from a set of "is" or purely factual premises. For a validly deduced conclusion cannot possess any surplus meaning not already present in the set of premises; however, a moral conclusion would possess prescriptive meaning not present in the purely descriptive meaning of a set of entirely factual premises.

Although I believe the preceding "is-ought" prohibition can be challenged on its own grounds, such a criticism would require an inquiry into the theory of meaning which space prevents me from pursuing in this study. In any case, the considerations I want to introduce can be established independently of a resolution of the meaning of value-judgments, and it is important to see this. Nevertheless, my analysis does take up where emotivists, prescriptivists (like Hare) and kindred ethical theorists usually leave off – namely, in an account of what one might call the quasi-theoretical relationship between ethics and psychology, or, more precisely, between judgments of moral obligation and assertions of psychological motivation. We might then, for the sake of argument, follow Hare in conceiving questions of the meaning of moral judgments to be those relevant to an understanding of the *logic* of moral discourse and agree with him that "logic cannot determine what we are going to be attracted by or averse from".[6] That is, whether or not we have "pro-attitudes" to whatever kinds of actions or objectives is a factual matter to be answered by the investigations of empirical psychology. But the conclusions of such an empirical inquiry never preclude the *logical possibility* of anyone being motivated to desire or judge good any goal or action whatsoever, regardless of whether such occurrences are *contingently* improbable or even empirically impossible.

But even if we grant the general validity of the preceding analysis of moral terms and judgments, it is at least misleading to the extent that it engenders an underestimation of the role of *empirical motivation* in the function of moral and other value-judgments in guiding actual human conduct. In general, if there were no connection between assertions of prudential or moral obligations and actual motivations to fulfill such obligations, normative systems such as moral codes would simply have no use in human life, as they would lack any *applicability* to concrete behaviour. Even if the meaning of "X is good" or "one ought to do A" is such that they do not logically imply any specific motivation to desire X or perform A, unless there is at least a *causal connection* between what individuals judge good and what they are psychologically motivated to desire, normative systems would be as empty of practical import as the conceptual structure of a physical theory would be of cognitive import without empirical conditions of application for its theoretical concepts. It is in this light that we can best tackle the question "Why ought I to be moral?" or the problem of the justification of an ethical system in terms of its psychological sanction. An understanding of this relationship between moral principles and motivation[7] can begin by examining simple cases of "practical reasoning". We might first consider an illustration outside of the context of consumer behaviour.

Suppose then, that an agent Jones is deliberating as to whether or not to join a wildcat strike at his plant. We might reconstruct his reasoning towards such a decision in the familiar form of a practical syllogism:

A: I ought to support activities which are likely to increase my wages significantly.

B: Joining the wildcat strike is likely to do so.

C: I ought to join the wildcat strike.

No doubt the normative (and major) premise of this syllogism presupposes a prior case of practical reasoning in which our agent Jones determines the desirability of increasing his wages, which reasoning we might schematize thus:

D. I ought to support activities which are likely to lead to my personal happiness.

E: Activities likely to increase my wages will probably lead to my personal happiness.

F: I ought to support activities likely to increase my wages.

Now our present concern is not with formal aspects of these cases of practical reasoning, but rather with what we might call the *epistemic status* of the normative major premises of the above syllogisms. What type of warrant or justification do these premises possess? The initial normative principle, A, is of course, inferentially justified – it can be seen to be *deduced*, in conjunction with a suitable minor factual premise, from our second normative major premise D. But, and this is the central question, what type of justification is there for Jones' assertion of D, on the assumption that D cannot be inferred from any logically prior normative principle?

The answer to this question takes one to the heart of moral philosophy in the British Utilitarian tradition. Suppose we characterize the class of principles exemplified by A as immediate norms or, in the context of our present analysis, as immediate reasons for actions, which norms have a *mediate* epistemic status, being derivable from the class of principles exemplified by D. We may characterize this latter class as *primitive* norms or primitive reasons for action in that *at least from the point of view of the agent*, they cannot be inferred from logically prior principles. In the final analysis then, and important matters of detail aside, we find that within the Utilitarian tradition the primitive norms of practical reasoning are justifiably accepted or asserted by an agent, on condition that the kind of actions prescribed by such a norm be an object of a certain kind of *psychological* state on the part of the agent – what Hume labelled a "feeling of approbation" towards A-type actions, or what some contemporary philosophers have called a "pro-attitude" towards such actions. Less cumbersomely, albeit more vaguely, we might simply classify this view as the doctrine that the justification of the primitive reasons for certain kinds of action, that is the agent's basic normative principles governing those actions, is furnished by the content of the agent's wants or desires with respect to actions of that kind.

But to *desire* or want something belongs to the category of motivation. That is, if an agent can correctly be described as desiring X, then he can be further described as being subject to a *disposition* to perform actions of which X is the consequence, and hence are means to the securing of X – or which actions can be described as doing X itself and hence are wanted as ends in themselves. Accordingly, we might put the above analysis of reasons for actions within the framework of our present topic by saying that, within the Utilitarian tradition, fundamental, i.e., non-derivative normative principles, demand and acquire a justification through agents being psychologically motivated to perform actions specified by such principles. Hence, unless a value system headed by normative principles can be supported by motivations to follow the principles, then the system is (at least partially) unwarranted.

Recent philosophical investigation has concentrated on the logical nature of this relation between obligation and motivation. On the one hand, some philosophers argue for a strong "internalist" connection, that is, that an agent's cognizance that he is subject to a particular norm or obligation *logically entails* that he is motivated to fulfill the obligation. On the other hand, other philosophers[8] have argued for a logically weaker "externalist" connection, that whereas it is not logically inconsistent to accept "I ought" without correspondingly accepting "I shall", nevertheless, given certain general truths about human emotions as articulated in empirical psychology, under certain circumstances, it is *causally* impossible for an agent to realize he is under an obligation and not be motivated, that is feel a disposition, to fulfill the obligation.

Without taking sides in the internalism/externalism controversy, an understanding of the dispute concerning the character of the relation between obligation and motivation can, nevertheless, help to elucidate a central problem in the reasons-causes controversy. We observed that a rationalization for an action centred on the justificatory aspect of an agent's reasons for acting as he did – that, as he viewed his "problem-situation", the course of action he selected was "the thing to do". Thus, upon analysis, we should find that the agent *valued* the action in itself or as leading to a consequence he valued. The basic question then arises as to whether and, if so, *how*, reasons can have causal efficacy. From a structural point of view the answer to this question primarily depends, as numerous philosophers have argued,[9] on our success in devising general laws of human action connecting an agent's *having* reasons (i.e., beliefs and desires) with the performance of actions rendered appropriate by those reasons. As our discussion in Chapter 2 of this study has shown, although there are conceptual problems in interpreting such laws – e.g., with respect to the question of their "non-contingent" truth status – we concluded that it was possible to formulate action-theoretic "laws" that were explanatorily adequate.

But from a substantive or ontological point of view, that is, with respect to the *determinate content* of reasons for action, our present discussion permits us to reinforce the conclusion that reasons (or better an agent's having of reasons) can operate as causes of his behaviour. For we have noted above that an agent's primitive reasons justifying his action-choices exhibit a type of "essential" relation to his affective or motivational states, to his desires, "pro-attitudes", or what earlier philosophers classified as his "inclinations" to perform certain kinds of actions. In effect, in a manner that appears paradoxical, at the level of primitive reasons as formulated in terms of ultimate normative principles, normative concepts, as it were, "phase into" descriptive ones. And, unfortunately, the paradox is compounded by the presence of alternative ways of interpreting this merging factor, which options play again on the normative-descriptive distinction. Let me explain.

On the one hand, we might, in an internalist vein, *identify* or equate primitive reasons with an agent's psychological attitudes. A person's primitive reason for performing an action simply *is* his possession of a "pro-attitude" or disposition to perform that kind of action. On this interpretation, an action is ultimately justified for an agent, because, as a matter of empirical fact, he has a positive psychological attitude towards a class of actions of which this one is an instance. Accordingly, some of those philosophers who have sought to defend this interpretation have, not surprisingly, included factors concerning psychological states such as a speaker's interests, desires, attitudes, etc. as part of the *meaning* of his utterance of normative principles.[10] In effect, his assertion of such principles *gives expression to* his reasons *qua* psychological states. Hence, on such an "internalist" account, it would *follow logically* from an agent's assertion of a basic normative principle that he was psychologically motivated to engage in action in agreement with the principle.

One might consider, on the other hand, that the basic normative principles themselves be taken to *be* primitive reasons for acting. And one might consider, further, that it is *logically possible* that an agent be conscious of the soundness of a normative principle constituting a primitive reason, and yet *not* be psychologically disposed to "internalize" the reason and thereby be subject to a motivational influence to subscribe to the principle in his actions. Nevertheless, such "externalist" reasoning, in concurring with internalism that normative discourse would be *pointless* unless somehow tied to motivations to act as the discourse prescribes, reaches a conclusion that, for the purpose of accommodating rational explanation within causal explanation, will suffice. Thus, although demurring from claiming that an agent's consciousness of, or utterance of, what he takes to be a sound normative principle governing his action *logically implies* a corresponding motivation, nevertheless, assertions of such principles "pragmatically presuppose" a motivating desire. Such a presupposition takes the form of it being *causally* impossible, in certain circumstances, for the agent to perceive what he ought to do and not be motivated accordingly. Otherwise, without even this *empirical* connection, the use of reasons *qua* normative judgments would be sterile, as they would be impotent in fulfilling their distinctive role of guiding human conduct.

It might seem that we are conflating an irrevocable distinction between contexts of explanation and justification here. But it is the import of our discussion that, with respect to primitive reasons or the ultimate normative principles conveying such reasons, the distinction itself must be bridged, that is to say a *synthesis* of explanation and justification must be developed. Thus, if the ultimate norms governing action-choices lack a motivational underpinning in the sense that agents cannot be moved to follow the norms, such norms would *ipso facto* lack a pragmatic justification or "vindication" in that they would not be able to fulfill their proper function of guiding actions. In this sense, an assent to an ultimate normative principle either logically entails or pragmatically presupposes the presence of a psychological state which both vindicates acceptance of the principle and causes or "excites" the agent to perform the action prescribed by the principle. But once such a vindication or psychological sanction is provided, we thereby are also in possession of a causal *explanation* why particular agents *do* subscribe to certain basic (non-derivative) norms. The category of justification, in other words, has a wider scope than merely the deductive subsumption of one proposition under a more general one.[11]

2. Restructuring Choice Theory:
Economic Rules and Psychological Sanctions

What bearing has the preceding discussion concerning prescriptive statements and psychological motivation on the logical status and value-theoretic foundations of CCT? None, if we were to listen to neo-classical theorists propounding the orthodox doctrine of value-neutrality in economic theory. For such theorists have conveniently ignored the question of the need for a motivational backing for normative principles or rules. Instead, influenced by emotivist and prescriptivist ethical theories, they have taken refuge behind the anti-naturalist foundation of these theories which we outlined above – that value-judgments have a different logic or meaning from descriptive statements and, hence, that one cannot validly infer normative statements from purely descriptive premises. On this issue, we may refer again, in amplified fashion, to the representative view of Klappholz, who, in an influential article, comments:

> The 'orthodox' position rests on Hume's observation that norms or proposals cannot be deduced from descriptive statements alone, a descriptive statement being defined as a statement which has truth-value (whether or not it is possible to ascertain its truth). Thus statements which have truth-value are value-free, in the sense that proposals cannot be deduced from these statements alone; *logically* they have no ethical implications. Since the scientific part of economics consists exclusively of descriptive statements, it cannot have any ethical entailments, and is therefore value-free.[12]

Most importantly, and revealingly, Klappholz deploys his endorsement of Hume's "is-ought" prohibition to classify as irrelevant, when tackling the problem of the value-neutrality of economic methodology, an examination of the "motives for, and psychological effects of using certain words". For such psychological factors do not, he claims, at all determine the "logical status" (by which he understands the meaning) or the truth or falsehood of an accepted statement.[13] Accordingly, for Klappholz and like-minded methodologists, concern with the psychological motivations for accepting an economic statement will, *ex hypothesi*, have no bearing on the question of whether or not such statements are purely descriptive or value-laden, this being an independent matter of the "logical status" or type of meaning such statements exhibit.

But, to my mind, such a conclusion grossly misrepresents the genuine "logical status" of the hypotheses of economic theory. In fact, the above account of the relation between moral obligation and psychological motivation provides, I think, the essential clue to ascertaining what kind of statements economic theory *does* comprise. Let me explain by returning to CCT in an attempt to set forth what I take to be, in the final analysis, the most accurate interpretation of the logical status of its statements.

Basically, I believe the most illuminating interpretation of the axioms of consumer choice theory to be a construal of them as, *in the first instance*, a set of *normative* principles in the form of *rules* for the consumption practices of an *ideally rational* consumer. The implications of this interpretation of the axioms of CCT with respect to the overall epistemic status of the theory will be deferred until later chapters. However, certain issues concerning the category of rules to which A_1-A_4 can be most suitably adapted, and the normative *cum* motivational status of these rules, need to be clarified in the context of the problems of the present chapter.

We might profitably begin by reconstructing A_1-A_4 in a form which more perspicaciously represents their initial normative dimension. Originally, it will be remembered, they were presented in conformity with their standard form in economic treatises, that is, as universal descriptive hypotheses or "assumptions". However, as normative rules they might be stated thus: (It would be useful for the reader to compare the following with the original list on page 7.)

R_1 (A_1) (comparability or completeness)	Any *rational* consumer, S, *ought* to form a comparative evaluation of any two alternative commodity-bundles, say A and B, that is determine whether he prefers A to B, B to A, or is indifferent between A and B
R_2 (A_2) (non-satiation)	S *ought* not to be content with any particular level of consumption – he *ought* to prefer more of any available commodity.
R_3 (A_3) (transitivity or consistency)	For any three alternatives, say A, B, and C, if S prefers A to B and B to C, then he *ought* to prefer A to C. In this sense, the rational consumer ought to be "consistent" in his choices.
R_4 (A_4) (diminishing marginal rate of substitution)	The amount of y S should be willing to give up to get an additional unity of x *ought* to become progressively smaller as the quantity of y diminishes. Rational consumers ought to be relatively stingy with relatively scarce goods.

What kind of rules, then, are R_1-R_4? It seems to me the most accurate classification, in the light of the *aims* of CCT, is to consider R_1-R_4 as *instrumental norms* or prudential maxims which a rational consumer would follow in order to most efficiently attain his intrinsically desired goal or ultimate end. No doubt, this claim is pregnant with most of the philosophical foundations of CCT. Of course, any unpacking of its content first demands that we focus on what constitutes the final end or goal of the rational consumer of CCT. In this way, we will be better placed to understand the sense in which the following of R_1-R_4 can be deemed a means for attaining the end, and, finally, to appraise the end itself. It is to our analysis of the relation between norms and motivation that we must turn in order to determine the final end of CCT.

We observed in that analysis that, at least according to the Utilitarian framework endorsed by neo-classical economics, an agent's psychological attitude, constituted by a standing want or desire, offered a terminating justification, in the form of a psychological sanction for an ultimate normative principle. In effect, such a sanction comprised an "exciting" reason or (causal) motivation to follow the norm, and thus to perform the kind of action prescribed by it. Hence, we might say that, within the Utilitarian tradition, a certain type of *psychological* ground provides the ultimate *justification* for (rational) action, or alternatively, *explains* why an agent's basic normative principles are the ones they are. Or we can clarify this viewpoint in another way by noting that logically primitive norms specify ultimate ends of human actions, that is, objects of desire which are desired for their own sake rather than as means to further objects. Hence, in our example on page 145, Jones wants to perform actions that are likely to increase his personal happiness, not for any "ulterior motive", but because to him his happiness is intrinsically valuable, that is, an ultimate end.

Now, it is to be observed that the instrumental normative content of CCT can be *summed up* in the equimarginal rule that a rational consumer ought to pursue a policy of purchasing directed toward allocating his income among combinations of commodities to the point at which the ratio of the marginal utilities of the various goods are equal to the ratio of their respective prices. This all-embracing or "omnibus" rule, O, can be deduced from the set of axioms of CCT construed, in the manner just adumbrated, as rules (R_1-R_4) for the rational choice of commodity-bundles. (In a sense, R_1-R_4 are "second-order" norms of consumer choice for they enable an agent to act in accordance with O.)

But the theory, thus reconstructed, *also* affirms a *motivational* buttress for its prescriptive rules. For CCT claims that the consumer whose behaviour *does* conform to its normative requirements (R_1-R_4 and, therefore, O) will attain a position of "equilibrium" where he will maximize his (material) utility, thereby satisfying his economic desires as far as possible, and, therefore, have no inclination to dispose of his purchasing power differently. And, the theory presumes, the expectation of attaining such a position is a motivational influence to which everyone is causally necessitated to yield. The desire to maximize utility thus serves as the psychological ground or "motivating reason" which both vindicates and explains the submission to the rules of rational consumer choice specified by the theory. It is evident, then, that the ultimate end or purpose, through a desire for which a rational agent would submit to the rules recommended in CCT, is the maximization of (material) utility, that is, the maximal satisfaction an agent could receive from the use of material commodities. Accordingly, the theory may also be construed as giving expression to the appropriate motivation *via* its tacit subscription to a further (Utilitarian) *categorical* norm prescribing the final end of a rational consumer – i.e., *homo economicus* ought to maximize his material utility.

In sum, therefore, CCT can best be interpreted as both:

(i)   recommending a set of instrumental norms or rules for rational consumer choice, and

(ii) setting forth the ground or reason for the actions of rational consumers in terms of the psychological motivation which would justify and/or explain submission to the normative requirements of the theory. And such a psychological vindication receives expression in the theory's commitment to a Utilitarian categorical norm. (Of course, the categorical norm of the moral theory of classical Utilitarianism is that an agent ought to maximize social, not private utility. But again,[14] neoclassical economics argues that the "invisible hand" mechanism of a perfectly competitive, free enterprise economy will bring about a ("Pareto" constrained) maximum social utility as an unintended consequence of the pursuit of maximum private utility by individual rational economic men.)

Interpreted in the proceeding way, we can see why an uncritical adherence to the "is-ought" injunction has tended to confuse methodologists in their understanding of the logical status of the statements of economic theory. For, as psychological assertions are themselves typically construed as factual or descriptive claims, and as descriptive assertions do not, according to the injunction, imply prescriptive ones, the critical *relation* of descriptive, psychological factors to prescriptive claims has normally gone unnoticed by those concerned with economic methodology. Indeed, since value-judgments remain pragmatically empty or *inapplicable* to human affairs without motivational underpinning, the acceptance of the "orthodox" division of facts from values, of descriptive claims from normative ones, has been more obscurantist than clarifying in attempts to make economic explanation intelligible, and, in general, is better abandoned as such a blunt *modus operandi* in the philosophical analysis of social scientific explanation.[15]

3. Historical Background: Mill's Proof

With respect to finding the basis of the reasons/causes problem in the relation between moral obligation and psychological motivation, one finds an instructive case study in historical Utilitarianism. Consider, for instance, Mill's discussion of both the "ultimate sanction" and the "proof " of his Principle of Utility or Greatest Happiness Principle in Chapters III and IV of *Utilitarianism*. In effect, Mill can be understood as arguing that a determination of the *psychological sanction* for the Principle of Utility, itself amounts to all the "proof" of which this "first principle" or ultimate standard of morality is capable.

To begin with, Mill is well aware of the elementary logical point that ultimate or non-derivative principles governing our conduct are incapable of proof in any strict sense – that is, by deduction from more general statements. Rather, Mill searches for a looser variety of justification for his first principle of morality in the form of what he calls "considerations capable of determining the intellect either to give or to withhold its assent to the doctrine".[16] And the notorious form which Mill's presentation of such "considerations" takes is, in sum, a) to claim that happiness is intrinsically good or desirable because everyone actually desires it, and b) no one ever desires anything else except happiness.

Of course, Mill's "proof " has been strenuously criticized, most familiarly by Moore who accused Mill of committing the naturalistic fallacy in the sense of defining the unique, unanalyzable property "good" in terms of natural or empirical properties – in Mill's case of equating the meaning of "good" with what people actually desire. For, Moore argues,[17] "desirable" means "what it is good to desire", and since "desirable" thus includes the moral predicate "good" in its meaning, it is fallacious to define "desirable" by means of the empirical predicate "what people do actually desire".

In a way, Moore's analysis can be seen as structurally similar to Hume's argument against deducing a prescriptive conclusion from purely empirical premises. For if, with Moore, we agree that, due to the unique, unanalyzable character of the moral predicate "good", its meaning cannot be identified with the meaning of empirical predicates, then Mill *would* be guilty of an illicit contravention of "Hume's Law" if he were to deduce "happiness as desirable" (i.e., intrinsically good) from the premise "happiness is desired", as there would be surplus meaning in the conclusion not already present in the premise.

However, it seems to me that Moore has unfairly and inadequately dealt with Mill's "proof" by interpreting it in a manner too closely corresponding to reasoning by deductive inference. Let us, for the sake of argument, grant Moore's charge that Mill is using "the desired" as synonymous with "the good". Nevertheless, by returning to a consideration of our discussion of the non-deductive justification of ultimate norms in terms of their sanction *via* psychological motivation, we may defend at least the *form* of "proof" Mill presents against the charge of naturalistic fallacy.

In effect, in appealing to the psychological fact that men do in fact desire happiness, Mill can be understood as seeking to exhibit the kind of justification for the maximization of happiness axiom that we have argued any non-derivative normative principle requires – that is, a sanction in the form of a motivation to which an agent is causally susceptible. It is such an empirical fact which, if believed to be true, would constitute "considerations capable of determining the intellect" of a reflective person. Moreover, it is beside the point that a proposition reporting the existence of such an empirical fact is not, as Moore complains, identical in meaning with a proposition affirming that happiness is intrinsically good or desirable. For Mill is not, in an "internalist" vein, attempting to find motivational implications by analysis of the meaning of an ultimate principle of moral obligation, which procedure might be put into the form of deductive inference. Rather, in the manner of "externalist" argument, Mill should be interpreted as drawing our reflective attention to the causal connection of the maximization of utility (happiness) principle with a motivational backing, consisting of a universal disposition of agents to follow the principle, that is, "that human nature is so constituted as to desire nothing which is not either a part of happiness or a means of happiness".[18] Of course, Mill's assumption here of the truth of psychological hedonism might be erroneous. In fact, such an error follows from what we have argued earlier.[19] Consequently, the *particular* "proof" which Mill provides is, therefore, not successful.

Nevertheless, it is incumbent upon any normative system that presumes to formulate ultimate standards of obligation to at least proffer the *kind* of "proof" or rational considerations presented by Mill. For, as we have noted, unless primitive principles of obligation can be shown to be connected with motivational influences, the normative system headed by these principles will be futile, lacking behavioural applicability. Indeed, Moore's own moral philosophy, postulating an allegedly non-natural property of goodness, accessible only *via* an intellectualist intuition, has been charged[20] (rightly, I think) with displaying just such a motivational lacuna.

The meaning and justifiability of Mill's "proof" has not been discussed merely for the purpose of historical exegesis. Rather, it seems to me that the nature and point of Mill's "proof" parallels the kind of interplay between prescriptive and descriptive-explanatory features of CCT. Again, the axioms of CCT can be perspicaciously interpreted, from an *initial* point of view, as recommending a set of rules for consumer behaviour, summed up in the equimarginal rule O. But the neo-classical theory of consumer choice can, on a second level, be instructively viewed as providing a "proof" or justification for these prescriptions (R_1-R_4 or O) in terms of motivational considerations. Thus, true to its origins in Utilitarian reasoning, CCT conceives of economic man as disposed, by nature, to maximize his happiness. Hence, a rational consumer would be susceptible to a reason or motive to assent to these rules if the theory could demonstrate to him that following them would have the desired consequence to the maximal degree – that is, would maximize his happiness. And, of course, this is precisely what CCT intends to do in describing the position of "equilibrium", which the consumer attains on condition that he conforms to R_1-R_4 (or, more generally, O), a position wherein the consumer maximizes his utility and, therefore, as we noted the economist Baumol put it, "has no motivation to revise his purchasing plans".[21] It is clear, then, that analogous to Mill's *modus operandi* in his "proof" of the utility maximization principle, CCT is to be understood as presenting a justification for a set of rules for a rational agent in the form of a motivational consideration to which it believes any such agent would be susceptible.

Moreover, the deployment of this rule-*cum*-motive schema for the description and explanation of actual economic behaviour is, so to speak, built into CCT's initial, or *logically prior* form as a normative system. For, according to the neo-classical theory, economic agents do not freely choose to seek their greatest possible utility. Rather their psychological make-up is conceived, in Mill's terms, as "so constituted" as to desire nothing else. And, CCT continues, if they are able to satisfy the appropriate rationality conditions postulated by CCT with respect to their information and preference-structure, they *will* regularly choose courses of action which do, in fact, result in the maximization of their material satisfaction.

An important point needs emphasizing before proceeding. By "prior" we do not mean *temporal precedence*. Indeed, since neo-classical theorists themselves have generally insisted, from the inauguration of CCT until the present day, that CCT aims at a descriptive account of actual consumer behaviour, a normative reading of CCT has rarely been articulated, let alone been the temporally first interpretation. Rather, by a normatively "prior" interpretation of CCT, we shall argue that such an interpretation is "logically" or "conceptually" prior in a sense that will be made increasingly clear in later chapters. Similarly, unless the context makes clear that a temporal inter-pretation is intended,[22] a non-temporal, "conceptual" interpretation should also be given to such cognate expressions as "initial", "in the first instance", "the original form", "introduced as", etc. whenever these phrases are used to characterize a normative interpretation of CCT in the remainder of this inquiry.

Chapter 10

The Problems Related

Upon review of our investigation of the philosophical foundations of the neo-classical theory of consumer choice, it is apparent that three underlying themes have continually surfaced to demand our attention.

a) The "analyticity" problem – to what extent, and in what sense, are the explanatory principles of CCT "necessarily true", rather than hypotheses describing contingent, "causal" connections that are falsifiable by empirical evidence?

b) In what sense does CCT exhibit the form of an "idealized" theoretical structure, and in what way does this pose difficulties for the task of explaining and predicting the actual behaviour of real-life agents?

c) What is the nature of the "normative" dimension of CCT in its concern to explain the behaviour of "rational" consumers? What kind of moral valuations, if any, are implied by this normative aspect of CCT?

Although the connections between these three problems have demanded some comment in the separate discussion of each of them, an elaboration of their *systematic relationship* has so far been postponed. However, it is to such a synthesis of the dominant themes of our investigation that I want to turn in this chapter. In doing so, it is hoped that an overview of the logical structure and moral foundations of CCT will be introduced.

1. Cognitive Idealization and its Affective Implications

We might usefully begin our attempt at synthesis by inquiring into the *source* of the idealized character of CCT. Why is it the case that CCT does *not*, in its canonical formulation without additional assumptions, account for the behaviour of real-life consumers engaged in actual purchasing activity?

The immediate reply to this question is to appeal to the implicit rationality assumption of CCT – that the theory seeks to explain the consumption only of the *rational* economic agent, one who distributes his income intelligently in enacting the appropriate means, given the economic situation as he finds it, to achieve his goal of maximum utility. Of course, as our previous analyses have made manifest, the simplicity with which this rationality assumption can be stated belies the extensive *evaluative* implications it exhibits, once its role within CCT has been unpacked. Thus, we have observed that CCT's concept of the consumer *qua* rational economic man is of an agent who systematically represses immediacy or spontaneity of desire, and who displays an unbounded acquisitive tendency to satisfy an ever-expanding, insatiable desire for material satisfaction. Both of these dispositions, we have argued, signify corrigible moral attitudes which need not be, and sometimes are not, instantiated by the actual dispositions of real consumers.

In other words, the very source or fundamental reason why CCT takes on its status as a theoretical idealization lies in its role as a *normative system*. Such a relationship occurs on two evaluative levels, the affective and cognitive. Both levels, furthermore, function so as to mutually reinforce the idealized aspect of CCT. Basically, the affective level, recommending suitable attitudes for the rational consumer, is conceived to *follow upon* certain cognitive traits of this agent. This dependency needs to be elucidated.

It will be remembered that the ideally rational consumer, as understood in CCT, has access to an extremely privileged cognitive state of complete information concerning his options – that is, he knows the content of all obtainable commodity-bundles, the utility or subjective satisfaction conse-quent upon purchasing any particular bundle, and on the basis of these utilities he is able to order bundles in terms of preference. Although such capacities constitute idealized properties which are rarely, if ever, realized by actual economic agents, the reason for their postulation in CCT can be found in the belief of neo-classical theorists that the Utilitarian norm prescribing the ultimate end of a rational consumer, namely the maximization of his utility, *demanded* such an idealized cognitive ability on the consumer's part in order that he completely comply with such a principle. Granted it can be argued that the viewpoint is misplaced;[1] nevertheless, neo-classical economists appear to have been under the impression that only if an agent had complete and certain knowledge of alternative action-choices and their consequences, would he be epistemically equipped to successfully follow the basic Utilitarian prescription to maximize his (economic) utility.[2]

Now, we have observed above the nature of the affective traits of rational economic man in referring to his calculating and aggrandizing attitudes – his dispositions to methodically suppress submission to random, spontaneous economic impulse and to seek continually more satisfaction from material consumption. Once again, these attitudes exhibit the consumer described by CCT as an "ideal type" – manifestly, not all actual consumers display the proposed ideal development of human nature constituted by such extreme calculatedness and acquisitiveness. But such attitudes, which we have argued in Chapter 5 involve commitments to significant moral options, are instructively construed as linked with the cognitive capacities of the ideal consumer. That is, such affective states can be viewed as *enabling* the rational consumer to accumulate the extensive information concerning commodity-bundle alternatives and purchasing consequences which he requires. For it is clear that neo-classical theorists[3] consider that the *lack* of such moral attitudes would prevent the development of the cognitive state of complete information which itself is understood as enabling the maximization of utility.

Moreover, we can agree that this consideration does have some plausibility. To the extent that a consumer has a psychological make-up which disposes him, in opposition to the calculatedness assumption implicit in A_3, to recurrently submit to his immediate consumption impulses, he would render himself incapable of ascertaining the comparative utility of other purchasing possibilities, since his capitulation to a *habit* of impulsive buying would bar him from such canvassing. Suppose, furthermore, that in contravention of the prescription to constantly aggrandize one's material utility, as embedded in non-satiation axiom A_2, a consumer sought a Stoic equilibrium of "lacking in nothing" by contracting his desires for more commodity satisfaction. Again, CCT can be usefully interpreted as proscribing such a policy on the grounds (amongst others) that it would needlessly circumscribe the cognitive capacity of the ideal consumer by preventing him from ascertaining the complete range of all commodity alternatives that would be available to purchase *if* only he *did* desire them.

In sum, CCT has taken the form of a theoretical idealization *because* of its dimension as a normative system, or, more precisely, a normative system of a particular kind. In effect, CCT construes the rational economic man as a classical *Act-Utilitarian* who considers it incumbent upon himself to review all obtainable action-alternatives with respect to the value of their consequences in the aim of choosing that alternative of maximum value. And in order to efficiently meet this severe cognitive demand of the Act-Utilitarian prescription, *homo economicus* endorses the derivative recommendations that he consistently manifest attitudes of calculated self-control and aggrandizing acquisitiveness in his desires for material goods.

Of course neither the cognitive directive nor its auxiliary affective rules are consistently followed by fallible mortals. In fact there is every reason to believe that it is empirically impossible for any agent to satisfy the governing cognitive demand, which impracticality has, of course, been the subject of trenchant criticism of Act-Utilitarianism as a moral philosophy.[4] Moreover, we have argued in Chapter 5 that the neo-classicist claim that submission to the affective rules presupposed by A_2 and A_3 is required to produce maximum satisfaction is itself a dubious one.

2. Normative Idealization and Necessary Truth

We may further elucidate the interrelation of the main philosophical aspects of CCT by examining the bearing our interpretation of CCT as an idealized *cum* normative system has on the alleged "analytic status" of the theory.

Again, an appreciation of the role of the "strong" rationality assumption, implicit in CCT, provides a key to understanding this connection. This assumption states that the rational economic agent possesses complete and infallible information of his "problem-situation", and chooses a course of action (e.g., the purchase of a commodity-bundle) that is appropriate to his situation.

In Chapter 2, we unpacked the content of the consumer's "problem-situation" in terms of his aim and factual beliefs as to the means of realizing his aim in the environment in which he found himself; and we analyzed the "relativized" kind of necessary truth exhibited by explanatory generalization G" governing his action-choices. Furthermore, we claimed that the necessity or "analyticity" involved was a feature of a highly abstract level of social scientific theory construction, and that empirically falsifiable explanatory arguments for contingent social phenomena could be found by giving specific content to the indeterminately specified mental events of G".

Although the conclusions concerning the "analyticity" of CCT reached in Chapter 2 do not need to be qualified in the present discussion, a further (but related) ground for a type of "necessary, a priori" truth status of CCT now demands examination. For, in distinction from our earlier analysis, wherein the source of the analytic necessity resided basically in implications of the meaning of the kind of explanandum-event at issue, viz., a human action, the present source of logically necessary truth lies in the character of CCT *qua* normative idealization, in particular in its aim of explaining the consumption patterns of *rational economic man*. Put another way, CCT limits the determinate content of its theoretical variables by confining the range of the direct applicability[5] of its axioms to *ideally rational* agents, those with the idealized cognitive capacities and affective dispositions described above. And it is just such a circumscription which is responsible for a kind of a priori necessity characterizing the truth conditions of CCT. Let us see why this is so.

Consider that we are dealing with the behaviour of the ideally rational consumer as conceived in CCT. The crucial point is that the behaviour which CCT predicts our ideal agent will enact, can be *demonstrated* a priori and with logical necessity to be the only behaviour such an agent would, or even *could* perform. Or, in other words, it can be demonstrated that it is *logically impossible* for the *rational* consumer to perform another action than the one predicated by the theory – that is, the purchasing of a combination of commodities which satisfies the equimarginal principle. Alternatively, from another epistemic perspective, we could validly claim that, given the meaning of *homo economicus qua* rational consumer, it is an analytic truth that he purchases a commodity-bundle in accord with the equimarginal principle (wherein the ratios of marginal utilities are equal to the ratio of the prices of the chosen commodities). That these important conclusions follow from the *kind* of theoretical idealization formulated by CCT can be substantiated by the following considerations.

To begin with, the subject under inquiry in CCT, the rational consumer, is understood as an agent who does subscribe to the Utilitarian rule defining his ultimate goal – viz., that he ought to maximize his material utility; hence, we may truly describe the action of this subject as one of seeking to maximize his subjective satisfaction from the use of material commodities. Of course, there is yet no prediction that he *will* maximize such utility without additional assumptions which further characterize his rationality. As we have seen, these assumptions are affirmed in CCT by the stipulations that the rational consumer follows a set of instrumental norms directed towards his final end of maximal utility, which norms we have constructed as R_1-R_4. And, hence, the conjunction of the descriptive counterparts of R_1-R_4, the original A_1-A_4, accurately *describes* this rational agent as one who prefers more of any available commodity, orders his preferences transitively, etc.

Suppose, then, that we gather together the implicit assumptions concerning the rationality of the agent investigated in CCT (his aim to maximize utility and his complete information) and those explicitly postulated (A_1-A_4). Let M represent the entire set of these rationality conditions. Consider, further, that the implicit ability constraints of CCT (call them C) describing the consumer as choosing freely and within the limits of a particular income, are conjoined to M. Accordingly, let us suppose that M and C form the antecedent conditions of a putative economic generalization. As a suitable consequent for this generalization, let us take a consumer choice consisting of the buying of a commodity-bundle satisfying the equimarginal principle (which action we will call A). For any consumer, S, then, our proposed generalization, H, would be:

$$H: (S)\,(A)\,[(M\ \&\ C) \rightarrow A]$$

or, verbally, if any consumer fulfills rationality conditions M, and meets the ability conditions C, then he will perform actions of kind A.

Two notes are worth mentioning here. We might first observe that, in effect, A_1-A_4 of M characterize the antecedent affective conditions of the rational agent – viz., that he is acquisitive, calculating, etc. in the precise manner implied by A_1-A_4.

Secondly, it might be asked in what way H differs from G". Indeed, the propositional content of H and G" are equivalent. In essence, H constitutes a *reformulation* of G" by *making explicit* the manner in which G" functions as a rationality postulate. Thus, the antecedent of H explicitly mentions the cognitive and affective properties defining a rational consumer, whereas the consequent explicitly identifies the kind of action-choice such a rational agent would make.

But what then is the logical status of the implicative connective ('$\rightarrow$') of H? Does it represent a uniform but contingent (empirically falsifiable) relation between, in effect, the pattern of wants of an unconstrained, rational consumer and the particular sort of purchase which he does make? Or is the relation a non-contingent one wherein the assertion of the antecedent condition *logically entails* the assertion of the performance of the type of action mentioned in the consequent?

The answer to this crucial question lies with the latter claim – the universal implication affirmed by H is a non-contingent, unfalsifiable one. It is a logically demonstrable truth, not a factual conjecture demanding empirical corroboration, that if an unconstrained consumer has the ability to buy, (C), and fulfills the rationality conditions, (M), he will purchase in accord with the equimarginal principle.

Ironically, although neo-classical economists generally continue to believe that the relation at issue is a contingent, empirical one, their mode of reasoning in presenting their theory of rational choice manifests that they are actually taking the relation to be one of deductive entailment, regardless of the fact that they classify it otherwise. For they argue in the following way.[6] First, proposed *counter-examples* to H are suggested – that is, cases of a consumer purchasing commodities in contravention of the equimarginal principle. It is then argued, for any such case, that a description of it is *inconsistent with the meaning* of one or more of the initial rationality

162

conditions, M. But, if such a form of argument *is* valid, the relation between the antecedent and consequent of H could not be a contingent, factually testable one, but must be one of deductive or analytic entailment between the meaning of the concepts employed in M (given C) and A. And since it can be shown that the arguments such economists articulate *are* valid, generalization H is a logically necessary truth.

Two related points concerning the kind of "analyticity" characterizing H need to be stressed. First, it is evident that the analytic relation is to be identified as holding, in particular, between the conditions defining the meaning of a rational consumer (M) and the kind of action such an agent would perform (A), *if he could.* In other words, the other condition C of generalization H, concerning consumer freedom and financial resources, simply spells out the content of the ability clause "if he could", which, if not fulfilled, would operate as an "interfering condition" precluding the performance of a whole range of actions (including rational and irrational purchases), and such actions would have no special connection with the meaning of M or A. Indeed, we might emphasize the irrelevance of C to the particular analytic connection of concern by relegating C to a familiar "ceteris paribus" status. Hence, we might formulate H as H' thusly:

H': (S) (A) [(M and ceteris paribus) → A]

or verbally, if any consumer, S, fulfills rationality conditions M, and other things being equal, then he will perform actions of kind A.

Secondly, it is instructive to compare the grounds for the logical necessity of H (or H') with those given for G' in Chapter 2. With respect to G' we noted that the reason for its "analyticity" lay basically in the consideration that this generalization formulates a principle for *categorizing* all human actions as events caused by some set of mentalistic wants and beliefs. Moreover, since accounts of the behaviour of a specifically rational consumer conceive it as caused by his wants and beliefs, this behaviour will also be covered by G' with its "impermanent" necessity arising from its "relativized" synthetic a priori truth status. In identifying the distinctive "analyticity" of H and H', however, we must focus on a different ground than that underlying G' or G".[7] And such a ground will issue in the fact that H is necessarily true a priori in an *additional more radical sense* than G'.

Essentially, the basis of the "analyticity" of H can be exhibited as the *deduction* (in the consequent of H) of a *policy* for an optimal action-choice, from the assumptions, M, defining a rational consumer (in the antecedent of H). For, given C, these assumptions, comprising a "meaning convention" implicitly defining the rational consumer of neo-classical economics, entail the consequent describing how such a *homo economicus* would act. In other words, for the very reason that the truth-claim of generalization H is *limited* to the action-choices of (perfectly) rational subjects, the description of the action mentioned in the consequent is non-contingently related to the description of the initial conditions mentioned in the antecedent. The truth of H is, therefore, guaranteed a priori – given the meaning of the rationality of consumers as conceived by neo-classical theory, no observational finding can impugn the truth of H. Validating H can be, and is, done in the armchair.

Of course, H shares the capacity of G' and G" to function in empirically testable *explanatory arguments*. For once the indeterminate wants of H are supplemented by a report of the determinate wants of a particular occasion, we can conceive of falsifications for proposed explanations of an actual consumer choice in terms of the particular course of commodity-purchasing being caused by a different set of specific wants or preferences than the ones which were in fact responsible.

However, the noncontingency in the truth status of H compounds, as it were, that of G', because it places *limits* on the kind of wants that might lead to a purchase. For the consequent of H describes a *rational* purchase (one which accords with the equimarginal principle), and such purchases are determined by a *single structure* of wants and preferences, namely those of the neo-classical rational consumer who orders his preferences in conformity with rules R_1-R_4. In enacting such a purchase, the rational consumer "could have done otherwise" only in the sense that the specific content of his wants might have been different. For instance, even though he actually did prefer bundle A (10 ties, 20 shirts) to B (15 ties, 15 shirts) to C (12 ties, 15 shirts), he could have had the reverse set of preferences – C to B to A. Nevertheless, no matter what the particular content of the variable wants which precede an equimarginal choice, such a choice is, for the rational consumer, necessarily or non-contingently connected with a set of wants satisfying the *structural relations* of A_1-A_4.[8]

In brief, the neo-classical theory of consumer choice (CCT) articulates an elaborate analysis of the meaning of the concept of an ideally rational consumer, wherein rationality is understood along classical Act-Utilitarian lines. The mainspring of the theory is normative – subsequent to defining the characteristic dispositions of a Utilitarian economic man in terms of (1) the overarching end (maximum material utility) to which he is committed and (ii) the affective attitudes he endorses (acquisitiveness, calculatedness), CCT deduces a strategy for allocating his purchasing power among alternative sources of utility (available commodity-bundles). But not only is the theoretical system initially constructed normative, but also an idealized one. For in order that he might fully attain his goal, the rational consumer, as articulated in CCT, is provided with a degree of omniscience, and consistency in affective dispositions, that is rarely (perhaps never) exemplified by the behaviour of actual agents. In other words, it is the demands put on the rationality of the agent under study that renders the theory an idealization.

3. Economics and Empiricism: Myrdal

If we reflect on the analysis of CCT as presented in this chapter, that is, as interpreted as a theory of the consumer behaviour of rational economic man (*homo economicus*), it becomes clear that our conclusions present a serious challenge to the tenability of aligning CCT with the theory of science formulated in the empiricist tradition. For we have observed that:

a) the explanation and/or prediction of the consumer behaviour of a rational agent are governed by generalizations that are necessarily true by virtue of the definition of economic rationality in the domain of consumption, and

b) a basic reason for such "analyticity" in CCT was due to the consideration that, *in the first instance*, the aim of CCT is best understood as that of constructing a normative theory prescribing the most advantageous rules to be followed by an ideally rational consumer *qua* Utilitarian man.

Needless to say, both of these aspects of our interpretation of CCT would be repugnant to traditional empiricists who insist on two cardinal tenets for the methodology of any science, natural or social, namely:

(1) that the generalizations which furnish any scientific theory with the capacity to explain its range of phenomena be contingent, empirical statements that are capable of observational disconfirmation. Accordingly, as Rudner puts this canon in the context of assessing idealized theories in social science, including theories of economically rational behaviour ... "If it were the explanatory or predictive power of *analytic* statements that confronted us, the puzzle of how such statements could have explanatory or predictive power would involve an obvious inconsistency".[9]

(2) that the corpus of an acceptable scientific theory comprises descriptive, as opposed to normative statements. Such theories report the movements of objects and the actions of persons, and account for such processes by

subsuming them under lawlike statements which describe regularities in the interactions of different kinds of entities. But there is (or should be) as little intent in scientific statements to recommend how humans ought to act as to (absurdly) seek to recommend the norms according to which physical bodies ought to move.

Well, in the light of our construal of CCT as, at least originally, an a priori, normative theory, we might be inclined to conclude that CCT is a hopeless aspirant for scientific legitimacy, in any case, according to the canons of empiricist methodology. As I see it, such a conclusion is premature and ultimately misguided. It is true that in limiting the applicability of economic generalizations to rational agents, CCT takes on an a priori *cum* normative status. And we must grant that the concept of a rational agent articulated by CCT is extremely strong, involving as it does "unrealistic" cognitive abilities and affective consistency. But this consideration serves merely to underline the fact that CCT is a theoretical idealization and is to be assessed by special criteria appropriate for such structures. Moreover, we have discovered that CCT is in fact a unique kind of idealization – again one with a priori *cum* normative truth conditions. And, as we shall argue later,[10] this type of idealization requires even more idiosyncratic criteria of assessment than the regular variety. A presentation of the grounds for this conviction will elicit a comparison of the *aims* of natural and social scientific enquiry. But, for now, it will be useful to examine Gunnar Myrdal's important criticism[11] of a bogus manoeuvre of some of those who have attempted to reply to empiricist critiques of the scientific adequacy of micro-economic theory.

Neo-classical economists who use the tactic Myrdal criticizes are motivated by the basic methodological difficulty we have outlined: the neo-classical theory of consumer behaviour seems to be necessarily true, if understood only as a theory of rational consumption. Or, more precisely, the general hypothesis H, embodying the "assumptions" of the theory, is true by virtue of the meaning of the concept of a rational consumer defined by its antecedent conditions. Not surprisingly, then, the threat of what according to empiricist canons would be a "factually empty" theory, barren of explanatory power, is resisted.

Resistance takes the form of attempting to supply synthetic "empirical content" to H by "rationalizing" *actual* consumer behaviour. That is, every-day consumer behaviour is claimed, "for the most part", to resemble the rational type described by our H of neo-classical economics.[12] As Myrdal puts it ... "the hedonistic model [our CCT] is thought to apply, by and large, to human behaviour. Ordinary people are believed to behave rather like economic men".[13] More precisely, the "rational action" reported in CCT is identified with "normal action" in the sense of average behaviour, where "average" is defined technically. That is, if we were to aggregate a large number of instances of actual consumer behaviour, it is maintained that the calculated average kind of behaviour would closely approximate the rational kind which CCT describes ... "We are asked to believe that the economic man is also the average 'man', for only then can the theory be applied to the world".[14]

But this assumption can only be justified by statistical evidence, and in a specific way. As Myrdal remarks, "deviant" or irrational cases of behaviour must be distributed randomly so as to cancel out and, hence, must show a normal frequency distribution. But, Myrdal continues, what observational evidence has been accumulated in this area tends to disconfirm this assumption. Accordingly the second tactic, although logically possible, has been empirically discredited, and should, therefore, be abandoned.

Myrdal's criticism here brings to mind a persistent confusion amongst social scientists of various disciplines with respect to a correct and intellectually honest use of the concept of "norm" or "normal". On the one hand, "norm" can be used purely descriptively, without evaluative presuppositions, as a statistical norm, defined technically, as a mean with respect to some property of objects in a certain reference class. In this sense, the identification of "normal consumer behaviour" would be an entirely factual question as to whether, for instance, individual consumers, as a mean, preferred more of any available commodity (consistently with A_2). On the other hand, "norm" can be used in an undeniably evaluative way, as a rule prescribing that a particular kind of behaviour *ought* to be occurring. "Normal" behaviour, in this sense, would be that which met some sort of evaluative standard, as, for example, that behaviour which complies with the imperative: "a (rational) consumer ought to prefer more of any obtainable commodity" (as recommended by R_2).

Unfortunately, this duality in the meaning of "normal" has entrapped social scientists into two sorts of error – fallacies of equivocation and "ideological" fallacies. In the first case, through simple semantic confusion, they have used the first sense of "normal behaviour", although intending to use the second (or vice-versa). The second case is one of theoretical treachery. Although actually intending an evaluative use of "normal behaviour", as behaviour which they believe ought to be occurring, but agreeing with positivist strictures that such normative discourse is scientifically inadmissible, an attempt is made (often successfully) to camouflage the normative intent by masquerading the evaluative language as purely factual discourse. That is, a morally approved imperative (norm in the second sense) is articulated as if it were merely a statistical discovery (norm in the first sense). Of course, whether the theorist is fully conscious of such theoretical subterfuge, or merely its unwilling victim, is something only his psychoanalyst knows for sure.

With these distinctions in hand, Myrdal's point can be read as indicating that neo-classical economists defending CCT are guilty of just such a confusion with respect to the use of "normal consumer behaviour", although his discussion leaves one unclear as to whether the fallacy is of the semantic or ideological variety. It would be a central import of our analysis, however, that the latter kind of fallacy is paramount.[15]

It is significant that Myrdal himself maintains that the "hedonistic model" applies only to the actions of rational economic man, and thereby issues in what he, somewhat misleadingly, calls a "circular" theory which contains all its conclusions concerning economic behaviour in its "assumptions" of rational agency.[16] Now, Myrdal's claim here is somewhat similar to a conclusion of our analysis wherein we argue that CCT has a type of necessary a priori truth status, in the sense that its implications concerning choice behaviour follow deductively from conditions defining a rational consumer. Myrdal, however, views such a conclusion, in conjunction with the falsehood of the thesis that the rational consumer is also the normal or "average" one, as jointly decisive reasons for abandoning CCT as a useful scientific theory.

We might summarize Myrdal's (rather paradoxical) reasoning here in the following way. In concert with conventional empiricism, since CCT is non-contingently true, Myrdal argues that the theory is a factually empty, untestable one, and, therefore, without even potential explanatory power. But, even if, *per impossible* it was, by the "average behaviour" tactic, given factual content and thus *potential* explanatory power, it would, in any case, be empirically false. But on either grounds of empirical vacuity or falsehood it fails a necessary empiricist criterion for the explanatory adequacy of a scientific theory, and ought, therefore, to be entirely abandoned.[17]

It seems to me, however, that CCT need not, on the grounds he offers, suffer the sorry fate Myrdal has in mind for it. In effect, the concerns of Myrdal typify a widespread recalcitrance amongst methodologists, working within the traditional empiricist conception of science, to find any merit in theories whose "laws" or generalizations are not contingent and descriptive hypotheses. Accordingly, general statements would come under empiricist censure if they had a priori truth conditions and/or lent themselves to an interpretation as normative statements. The first unwelcome trait is understood to militate against the empiricist canon of the experiential falsifiability of all genuine scientific theories, the second against the Humean exclusion of value-judgments from the sphere of an empirical science whose aim is to report and explain matters-of-fact. But, our analysis has concluded that the underlying general statement of CCT, i.e., H, can be interpreted as both a priori true and normative. Is there any non-arbitrary way, then, in which the legitimacy of CCT might be rescued from objections directed against the theory from the camp of empiricist methodology? Or to focus this question more precisely – is it possible, and if so, in what sense, for a necessarily true, normative theory, such as CCT, to have significant scientific utility? I think the answer to this crucial question is affirmative, and we are now in a position to begin elucidating the reasons for such a positive stance. In the end, we shall see that an empiricist method of inquiry can be sustained for CCT, but only one of a "liberalized", not conventional sort.

4. Ideal "Facts"

A full-fledged response to empiricist censure must await Chapter 14. But, as a first step in this chapter, we may observe certain epistemic implications of our interpretation of CCT that resist conventional empiricist critiques. Insofar as we have understood CCT as an ideal-*cum*-necessary-*cum*-normative theory, it is clear that this theory would often be false of the behaviour of *actual* consumers. However, it should be noted that, properly understood, CCT does not make any *claim* to be generally true of this kind of behaviour;[18] nor, *a fortiori* does it intend to directly[19] explain or predict such behaviour. Hence, any appeal to the failure of generalization H of CCT to successfully predict the actual choices of real agents as conclusive grounds for rejecting CCT would be misplaced (*pace* Friedman).[20]

No doubt, a standard empiricist might reply, upon noting the inaccessibility of CCT to observational validation, that this point simply reveals that CCT is not an empirical theory, that it is without factual content, and it is for this reason not informative about, let alone true of actual economic behaviour. Rather, such an empiricist would continue, the axioms of CCT only make explicit the implications of the meanings neo-classical economists have conventionally assigned to the basic concepts of consumption – "utility", "preference", "choice", etc. Consequently, he would claim we must wait upon empirical observation of economic behaviour to determine what regular connections, if any, actually do obtain between specific price-income situations and certain types of consumer choice.

However, this empiricist response, although partially correct, is not entirely convincing. For, in one crucial case, CCT *does* imply predictions (or explanations) of the choices of an individual consumer. I refer here to the fact that the predictions of all the purchases of the completely rational agent[21] – *homo economicus* – *are* derivable from H alone. But H is necessarily true. Hence, prediction (and explanation) of maximally rational consumption is a matter of a priori analysis, not empirical discovery. CCT, in other words, does provide information about extra-linguistic, albeit ideal, "facts". Such a derivation of predictions from necessary propositions alone is not, however, something our conventional empiricist can countenance, if he is to remain consistent in his use of received methodology. (We might say that, in a perhaps paradoxical sense, perfectly rational agents lack the "freedom" of their less rational counterparts to "do otherwise than they do" – viz., they have no "options" other than completely rational choices. Consequently, unlike the case for actual agents, we have no need to undertake observations to ascertain how completely rational agents will behave.)

Of course, CCT and its predictions will be "nonfactual" in the sense of "ideal" since *homo economicus* refers to no actual entity. However, as explicated earlier,[22] ideality does not in itself remove descriptive empirical content from a theoretical system. (In this respect it is significant that it is only empirically, not logically, impossible for real-life agents to consistently exemplify the defining characteristics of the completely rational economic man.) We might elicit the epistemic significance of this point in observing that H *is* descriptively true of real consumers under those conditions where they *are* completely rational. Again, for such (ideal) circumstances, general-ization H is informative about extra-linguistic fact. And yet, H has also been seen to be a necessary, a priori proposition. In sum, we are led to understand a theory of (maximally) rational economic behaviour in a manner that would be unacceptable to our standard empiricist.

But it is just this epistemic singularity of CCT that grounds its basic normative role. Understood as a descriptive theory, we have seen that CCT is true of the actions of *homo economicus*. But the purchases which CCT asserts he will make in any particular situation are *a priori* guaranteed to be maximally successful. Hence, the behaviour ascribed to *homo economicus* sets a (normatively) ideal standard of choice for any price-income situation which an actual consumer might find himself confronting. Since actual consumers are assumed to share the same goal (maximum utility) as their ideally rational counterpart considered in CCT, then they *ought*, insofar as they can approximate, to imitate the behaviour of this counterpart. For the latter has the requisite omniscience and temperamental consistency to regularly identify, from a range of alternatives, the optimally efficient course of action for securing the goal he is presumed to share with less endowed real-life agents. Indeed since the choices of *homo economicus* are necessarily rational, real-life consumers are a priori assured independently of awaiting the empirical outcome of patterning their purchases after him, that such a strategy offers the best possible choices in any "problem situation" in which they find themselves. Accordingly, CCT can serve, where its (ideal) behavioural implications are compared with instances of the behaviour of actual agents, to *assess* the rationality of the latter.

Chapter 11

Essential Statements and Holisitic Theory

We have mentioned that it is the nature of theoretical idealizations to be typically false of empirical phenomena within their domain. And we have observed that, as an idealized structure, the theory of consumer choice (CCT) is no exception to this rule.[1] In fact, economists have developed the theoretical model of consumer choice in examining the implications of the theory when any of A_1-A_4 are relaxed or considered not to obtain. But we need to reply to a significant objection that can be raised in this context. It might be claimed that not each of A_1-A_4 has "axiomatic" status; in particular, it might be contended that axiom A_2 of non-satiation and A_4 of diminishing marginal rate of substitution are of a lesser "subsidiary" status used to generate "well-behaved preference orderings". After all, the axioms of completeness (A_1) and "consistency" (A_3) are the primary principles for the construction of an ordinal preference ranking. Part of such a challenge might be the claim that A_2 and A_4 are less empirically substantive claims than auxiliary "technical" assumptions, simplifying the theory of choice and rendering it more "mathematically tractable".

In our view, the objection is not, all things considered, compelling. But it is an important challenge, as shown by the fact that our response will demand that we undertake a deeper examination of our "conceptually prior" interpretation of CCT as a normative system, the character of the empirical confirmation of a scientific theory, and the relation between these perspectives.

1. Relaxing the Axioms of Choice Theory

We have argued that non-satiation axiom A_2 embeds a significant commitment to a serious moral option; let us begin, then, by examining the extension of CCT to represent consumer satiation. In this context, our indifference curve analysis could be adjusted to cover cases of satiation with respect to some particular good(s), or with respect to all goods. As our Stoic moral alternative expressed the pursuit of individual satisfaction in the actual reduction of material desire, it will be most appropriate for our purposes to examine the latter case. Thus, to take the simplified case of a two-commodity (x,y) bundle, and referring to figure 11.1 on this page, the individual, S, would be at a point of complete satiation, or absolute maximum satisfaction with respect to all goods at his "bliss point" B.[2] The indifference curves of S are closed curves; curves closer to B represent higher levels of subjective satisfaction or utility. Clearly if S's bliss point occurs at a point less than the boundary of his budget constraint, he will not spend all his income in choosing bundle B. This is the case in figure 11.1 where his budget constraint is MM':

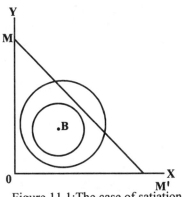

Figure 11.1:The case of satiation

Axiom 4 affirming diminishing marginal rate of substitution is the contemporary "behavioral" descendant of the celebrated law of diminishing marginal utility. The original psychological principle referred to a certain degree of urgency of material wants as measured by introspectable conscious pleasure following upon the purchase of goods: at a certain point, incremental increases in quantities consumed were accompanied by decreasing amounts of experienced satisfaction. The transition to the formulation of A_4 in terms of the marginal rate of substitution expresses the tough-minded "externalization of mind" we have seen is characteristic of economic behaviourism. Hence, as we have interpreted A_4 in Chapter 2, the axiom simply refers to the publicly observable disposition that the consumer is willing to give up diminishingly less of y to get more and more of x; alternatively put, the more one has of a commodity y the less one is willing to forego other goods to purchase even more of y. More generally, A_4 implies a preference for a variety of goods in the combination of commodities one consumes in precluding behaviour patterns in which the "extreme" of a single good is chosen when a bundle of mixed commodities is available. Choice behaviour satisfying A_4 is captured in mathematical terms by the "convexity" of a preference-ordering satisfying A_4 – i.e., if a bundle is varied along a line segment in the "space" representing commodity-bundles, one of the end points is least preferred.[3] Geometrically, diminishing marginal rate of substitution implies the property observable in figure 2.1 on page 9 that indifference curves are "convex to the origin" – in fact A_4 is often referred to in the literature by its technical name of the "convexity assumption". It follows from what we have said that a convex preference ordering would be inconsistent with, for example, preferring meat alone to meat and vegetables.

On the other hand, figure 11.2 below portrays the non-convex indifference curves of a consumer who violates A_4 for the case of a two-commodity bundle:

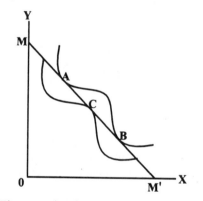

Figure 11.2: The case of non-convexity

Here, a rational maximizing agent would not choose commodity-bundle C since there are bundles A and B that are within his budget constraint MM', but are in the convex part of a higher indifference curve that represents greater utility. However, between points A and B there is *indeterminacy* of choice: there are no grounds for the rational agent to choose between the combinations of x and y corresponding to these points of tangency – either bundle may be chosen.[4] On the other hand, with a (strictly) convex preference ordering, we can be assured that any particular or "local" position

174

of maximal satisfaction for the consumer is also a "global" or absolute one – geometrically, that there is a *unique* point of tangency between an indifference curve and a budget line.[5]

2. Well-Behaved Orderings and Well-Behaved Individuals

The foregoing rehearses the theoretical modelling of violations of A_2 and A_4 within neo-classical economics itself. But what then are we to make of the methodological significance of the retention of the assumptions of non-satiation and convexity within standard formulations of neo-classical theory? Again, do they, upon reflection, really lack "axiomatic" status: are they merely auxiliary "technical" assumptions included to make the theory "mathematically tractable"? I think not. Reasons for this conclusion will require a closer look at the basic "logical structure" of the axioms of CCT and an inquiry into the "holistic" character of the validation of scientific theory in general.

As mentioned previously, consumers sometimes transgress any of the axioms A_1-A_4 in their actual behaviour. But it is important to remember that this is a point which is central to *our own analysis* of CCT under its interpretation as a descriptive science. However, in our view, the propositions A_1-A_4, *including* A_2 and A_4, are axiomatic or essential to the "conceptually prior" interpretation of CCT as a *normative system* defining and prescribing the rational agent of neo-classical theory.

We may begin here by observing that neo-classical economists do understand each of A_1-A_4 as necessary to generate "well-behaved preference orderings". But it is arguable, as some economists have themselves stressed,[6] that the rational individual of non-classical economics is *identified with a set of well-behaved preferences*. What is it, then, that makes such an ordering "well behaved", what connection does such a regimentation have with normative demands on rationality of choice, and what contribution does each of A_1-A_4 have to meeting such demands? As we shall see, a full answer to these questions requires that we view them from the point of view of *both* individual and social choice. But we shall commence with some preliminary remarks that focus only on the perspective of the individual.

From this vantage point, CCT conceives an ordering of options well behaved if, from the alternative actions open to an individual, the agent is able to choose a "best" alternative; and a "best" alternative is given normative content in being understood, as we have seen, along Utilitarian lines – as that action which will enable the agent to maximize his subjective satisfaction.

Hence, leaving technical details of explanation aside, the completeness and transitivity axioms (A_1 & A_3) are construed as logically essential for an agent to select a best alternative, as these axioms are understood to be conceptually/mathematically necessary to ordinally rank all his options from the most to least preferred.

The justification of diminishing marginal rate of substitution (A_4), or the convexity of a preference ordering, as an essential postulate of rationality for individual choice, integrates psychological and logical considerations. Here, it is recommended that a prudent consumer give priority to the satisfaction of more urgent material desires in conserving his relatively scarce goods by being less willing to exchange a desired commodity for others as he possesses a decreasing quantity of it. Arrow explains such a warrant for A_4 in linking the axiom with its historical precursor, the principle of diminishing marginal utility:

> The older discussions of diminishing marginal utility as arising from the satisfaction of more intense wants first make more sense, although they are bound up with the untenable notion of measurable utility. However, their fundamental point seems well taken. We must imagine the individual has the choice of alternative uses of a given stock of goods to maximize his well-being. The preferences for alternative bundles rest then on the *best* use that can be made of each. This preliminary maximization, so to speak, gives rise to the convexity of the indifference curves.[7]

But the wisdom of such a psychological disposition is reinforced by the basic logical consideration that unless an agent satisfies A_4 such that his preference ordering is (strictly) convex he will also not be in a position to exercise the final maximization – viz., he will not be able to clearly identify a globally best alternative from among *all* the action-choices open to him.

In examining the case for the essential theoretical role that non-satiation axiom A_2 plays within CCT as a norm of rationality for individual choice, we may build on our earlier discussion in Chapter 5, section 1. In effect, neo-classical theorists have assumed that non-satiation contributes to a well-behaved preference ordering for material goods by enabling an agent to *increase* his total level of utility – but in a suitable way. As we have argued previously, by postulating A_2, neo-classical economists have aligned themselves with Benthamite Utilitarianism in endorsing an exclusively "expansionist" form of maximization *per se* – again, that an individual can increase his total utility only by increasing the quantity of his satisfied desires. Of course, we have challenged the canonical character of such a

Benthamite principle in drawing upon Stoic ethics to recognize a more reasonable alternative to the structurally expansionist type of utility maximization implicit in A_2 – thus, we saw (qualified) wisdom in the contraction of desire for material goods. But such wisdom is not countenanced by CCT. In prescribing that a consumer ought to prefer more obtainable commodities, the normative reading of A_2 expresses an understanding of economic rationality that is essential to the neo-classical conception of growth in personal well-being in the domain of consumption: individuals advance their own good only by expanding their quantity of fulfilled desires for purchasable commodities, rather than being satisfied with a current level of consumption, let alone seek a final equilibrium by reducing that level. As David Gauthier succinctly observes in characterizing the agent of conventional economic theory ..."Appropriation has no natural upper bound. Economic man seeks more".[8]

3. General Equilibrium:
Well-behaved Individuals and the Common Good

The full force of the "axiomatic" significance of the assumptions of non-satiation and "convexity" in the field of consumption can only be appreciated by viewing individual choice within the larger picture of the "social choice" of a form of economic organization. Our inquiries here will permit us to instructively broaden our analysis of the neo-classical theory of rational choice. For we shall be able to place CCT within the overall framework for the economic system provided by general equilibrium theory, and observe the connection of this theory with welfare economics in the vindication of a competitive free-market economy. In moving to this more general viewpoint, moreover, we shall be able to further our understanding of the epistemological foundations of CCT; in particular, we shall be able to see the critical implications of the "holistic" nature of the testing of a scientific theory for the confirmation of the individual axioms of CCT.

Now the theory of consumer choice has itself been a "partial equilibrium analysis" insofar as it examines the equilibrating behaviour of individual decision-makers – i.e., consumers – and individual markets in consumer goods, seen as isolated units. In re-focusing on the interconnections among decision-making units and among distinct markets, general equilibrium theory studies conditions for simultaneous equilibria for all economic actors and all markets.[9] As implied by our earlier discussion in Chapter 7, section 4, an equilibrium state would obtain for a market if there were no tendency for the variables comprising the market to change. More particularly, within general equilibrium analysis, neo-classical economists concentrate on the conditions sufficient for a competitive price system to ensure the existence of a general equilibrium.

By a "competitive" market we shall refer to the fact that each decision-maker, i.e., consumer or firm, takes prices as given and not subject to its decision. Broadly put, then, a general competitive equilibrium would be one wherein there existed a set of prices for all commodities such that for each commodity the total goods demanded by consumers equalled the sum of the quantity originally available and the total produced by all firms.[10] Furthermore, and importantly, there would be no tendency for the economic system to move from such a position because, once attained, all agents within the economy would be maximizing the value of their objectives: i.e., each producer would be maximizing his profit from producible commodities, and each consumer his satisfaction from the use of attainable commodities. Of course, in order to secure such maximization, agents within different sectors of the economy must be acting in rational ways. For instance, technical formulations aside, any firm must invoke the best available technology in combining its input of factors of production across the commodities it produces such that it maximizes net output for its total financial outlay.[11] The appropriate behaviour of the consumer implied by general equilibrium analysis will be examined shortly.

We have already observed an essential link between general equilibrium for the entire economy and optimality for individual agents within the economy – i.e., at a competitive equilibrium, producers will maximize profits and consumers will maximize utility. But in its link with welfare economics, general equilibrium theory can well be considered to provide the normative capstone of neo-classical economics. For, within such a context, competitive free-market economies are connected with *socially desirable* states. Thus, under certain assumptions, it is demonstrated that a perfectly competitive market will deliver a general equilibrium; furthermore, the two parts of the "Fundamental Theorem of Welfare Economics" are proven: i) any competitive equilibrium is shown to be "Pareto-optimal" and ii) any Pareto-optimal social state is, under certain conditions, shown to be a competitive equilibrium.[12] By a Pareto-optimal state is meant one any movement from which will make some consumer(s) worse off: more specifically, the distribution of commodities among consumers is such that any re-distribution would increase the utility of some consumer(s) only by decreasing that of at least one other. The findings expressed by the Fundamental Theorem are of the first importance to the general normative force of neo-classical economics. Why?

Basically, the demonstration of a connection between general equilibrium and social optimality provides the contemporary case for the "system of natural liberty" classically formulated by Adam Smith. Within the tradition defined by such "natural liberty" there is avowed nothing less than a "general frame" or "underlying vision" of a form of socio-economic life. In fundamental terms, individual liberty is seen as the instrument of social harmony: free, but rational individuals, motivated solely by the concern to maximize the satisfaction of their own self-interest, and interacting only through voluntary exchange, will, nevertheless, attain an aggregate outcome that is beneficial to all. Though such an outcome not be part of the intentions of the individual agents, nevertheless, the market forces of a perfectly competitive system will so allocate resources as to lead participants, as if by an "invisible hand", to a coherent economic order of mutual advantage.[13] Put in terms of the neo-classical offspring of the classical vision offered by general equilibrium analysis: the equilibrating processes of a decentralized economy working through a competitive price system will bring about a "Pareto-efficient" social outcome.

The normative import of the contemporary version needs to be clarified. The term "Pareto-efficient" should not mislead us, as some have been, into assuming there is only an instrumental value, of no real moral significance, to the conclusions of general equilibrium theory. On the contrary, the equation of general equilibrium with Pareto optimality addresses the *consequentialist* dimension of moral assessment – i.e., one wherein actions or institutional practices are judged desirable to the extent they bring about an end deemed morally valuable. In the case at hand, then, a form of economic organization, a perfectly competitive market economy, is appraised as morally commendable on the grounds that it is efficiently conducive, in a well-defined sense, to a good end. But wherein lies the end? In response to this question, neo-classical economists have modified the classical utilitarian answer – the maximization of total social utility – on the grounds that it involves an untenable notion of measurable interpersonal comparisons of utility. In effect, this classical consequentialist criterion is revised through the provision of a "Pareto optimum" measure of the good end that is co-ordinated with the principle of consumer sovereignty. Put in summary fashion, the general equilibrium "centrepiece" of neo-classical theory can be understood to imply that if individual producers and consumers are left free to act in a solely self-regarding fashion to maximize their own profits and utility in a perfectly competitive market economy, then, as a consequence the common good or social utility will be "Pareto" maximized. More precisely, "common good" is here defined as the maximal satisfaction of the totality or aggregate of given individual consumer desires, but as consistent with the Paretian *distributive constraint* – namely, any movement from such an end-state would make some consumer worse off in terms of the satisfaction of his *de facto* wants. And such a social outcome is considered eminently valuable. For, as Koopmans explains,

> the idea that perfect competition in some sense achieves efficiency in the maximization of individual satisfaction runs through the whole of classical and neo-classical literature.[14]

Of course, assuming the demonstrations of the Fundamental Theorem are valid, such consequentialist reasoning is far from the whole moral story. Serious questions of ethical fairness or distributive justice have traditionally haunted consequentialist conclusions in applied ethics. And the situation in neo-classical economics is no exception to this rule. We may agree that general equilibrium theory does prove that a perfectly competitive market will deliver a Pareto-efficient equilibrium. But the theory also demonstrates that there will be a set of such equilibria that are generated by different given distributions of "original endowments" – i.e., allocations of ownership of the factors of production across the individuals of a particular society. Hence, a final moral appraisal of the various possible Pareto-optimal social outcomes cannot be made unless and until a defensible criterion of fairness is provided to determine an ethically acceptable initial distribution of factor endowments and, thus, the comparative moral worth of the distinct Pareto-optimal consequences to which different distributions lead. Nevertheless, it should be said that neo-classical economists are well aware of the remaining moral agenda and may plausibly argue that, from a consequentialist perspective, the reasoning establishing the Pareto-efficiency of the social outcomes of a competitive free-market is an important first part to the full moral story.

4. Well-behaved Orderings and the Common Good

We are now equipped to take up a critical question for our methodological position. What is the specific character of the rationality of the individual consumer postulated by general equilibrium analysis? To answer this question we need only summarize the assumptions characterizing consumers in the standard proofs of a competitive equilibrium. In outline, such individuals are completely self-regarding agents who also exhibit well-behaved preference orderings. In specific terms, with respect to the first trait, such agents express no "interdependent utility functions" – viz., each is moved solely by concern for the satisfaction he expects to receive from the commodity-bundles allocated to himself and is indifferent to the satisfaction secured by others.[15] And, most importantly for our concerns, such rational individuals possess well-behaved preference ordering precisely insofar as (versions of) the axioms of CCT are true of them, including non-satiation (A_2) and "convexity" (A_4). Moreover, non-satiation and convexity are essential or ineliminable assumptions in the explanation or prediction of a general equilibrium and in the demonstration of its connection with the normative ideal of social optimality. Let us see how.

Consider first the theoretical role of non-satiation within general equilibrium analysis. Most critically, a logically weaker variant of our A_2, call it A_2', i.e., that no consumer be sated with respect to all goods, is required such that "Walras' Law" obtains,[16] which latter principle is a necessary, basic assumption in the proof of the existence of a competitive equilibrium. Walras' law affirms that the total market value of commodities supplied equals the total demanded for any set of prices.[17] Clearly we need to explain further the relation of Walras' law with equilibrium, why the violation of A_2' is inconsistent with the assumption of the law, and why the move to a logically weaker version of A_2 does not significantly weaken the evaluative presuppositions of A_2.

It will be instructive to address the first question in general terms. As Koopmans aptly puts it, a competitive equilibrium is to be conceived as a "balancing bundle of choices".[18] Fundamentally, such choices are to balance between two sets of economic agents – firms choosing bundles of commodities to produce and sell, and households or consumers choosing bundles to purchase. Logically, such choices will balance if and only if the bundles chosen by producers and those by consumers are such that, for each commodity, aggregate production (plus those held as initial resources) equals aggregate consumption. Operationally, this will only happen if the total value of all purchases planned by households is the same as the total value of sales planned by firms – in other words, that Walras' law is satisfied. But we have already observed that producers, as rational profit-maximizers, will maximize output for given monetary outlay. How then could consumers, as rational, *balance* such a maximizing choice? Only if each chooses to purchase the "largest" commodity-bundle consistent with his purchasing power – i.e., each spends all his income on consumption (purchases at the boundary of his budget constraint). Psychologically, this will only occur if all consumers have the incentive or motivation to pursue such choices. But this implies that at any level of consumption, the rational consumer is unsatiated in that he prefers to possess more of some good(s) – in conformity with A_2'. Put another way, only if the rational consumer remains unsatiated will his utility-maximizing pattern of motivation be *compatible* with the profit-maximizing motivation of rational producers such that the level of commodities demanded *will coincide* with the level of commodities supplied in all markets. Contrariwise, if some consumers have reached a point of bliss or complete saturation such that they are not disposed to exercise their full purchasing power in spending all their income, there will be excess supply ("negative excess demand") in the market of some product(s), thereby thwarting general equilibrium and wasting resources by producing unwanted commodities.[19] (Technically, neo-classical theorists sometimes permit a mathematically expressed equilibrium to be preserved for such circumstances by conceiving the surplus commodities as free goods with zero prices, and assuming the existence of a costless or "free disposal" for such unwanted products;[20] however, such exceptional conditions are empirically very unlikely to obtain.)

Assumption A_2' also plays a key role in establishing the normative import of a competitive equilibrium's connection with Pareto optimality. As mentioned above, the first part of the "Fundamental Theorem" asserts the proposition (call it F) that a competitive equilibrium guarantees Pareto optimality. Now, from a purely formal point of view, since the question of the actual existence of an equilibrium can be begged, *as a group* the assumptions concerning preference orderings are not required in proving F – although they are needed to ensure that an equilibrium exists. However, the particular non-satiation axiom, A_2' *does* have an essential use in the indirect proof of the proposition. For, after assuming that F is false, it is critical in constructing the proof to derive a contradiction *via* the presumption that the rational agent will not spend less on goods than he receives in income – which presumption is satisfied on condition that rational individuals are not satiated as specified by A_2'.[21] Furthermore, in demonstrating the second part of the Fundamental Theorem – that any Pareto-optimal outcome can be achieved in a competitive equilibrium for some initial distribution of factor endowments – it is necessary to re-assume the assumptions used to prove the existence of general equilibrium, including non-satiation in the form of A_2'.[22]

Nor does the logically weaker form of A_2' as contrasted with A_2 substantively weaken our conclusion that the assumption of non-satiation in neo-classical economics presupposes a commitment to a substantive moral option. We may grant that in assuming that the rational consumer prefers more of some good(s), not simply more of *any* purchasable commodity, general equilibrium theory extends, in A_2', the empirical applicability of A_2 of CCT. However, neo-classical theory does not thereby forsake a commitment to insatiable material wants in the form of an endorsement of what we have called an expansionist form of utility maximization. Most importantly, it would still be a violation of the modified non-satiation assumption A_2' of general equilibrium theory for a rational neo-classical agent to invoke the Stoic moral option outlined in Chapter 5, section 1, and reduce or *contract* his general level of desire for consumer goods. For the acceptance of such an alternative could very well dispose such an agent to spend less than his purchasing power permits, to be content with the allocation of a commodity-bundle that left a slack in his budget constraint. But then his pattern of choice would *not* balance that of self-interested, profit-maximizing producers seeking maximum output from the available technology. And thus the provision of a Pareto-optimal competitive equilibrium would be frustrated. Rather, the rational actor of equilibrium analysis must, in consistency with the expansionist imperative, continue to prefer some "larger" commodity-bundle to any smaller one. More exactly, for each bundle within his attainable set there must be some other preferred to it which has at least one more unit of some good, and no less of any other – even though he may be sated with respect to any particular good or set of goods. We may say that once CCT is subsumed within general equilibrium theory, with A_2 modified to A_2', the rational individual remains a "possessive individualist" who pursues unlimited material gain for himself in consumption (or production); however, he is not as *indiscriminately* insatiable as in his original characterization in CCT. In sum, although the rational economic man of neo-classical theory may not want more of everything, he does want more.

Viewed through the lenses of its incorporation within general equilibrium theory, we can be more direct about the essential, indispensable role of the "convexity" assumption of CCT as embodied within the axiom of the diminishing marginal rate of substitution (A_4). Again, within equilibrium analysis, neo-classical economists seek to determine a system of prices for a competitive market that provides for optimizing choices in the production and consumption sectors of the economy, and which decisions in the different sectors are compatible with each other. In order to so optimize, each rational consumer will allocate his full income among attainable commodities such that he reaches a state of maximum utility within the limit of his purchasing power; in order to so optimize, each rational producer will utilize his factors of production such that he reaches a state of maximum profit for his outlay on factor inputs. But consider that there are nonconvexities for certain individuals in their preference orderings or for certain firms in their sets of technologically possible production bundles.[23] It follows that there will be a serious indeterminacy in the identification of optimal states for consumers or producers placed in such circumstances. For, from what we have said earlier, we may expect that the functions representing either preference orderings or production possibilities with nonconvexities will contain multiple "local" maxima, without a means of determining whether a local maximum is also an absolute one. Consequently, under the empirical conditions generating nonconvexities in production or consumption, producers will not be in a position to identify specific production bundles that maximize profits, and consumers will not be able to identify particular consumption bundles that maximize utility. *A fortiori*, the requisite empirical conditions will not be satisfied such that the economist can explain/predict the existence of a general competitive equilibrium – i.e., a social state from which the primary actors in a market economy have no tendency to move. For neither producers nor consumers will be positioned so as to exercise optimal choices. Or from the normative perspective of individual rationality, particular producers and consumers cannot be confident of doing as they ought to do in order to secure their valued ends. And the communal rationality promised by market decision-making fares no better. For we cannot be assured that a determinate general equilibrium exists that furnishes a socially desirable Pareto-optimal state; nor without the satisfaction of the convexity conditions can we establish that any Pareto-optimal state can be decentralized into a competitive equilibrium.[24] In upshot, parallel to the denial of non-satiation, the failure to satisfy the convexity assumption, A_4, of CCT (or convexity in production) puts at serious risk the most significant normative claims made for the competitive market economy within neo-classical economics. As Koopmans puts the centrality of these assumptions ... "the convexity assumptions made about supply or production possibilities and about preferences are in some sense minimum assumptions ensuring the existence of a price system that permits or sustains compatible and efficient decentralized decision making."[25]

5. Empirical Realism and Mathematical Rigour

The preceding analysis can be reinforced in the context of a specific issue. The deployment of postulates A_2 and A_4 within CCT, or within this theory's incorporation within general equilibrium theory, are formally expressed by the mathematical properties of the "monotonicity"[26] of A_2 and the "convexity" of A_4. But then are we simply once again in the presence of the long-standing methodological problem in economics of trading empirical "realism" for mathematical "rigour" in theory-construction? Plainly, general equilibrium theory resembles CCT in being a theoretical idealization whose truth-conditions are only approximated by actual human behaviour. Moreover, we have ourselves explained in Chapter 1, section 1, that it is characteristic of the explanatory systems formulated by theoretical idealizations to employ simplified hypotheses that abstract from the complexity of empirical phenomena. Such simplicity, furthermore, could often be understood as a "cognitive utility" in theory-construction in that it eased the mathematical expression of hypotheses, which mathematical formulation was typically a necessary condition for the deductive systematization of the theory, which in turn facilitated the verification, predictive power and applicability of a scientific theory. Can we not, then, underwrite the employment of A_2 and A_4 in general equilibrium theory on just such important grounds of theoretical simplicity *cum* mathematical tractability?

There is certainly something to be said for this perspective. It would clearly be quixotic for an economist to attempt to provide a formal proof of the existence of a general equilibrium state without a mathematical formulation of the assumptions from which he intends to deduce his required conclusion. But the point that needs to be stressed here is that an appeal to the mathematical tractability of the assumptions of general equilibrium, including the monotonicity of A_2 and the convexity of A_4, does not thereby render these principles less "essential" or "axiomatic", for either descriptive/explanatory or normative uses of general equilibrium theory. Granted, as with other idealized theories in science, simplicity *cum* mathematical expressibility will be purchased at the expense of a degree of descriptive truth or "realism" – not all consumers prefer larger commodity-bundles in the sense required by the "monotonicity" of A_2' or prefer mixed bundles in the sense demanded by the "convexity" of A_4. Nevertheless, as explained in the preceding sections, A_2' and A_4 play an essential or necessary role for both the explanatory and normative functions of neo-classical choice theory and its connection with welfare economics *via* general equilibrium analysis. As these points are critical ones, we might usefully summarize and amplify them.

Barring the technical gymnastics of free goods and costless disposal, we have seen that unless any consumer remains unsatiated with his level of consumption, then he will not be disposed to expend all his income on his choice of commodity-bundles such that there will be, in Koopmans' terms, a "balancing bundle of choices" – i.e., a bundle chosen by utility-maximizing consumers which matches the production-bundles chosen by profit-maximizing producers. But such a compatibility of demand and supply decisions is definitive of a competitive equilibrium. Hence, A_2' plays an indefeasible role in explaining or predicting the existence of a competitive equilibrium. Furthermore, only by preferring "more to less" in accord with A_2' will any consumer be in a position to reach an equilibrium state such that, within the limits of his budget constraint, he maximizes his utility in the canonical "expansionist" sense of the highest quantity of satisfied desires for material goods. And only thus will there be a general equilibrium state for all consumers that is socially valuable in the Pareto-optimal sense. Again, there-fore, A_2 must be understood as a necessary or essential postulate for the normative function of neo-classical choice theory.

We reached similar conclusions with respect to A_4. For both explanatory and normative purposes, it is crucial in the construction of general equilibrium theory to avoid indeterminacy. That is to say, we wish to explain the existence of a decentralized price system that will ensure a determinate state of competitive equilibrium for both consumers and producers. And since such a state would simultaneously guarantee that each consumer would achieve his valued end of maximum utility and that each producer that of maximum profit, clearly a competitive equilibrium expresses a compatible normative ideal for such decision-makers. But the assumption of diminishing marginal rate of substitution (A_4), as mathematically expressed in the "convexity" of indifference curves, is essential or unavoidable for ensuring that such a determinately optimal equilibrium obtains, for guaranteeing, along with convexities in production bundles, as Koopmans explains, in terms of his own equilibrium analysis ... "When Proposition 3.1 states about a point that it maximizes profit in the production set, or when Proposition 3.3. states that it is a best point within a [consumer's] given budget restraint, then the statements mean just that".[27]

Let us return, then, to the question of "trading" factual truth or "realism" for simplicity and mathematical rigor. We may grant that sometimes in the con-struction of economic theory a degree of factual truth has been exchanged for simplicity in the statement of hypotheses in order to facilitate their mathematical formulation. Moreover, we have recognized that there is frequently methodological advantage to such an exchange in scientific theory-construction generally. But the *primary* grounds for the use of A_2 and A_4 in CCT and general equilibrium theory is of a different logical order than found in the merits of such trade. Again, the preference-structure of the rational consumer of CCT *is* a simplified idealization from the variety of preference-orderings of actual consumers. But, in this case, A_2 and A_4 are not originally introduced as members of the axiom-set for consumers in order to function as "secondary principles" or "auxiliary formal assumptions" such that, along with the authentically first principles of "completeness" (A_1) and "consistency" (A_3), analytical mathematical methods may be used to conveniently systematize choice theory. Rather, A_2 and A_4 (help) generate a well-behaved preference ordering that is, in the first instance, well-behaved, for the substantive explanation of the *empirical truth-conditions* of a competitive equilibrium, and for elucidating the normative appeal of such an equilibrium for both the individual participants and collectivity of a free-market society. Fortunately, if A_1-A_4 are satisfied, this axiom-set will also be mathematically "well-behaved": a utility function will be constructible, unique up to a linear transformation, which assigns a real-valued utility index to each action-choice.[28] And such a mathematical framework, of course, enormously facilitates the deductive systematization of economic choice theory, especially for the purposes of calculating optimal choices. However, the mathematical formulation exhibits a *derivative* status. The factual properties of an equilibrium state obtain, and obtain with their normative implications, on condition that preference axioms A_2 and A_4 (and other consumption and production postulates) are empirically true. Hence, an adequate utility function will serve to numerically *represent* such nonmathematical orderings. In brief, the preference-ordering of a rational consumer does not have the properties it has in order to reflect the properties of a well-behaved utility function; rather a suitable function has the properties it has because of those that are already factually true of the well-behaved preference-ordering of a rational consumer.

6. Microeconomics and the "Quine-Duhem" Thesis

The above discussions of the entrenchment of the non-satiation and convexity axioms within neo-classical economics provides us with an informative setting to address the important question of the import on economic theory of what has come to be called the "Quine-Duhem" thesis.[29] The fundamental aspect of this thesis that bears on our present concerns is the *holistic* character of scientific theory-construction with its crucial implication of an equally holistic character to the confirmation or empirical test of a scientific theory.

Let us agree that any scientific theory embodies a conceptual system, typically mathematically expressed, for the interpretive representation of some domain of sense-experience. As far as theory-construction in science is concerned, the basic holistic claim of the Quine-Duhem thesis can be put in terms of a "network model": theoretical interpretations of observed events are united with other such interpretations by means of a network of laws that constitutes a *total* theoretical system for the (mathematical) representation of a range of experience. The emphasis, then, is on an understanding of a scientific theory as a *coherent whole* whose constituent hypotheses are logically connected to form a unified total system. Most importantly, such a conception has crucial implications for the nature of empirical confirmation within science. As Quine comments, "... our statements about the external world face the tribunal of sense experience not individually but only as a corporate body".[30] In other words, it is a total theoretical system of hypotheses that faces the test of experience through verifying or falsifying observations; individual scientific hypotheses comprising the system are not in themselves so confirmable or refutable. Put thus bluntly, the meaning and validity of the Quine-Duhem thesis has, unsurprisingly, received a good deal of critical scrutiny.[31]

There is, however, a more specific corollary to the thesis that is clearly borne out by the history of scientific practice, including that of economics. I refer to a deliberate *conservativism* in the practice of the validation of scientific theory: in Quine's terms, we have a "natural tendency to disturb the total system as little as possible".[32] More precisely, suppose certain particular propositions are of prime importance to the credibility of a theoretical system considered as a whole. In such a situation, scientists are generally disposed to persist in holding such statements to be true; accordingly, when confronted with recalcitrant experiential evidence for such propositions, rather than re-evaluate them, they are likely to make adjustments elsewhere in the total network.

In my judgment, the pragmatic conservativism implied by the Quine-Duhem thesis has played a significant role in determining the nature of the confirmation of economic theory. In order to elucidate this issue, let us first view general equilibrium theory as constituting the most comprehensive articulation of the total theoretical system of neo-classical microeconomics. From this perspective, it is readily understandable that axioms asserting insatiable wants and diminishing marginal rates of substitution (A_2 and A_4) find themselves entrenched within neo-classical theory. For their displacement or substantive revision, even when faced with contrary evidence, would lead to a significant disturbance in the total theoretical system of neo-classical economics. In particular, as we have argued, A_2' and A_4 are essential assumptions within general equilibrium theory in demonstrating the existence of a determinate competitive equilibrium, whose existence is sufficient for Pareto-optimality and conversely. Contrariwise, if we were to forego A_2' and A_4 such implications would not be forthcoming. But the failure of such implications to obtain would undermine the total theoretical system of neo-classical economics at its core.

We may best recognize such a dramatic consequence in remembering that equilibrium analysis inclusive of its welfare implications provides the most rigorous expression of what we have called the "general frame" of neo-classical economics, a frame which, moreover, integrates factual and normative objectives. From the point of view of an explanatory, descriptive science, general equilibrium theory identifies the causal conditions for a system of interrelated markets to regularly and simultaneously be in a state wherein there is no tendency to change in the variables comprising such markets. But it is the purposive actions of intentional agents that constitutes the behaviour of markets. Hence, a general equilibrium state will only be secured *via* the pursuit of the positively valued ends of individual actors informed by the morally approved common end(s) of the society they populate. Thus, empirically, a general equilibrium expresses a "rest state" for a free-market economy insofar as the systematic order the competitive market provides reconciles the intentional activities of individual agents. But this it does by furnishing a normative consistency at two levels: a) the level of *individual agents* wherein the valued goal of particular producers (maximum profits) is rendered consistent with that of particular consumers (maximum utility); and b) the level of the economic *community* wherein the goals of individual actors are brought into consistency with the social ideal or common good as understood by a classical liberalist perspective: a maximization of the aggregate satisfaction of the preferences of freely interacting individuals (as defined and constrained by Pareto-optimality).

If such full normative consistency can be realized, the general frame or "underlying vision" of neo-classical economics will be empirically actualized. In effect, the celebrated "natural harmony of each with all", as conceived by both classical and neo-classical thought for a competitive free-market economy, will be put in place – surely the most prized and tenaciously held principle of the theoretical network considered as a whole. From the point of view developed in this study, neo-classical economics would lose its "point" or basic *raison d'être* if this principle of natural harmony were to lose its credibility.

Now, we may grant that as each household is relatively small compared to the entire economy, instances of "pathological" behaviour exhibited by any particular consumer will not significantly affect the existence of a Pareto-optimal competitive equilibrium. However, as explained, unless there is a general disposition across individuals to express an insatiable desire for material satisfaction in the expansionist sense defined, and a similar tendency to be parsimonious with relatively scarce goods (i.e., conform to A_2 and A_4), then the occurrence of such a socially optimal equilibrium would be seriously arrested. But without an essential connection between general equilibrium and social optimality, the neo-classical case for the classical principle of natural harmony as endemic to perfectly competitive free-markets would be severely frustrated. And without a well-founded principle of natural harmony the total network of neo-classical theory would lose its focus.

We may usefully close this chapter with a quotation from Arrow and Hahn which suggests the cost to the classical tradition in neo-classical thought of such a loss of focus:

> There is now a long and fairly imposing line of economists from Adam Smith to the present who have sought to show that a decentralized economy, motivated by self-interest and guided by price signals would be compatible with a coherent disposition of economic resources that could be regarded, in a well-defined sense, as superior to a large class of possible alternative dispositions. Moreover, the price signals would operate in a way to establish this degree of coherence. It is important to understand how surprising this claim must be to anyone not exposed to this tradition. The immediate "commonsense" answer to the question "What will an economy motivated by individual greed by a very large number of different agents look like?" is probably: There will be chaos. That quite a different answer has long been claimed true and has indeed permeated the economic thinking of a large number of people who are in no way economists is itself sufficient grounds for investigating it seriously.[33]

Chapter 12

Economic Uncertainty and Logical Structure

We have analyzed the fundamental "logical structure" of the neo-classical theory of choice (CCT), in its conceptually prior form, as a necessarily true, normative idealization. Now it is to be remembered that we have understood CCT as assuming that the individual consumer chooses under conditions of certainty. But the theory of economic choice has been developed by neo-classical theorists to also deal with cases in which an agent must deliberate on the basis of uncertain evidence. The most entrenched theory in neo-classical economics for situations of uncertainty focuses on conditions of risk: here no unique outcomes can be predicted with certainty for alternative action-choices, but probabilities can be assigned to all the possible consequences of each of the available alternatives. As the theory of choice under risk provides the most settled analysis of uncertain choice in contemporary economics, our investigations in this chapter will concentrate on this model. (From this point in our discussion, when reference is made to uncertainty, the specific conditions of risk shall be understood.) More particularly, we shall begin by arguing for a *ramification thesis* – viz., that our conception of the basic features of the "logical structure" of the neo-classical theory of choice under certainty (CCT) need not be modified, but is indeed reinforced in moving to the neo-classical model for choice under uncertainty. This investigation will be followed by an examination of proposals by certain economists themselves for alternatives to the conventional maximizing models of choice in an uncertain environment: Simon's "satisficing" framework and Loomes's and Sugden's "regret theory".

1. Uncertainty and Normative Idealization

In extending the structure of CCT to deal with cases of risk, neo-classical theory re-conceptualizes the agent as attempting to maximize *expected utility* – i.e., the sum of the products of the utility of possible consequences of feasible actions weighted by the probability of the occurrence of each consequence. In addressing the question as to the logical structure of the revised conceptual scheme for choice theory, then, it is incumbent upon us to clarify the meaning of the basic elements of expected utility – in particular, what are the concepts of probability and utility being employed?

Most consumers deliberating as to risky choice from among alternative combinations of commodities would tend to make subjective estimates as to the likelihood of the different possible outcomes of their purchasing options; for, generally speaking, they would lack sufficient evidence from past experience of the "relative frequencies" of certain types of consequences following particular kinds of purchases to be equipped to assign an objective probability distribution to future outcomes. In any case, as Sugden observes,[1] the concept of probability preferred by neo-classicists is the subjective or personalistic one, especially as formulated by Savage.[2] Here, an ascription of probability measures the degree of belief or confidence that an individual has in the truth of a proposition. Operational meaning is provided for such subjective hunches by defining them in terms of overt behaviour. Classically, the behaviour selected as a criterion of a subject, S's, degree of confidence in a proposition, P, is that of his betting behaviour: specifically, what are the least odds that he would be willing to offer in betting on the truth of P obtaining, as against not P. Hence, if S is disposed to wager \$2 as against \$1 in affirming that the Montreal Expos will win the next World Series, we may conclude that his belief in this proposition (P) is measured by the odds of 2 to 1, or, in the language of probability, that he assigns a probability value of 2/3 to P.

It is a significant property of subjective probability judgments that two individuals, both of whom are reasonable and acknowledge the same evidence, may, nevertheless, have different degrees of confidence in the same proposition and, hence, impute different subjective probabilities to it. However, the subjective theory directly applies only to reasonable or rational subjects understood as individuals whose degrees of belief across a body of related statements are not only logically consistent, but *coherent*. True to the methodological spirit of the subjectivist theory, coherence is provided with a behaviourist criterion: no reasonable individual, S, would distribute his bets across a set of propositions such that a "Dutch book" could be made against him – i.e., that S would not accept odds for the individual propositions such that he was bound to suffer a net loss of something he valued whatever the outcome of events. And it has been proven that a necessary and sufficient condition for such coherence is that an agent distribute his degrees of belief (subjective probabilities) such that they satisfy the rules of the probability calculus.[3]

We may agree that, by definition, no rational agent would want to undergo a net loss of positive satisfaction no matter what consequences of his choices obtained in the world. It is clear, then, that in its insistence on the construction of a coherent body of beliefs, the theory of subjective probability would function as a *normative* theory recommending a certain kind of rule-defined regularity in the manner in which we unite some beliefs with others. Accordingly, insofar as our actual assignments of subjective probabilities to a set of propositions is incoherent, the theory prescribes norms of adjustment for the probability values of some of the propositions; in this way such irrational real-life behaviour can be brought into conformity with the normative requirements of the theory. Indeed, the interpretations of the architects of the subjectivist theory confirm an understanding of the theory as an essentially normative structure. As Savage, for example, characterizes the postulates of his model:

> Two very different sorts of interpretations can be made of P, and the other postulates to be addressed later. First, P can be regarded as a prediction about the behaviour of people, or animals, in decision situations. Second, it can be regarded as a logic-like criterion of consistency in decision situations. For us the second interpretation is the only one of direct relevance, but it may be fruitful to discuss both, calling the first empirical and the second normative.[4]

It is plain that, from one point of view, the conception of subjective probability integral to (subjective) expected utility theory places lesser demands on the cognitive abilities of the rational agent than our original CCT. For, within the new model of choice, an agent is not required to know with certainty the objectively unique outcome of each possible choice. It is only necessary that he be equipped i) to express subjective estimates of the likelihood of the outcomes of his various options, and ii) to do so in a technically coherent manner. However, this is not a context for the rational agent to relax. For it is important to observe that i) and ii) remain very severe cognitive requirements for ordinary mortals. For example, an actual consumer, if he is to be rational, must still know all purchasable commodity-bundles, be capable of determining all possible consequences of his feasible purchases, be able to identify the least odds he is willing to bet on each consequence occurring, and always combine his bets such that they are consistent with the probability calculus. But, clearly, the typical actual consumer will rarely be capable of completely following such rigorous demands on his intelligence, but only of approximating them. Hence, in a pattern we have found familiar in our analysis of CCT, in order to meet the requirements of subjective probability as a normative system recommending rules for the behaviour of rational individuals, the theory also takes the form of a theoretical idealization in accounting for the behaviour of actual agents. To return to Savage:

> Subjective probability refers to the opinion of a person as reflected by his real or potential behaviour. This person is idealized; unlike you and me, he never makes mistakes, never gives thirteen pence for a shilling, or makes such a combination of bets that he is sure to lose no matter what happens. Though we are not quite like that person, we wish we were.[5]

Let us now turn to a consideration of the logical character of the other basic element of subjective expected utility theory (to be abbreviated as SET) – i.e., utility. In the first place, we should note that the ordinal utility scales that suffice to rank preferences for possible actions in the case of the theory of choice under certainty (CCT) are not adequate for the ranking of such options under conditions of uncertainty where each action is correlated not with a definite outcome, but with a set of possible ones. Basically, in the latter case, we need to know not only the absolute order of preference as in CCT, but also the relative strength of the preferences between alternatives – by how much more (less) A is preferred to B than B is to C, etc. We need, that is, a utility function that provides an "interval" measure of the value of alternative action-choices. This, in turn, will be available if we can provide an interval utility scale of our order of preferences for the possible outcomes of each feasible action.

In order to construct such a measure, neo-classical economists standardly deploy the utility function for choice under uncertainty introduced by von Neumann and Morgenstern.[6] This approach takes its bearing from the determination of an individual's attitude towards betting or risk-taking generally. Briefly, consider that we must identify an interval utility measure for John's preferences over action A, B, and C. First, we should conceive of each action as a gamble or lottery with its related outcomes as its possible "prizes". An agent's preferences for particular actions depends entirely on his preferences for the outcomes and their probabilities. Thus, suppose that action B, say, is known by an agent to have possible consequences X, Y, and Z in that (transitive) order of preference. In order to ascertain an interval utility measure of John's preferences over these outcomes we first assign a utility of 1 to the most preferred outcome (X) and 0 to the least preferred (Z). The utility of the "middle preference" (Y) is then determined by identifying the risk John is willing to take to attain it: more particularly, which lottery would he accept with X and Z as prizes that he considers indifferent to the choice of Y. If, for example, he would accept a lottery with an 80% chance of receiving X to 20% for Z as one that is indifferent to a certainty of obtaining Y, then the utility for Y may be fixed at 4/5. (In effect, John can be seen to prefer Y a good deal more than Z.) Then our scale X:1, Y:4/5, Z:0 can be expressed by a utility function, u, that provides an interval measure of John's preference over X, Y, and Z (where u is unique up to a positive linear transformation).

It is to be noted in our example that since John is indifferent between Y and the proposed lottery, the utility of the lottery is also 4/5. However, since on our scale outcomes X and Z have utilities 1 and 0, the *expected utility* of the lottery will also be calculated to be 4/5 (i.e., 4/5 X 1 + 1/5 X 0). In general, in the construction of von Neumann-Morgenstern interval utility functions, the utility assigned to any lottery can be identified with its expected utility. But we have also observed that each action in a choice under uncertainty may be understood as a lottery with its possible outcomes as prizes. Hence, the utilities of alternative action-choices will be their expected utilities. Accordingly, insofar as the rational agent *qua* rational seeks to maximize his utility, such an agent in uncertain circumstances will attempt to maximize his expected utility.

In upshot, we may conclude that von Neumann-Morgenstern utility theory is, in its most direct interpretation, a *normative* theory recommending uniform choice behaviour for uncertain circumstances – viz., a rational agent ought to choose that action with the highest expected utility from among the feasible alternatives. Since this action is understood as a lottery, in so deciding, he will *ipso facto* be choosing that action with the highest utility from among the feasible alternatives; and such an action will be the one he most prefers.

Not that most actual agents will find themselves with sufficient affective consistency and discriminating power to meet the demands on decision-makers required to satisfy the principles of von Neumann-Morgenstern utility theory. Consider in this context the rational consumer of neo-classical economics facing choice under conditions of uncertainty. He must, to begin with, be able to order his preference in conformity with rules R_1-R_4 of the theory of choice under certainty (CCT). But further claims on his ability to arrange his preferences are made in the extension of CCT, via von Neumann-Morgenstern, to uncertainty conditions. In the first place, he must be able to fix his preferences in accord with R_1-R_4 not only for outcomes but for lotteries over outcomes. However, the uncertain, but rational individual must be equipped to satisfy the following further conditions on the ordering of lotteries and outcomes – roughly:

a)   continuity: given any three consequences, X, Y and Z in that order of preference, there is one and only one lottery, with X and Z as prizes, such that S is indifferent between it and Y.

b)   monotonicity: if two lotteries, A and B differ solely in the respect that the "most preferred" prize in A is preferred to that of B, then S prefers A to B. Similarly, if two lotteries A and B differ solely in the respect that there is a higher likelihood in A of winning the most preferred prize, then S prefers A to B.

c)   reduction: S is indifferent to a compound lottery and its reduction to a simpler one, as long as the reduction conforms to the probability calculus.

Obviously, these new conditions put severe requirements on the ability of actual agents to know and order their preferences in addition to the already rigorous demands of CCT. For instance, in order to meet the further conditions of the von Neumann-Morgenstern perspective, uncertain rational agents must not only be able to order the possible consequences of alternative choices, but also all lotteries with those consequences, all compound lotteries of the original lotteries, all lotteries compounded from this last set, etc. But it is evident that real-life decision-makers could not completely measure up to such extreme claims on their practical intelligence, but only attempt to approximate them. Thus, once again, in order to specify the conditions according to which rational agents would follow the rule to maximize expected utility enjoined by von Neumann-Morgenstern utility theory in its conceptually prior form as a normative system, the theory acquires the status of a theoretical idealization in the explanation of actual behaviour.

Let us put the components of probability and utility together and return to the full subjective expected utility theory (SET). In extending the scope of the traditional theory of choice under certainty (CCT) in order to deal with situations of uncertainty, we have shown that both components of SET reaffirm the conceptually prior status of neo-classical choice theory as a normative idealization. In fact, any initial impression we may have had of the attenuation of the idealized character of CCT in moving from certainty to uncertainty has been shown to be misleading. Since it is no longer required that the rational agent have certain knowledge of a definitive outcome for each alternative action, it is true that SET is "qualitatively" less demanding than CCT. Nevertheless, in the number of capabilities demanded of an individual such that he be able to assign coherent subjective probabilities, a case can be made from the "quantitative" perspective that SET is even more exacting than CCT. Moreover, it is explicitly evident that the demands placed on practical reasoning within von Neumann-Morgenstern utility theory to order preferences over outcomes on an interval scale require significantly more idealized agents than the ordinal rankings of CCT. In effect, in the "operationalization" of SET, clear, empirical criteria of application for the basic concepts of probability and utility are purchased through a severe idealization of the theory.

2. Uncertainty and Necessary Truth

We have yet to examine the status of the other fundamental feature of the logical structure of neo-classical choice theory once we make the transition from decision-making under certainty, as expressed in CCT, to that of uncertainty. In its conceptually prior form, we have analyzed CCT as formulating a necessarily true theory that was not subject to observational confirmation or falsification by empirical test. But do such non-contingent, a priori truth conditions also characterize the theory of choice once it is extended to conditions of uncertainty? Again, our answer shall be clearly affirmative.

In defence of this answer, we may return to an examination of G", the basic explanatory generalization of CCT which we introduced in Chapter 2, section 2. More particularly, it will be useful to further clarify the knowledge constraint (antecedent conditions 3 and 4 of G" on page 20) as it bears on the question of the "analyticity" or necessary truth of G". Suppose we were to relax this constraint in the transition from a model of consumer choice under certainty to one of choice under uncertainty; more precisely, let us again assume the conditions of risk where, as noted above, the consumer is not certain as to the consequences of his alternative action-choices, but can ascribe (subjective) probability values to such outcomes. Now we have seen that neo-classical theory formulates the general decision problem as one wherein the rational economic agent seeks to maximize his utility. But in the standard neo-classical adoption of the von Neumann-Morgenstern approach to the conception of uncertainty, we have also observed that in the conception of actions as "lotteries", the utilities of actions are identified with their expected utilities. Hence, in a logically continuous extension of CCT, neo-classical theory *re-formulates* the decision problem as one wherein the rational, but uncertain, consumer seeks to maximize expected utility. Accordingly, in the uncertain circumstances of risk, the consumer is understood to choose that action (purchase of a particular commodity-bundle) from among the feasible ones that will provide him with the highest expected utility. But suppose, then, we were to construct a counterpart to G" to cover these cases of uncertainty (let us call this counterpart Gu"). It is clear that similar grounds to the ones which indicated the logically necessary character of G" under conditions of certainty *would continue to do so* for Gu". In particular, knowledge conditions 3) and 4) of G" would revert to belief conditions resembling those of 3) and 4) of G' (see page 18 above). More precisely let us assume that conditions 1), 2) and 5) of G" remain the same for its counterpart Gu" for cases of uncertainty. However, conditions 3) and 4) would change as follows:

3) S believes p, that action B, the choosing or purchasing of X, to be a means, *with an expected utility*, e, of realizing K.

4) S believes that no other action is a better or equally efficient means of achieving K than B, i.e., that B has the highest e compared with feasible alternatives.

But, as in the case of G", S's performance of action B, expressed in the consequent Gu", would be analytically entailed by the satisfaction of antecedent conditions 1-5. As a matter of conceptual meaning, if an agent wants the satisfaction or utility found in the consumption of commodities, if in uncertain circumstances such utility can be identified with expected utility, if he has no preferred want, and if he believes a feasible action, B, to be maximally efficient in securing expected utility, then there would be no possible countervailing condition, empirical *or* logical, to the enactment of B. In short, the problem of the "analyticity" of potential explanatory generalizations *recurs* for a theory of consumer choice under conditions of uncertainty.

Not that this should come as a surprise, given our discussion of the connection between normative idealization and necessary truth in Chapter 10, section 2. In that discussion, we reconstructed G" as H to better reveal the way in which G" functions as a normative principle or rationality postulate. Briefly, H was interpreted as emphasizing that the direct applicability of G" is limited to the purchasing pattern of an *ideally rational consumer* qua Act-Utilitarian agent. And the conditions defining such normative ideality in the antecedent of H were found to *logically entail* the consequent specifying the kind of purchase such an economic man would make in order to maximize his material utility. But, the logical substance of our analysis in that section also applies, *mutatis mutandis*, to the lesser but still idealized rationality of economic man deliberating in an uncertain purchasing situation. Thus, suppose we were to construct a counterpart to generalization H, call it Hu, to represent the uniform choice-behaviour of *homo economicus* confronting uncertain conditions in consumption. We should expect that the kind of purchase our ideal agent would make in order to maximize his expected utility is *logically necessitated* by the conditions (M) defining his rationality in the uncertain circumstances (of risk) as specified in the antecedent of Hu – including the "coherence" of his probability estimates, the monotonicity of his preferences over lotteries, etc. And such an expectation would not be disappointed.

By bringing together the specific conclusions we have reached in the last three sections, we may see that our ramification thesis has been established. For in extending the traditional theory of rational choice under certainty (CCT) to cover uncertain conditions, the fundamental characteristics of the logical structure of such neo-classical theory are preserved. More particularly, in accounting for cases of uncertainty, the application of subjective expected utility theory (SET) to consumer behaviour continues to apply a theory whose conceptually prior form is that of a normative idealization that is necessarily true a priori – indeed in its idealized character SET only amplifies the ideality of CCT. In sum, none of our major conclusions concerning the logical structure of rational choice theory need be *displaced* in moving to SET from CCT.

3. Simon: Maximizing and "Satisficing"

An important critique of neo-classical choice theory may be introduced by the comment that when dealing with problems of rational decision, the descriptive inaccuracy due to the pronounced "ideality" of the theory could lead to a serious weakening, if not elimination, of its normative force. I refer here to a familiar criterion of adequacy for any normative system: for any norm to be binding on an agent, it must be logically and empirically possible for the agent to enact the norm. Or, as von Wright puts this fundamental principle: "That there is a prescription which enjoins or permits a certain thing, presupposes that the subject(s) of the prescription can do the enjoined or permitted thing."[7] But, *prima facie* at least, it appears that CCT cannot satisfy this basic meta-normative postulate. For instance, we observed that CCT assumes that an economic agent possesses "complete knowledge", that is, that he is not only cognizant of all alternative actions available to him but also able to calculate the definite outcome of all these possible options. However, not only is such an assumption descriptively false of actual economic agents, but it is reasonable to conclude that such knowledge and computational ability are empirically impossible to realize as it is simply beyond the capacity of any human organism even when assisted by mechanical technology. Moreover, we observed that SET shared such an implication of its cognitive idealization.

In an attempt to resolve this apparent defect in classical choice theory, inclusive of both CCT and SET, Herbert Simon has proposed what he considers to be a theory of rational decision that is scientifically preferable to the classical one. Basically, Simon's intention in devising a new model is to construct a theory whose principles more accurately or "realistically" describe actual human deliberation and choice. Hence, the postulates of the new theory would not imply impossible prescriptions for human agents. As Simon states his aim:

> Broadly speaking, the task is to replace the global rationality of economic man with a kind of rational behaviour that is compatible with the access to information and the computational capacities that are actually possessed by organisms including man in the kind of environments in which such organisms exist.[8]

Now it can be seen that the economic theory of choice, as set forth in this study, conceives consumer behaviour as the maximization of a value (utility or subjective satisfaction) subject to certain constraints. These constraints comprise a given income, a set of possible commodity-bundles as objects of alternative action-choices (purchases), and the extent of the consumer's knowledge as to presence of the alternatives and their consequences in terms of their comparative utilities. Only some of these constraints are unalterable: the particular income, prices and available set of commodity-bundles are incorrigible givens in the sense that they are beyond the present ability of the rational consumer to control. However, the information or knowledge of available choices and outcomes *is* within the control of an economic agent in that he has the power, by investigation and computation, to increase this knowledge.

The crux of Simon's objection to conventional economic theory is that the knowledge constraints placed upon the agent are hopelessly unrealistic. In a situation of certainty, such as that assumed by CCT, we have observed that the traditional theory demands that the rational agent possesses complete or perfect information such that he is intelligent enough to calculate the unique outcome of each possible choice. Simon, however, emphasizes that in actual choice situations of any complexity there is no empirical evidence that any agents are capable of such knowledge. Nor, for Simon, does the lesser demand on an actor's knowledge required by the conventional neo-classical theory of decision under certainty (SET) sufficiently relax the required degree of information acquisition such that SET at least provides a reasonably approximate conceptualization of concrete choice behaviour. In this Simon would agree with our ramification thesis defended in the last section – for example, he draws attention to the severity of the demand that the economic agent be able to assign a definite probability distribution to the possible consequences of particular choices.[9] And as he comments in a recent paper:

> It is cold comfort to know that if human beings followed the dictates of subjective expected utility, or some other idealized theory of rationality, they would then be able to make wholly consistent and transitive choices. It is cold comfort because I know that, as a human being, I live in a world that is orders of orders of magnitude too complex for the process of calculation called for by the theory to work.[10]

Given their extreme conceptions of a rational agent's knowledge and calculational ability, Simon concludes that neo-classical choice theories, for both certain and uncertain conditions (CCT and SET), cannot adequately explain or predict actual economic behaviour.

In virtue of this judgment, Simon opts for a new theory of rational choice, one in which the "global rationality" of the classical models, requiring in his view "virtual omniscience and unlimited computational power",[11] is replaced by a more limited "bounded rationality" in line with the level of information and calculational ability rational agents actually do possess. In other words, Simon's alternative theory of rational choice would consider a subjective psychological property, the final *limits* to an agent's acquisition of knowledge as included among the constraints taken as given or uncontrollable, rather than construing his knowledge as entirely a "strategic" variable subject to his control.

According to Simon, the "global rationality" embedded in neo-classical analysis conceives of economic actors as "substantively rational" – i.e., as choosing an action that is appropriate to a given goal within the limits of given environmental conditions. Hence, within CCT, once a goal of maximum utility and the external limits of purchasing power (income) and available goods are posited, there is only one substantively rational choice for any agent – the one which satisfies the equimarginal principle. Such a conclusion is mathematically compelling irrespective of whether mere mortals are empirically capable of enacting procedures to find the rational choice in practice. However, as Simon is completely sceptical of the existence or development of such capability, he recommends that economic theory-construction replace its commitment to substantive rationality by one of *procedural rationality* wherein the latter is understood as behaviour which results from suitable deliberation.[12] Such procedural rationality will concentrate on detailed empirical studies of the actual processes, especially the heuristic procedures, that real-life actors use in finding adequate action-choices. Furthermore, by recognizing more realistic assumptions concerning the constraints under which an agent chooses, Simon believes that a research programme based on procedural rationality facilitates the construction of a theory of choice that predicts and explains concrete human behaviour more adequately than does neo-classical theory, and is, therefore methodologically preferable.

It seems to me, however, that, in an important respect, Simon does not make his case. In particular, I want to take issue with an interpretation Simon places on his "behavioural" theory of choice in contrast to the classical one. For Simon construes his theory as a "satisficing model" of rational behaviour in contrast to the "maximizing model" of traditional economic theory. As he states: "the key to an effective solution appeared to be in substituting the goal of satisficing, of finding a good enough move, for the goal of maximizing, of finding the best move."[13] But, as I see it, Simon's theory of satisficing behaviour *is no different in kind* from the neo-classical theory. In particular, we shall see that, upon analysis, contrary to Simon's intention, his behavioural model *also* describes a maximizing agent.[14] In effect, Simon's rational individual still seeks an optimal or best outcome in that his choice is the most preferred one, *given* the limited state of knowledge imposed by the fixed constraints under which he chooses. And, thus, the logical structure of the means-end relationship remains within a maximizing framework. This is so even though, given the more complete knowledge assumed by the neo-classical models, the same rational agent, in the same external circumstances, might very well have settled on a different choice as most preferred or as expected to provide maximum utility (or expected utility). Let me elucidate my criticism in commenting on a paradigm example which Simon himself employs with the intention of establishing a generic difference between his model and a maximizing one.

Simon, then, presents the case of an individual whose decision-problem is the choice of a price at which to sell his house.[15] Of course, if the neo-classical theory of choice were operative in this situation, the rational agent would accept the highest price a potential buyer would be willing to offer, since such a price would be preferred more than any lower price and would, by definition, bring maximum possible utility. Moreover, since the classical economic agent of CCT would possess complete knowledge of all the alternative prices potential buyers would offer, it would be possible for this agent to realize his optimum prospect, or maximize his utility, by waiting for and then accepting the highest price offered. However, real-life economic agents do not typically possess such impressive knowledge, even in the attenuated sense of being able to assign a coherent probability distribution to the particular offers which might be made (and thereby be equipped to maximize expected utility). In lieu of the practically omniscient agents of neo-classical theory, Simon affirms the actual existence of agents who, before deciding, set a goal which is "good enough" or "satisfactory", even though it might not represent an obtainable goal which would maximize gain (or expected gain). For instance, he might designate $125,000 as a satisfactory or acceptable offer or price for the house, even though there do, in fact, exist, beyond his cognizance, potential buyers willing to pay as much as $150,000, which "objectively" would provide an optimum or "maximizing" price. In sum, Simon's "satisficing" agent would find any offer equalling or surpassing $125,000 as satisfactory. Any such offer would fulfil his subjective "aspiration level".

However, Simon is simply mistaken in conceiving the behaviour of this house-seller as the pursuit of a non-optimum or non-maximizing goal. For the acceptable price of $125,000 (or more) *does* represent the object of his most preferred want, since such an object *is* a function of the information he actually does possess. Simon's error lies in his implicit belief that the optimum or maximizing goal is that goal which, if attained, would, as a matter of *objective* fact, maximize our agent's utility *regardless* of whether or not the agent knows this fact. But the goal an agent consciously pursues, and the courses of action he adopts as means to such ends are subjective, relative concepts in the sense that they are a function of the agent's intentional credal states – he must be aware of the goal and believe certain actions conducive to its attainment. But if he does have such awareness and belief, he will never adopt a course of action he consciously believes to be less conducive to his goal than an alternative course of action of which he is also cognizant and able to perform. Granting ability, if he does not choose the optimum course of action, he is either ignorant of its existence, or is intentionally pursuing a different, preferred goal; conversely, if the agent is cognizant of the best feasible course of action, and has no preferred goals, he will choose that action. That is, as our analysis of G' in Chapter 2, section 2, established, as a matter of "conceptual necessity", he will act as a maximizer.

Hence, the reason why Simon's house-seller would find $125,000 an acceptable price even though $150,000 is objectively available, is, barring other constraints, simply that he does not know of the availability of the offer of $150,000. It is not that he is *intentionally* selecting a "good enough" action; for if he *did* know of the existence of a buyer willing to pay $150,000, he undoubtedly would accept his offer. Indeed, in suggesting that his satisficing model is especially appropriate in "dynamic contexts" in which, say, the house-seller receives a ..."sequence of offers, and may have to decide to accept or reject each one before he receives the next",[16] Simon himself indicates a situation in which the agent would likely be unaware of the best offer that would be made. Moreover, the indefeasible maximizing aspect of rational choice is further evidenced by the fact that, even within the range of the allegedly "satisficing offers" ($125,000 or more), one would correctly predict that if two prices were simultaneously offered the seller, he would choose the higher price. In short, in reducing the knowledge possessed by decision-makers to more realistic proportions, Simon's "satisficing" model of rational choice will frequently predict that an agent will choose an action which, from an "objective", completely informed point of view, is suboptimal. Nevertheless, as a function of the information-basis or point of view of the agent himself, he is selecting the optimal or maximizing course of action. And the conception of rationality embedded in the notion of maximizing behaviour *is* from the point of view of the agent.

It follows from what has been said that proposals for sub-maximal principles to conceptualize and explain human choices will be in contravention of the "necessary truth" of action-theoretic generalization G' (or G" for the special case of economic choice). And it needs to be emphasized that we are not engaged in mere quibbling over linguistic niceties here. The heart of our case against Simon turns on a deep Aristotelian principle underlying the conceptualization of human choice: if an agent is not subject to physical or psychological disability (including weakness of will), he will not, as a matter of logic, substitute an option he perceives to be less valuable for one he perceives to be more valuable.

It is in this light that we can agree with critics of Simon's notion of procedural or "bounded" rationality that it provides no adequate means of objectively appraising an individual's own ascription of rationality to his behaviour as long as he believes it "good enough" or appropriate to his subjective level of aspiration.[17]   Or, as Levi argues,[18] even in terms of procedural rationality, without reference to an "unbounded" ideal criterion of rationality, such as that intended by maximizing models, there does not seem to be any intelligible purpose to investigating heuristic search procedures directed towards *improving* our calculational capabilities.

Nevertheless, in his attack on maximizing models, Simon prompts us to raise an important general issue whose discussion will serve to further explain the nature of theoretical idealizations with normative import such as that of CCT (or SET).

The pertinent issue can be developed from a distinction introduced by Bales to counter a certain kind of argument against Act-Utilitarianism.[19]   But this argument might as well have been levelled against CCT, for we have noted earlier that CCT can be construed as an application of the Act-Utilitarian standard of a prudentially justified action to the realm of economic actions. (Thus, both Act-Utilitarianism and CCT prescribe that a rational agent ought to choose that action, from among obtainable options, which maximizes his utility, where CCT specializes the utility function to include only the satisfaction that the agent derives from the use of material commodities.) In any case, the type of criticism to which Bales replies is the one we have been examining in our response to Simon – viz., that it is empirically impossible to *apply* a maximization of utility standard in order to formulate a rational decision in a concrete situation. Some critics even ascribe a "stronger" logical impossibility to maximization policies: one form this objection takes is that an infinite regress is ineluctably generated by any attempt to specify a tractable set of alternative actions from an unmanageably large set of possible options. As Michalos explains, the aim of a maximizer in any such delimitation is to isolate a maximally efficient set of alternatives in the sense of "the set that contains the maximally efficient alternative from the set of all logically possible alternatives and as little extra as possible".[20] But, Michalos continues, such a procedure leads to an infinite regress since in order to delimit the preferred set of alternatives one must identify the maximally efficient alternative, which in turn requires that one delimit the preferred set of alternatives, and so on *ad infinitum*. Accordingly, since the quest for a maximally efficient set of alternatives generates a logically intolerable infinite regress, Michalos concludes that ... "there can be no choice of a maximally efficient set of alternatives. Hence there can be no rational action according to the maximizer's proposal."[21]

Bales' reply to both logical and empirical objections is to charge that they rest on a failure to preserve an important distinction between i) an explication of what makes acts right (or, for our present concerns, rational), and ii) an effective decision-making procedure which would enable one to identify a course of action, from the available options, which possessed the right-making or rational-making characteristics spelled out in i).[22] Since, according to Bales, i) and ii) are logically distinct notions, it is not to be supposed that an adequate answer to i) necessarily entails a useful answer to ii). But just this illicit supposition, Bales argues, is at the heart of empirical or logical "impracticality" arguments against the maximization criterion of rightness or rationality.

For our purposes Michalos provides an important rejoinder to Bales. Although granting the validity of the distinction Bales draws, he nevertheless demurs from accepting his conclusion that impracticality objections to utility maximization err through failing to observe the distinction. In support of his position, Michalos first provides a general classification of the distinction as one between the *meaning* of a concept such as rationality and a *criterion of application* for the concept, but then draws an important connection between the items distinguished: no explication of the meaning of a concept should imply the impossibility of supplying an effective criterion of application for it. But, Michalos continues, impracticality arguments show that the analysis of the meaning of the concept of rational action in terms of maximization are guilty of just such an a priori preclusion of the application of the concept.[23]

We can agree that Michalos' premise concerning the relation between meaning and criteria of application is correct and important. In the context of explications of the meaning of norms this premise can be construed as reiterating the dictum of "ought implies can". Again, it is futile to define the meaning of a norm such as that prescribing the rationality of an action if it is impossible for reflective agents to follow the norm so defined. However, Michalos is misguided in maintaining that the truth of his premise entails the futility of maximization accounts of rationality. For he is unwarrantedly pessimistic about the capacity of a maximizer to delimit a manageable set of alternatives from which to choose a rational action in the form of one which maximizes his utility. Michalos, along with many other decision theorists, understates the importance of the fact that all maximization problems confronting actual agents in concrete situations are those of *constrained* maximization, and, hence, only maximization of this type is of concern to social scientists attempting to explain or predict the choices which maximizing agents make. And, most importantly, it is in the nature of the constraints within which a decision-maker is operating, to dictate, as it were, a tractable set of alternatives out of all logically possible ones, from which set the rational agent can choose a maximally efficient course of action. Let me explain in examining the implications of the constraints involved in the decision situation of the maximizing consumer of CCT.

To begin with, CCT itself explicitly describes a consumer as attempting to maximize his utility subject to his budget constraint. Thus the options, consisting of purchases of commodity-bundles which are open to the consumer, are already significantly circumscribed by the set of bundles which he can afford to purchase. Of course, CCT itself specifies no further constraints for the reason that within the theoretical content of the theory none are needed. That is, the idealizing assumption within CCT claiming that an agent chooses under conditions of certainty implies he will be capable of surveying all purchasable alternatives and infallibly identifying his order of preference among them. Similarly, in the conventional model of choice under uncertainty, SET, we have observed that he must exhibit the exceedingly idealized intelligence required to identify the action-choices which will maximize expected utility.

Of course, an equivalent way of characterizing an idealizing assumption is to say that it is an unrealistic one – for example, we can agree with Simon that consumers do not possess such "virtual omniscience and unlimited computational powers". It might seem, therefore, that the idealizing aspect of CCT plays into the hands of the kind of objection to maximizing models which Simon, Michalos and others raise – that is, that it is impossible for real-life agents to apply the maximization criterion to actual situations. However, such a conclusion is premature until it is conclusively argued that the kinds of factual constraints that must be introduced in order to remove the idealized dimensions of maximizing models such as CCT or SET, and thus make choice theory practicable, render such models otiose. But I do not think such an argument can be provided.

The reason for my scepticism is that the introduction of the additional constraints would presage no need to abandon the theoretical framework of a maximizing model. To see that this is the case, we might first examine the content of the additional constraints. Besides income or general purchasing power, then, actual consumers attempt to maximize material utility subject to the constraints of the limited character of the time, energy and information accessible to them in real-life choice situations. In effect, these new constraints require the consumer to *economize the decision-making process itself*, that is, to administer the surveying and evaluative ordering of alternatives in an efficient manner. Since the information-gathering processes themselves bear costs that will affect the utility-benefits derived from consumer choices, these processes must also be efficiently organized in order that such utility will be the maximum possible. But how? How many and which alternative actions should be identified and evaluated prior to choice? At first sight, a dilemma threatens to undermine a coherent answer to this question. On the one hand, an answer consistent with utility maximization demands that the agent at least select the maximally efficient set as it includes the maximally efficient action. But this answer is directly subject to the regress arguments of the kind Michalos has outlined. On the other hand, if information gathering needs are economized such that it is permissible to exclude the maximally efficient set, has not, as Simon and Michalos would charge, the policy of maximization been abandoned in favour of a weaker policy?[24]

The way out of this dilemma, as I see it, is to challenge the credibility of the second horn. And the basis of the challenge lies in an appreciation of the general relationship between idealized theories and conditions for their successful application or practical employment.

Suppose, for instance, that a rational consumer, following a maximizing policy, was required, as Simon and Michalos would have it, to isolate the maximally efficient set of alternatives, even while attempting to economize his information gathering. The common experience of agents in choice situations reveals that such a requirement, demanding as it does severe costs in the time and energy expended in calculating and evaluating, would be self-defeating. Rather than ensuring that a purchase which maximized utility would ensue, such an "all-or-nothing" approach would so diffuse the allocation of available time and computational energy that the prospect of deciding upon a maximally efficient set would be rendered very improbable. Consequently, such heuristic procedures or "rule of thumb" measures as comparing and selecting alternatives which had satisfactory or "good enough" consequences when chosen in similar price-income situations in the past, are adopted.

Although such a rule of thumb procedure would obviously husband the scarce resources in time and energy of the decision-making consumer, it is admittedly possible, even likely, that, *on some occasions*, it would permit the selection of a set of alternatives that was not the maximally efficient one, i.e., that did not include a maximizing alternative, and, therefore, brought about purchases which did not maximize the consumer's utility. Does this possibility, therefore, entail, as Simon and Michalos argue, that rule of thumb procedures are inconsistent with a model of utility-maximization, on the grounds that they prescribe a logically weaker policy for rational choice?

I think not. Although, on the surface there is an air of paradox in setting aside, for practical purposes, all-or-nothing approaches to the acquisition of information in decision-making within maximization frameworks, such a paradox can be successfully dissolved. For the crucial consideration is that, in the long run, a rule of thumb approach to alternative set-selection would be *more conducive* to the performance of acts (purchases) which *maximized* a consumer's utility, than would an all-or-nothing procedure. Given that neo-classical theories of consumer behaviour postulate a final end of utility-maximization for rational consumers, it would be inconsistent, in applying the prescriptive implications of the theory to actual choice situations, *not* to jettison an all-or-nothing policy requiring an information gathering procedure which, although, as a theoretical ideal, would uniformly elicit a maximizing alternative, nevertheless, when put into actual long run practice, would be less likely to provide maximizing alternatives than rule of thumb procedures. Hence, the *inverse* of the claims of inconsistency of Simon and Michalos is closer to the truth. Of course, on these grounds, we too can see the wisdom of Simon's study of effective heuristic techniques or rule of thumb procedures; it is just that there is good reason to believe that such procedural rationality can still be conceptualized and regulated by the ideals of a maximizing theory of rationality.

But this should come as no surprise. For, as we have explained, both CCT and SET formulate theoretical idealizations and, as in the case of the idealized theories of natural science, the requirement of accessibility to empirical *actualization* is needlessly strict. We might put this issue in terms of the explanatory status of idealized scientific theories and take note of a specialized criterion of adequacy for scientific explanation when modified for the exceptional case of theoretical idealizations. This criterion has three approximation conditions: Adapting Hempel,[25] we may require i) that the extreme conditions characterizing the statements of tenable scientific idealizations can at least be increasingly empirically *approximated*; ii) that there be a clear measure of the distance of actual states from the ideal; and iii) that whenever such approximation occurs, the statements be confirmed to the appropriate degree. In this way, the explanations furnished by acceptable idealized theories would fulfil Hempel's R_4 condition of truth or "factual correctness" for the adequacy of a scientific explanation,[26] as adjusted for idealizations.

For the case of CCT, construed normatively, in order to satisfy the second condition, it must be possible to clearly specify, when the theory is applied with the intent of guiding an actual consumer in making a rational choice, the degree to which the actual utility, resulting from choices generated by decision-making procedures involving rule of thumb techniques for the acquisition of information, approximates the ideal result postulated by the theory. But CCT, by formulating precisely the formal conditions under which the ideal result (goal) is attained, makes possible an exact measure of the approximation of actual results to the ideal. That is, according to the equimarginal principle defining the ideal case, actual purchases will approximate to the ideal to the extent that the marginal utility per dollar's worth of each commodity purchased approaches equality. Moreover, in conformity with the first and third approximation conditions for idealizations, as actual circumstances for acquiring information do more closely approximate the ideal conditions mentioned in the theory (especially unlimited computational power), the consequences of consumer choice more closely approximate the result predicted for the ideal case (maximum utility as defined by the equimarginal principle).

The reason behind the mistaken refusal of Simon and Michalos to see decision-making procedures that, *within* a maximizing theory, permit deviations from maximizing behaviour, perhaps lies in their failure to fully recognize just this general relationship between the construction of idealized theories and their practical employment. There is no sufficient reason to reject such idealizations, in the manner of Simon and Michalos, on the grounds that it is impossible to provide means of applying the theories to concrete cases, which means *preserve* the idealized content of the theories. For, as long as the approximation conditions for defensible idealizations can be satisfied, as they can in maximizing choice theories such as CCT or SET, that is sufficient. Indeed, if one were to generalize the principle underlying bounded rationality and require that the meaning of all idealized theories in science permit criteria for their exact application, such a generalization would provide a *reductio ad absurdum* of the demand. For no such idealized theory in science (e.g., concerning motion in a vacuum, or expansion of perfectly elastic gases) permits a criterion for the empirical application or instantiation of its principles *as idealized*, but only a criterion for identifying the approximation of empirical phenomena to the values of the idealized principles. Indeed, to insist on a more congruent correspondence between the meaning of idealized theoretical principles and criteria of their application is to make demands that are empirically impossible to meet. For an acceptable scientific idealization will be underpinned by empirical postulates which account for deviations between ideal and actual cases, as the truth of these postulates entails the empirical impossibility of the properties of actual phenomena coinciding with the meaning of the idealized theoretical concepts.

4. Maximizing and Regret Theory

A significant alternative to conventional expected utility theory for decision-making under uncertainty that has been recently developed is that of "regret theory", particularly in the form articulated by Loomes and Sugden.[27] It will be illuminating to examine this theory, especially as it returns us to significant issues concerning "mechanistic" as contrasted with full-fledged "intentionalist" frameworks for understanding rational choice that have occupied us in this study. Let me begin with a brief explanation of Loomes and Sugden's model.

The core of Loomes and Sugden's argument against expected utility theory, whether it deploys an objective or subjective conception of probability, is that it provides a seriously *incomplete* conceptualization and explanation of choice behaviour. In particular, the conventional theory offers an impoverished conception of the structure of the *valuations* that motivate rational agents to make choices between alternative actions. As Loomes and Sugden stress,[28] alternative actions are ranked or comparatively valued by expected utility theory entirely on the basis of the probability-weighted consequences of each action and the individual's pattern of tastes – in this way, an expected utility number is assigned to each action rating its value. Most importantly, the valuation and ranking of any available action will be *independent* of the valuation of any feasible *alternative action*. However, according to Loomes and Sugden, this is a substantive defect in expected utility theory for both explanatory/predictive and normative uses of a theory of rational choice.

From the former perspective, Loomes and Sugden draw our attention to the fact that many subjects actually have the psychological experiences of regret and rejoicing, and that such experiences do make a significant difference to the valuation of the consequences of optional actions in choice under uncertain conditions. More specifically, the value or "utility" such agents find in experiencing the consequence of an action is determined not only by realizing that outcome but also by the regret/rejoicing that they feel in recognizing the more/less pleasurable consequences that *would have* ensued from the alternative actions that they have rejected. As Sugden puts it: "the fundamental idea behind this theory is that the psychological experience of 'having x' can be influenced by comparisons between x and the y that one might have had, had one chosen differently."[29]

Formally, consider the agent of standard neo-classical expected utility theory (our SET) for whom, as Loomes and Sugden explain, there is a "choiceless" utility function $C(.)$ that assigns a utility index to each possible consequence x_{ij} associated with all actions i in all states of the world j. Such a function is understood as "choiceless" in that it conceives of such utility as the value of the consequence to the subject independently of having chosen it. However, suppose that in choosing action A_i an agent S must reject action A_k, and that outcome x_{ij} with "choiceless" utility C_{ij} occurs. According to Loomes and Sugden, the actual utility experienced by S will be his modified utility m_{ij}^k, that is, his choiceless utility as adjusted for the loss or increase in such utility as S experiences the regret or rejoicing due to his reflection on the utility he would have realized had he chosen A_k – where regret or rejoicing is the difference between the utilities of the outcomes of the chosen and rejected actions for a particular state of the world (C_{ij} - C_{kj}). Accordingly, within regret theory, it is asserted that S will choose between alternative actions in order to maximize the mathematical expectation of modified utility: thus evaluating alternative A_i with respect to alternative A_k,

$$\text{expected modified utility} = E_i^k = \sum_{j=1}^{n} p_j m_{ij}^k$$

First, a comment on the logical structure of regret theory. On the one hand, the substantive content of the valued objective that is to be examined *is* clearly different in kind from that of conventional expected utility theory. For the latter model simply does not include feelings of regret/rejoicing among the values which motivate action choices. Thus, in terms of their mathematical expression, there are distinct objective functions that are maximized within the two theories. This point is highlighted by the fact that if an agent experiences *no* regret or rejoicing, regret theory reduces to that of expected utility theory.[30] From the point of view of its substantive empirical content, then, regret theory is a *bona fide* alternative to the customary maximization model for choice under uncertainty. On the other hand, as far as the logical structure of its means-end framework is concerned, regret theory remains, as with the satisficing theory of the last section, within the generic classification of a maximizing model; indeed, insofar as the agent of regret theory perceives an end of modified utility, inclusive of expected regret/rejoicing, as less/more valuable than one of choiceless utility, it is difficult, as a matter of conceptual possibility, to see how it could be otherwise.[31]

We have mentioned that Loomes and Sugden find regret theory superior to expected utility theory for both explanatory/predictive and normative purposes. In the former context, it is argued that regret theory has greater explanatory scope/predictive power than traditional expected utility theory in that the former can predict and account for the same choice behaviour as the latter, but can also subsume a wider range of such activities. In particular, its principles can predict or explain choices that are considered anomalies for the traditional theory – such as those expressing intransitive preferences in certain cases of betting behaviour.[32] Suppose, then, such allegedly anomalous behaviour occurs because of the role anticipated regret/rejoicing plays in an agent's deliberations as to how he ought to choose between options. It is not surprising, then, that expected utility theory has less explanatory or predictive capability than regret theory as it ignores a significant motivating factor in human behaviour. Moreover, Loomes and Sugden insist that there is nothing irrational about, say, intransitive preferences issuing from the integration of regret/rejoicing into the agent's practical reasoning.[33] Individuals *do experience* the sensations of rejoicing/regret, which experiences they find desirable/undesirable and, hence, to which they impute positive/negative values. Consequently, they are in fact acting as normal *rational* agents in anticipating such feelings in their deliberations as to the full content of the outcomes of their alternative action-choices, and including them in their calculations as to their optimal course of action. To not do so would be to overlook a real source of value/disvalue for their prospective well-being; consequently, Loomes and Sugden conclude that conventional expected utility theory is guilty of an unduly limited conception of rationality for just such an oversight. Hence, such theory is also found wanting under a normative construal recommending a pattern of choice for economic agents.

It strikes me that the phenomena of regret and rejoicing are undeniably real and significant objects of human valuation and that Loomes and Sugden, in particular, are to be commended for extending the conceptualization of rational choice under uncertainty to take account of these phenomena. However, I have a mixed response to the actual identification of the *specific content* or nature of regret and rejoicing by Loomes and Sugden, and my reservations on this issue make a significant difference to an appropriate understanding of these phenomena as dimensions of human rationality.

In specifying the content of the basic notion of "choiceless utility" in the construction of regret theory, Loomes and Sugden advise[34] that we understand this notion as equivalent to the classical nineteenth century concept of utility – as we have seen in earlier chapters, the psychological experience of pleasure associated with the satisfaction of desire. And such utility is believed to be determinable through introspection by the conscious subject. Perceived difficulties with the exact measurability, interpersonal comparability, and especially, as we have seen,[35] the testability of hypotheses incorporating such an introspective concept, have led contemporary economists to abandon it in the construction of their choice theories. However, insofar as this movement has led to mechanistic reductions of choice theory *via* behaviourist definitions of theoretical vocabulary, we have argued in Chapter 4 that such a development has been regressive in arresting both the explanatory scope and normative capability of economic theory. And, irrespective of the methodological wisdom of reviving the classical concept of utility *qua* introspectable pleasure, it is apparent that Loomes and Sugden find the behaviourist conceptions of utility underlying conventional expected utility theory too restrictive in similar ways – more particularly, it prevents rational choice theory from either accounting for the important phenomena of regret or rejoicing, or recognizing that these experiences are integral factors in the considerations of rational agents deciding how they ought to behave. In this implication of regret theory, our own arguments against behaviourist concept formation in neo-classical choice theory would lead us to be in considerable sympathy with Loomes and Sugden.

As I see it, however, Loomes and Sugden have too restricted a concept of the empirical content of regret itself, and one which unduly limits their vision of the deeper role that the consideration of regret may play in characterizing the rationality of human choice, including that of the consumer. In particular, they have not gone far enough in liberating the phenomenon of regret from an overly "mechanistic" modelling of individual choice. For it is to be remembered that they conceive regret as a "feeling", a psychological experience in the form of a painful *sensation* linked to the frustration of a desire for the consequence of an alternative action, which outcome that agent has had to forego in enacting the option he did choose.[36] Again, we can agree with Loomes and Sugden that such a qualitative element of experience is an "internal" mental state that conscious subjects do find undesirable and, hence, a "disutility" whose real prospect rational individuals should include in their evaluation of options prior to choice. As Loomes and Sugden sensibly comment ... "if an individual does experience such feelings, we do not see how he can be deemed irrational for consistently taking those feelings into account."[37]

214

So far, so good. But this form of regret theory remains within the boundaries of *instrumental* rationality. Given the generic end of maximal experienced pleasure, regret theory recommends the most efficient means to attain it – even though, as contrasted with conventional economic analysis, such efficiency now takes prudent account of the pleasure/pain associated with awareness of rejected alternatives. In so limiting the phenomenon of regret to this category of experienced sensation, Sugden's conception of the phenomenon in the following terms is appropriate: "On a Humean view of rationality, regret is just another kind of passion, to which reason must be a slave: there is no sense in which the feeling of regret can be called reasonable or unreasonable."[38] However, human beings *qua* full-fledged persons are not so confined in their purposive deliberations or practical reasoning to the mechanical calculations of the optimal means to satisfy existent "passions" that must, à la Hume, simply be taken as given.[39] Moreover, the occurrence of regret is a prime confirmation of the failing of a Humean limitation to instrumental rationality, not a reinforcement of the sovereignty of such tunnel vision. We may best elucidate this point by examining an illustration of the important contexts in which regret is more perspicaciously conceived as a *rational attitude*, rather than simply an experienced sensation.

Consider an example of the logic of the situation discussed in Chapter 5, section 3, wherein I have to allocate my financial resources (income) over a variety of possible purchases (commodity-bundles), but where I must do so over a period of time such that I am confronted with a sequence of action-choices. As we observed Marshall arguing, as a rational agent I would show no temporal preference as such in "discounting" for future consumption options by ascribing less value to them than if they were now present, other than can be justified by the likelihood of them not obtaining as indicated by mortality tables, catastrophe statistics, etc. But suppose I am one of Marshall's "uneconomic men", and that my moral character is such that I am generally disposed to the incontinence or impulsiveness in consumption of dissipating most of my income in immediate consumption, leaving myself bereft of financial resources to meet future consumption needs. Well, no doubt, upon frittering away my income on current purchasing, I may very well undergo regret in Loomes and Sugden's sense of a felt painful sensation in reflection on a whole range of future consumption options that I have rendered inaccessible through my incontinence. Moreover, as an instrumentally rational agent, I may take cognizance of such personal impulsiveness, anticipate the regret it induces, and attempt to reduce such "dissonance" through some type of "self-binding" policy[40] such as an unbreakable

215

arrangement wherein my spouse is legally granted allocational control over the bulk of my income. And thereby I would provide myself with more efficient means to realize my desired end – now understood as the maximization of my expected "modified utility".

But this is much too "minimalist" an account of the rationality embedded in self-binding practices. In order to appreciate this fact, we might, in our example, ask for the specific *reason* for my expectation of regret prior to engaging in an impulsive course of consumer choice. Again, it *may* be, with Loomes and Sugden, that, on the basis of past introspective evidence, I fear the prospect of placing myself in a situation where I shall have the painful sensation of desirable options foregone. But it is just as empirically plausible that, through incontinent consumer behaviour, I expect to regret that I shall not live up to the image of the kind of "self" that I will to be – say, one of discreet moderation. In such a predicament, I am not primarily concerned, as Loomes and Sugden's account would suggest, with some lack of instrumental rationality – with a failure to choose the most efficient means to secure a given end of maximal modified utility *qua* pleasurable sensations. Rather, I am anxious that my impulsiveness will portray a miscarriage of *expressive* rationality.

As briefly alluded to earlier,[41] this form of rationality is concerned with an individual's effort in his action-choices to develop his autonomy or self-mastery, to enact strategies of choice that are "self-directive" and that will define the kind of person that he wills to be. Of course, we may anticipate replies of neo-classical economists that would seek to re-define expressive rationality as a variant of the instrumental sort (in, say, classifying self-respect as a given end for the choice of efficient economic means). But such replies would be misdirected, for expressive rationality is better understood as characterizing certain actions as ends-in-themselves, as giving expression to the agent's self-identity in the very action itself. Furthermore, certain basic economic practices are explained in a severely truncated way unless the role of expressive rationality is integrated into the explanation. Thus, an adequate explanation of a range of consumer behaviour is provided only if it involves an account of the manner in which the purchase of particular commodities and services instantiates a strategy of the agent to communicate the expressive meaning of his consumption to himself and others, that is to symbolize in his style of consumption the kind of person he is.[42]

In terms of our illustration, then, my indulgence in the immediate gratification of current consumption shows a miscarriage of expressive rationality in that such profligacy publicly symbolizes the opposite of the self that I seek to be and to exhibit – again, one of discreet moderation. And insofar as I attempt to improve my expressive rationality through the self-binding involved in transferring my disposable income to my spouse, I do not do so with the intention of increasing the expected value of my future introspectable pleasure – although this might be a foreseen, but unintended, consequence (a so-called "second effect"[43]). Rather I do so with the conscious intention of supplying a means for my character development, of strategically manipulating my observable empirical self such that it might become more in accord with the ideal self or person I aim to be. Most importantly, it is my reflection on my lack of *ethical integrity*, the failure of the self that I actualize in my choice behaviour to match the morally better self with whom I identify that is the basic ground of my regret. In this "what might have been" compared to "what is" lies the actualization of my self-identity as an autonomous agent or complete person. Understood thus, regret is a rational moral attitude towards my behavioural dispositions, not merely a painful sensation, not just another kind of Humean "passion" that "in no sense ... can be called reasonable or unreasonable".[44]

We have agreed with Loomes and Sugden that regret theory is both a predictive/explanatory and normative advance over conventional expected utility theory. But our criticisms lead us to conclude that both the explanatory scope and normative credibility of regret theory itself would be advanced by an integration of criteria of expressive rationality into the conceptualization of regret for the purposes of constructing an alternative theory of rational choice under uncertainty. For human beings are in fact motivated in their economic behaviour by anticipating regret due to a loss of their moral self-identity – and so they should be.

The preceding considerations of ethical moment lead us to consider more generally whether the extension of a theory of economic choice under conditions of certainty to one which comprehends uncertain circumstances brings further, and basic, moral implications. Our answer to this question is robustly affirmative, and to whose explanation we shall proceed in the next chapter.

Chapter 13

Economic Uncertainty and Consumer Autonomy

We observed in Chapter 11 that the integration of general equilibrium theory with welfare economics provides neo-classical economics with the contemporary version of Adam Smith's "invisible hand". Within a perfectly competitive market economy, the different "parts" of the economic system – production, exchange and consumption – so adjust to each other that a general equilibrium state is secured that is to the mutual advantage of all agents within the overall system, even though such a collective optimum is not intended by the participating actors. Of course, in real empirical terms, such an "invisible hand" is not the instrument of some actual "deus ex machina" guiding the free-market. There is no omniscient, benevolent spectator who fully understands the nature and consequences of each individual economic activity such that he can steer the entire market system towards an end-state wherein there is a harmony of each with all. In the real-life competitive economy whatever mutually advantageous states do ensue for its participants will be the outcome of the uncertain choices of the fallible mortals who are actually engaged in production, exchange and consumption.

However, standard models of "general competitive analysis" express theoretical idealizations that, in effect, salvage the omniscience of an external spectator by re-locating it as a property of the calculations of decision-makers within the perfectly competitive market. More precisely, producers and consumers exercise their respective rational choices under conditions of certainty or perfect information. Accordingly, on the subsumption of CCT within a general equilibrium theory, consumers are assumed to know all available commodity-bundles and can completely rank them in terms of their preferences; moreover in the hypothetical context of "pure exchange" within general equilibrium analysis, individual consumers would be able to ascertain mutually advantageous trades with other individuals such that the marginal rate of substitution of commodities would be equalized across consumers. Similarly, rational producers will know all current and future production possibilities with fixed inputs and technology, and be able to identify that allocation of resources wherein the marginal rate of technical substitution between factor inputs in the production of each commodity is equal.[1] Decision-makers within the economy are also assumed to know all present and future prices for consumer goods and factor services. Clearly such epistemic attributions are idealized traits that are beyond the cognitive capacity of actual economic agents to fully exemplify.

In the light of such idealization, it might appear that the relevance and applicability of general equilibrium analysis to actual market economies was rather remote. However, according to many advocates of a free enterprise economy, it is a consideration of the first importance that a competitive market itself functions so as to narrow the gap between the kind of complete knowledge ascribed to the virtually omniscient actors of general equilibrium theory and the fragmented, incomplete information possessed by their real-life counterparts. In effect, the internal or "endogenous" operations of a free-market system are understood to provide a second-best surrogate for an omniscient, external spectator guiding the economy to a socially optimal general equilibrium expressing his benevolent design.

1. Hayek: Market Knowledge and Spontaneous Order

Perhaps the foremost defence of the above conception of the epistemic virtue of the market economy is to be found in the work of F. A. von Hayek.[2] As Hayek's views have been finding an increasing number of recent sympathizers,[3] it will be useful to review Hayek's major theses as perhaps the classic defence of the "informational efficiency" of the free-market system.

Hayek's arguments are especially instructive for our purposes as they begin with a generalization of a fundamental epistemological conclusion we have reached (for our own reasons) in our analysis of CCT. In particular, Hayek claims that the "pure logic of choice", extended in equilibrium analysis to include both consumer and entrepreneurial decisions, is necessarily true a priori.[4] However, according to Hayek, such equilibrium analysis can only have relevance for the explanation of economic activities in the real world once such "formal analysis" is complemented by empirical causal statements about the *acquisition and communication of knowledge*. Such an integration of empirical content within formal analysis is critical if we are to understand the normative force of equilibrium theory – viz., how actual general equilibrium states are in fact attained that satisfy the optimality conditions providing maximum profit for producers and Pareto efficiency for aggregate consumer utility.

It is in this important context that the epistemic virtues of the competitive market come to the fore. Thus, in Hayek's view, it is precisely the voluntary competitive activities of self-interested individuals within a free-market economy that provides the essential system of communication to secure equilibria that are also social optima.[5] More particularly, it is the response of rivalrous individuals to the information provided by the signals of the price system endemic to a free market that enables the overall economy to converge towards an efficient competitive equilibrium. For instance, it is only through the process of competition that prices are established for resources that inform entrepreneurs of least cost combination of inputs; similarly, it is market exchanges issuing in commodity prices that instruct consumers of the alternative expenditures of their income on the basis of which they can maximize their satisfaction from the use of material goods.

It is through such a transmission of useful knowledge imparted to relative prices that competitive market exchanges provide a coherent and efficient *order* for the economy. For Hayek there are two critical and logically connected factors in the provision of such competitive organization. First, Hayek directly challenges the import of the assumption of perfect knowledge or foresight implicit in traditional models of competitive equilibrium analysis: perfect foresight of each of the plans of others is not, as traditionally assumed, a necessary condition of securing general equilibrium. Rather complete compatibility of expectations is definitive of the harmony of a general equilibrium state itself. But any approach of the actual economy towards such an idealized order must turn on the use made of an existing dispersion of fragmented, imperfect knowledge among many individual decision-makers. And it is just the virtue of the market price system to serve as an uniquely efficient means whereby the isolated, imperfect "bits of knowledge"[6] of diverse individual agents can be corrected and co-ordinated such that the different sectors of the economy will tend towards a socially optimal general equilibrium. As such an idealized state is approached, impersonal price mechanisms will ensure that the expectations of economic actors concerning each others' beliefs and intentions come progressively into agreement. As Hayek explains ... "Correct foresight is then not, as it has sometimes been understood, a pre-condition that must exist in order that equilibrium may be arrived at. It is rather the defining characteristic of a state of equilibrium".[7]

Secondly, Hayek, echoing Adam Smith, emphasizes that the economic order engendered through the market's diffusion of knowledge is a *spontaneous* one. Although a co-ordination of economic expectations through the price system is an effect of the intentional actions of individual producers and consumers, it is *not* the outcome of anyone's conscious design, or an intentional end-in-view that an individual or society deliberately seeks.[8] Self-interested individuals, motivated by expectation of their own gains in profits or utilities, transmit their privileged knowledge of their own private ends to other agents through publicly observable changes in the relative prices of resources and consumer goods. But the coherent organization of production, exchange and consumption such an efficient transmission of information provides is not deliberately planned by individual participants in the market economy: they are simply sending and responding to price signals.

Finally, and most importantly, Hayek and like-minded economists argue a fundamental link between the optimal dissemination of economic knowledge within a society and the provision of freedom of individual choice within the economy. No single mind, or "central planning authority", has, or even can have, adequate knowledge of the complexities of the myriad production functions or preference structures required to engineer the movement of different sectors of the economy towards an efficient general equilibrium state. Such knowledge would require a virtual omniscience concerning *particular circumstances* of time and place which is never given to a central "mind".[9] On the other hand, such specific information *is* found in the unique possession of the "micro-units" of individual producers, consumers, and resource holders. However, effective use can be made of such real, "local knowledge" only if activities dependent on it are left to the free decisions of the respective, self-motivated individuals. For on this, and only this, basis of individual freedom of choice can the market price system function so as to disseminate to all interested parties the information dispersed among many individuals, and thereby co-ordinate the plans of separate decision-makers. Thus freedom is the handmaiden of that knowledge which provides the guidance for the invisible hand of the impersonal price system to move the different participants in the economy towards a mutually advantageous general equilibrium. As Hayek expresses this refashioning of Smith's "system of natural liberty", ... "the essential utility of the price system consists in inducing the individual, while seeking his own interest, to do what is in the general interest".[10] It is, furthermore, precisely the pre-eminent capability of the equilibrating processes of the market price system to supply the information necessary for socially beneficial decision-making that renders a free enterprise economy clearly superior to a socially planned one. The demands which would be put on the latter form of economic organization to acquire and process the knowledge necessary to match the social optimality delivered by the "natural harmony" of the competitive market, are irredeemably beyond the limits of human ingenuity, even when aided by machines.

2. Consumer Sovereignty and Epistemic Individualism

Given the intentions of this study, we need not take issue with Hayek's basic view that the competitive market operates with a singular economy of information to furnish the common knowledge required for a political economy to function efficiently. Indeed, we may agree that Hayek's work offers a deeply insightful account of the role of human knowledge in the free-market system. Nor are we especially concerned with the specific features of Hayek's personal viewpoint. Rather, we may take the Hayekian account as the *locus classicus* of the contemporary argument for the "informational efficiency" of economic organization through a system of voluntary exchange in an uncertain world. Moreover, on this score, it would be the consensus of neo-classical economists to concur with Hayek and the "Austrian school" – in fact, we have seen that Hayek provides a conceptualization, in epistemic terms, of the traditional vindication within orthodox economics of the free-market that traces its historical roots to the founding principles of the system of natural liberty expounded by Adam Smith.

For our present purposes, one feature of these principles requires special emphasis: the ultimate legitimation of the economic order delivered by a competitive free-market economy is taken to be its optimal provision for the well-being of the "sovereign individual". On the assumption that individual subjects, as least in their economic behaviour, are motivated by a desire to maximize the fulfilment of their self-interest, Hayek and neo-classical theorists are at one in continuing the classical tradition in arguing that a competitive free enterprise economy will meet this goal of individual agents to a greater degree than other forms of economic organization. More precisely, competitive market processes are claimed to bring about maximal satisfaction of the given desires of individual consumers. Earlier we observed this point of view encapsulated in the neo-classical doctrine of "consumer sovereignty". And we have also seen the full-blooded development of this framework in general equilibrium theory *cum* welfare economics. However, from the perspective of this chapter, we are concerned in particular with the role that the processing of information plays in these general arguments for the social optimality of the market economy.

In the present context, the critical factor to note is that neo-classical theory assumes a *direction* to the processing of information in the decentralized decision-making of the free-market. In particular, economic information originates in and is directed by the actual preference-orderings of individual consumers. In the words of the economists Walsh and Gram:

> the most important aspect of neo-classical theory lies in showing the effects of differences in demand on prices and allocations. The unique view implicit in the theory is that, by taking resources and technology as given, individual consumption choices can be regarded as determining all important variables: factor allocation, prices, incomes, and commodity allocations. This explains why, for the neo-classicists, the theory of choice is the core of economic science .... The decisions of households, or more generally of consumers/ resource owners, are so basic to the interpretation of neo-classical theory that the phrase "consumer's sovereignty" is used to emphasize their central role.[11]

It would be congruent with our entire study to be in sympathy with the claim of the preceding quotation. In fact, the desires of consumers for specific goods and the prices they are disposed to pay has dual import: it sets in motion the information so adroitly conveyed by market prices, but the optimal servicing of these desires also provides the final vindication for the bill of goods supplied by producers. Consumer sovereignty, in short, finds its traditional justification in both instrumental and substantive normative terms. As Hayek argued, respecting the uncoerced preferences of individual consumers brings about a maximally efficient diffusion of the particular, specific information necessary for deciding the actual combination of commodities to be produced by the economy; but the production of an array of goods that did reflect the free choices of individuals acting on their strongest preferences would constitute an ethically desirable political economy of the highest order.

The preceding discussion enables us to usefully address a general question of social values. Should *individual* consumers be taken to be the arbiters of the kind and quantity of economic goods a society ought to produce? The doctrine of consumer sovereignty would imply an affirmative answer to this question. To repeat: according to the doctrine the extent and form of the productive processes of a community is to be justified by the capacity of those processes to satisfy the given desires for material consumption of the individual members of that community; these members, moreover, are held to be best equipped, *as individuals*, to know the quantity and kinds of commodities which *will* satisfy their wants, and ought, therefore, to be left free to choose them. "Freedom" here is to be understood in the so-called "soft determinist" sense of being externally unconstrained. That is, an individual is not prevented from doing what he desires or coerced to do what he does not desire. Indeed, provision for such self-determination or "autonomy" on the part of the individual consumer should be considered an essential element in the "sovereignty" of consumer sovereignty.

ECONOMIC UNCERTAINTY AND CONSUMER AUTONOMY

We have found that the principle of consumer sovereignty has been a mainspring in the attempt to justify an organization of economic activity in the form of a competitive market system. Of course, this perspective has had a social corollary in terms of the ideal political structure to underwrite such an organization – i.e., a laissez-faire, liberalist political framework ensuring that the economic processes of production, exchange and consumption be free from governmental or centralized control. Typically, it is conceded, indeed stressed, that orthodox economic science itself makes no evaluations concerning the most desirable political system; however, given the primary goal of economic activity, that is, maximum "welfare" for individual consumers, orthodox or neo-classical economic theory argues that a laissez-faire political system promotes the achievement of this end better than any alternative.

We might focus the issue of concern then in terms of the following question. Is the end of maximum utility for individual consumers better attained within a "liberalist", laissez-faire political structure which guarantees that the individual agent is externally unconstrained, or left free to make his own choices of consumer goods, or within a broadly speaking, "paternalist" or "command" framework, wherein certain consumption "experts" prevail upon the individual consumer to buy certain sets of commodities for his own good? For our purposes, we will restrict our inquiry into this very general question by focusing our attention on a pertinent implication of CCT.

No doubt, as far as CCT is concerned, it is true that laissez-faire political policy would be more conducive to consumer utility, but the critical point is that it is *trivially* true. For, as we have seen, CCT assumes the economic *omniscience* of the consumer, as he chooses under conditions of certainty. That is, he has complete knowledge of all alternative purchases and can correctly predict the outcome in terms of his utility or subjective satisfaction resulting from each alternative. But it is also, as we have argued in Chapter 2, a necessary "conceptual truth" that, under such perfect epistemic circumstances, a consumer whose strongest desire is for maximum material satisfaction, and is free or unconstrained in his choice, *will* choose that set of commodities which leads to such maximum satisfaction. Granted the truth of this necessary proposition, to continue to wonder whether, given CCT, on grounds of empirical fact, a laissez-faire policy is more optimal than a paternalistic one, is a redundant exercise.

Of course, in the market economy as a whole, the individual consumer is competitively interacting with other individuals as consumers, resource owners and producers in pursuit of his goals. And perhaps such generalized

224

interaction would introduce limitations of the options available for certain consumers that even perfect knowledge of the remaining feasible choices would not compensate. But, as we have seen, it is the normative import of general equilibrium theory to deflect the significance of such a prospect for either the individual or society. Assuming producers and consumers meet the conditions of the theory, which includes satisfying the axioms of CCT and choosing under circumstances of perfect information, a perfectly competitive economy will bring about a general equilibrium state that maximizes both the utility of individual consumers and aggregate social utility in terms of the "Paretian measure" – i.e., any movement from such a Pareto-optimal states will make some consumer worse off in terms of the satisfaction of his *de facto* wants.[12] Such general equilibrium analysis, we observed above, provides neo-classical economics with a contemporary conceptualization of Smith's "invisible hand". Economic individualism promotes the common good: the equilibrating processes of the competitive market lead free, self-regarding individuals, on the basis of the information communicated through the price system, to engage in voluntary exchanges that are conducive to a socially optimal state whose realization was not part of their original intentions.

Nevertheless, the liberal individualist is not home-free. For a significant empirical question remains – viz., to what extent actual consumer choices *are*, in fact, performed under conditions of certainty, or conditions even closely approximating certainty. And there is ample factual evidence to indicate that the correct answer to this question is *rarely*, if ever. But it is *not* now a trivial truth that, within the *imperfect* epistemic circumstances of the real economic world, an agent whose strongest desire is to attain maximum material satisfaction, and who is left free in his choice, will choose a commodity-bundle which secures the object of his desire. (Let us call this real-life hypothesis M.) On the contrary, if M intends to state an exception-less universal truth, it is, in fact, a contingent falsehood. Of course, the central question with respect to the preferability of laissez-faire as opposed to paternalist policies is whether or not M is at least a statistically true generalization, and, therefore, a suitable premise for practical decisions concerning optimal social decision-making systems. More precisely, is it even probably true that an unconstrained individual, left to his own deliberations under conditions of uncertainty or imperfect information,[13] would make a choice of a collection of commodities that generated greater utility for him than if the choice was prescribed or made for him, by the decision of an external group of consumption "authorities"?

As we shall see, the preceding question raises especially difficult problems concerning the relation between individual liberty, personal welfare and the common good within neo-classical economics. In order to clarify these complex issues, it will be helpful to approach them at different "levels" of analysis. But our elucidation will also be served by tracking a basic theme that unites these levels: Is the individual, at least in his consumer choices, in the best position to *know* what is good for him? Let us call an affirmative answer to this question the *principle of epistemic individualism*. Arguably, it is the assertion of this principle that supplies the fundamental premise supporting neo-classical defences of "liberal individualism". Thus, Jerome Rothenberg maintains that across a large group of individuals, say a particular society, correct consumption decisions will be made with greater frequency by individuals acting autonomously than by external authorities. On this basis, furthermore, Rothenberg proceeds to draw the relevant normative conclusion favouring liberal or laissez-faire individualism:

> There is sometimes a discrepancy between the individual's preferences and his own welfare. His own valuations are likely to be only an imperfect projection of what is good for him .... On the level of the particular individual, there can sometimes be found a more perspicacious outsider. But on the level of the population as a whole, no concentrated group of outside evaluators can be found which comes anywhere near as close to expressing what is good for them as the individual members of the population themselves [H₁]. Thus the set of individual preferences becomes accepted as the arbiter of their own welfare. *Descriptive individualism in positive economics becomes transformed into normative individualism in welfare economics.*[14]

Clearly the critical premise in Rothenberg's argument for what he calls "normative individualism" is his version of epistemic individualism (labelled H_1 in the quotation). But *is* H_1 factually true – is it the case that more often than not the individual is a more reliable judge of the set of goods which will lead to his maximum utility than an "outside evaluator"? Again, it will prove useful to investigate this general question in a "stratified" way.

3. Product Complexity and Information Vector

At the first level of analysis, we shall employ the simplifying assumption that the consumer has entirely accurate beliefs as to the content of his desires for material commodities, in the sense that he knows what kinds of utility or satisfaction he actually does want to secure from the purchase of economic goods – that is, that he really does desire the satisfaction derived from the comfort, or novelty, or beauty, or prestige, or durability, or physical comfort, etc., in pursuit of which he makes his purchases. However, even if we accept this (not unquestionable) assumption, it remains an *open empirical question*, as to whether the consumer himself has more reliable beliefs than an independent "expert" concerning which *types of commodities*, and in what quantities, will as a matter of fact satisfy his given wants. Granted, the fact that only the individual consumer immediately experiences the consumption of products does lend some support to hypothesis H_1, that he himself is best equipped to judge the satisfaction-giving qualities of commodities. However, there are certain pervasive phenomena of contemporary market economies that tend to warrant the contrary hypothesis H_2 – that external authorities, informationally placed to analyze the properties of commodities, would be in a better epistemic position than the consumer himself to make accurate predictions as to what particular collection of which commodities would bring the kind of utility the consumer desires.

One such phenomenon, perceptively analyzed by Scitovsky,[15] is that of the mass production of products following upon the economies of scale which technological developments have facilitated in modern capitalist economies. Techniques of mass production engender economies of scale in ensuring that the more a particular type of good is purchased, the more cheaply it can be produced. In terms of efficiency, then, producers seeking maximum private profit, are only being rational in concentrating on the mass production of goods exhibiting such economies of scale. But goods that are mass produced find markets by serving the kind of desires that are shared by many. Such desires will be of the commonplace, unsophisticated sort, and the commodities catering to their satisfaction will, similarly, be of the "standardized", pedestrian kind. Hence, those persons with cultivated, atypical tastes will find, in an economy typified by mass production, that either their consumption desires will go unsatisfied through the provision of only standard products or a prohibitive price will be charged for the specially produced goods that could fulfil their material needs. The inaccessability of estimable works of art, even those of the performing arts, to all but the relatively wealthy is a clear example of this contemporary predicament.

This reminder of a current cultural malaise does challenge the principle of consumer sovereignty in terms of its distributive fairness, since in economies of mass production, on average, the "votes" of individual consumers of eccentric or sophisticated taste will count for less in determining what is produced than the tastes of those expressing a common denominator. But the cultivated here share a plight that the relatively impoverished have always known within a capitalist market economy. In any case, the assumption of primary concern for us, that the individual knows best what is good for him has not so far been undermined. Even though the sophisticate of moderate income will find his consumer wants usually by-passed by technologies of mass production, he will be under no illusion in concluding that his consequent general dissatisfaction is not in his own best interests.

In practice, however, modern market economies do tend to undermine the credibility of our principle of epistemic individualism. Moreover, they do so in a way which impugns the critical "vector" of the "underlying vision" of competitive market theory outlined above. For we shall find that the price system no longer encodes a communication of information respecting consumer sovereignty – viz., one moving primarily in the direction from consumer to market to producer. Now both strong advocates of free-market economies such as Hayek, and those who have strong reservations such as Scitovsky, would agree that it is only through market prices that we can have a uniform index of the valuations consumers place on the satisfactions they receive from commodities. But what *level and kind* of information concerning the consumer's "welfare", and the relation between his welfare and his autonomy, are embedded in those prices? Are the consumer preferences conveyed by actual market prices and the neo-classical theory representing such practices an *adequate indicator* of either the consumer's own good or his autonomy or the relation between these values? If we could assume both a) that the actual choices of individual consumers within concrete free enterprise economies expressed their authentic self-determination, and b) an implication of the principle of epistemic individualism, i.e., that their own unconstrained preferences were the best evidence of what was good for them, we could answer the preceding question straightaway in the affirmative. But the answer to our fundamental question is anything but straightforward.

One note of scepticism is sounded in observing certain consequences of the consumption of the kind of commodities characteristically produced by technologies of mass production. Even the consumer of limited taste is likely to become easily bored with the monotony of a commodity produced in great quantity at reduced cost through economies of scale. Accordingly, a common tendency within mass production in order to sustain (indeed increase) the consumption of goods has been to introduce a perceived "complexity" in the properties of goods through increasing product differentiation. And the techniques of modern advertising are elicited in order to "inform" consumer desire of the features apparently distinguishing a product from its closest competitors. One thinks here of the sophisticated

228

salesmanship deployed to lure consumers with the myriad "options" of competing brand-name electronic stereo music players that serve basically the same function to the same degree. Such practices are a stock feature of our contemporary consumer culture. But their implications for the normative force of the traditional principle of consumer sovereignty are of singular importance. For the direction of flow of information that has conventionally underwritten the principle in both neo-classical theory and free-market practice starts to change. In the face of the increasing complexity of the available products, the individual consumer is rendered no longer confident in his own knowledge of the sort of goods that will satisfy his specific desires, and begins to place such knowledge in the hands of the producer. Consequently in what Galbraith calls the "revised sequence",[16] or Scitovsky labels "producer's preference",[17] the exigencies of productive efficiency and growth, rather than consumer demand, are better understood as the *origin of the signals* that determine the kind and quantity of goods that a society will produce. As Scitovsky comments:

> Increasing specialization inevitably deepens the gulf between the producer's specialist expertise and the consumer's generalist ignorance of the nature and design of manufactured products; it is only natural that producers and consumers alike should have greater faith in the former's judgment of what it takes to give satisfaction.[18]

The bearing of this change in the direction of effective knowledge on the credibility of the doctrine of consumer sovereignty is clearly of significance. For the supportive principle of epistemic individualism has been attenuated: in behavioural terms the consumer has conceded that not he, but the producer, knows best what type of commodities are good for him. Hence, the consequences of the phenomenon of increasing product differentiation suggest that our empirical question as to whether the individual, as consumer, or an external authority, has more dependable beliefs as to what goods will fulfil the former's given wants should be answered in favour of the latter – in this case the producer. However, at this level of our analysis, we may grant that the challenge to the normative adequacy of the principle of consumer sovereignty is not *decisive*. For the individual consumer may still reserve for himself the basic premise that he at least has "epistemic privilege" as to the specific content of his material desires – that he alone knows best what kind of satisfaction he seeks from the consumption of commodities (that he really does want the novelty or comfort, or beauty, etc., in pursuit of which he makes his purchases). In general defence of this premise, he may even invoke the philosophical principle of the "privileged access" of a subject, viz., that he has incorrigible knowledge of his own conscious mental states, including economic preferences, since he is immediately aware of such states.[19] Admittedly, given extensive product differentiation, the producer may be better informed than the consumer himself to make accurate determinations as to what particular qualities of which goods would bring the kind of satisfaction the consumer prefers. But the individual consumer would remain his own master in determining and ordering his own material wants, while the producer would continue to respect such sovereignty. It is just that in a mass production economy of diversified products only the latter may have the necessary expertise to identify and supply the goods with the properties that will most fully serve the kind of satisfaction the former desires. And towards this end, advertising would have the entirely benign function of facilitating the movement of appropriate information – of instructing potential consumers of the elaborate qualities of the sophisticated products that would fulfil their given wants.

So far, then, it is arguable that there is in our analysis no implication of the *essential* forfeiting of the individual autonomy or self-determination definitive of consumer sovereignty. In Spinozistic terms, the command of information reserved to the producer need not transgress the consumer's self-command of his own desires. Even though the complex commodities supplied are decided by the favoured knowledge of the producer, the productive system may still serve wants original to the consumer. But, of course, this is not the final word. Accordingly, I would like to proceed to a deeper level of analysis in examining certain forms of economic life that really are decisive in undermining the doctrine of consumer sovereignty, especially its supporting principle of epistemic individualism. In this inquiry, we shall see that the meaning and relations between the basic concepts of knowledge, autonomy and welfare are more subtle and problematic than is typically understood in neo-classical theory, including the theory of consumer choice (CCT).

A qualifying remark is necessary before proceeding. In saying that wants are "original" to the consumer, we are not claiming that they must be innate; nor are we denying that they may be socially learned. Rather we are implying that such affects are autonomous, that is, they are within the reflective determination or self-critical control of the individual consumer. (More will be said about such reflective rationality in Chapter 16.)

4. Inverting the Frame

One clearly visible problem for the normative integrity of free markets is posed by the question as to whether the advertising undertaken by producers in the marketing of diversified products not only conveys information of a commodity's actual properties, but also creates or "manufactures" the individual's *desire* for these qualities and, hence, for the commodities that embed them. For instance, it might be claimed that through the advertising technique of "product imaging" a psychic desire is "synthesized" for a quality of a commodity that is even fictive. Whether or not an individual has an original desire for the "virility" or the "urbanity" present in the consumption of different brands of mass-produced ale, whose observable differences in taste are vanishingly small, both the desires and the qualities can be synthesized through clever marketing in any case. If so, as has been stressed by different writers,[20] the "frame", "underlying vision" or "social purpose" of neo-classical economics is put at serious risk. No longer are resources being allocated or productive processes being organized to provide optimal fulfilment of the autonomous desires or preference-orders of individual agents; rather individual choices are fulfilling consumer wants originated by producers to sustain productive activity or assimilate growth in productive capacity. Jean Baudrillard expresses this "inversion" of the conventional frame as emphatically as anyone:

> the needs invested by the individual consumer today are just as essential to the order of production as the capital invested by the capitalist entrepreneur and the labour power invested by the wage labourer. It is *all* capital.[21]

The consequences of such management of consumer demand for the displacement of the "general frame" of neo-classical economics as presupposed by the principle of consumer sovereignty are of the first order of significance. Put summarily, there would no longer be an empirically sound or logically coherent basis to vindicate a competitive market economy on the grounds that, compared to alternative forms of economic organization, it was most conducive to the material well-being of individuals. More particularly, general equilibrium theory would be divested of considerable normative force. No longer would it make sense to maintain that, given initial resource endowments, a competitive price system ensured a general equilibrium state that was socially valuable in terms of Pareto optimality – i.e., that a decentralized market economy most efficiently serviced the satisfaction of individual consumer preferences. For quite simply, on the evidence of the effect of advertising, salesmanship, etc. on the affective states of individuals, the tastes and preferences of the consumer would not be his own. In terms of logical structure, productive marketing technologies would be creating the individual wants neo-classical theory conceptualizes production as directed towards serving. Seen in this light, resource to the basic premise of epistemic individualism in support of consumer sovereignty would be futile. For particular consumers, *qua* individual subjects of experience, would have direct first-personal knowledge of private desires that had been externally fabricated in any case.

The preceding conundrum of orthodox economics can be placed against more general background considerations. As we have seen, the traditional justification of consumer sovereignty is fashioned within an understanding of an efficient diffusion of information when decisions are made under realistic conditions of uncertainty. But such communication had both causal-empirical and normative-ethical meaning. From the causal perspective, as we observed with Hayek, it is only if ultimate economic decisions are left to agents with adequate knowledge of particular production and utility functions, i.e., individual firms and consumers, will the information transmitted by price signals suffice to bring about an equilibrating order among market participants. But from the normative perspective, such dissemination of information had to have a particular direction. Only if the information supplied by the particular desires and preferences of individual consumers set in motion productive activity would an emergent market order be socially desirable. For only then would competitive market activity show that the moral value of individual freedom was itself in the service of a (constrained) Utilitarian moral standard of maximizing social utility – that the free choices of producers and consumers would, given constraints of available resources and technology, bring about a "Pareto-optimal" satisfaction of the totality of given consumer wants. But, of course, if the information represented and communicated by indifference maps was not indicative of desires and preference-orderings originating with individual consumers, but with producers, the conventional attempt to justify consumer sovereignty as an economical means of transmitting information conducive to the common good would be rendered a hypocritical non-starter.

The preceding problem has an important reflection in a fundamental political norm of the liberal-democratic framework aligned with neo-classical economics. According to a traditional principle of democratic liberalism, an individual should be entitled to be a "dictator" with respect to his "private zone" – that is, concerning his personal wants or interests the realization of which does not interfere with a similar realization on the part of others.[22]

Arguments for this principle have integrated both ethical and epistemic considerations: the moral value of individual autonomy presupposing, once again, that the individual is the most informed judge of his own wants. However, if the above consequences of the marketing practices of certain forms of industrial planning obtain, the necessary condition for the application of a sovereign "private zone" to individual consumer choice would be removed: the individual agent would not be epistemically endowed to know his own consumer wants best as such wants would not be within his self-determination, but externally determined for him by techniques of modern advertising, salesmanship, etc.

5. Consumer Bondage: Akrasia and Self-Deception

In the last two sections we have investigated the difficulties posed for conventional conceptions of consumer sovereignty by the "promotional culture" of productive planning systems in current market economies. At this point it will prove instructive to examine in more depth the implications of this promotional culture on the logical coherence of the connection between the concepts of knowledge, freedom, and human good or "welfare" within CCT. Such thorny issues can be usefully addressed in our "stepwise" fashion in terms of the seriousness of the challenge to the logical integrity of the relations between these fundamental philosophical concepts. In particular, we shall probe the relevant implications in economic situations of i) akrasia (weakness of will), and ii) self-deception.

i) For our purposes we may suitably characterize economic contexts of akrasia as those wherein the principle of epistemic individualism may apply, even though it is causally impotent. That is to say, even if we may assume that the individual consumer has privileged knowledge of both the objects and intrinsic character of his material wants, he is unable to act on such information. Even when the particular consumer knows best the kinds of satisfaction he wants, his order of preference among such affects, and the ranking of commodity bundles as to their capacity to satisfy his wants, nevertheless, through weakness of will, he is incapable of acting in what he knows to be his own best interest. In short, under akrasia, the consumer knows best what is good for him but cannot *do* it. The explanation of such a situation is most plausibly viewed as one wherein it is psychologically impossible for the akratic agent to do what he judges he rationally ought to do because he is causally "driven", perhaps unconsciously, by certain uncontrollable emotions.[23]

Perhaps the most straightforward illustration of the use of akrasia by a productive planning system would be the promotion of "addictive preferences" by appropriate marketing technologies. Consider, for instance, the inducement of a reflectively irrepressible appetite for cigarette consumption, originally engineered in advertising by an association, say, of cigarette products with an image of sophistication the consumer would be expected to desire. Whatever the marketing technique, it is important to recognize that once an akratic agency has been manufactured, the "voluntary exchange" of the consumer is no longer an autonomous one as he is no longer actively self-directive in his behaviour; on the contrary, in his choice of economic goods he is better conceived as a passive instrument of unconscious "drives", rather than a full-fledged agent consciously enacting his strongest intentional desire. It is important to note, moreover, that under akratic conditions of motivation, the "revealed preferences" of the consumer, technically defined, as we observed in Chapter 4, section 1, in terms of his overt purchasings, will not accurately reveal his actual strongest preferences, even as known to him, but induced appetites he would resist if he could. Hence, insofar as his utility function measures such revealed preferences, it will not be a sound gauge of his rationality within CCT understood as the maximization of the satisfaction of his actual preferences. *A fortiori*, the information about his subjective utility which the market price system so efficiently communicates will, nevertheless, be *distorted* information as to his – or other akratic individuals' – personal welfare. Hence, general equilibrium states, which include the aggregation of akratic utilities, *will not be genuinely Pareto-optimal*: akratic individuals can be made better off, without making someone else worse off, by moving to a position where only their actual consumer preferences, divested of the motivational force of akratic drives, are realized. Consequently, we may conclude that the role of industrial marketing in promoting akratic consumption is, *in the exact sense defined by neo-classical theory itself*, economically inefficient or sub-optimal.

ii) In turning to the problem of self-deception within consumer behaviour, we may return more explicitly to choice under conditions of uncertainty. But the above discussion of akratic consumption provides a useful preamble to the examination of self-deception.[24] For, as I see it, the latter more complex phenomenon may be understood as a case wherein the agent is "akratic" with respect to *both* affective and cognitive states, or more precisely, wherein emotive drive weakens epistemic probity or integrity of belief. This point requires elucidation.

CONSUMER BONDAGE: AKRASIA AND SELF-DECEPTION

Basically, in contexts of self-deception, I must decide between two conflicting beliefs on the basis of the available evidence. Although neither belief is justified as certain by the incomplete evidence, nevertheless, I consider one belief as warranted by the evidence whereas the other is unwarranted. However, through a process that has remained rather paradoxical to philosophical analysis, my affective states induce me to "turn a blind eye" to the belief I regard as well-founded and to "deceive myself" into "intentionally" believing the belief which is not adequately grounded. In effect, my desires distort my belief formation *via* a form of "wishful thinking". I somehow "will to believe" what I realize has insufficient evidence in its favour because I strongly prefer the state-of-affairs in which such a belief would be true to the one in which the contrary but warranted belief is true.

It is critical to observe that through self-deception the agent himself, so to speak, forfeits any personal claim to the principle of epistemic individualism. By evading the foremost requirement of inductive reasoning to base one's belief on sufficient evidence, he places himself in a position where he is not a competent, let alone best, judge of what is good for him. Characteristically, such cases arise in circumstances in which one finds an image of oneself that is confounded by the empirical data one accepts as, nevertheless, irresistibly desirable.

The last point quite naturally plays into the hands of certain marketing procedures of modern production planning. In this context, the producer utilizes suitable advertising technology to introduce into the deliberations of the prospective consumer an image of himself that prompts self-deception: even though the consumer recognizes such a conception of himself to be inconsistent with the perceived evidence, nevertheless, he disregards the belief validated by the evidence in accepting the belief that agrees with the self-image he cannot refuse. Perhaps the clearest illustration of such a "play on emotions" is found in the marketing techniques of the contemporary fashion industry which accompany the producer's "planned obsolescence" of goods in order to ensure an adequate "turnover". Here a buyer may well see that a belief in the sexual prowess advertised for him in the purchase of the newest brand of jeans, say, is ungrounded in the evidence; nevertheless, he adopts this belief despite the data as his reason for purchasing the good as he is unable to forego a conception of himself as the sexual athlete he is to become in wearing the jeans.

Once again, however, the normative purport of the connection between the classical concepts of consumer sovereignty, general equilibrium and social optimality are undermined by such an engineering of self-deception, and at a deeper level than that of induced akrasia. As a consequence of the wishful thinking endemic to self-deception, the individual consumer is no longer uniquely endowed with the local knowledge of his own particular utilities to communicate undistorted information through his sovereign choices in the market. Nor, under such conditions, could the general equilibrium states brought about by a competitive price system be socially desirable in a Pareto-optimal sense. For let us accept the plausible principle that, at least in the long run, an individual will maximize his satisfaction by acting on desires that are based on true beliefs about himself rather than the false beliefs caused by self-deception. With this principle in hand, and parallel to the case with akrasia, it follows that a general equilibrium state that represented an aggregation of consumer utilities some of which arose from the preference-orderings of self-deceived agents, would be an equilibrium position from which such agents would likely be better off in moving, and could do so without bringing about less utility for others. For the most part, it is not in an agent's best interests to have no tendency to move from a state in which his utility is predicated on an illusory image of himself.

When a consumer is subject to externally contolled akrasia or self-deception in his market transactions, we may say that the system of natural liberty degenerates into a system of contrived bondage, wherein "bondage" is aptly understood in Spinoza's terms as ...

> man's lack of power to control and check the emotions. For a man at the mercy of his emotions is not his own master but is subject to fortune, in whose power he so lies that he is often compelled, although he sees the better course, to pursue the worse.[25]

6. Autonomy and Adaptation

The preceding three sections may be read as cautions not to be lulled by the undeniable elegance and mathematical rigour of general equilibrium theory into naive conceptions of individual autonomy, human good, and the connection between them. One further form of gullible naiveté would proceed as follows:

Let us assume that the anomalous conditions of producer management of consumer desire, including the induction of akratic and self-deceptive pre-ferences, do not obtain. Given such circumstances and insofar as the utilities aggregated towards the formation of a "social welfare function" are those standing for the given preference-sets of actual individual consumers, we may affirm that at least the moral value of the autonomy or self-determination of individual agents is respected by the social choice mechanism. The only fundamental limitation on such personal freedom is to be found in the individual's income share based on his initial endowment of factor ownership. It is only this which provides the "constraint of necessity" within which individual freedom of choice may be realistically exercised. In technical terms, it is one's relative income which determines the "boundary" of one's "budget constraint" and thereby delimits one's feasible set of commodity-bundles from the larger global set that is limited only by the technological capacity for the production of goods. Hence, the only serious remaining ethical problem is that of determining a *morally just distribution* of either the final product or original endowments (and thus income), such that each individual has access to the maximum level of material satisfaction consonant with his fair entitlement to such welfare. Indeed, it is this particular moral perspective upon which the conditions for the construction of a neo-classical social welfare function have been founded.[26]

However, there is a significant "logical trap" to the preceding line of thought in neo-classical economics. Basically, the coherence of such practical reasoning requires that the desires and preferences ascribable to a particular agent be *separately determinable* from the constraints determining the feasible set or what it is possible for him to consume. But in an important class of cases preferences are not so determinable. In the practice of what Jon Elster has labelled "adaptive preferences",[27] an agent's desires and preferences are adjusted to his material possibilities themselves; put technically, his preferences are shaped by his feasible set. The type of cases most pertinent to the present context are exhibited by those agents who frame choices on the basis of a relatively impoverished original endowment or allocation of income. It is often characteristic of such individuals that they constrain the level and character of their wants to objects they can afford out of habituation and resignation. In Sen's terms, "The hopelessly deprived lack the courage to desire much."[28] And, as Elster well argues,[29] such cases of adaptive preferences are typically generated by non-conscious causal drives operating "behind the back" of the agent rather than through his own intentional character planning. Hence, we may see that such adaptation is clearly to be distinguished from the Stoic "contraction of desire" discussed earlier[30] as the latter arises out of deliberate moral choice. Furthermore, there is typically an element of self-deception in the causation of adaptive preferences. In subconsciously reducing the "cognitive dissonance" associated with the existence of purchasing options beyond their financial reach, the economically deprived will frequently downgrade the utility of such possibilities in a manner inconsistent with the perceived evidence.

It is plain that in circumstances where desire and preference are unconsciously adapted to possibilities, "free market" activities are not those of free men. Clearly, the autonomy of desire, essential to the principal of consumer sovereignty within a market society, wherein the individual is self-determining with respect to the character of his wants, is displaced by the attenuation *cum* distortion of individual desire by "blind" causal forces. *A fortiori*, since he is no judge at all in such circumstances, the individual is not the most knowledgeable judge of what is good for him; the principle of epistemic individualism is simply inapplicable to such contexts. Accordingly, in situations of adaptive preferences, the normative presumption of neo-classical welfare economics, that a competitive market economy optimizes the satisfaction of individual wants for a given distribution of original factor endowments lapses into incoherence. For individual wants have been *causally adapted to these very endowments themselves*.

7. Autonomy and Paternalism

We may observe that the self-deceived, akratic and adaptive individuals discussed above share a similar plight which Donald Davidson has perceptively characterized as one wherein ... "an actor cannot understand himself: he recognizes in his own intentional behaviour something essentially surd."[31] But Davidson's remark here is a useful reminder that such situations are only especially paradoxical cousins of a spectrum of similar cases for choices under uncertainty: often the actual or "manifest" preferences of the agent, those normally revealed in his overt choices,[32] are not an adequate measure of his "true preferences" or "real interests", those whose realization would bring his fullest personal well-being. An identification of true preferences is best put in the form of a subjunctive conditional – viz., the preferences the individual would have if he subjected his actual preferences to consistent and critical reasoning, and he was apprised of all the relevant factual information. And in such cases where his actual or given preferences are not his true ones, our subjunctive conditional would also be a counterfactual one.

Philosophers and economists writing on rational choice theory have stressed various related dimensions of the appraisal of actual preferences from the reference frame of an agent's true preferences.[33] Some have identified the ideally rational agent as one who has "preferences over preferences", or "second-order" preferences – i.e., a commitment to the kind of preference-ordering he believes a rational actor would want to have move him. In a cognate vein, Amartya Sen has advocated a capacity for "meta-rankings", or "ranking of preference rankings", such as a moral ranking of alternative rankings of action-choices.[34] These more elaborate structures for the ordering of options require fuller sources of information on an agent's rationality and good than that available in "mechanistic" modellings of choice from revealed preferences in terms of overt purchasing.[35] They also point to a critique of neo-classical accounts of rationality which seek to preclude the rational assessment of basic desires or final ends. An extensive examination of such limitations must await Chapter 16. There is, however, one fundamental issue that it would be appropriate to raise at this juncture: Would the recourse to "true preferences" as a more suitable criterion of the agent's well-being leave neo-classical choice theory vulnerable to a degenerate form of political paternalism?

By political paternalism we shall understand a system of social control wherein an individual's action-choices are impeded or induced by some external authority for the agent's own good. A degenerate form of such paternalism would be one wherein such constraints thwarted rather than furthered individual well-being. In order to gain some purchase on this classic problem that is relevant to our particular concerns, we may return to the subjunctive formulation of true preferences or real interests as the pre-ferences the agent would have if he reasoned consistently and critically and utilized all pertinent factual evidence. The pivotal difficulty with such an analysis is the common insistence as represented, for example, by Harsanyi, that true preferences be wedded in a defensible theory of rational choice with *autonomous preferences*.[36] But, classically, in both abstract philosophical and concrete historical terms, such a union has always been threatened by acrimonious divorce. Let us see why.

Even though they may not be an individual's actual preferences, in order to satisfy the condition of autonomous preferences an individual's true preferences must, nevertheless, be *his own* preferences.[37] Moreover, as neo-classical economists work within the liberal-democratic political tradition, they would and do require that in the context of social choice or public policy formation the principle of preference autonomy be respected. As Harsanyi puts this requirement... "in deciding what is good or what is bad for a given individual, the ultimate criterion can only be his own wants and his own preferences."[38] But we have identified, as Harsanyi himself does, the criteria of true preferences or real interests in terms of the familiar standards of reason: formal consistency, inductive evidential adequacy, and critical reflection. However, such principles have traditionally been understood to have *universal, impersonal authority*. Hence, so understood, external judges, as long as they were capable of reasoning soundly, would be as equipped as the agent himself to submit his *de facto* pattern of desires or preference-orderings to the appropriate canons of reason or rationality. They might even be better equipped, if the agent himself, blinded as he was by irrational impulse, was incapable of applying the appropriate criteria of rationality to discern his real interests. Put in relation to the concept of the person, insofar as my actual economic interests are not my real interests, the given wants or preference structures of my empirical self might fail to satisfy the principles of reason that my "real self" or ideal other self would apply.

In my judgment, although the issue has been the subject of considerable debate in recent years and we cannot go into the argumentative detail here,[39] criteria of correct reasoning *are* universally applicable across human subjects. More particularly, if person A and person B are placed in relevantly similar circumstances, and if both reason soundly, they must reach the same conclusion. If they do not, one of them must be in error. The bare fact that they are distinct subjects or "reflective indexicals" is not a sufficient ground to warrant diverse conclusions for uniform contexts. Otherwise, reason would lose its essential normative force: the invocation of particular considerations as reasons for believing p or doing a in particular circumstances would fail to make a claim on our inferences and decisions that would be binding.

However, as Isaiah Berlin forewarns,[40] we are on the verge here of supplying the classic philosophical backing for the degenerately paternalistic political systems that have wreaked dreadful havoc in concrete human history. We are, that is, running the risk of lending analytical support to the pretensions of certain historically activist states that have perpetrated immense human misery by repressing the satisfaction of the actual interests of their existent subjects in pursuit of the real interests of the rational selves that these subjects really willed to be – for, as Fichte ominously put it ... "No one has rights against reason."[41]

What has gone wrong with such paternalism? Fundamentally, the error lies in the failure to fully appreciate that sometimes autonomous preferences can be in *intractable* conflict with the true preferences of any particular agent. We may grant that what an actual individual would prefer if he were ideally rational may well differ from his manifest preferences. But part of what it means to be an *actual* self-directed individual is the recognition that at times it will be empirically impossible to become one's ideally rational counterpart. Granted, if one did choose under conditions of certainty, such a limitation need not apply. But then, as we have observed previously, usually the demands of certainty or complete knowledge are beyond the reach of real-life mortals. Indeed, an adequate understanding of this very constraint, that we are typically restricted to forming choices under conditions of uncertainty, would bring with it an appreciation of the fact that we *must* accept the hazard that our manifest preferences, as revealed in our actual choices, may not converge to the true preferences that our "higher" rational self would reveal.

In other words we must recognize the full import of the meaning of the "rational self" as an *idealized abstraction*. Admittedly, my rational self would, by the very nature of reason, exhibit my true preferences. But I may be empirically incapable of fully realizing my abstract rational self. My actual capabilities of "self-command", or that of any other person, are subject to limited horizons. Nevertheless, my autonomous self, even though engaged in the project of self-determination through reason, never extends beyond my own horizons; consequently, my autonomous self *remains* this existent self, however imperfect an image of its ideally rational, abstract counterpart. And it is precisely here that the worm turns in the characteristic practices of repressive paternalism. For invoking the sound consideration that the principles of rationality are universalizable, the fallacious and disastrous inference is drawn that anyone's autonomous self *is* his ideally rational self. In effect, the pretence is put forth that, since reason has universal authority, it can detach the very autonomy of the agent from his existent personhood and place it in his "real", entirely rational self. But the pretence is a large and pernicious fraud. Of course, *qua* autonomous agent, I will to be my completely rational counterpart. But it remains the existent, actual 'I' that must do the willing, and who continues to be the conscious centre of the experience of the satisfaction of my interests, however approximate such satisfaction might be to the satisfaction following upon the complete "self-mastery" of my abstract idealized self. Or, perhaps more to the point of the present discussion, it is only the actual 'I' who experiences the frustration of my own existent interests, indeed the pain of induced distress, by external authorities who cynically invoke the universalizability of reason to impose real misery on my affective life such that I might express the true preferences of a spuriously abstracted autonomous self. But no such fictitious self is a

241

reasonable replacement for my own self, however incomplete my autonomy or self-determination.

In the light of the above, we may understand repressive forms of political paternalism as re-enacting a familiar pattern of philosophical prejudice wherein recourse is made to the abstractive function of reason in order to confound a legitimate ontology. We may press home this lesson by a closer examination of the logical form of the subjunctive conditional we introduced on page 238 to explicate true preferences. In order to avoid an analytical slide into support for degenerate paternalism, the logical form of such conditionals should remain what logicians classify as "singular statements": they are statements reporting the preferences that some *actual named individual*, say John, would have if he were to undertake to subject his actual preferences to consistent reasoning, full evidence, etc. Symbolically, where R summarizes the incorporated procedures of reasoning, C the particular circumstances, P someone's preferences, and "a" names an actual individual such as John, the relevant formula would be:

i) $(Ca.Ra) \rightarrow (\exists y) (Py.May)$ – roughly: if a were in circumstances C and a undertook rational deliberation, he would manifest preferences P. However, since the principles of rationality summarized by R are universalizable, it is all too easy to displace the real individual referred to by 'a' for an impersonal abstration by substituting (perhaps inadvertently) a universally quantified variable 'x' for the individual constant 'a' Thus, symbolically, singular statement i) would be illicitly transformed into the universal generalization:

ii) $(x) [(Cx.Rx) \rightarrow (\exists y)(Py.Mxy)]$ – for any individual x, if he were in circumstances C and undertook rational deliberation, he would manifest preferences P.

But with this ill-advised logical form of true preferences in mind, it would be only natural for external authorities to lose sight of the need to link true preferences to the autonomy of an individual *qua* actual, existent individual, and legislate for him the rational preferences of an abstracted "everyman" as if they were his own. (In this regard, it is important to recognize that the value of 'Py' in formula i) need not be identical with the value of 'Py' in formula ii). Formally speaking, in transforming i) into ii), we might say there has been an invalid use of the quantification rule of "universal generalization" by violating one of the restrictions on the use of this rule; in particular, universal generalization can only be applied by quantifying over some *arbitrarily selected individual*, not simply any specific actual individual such as the one (John) named by the constant a of i)[42].)

What then are the normative implications of the preceding considerations for the practical issues of social choice and political policy? Although it is not possible to discuss this subtle and complex problem extensively here, our analysis does suggest a moderate perspective. Procedures for collective choice internal to neo-classical economics that simply aggregate the utilities representing the manifest preferences expressed in the observable choice of individuals suffer from informational anaemia. For such "revealed preferences" fail to communicate the evaluative content of the more rational wants that these very same individuals might have espoused had they reasoned more consistently, reflectively, etc. On the other hand, an adequate understanding of the *integration* of preference autonomy with rational desire requires that public policy only support social choice procedures that aggregate utilities representing the preferences of individuals as likely to be "filtered" or corrected for by the reasoning of these actual individuals themselves. Respect for the authentic autonomy of persons demands that the censoring of the preferences of "moral adults" be that of the self-censorship of these individuals, not the perversely paternalistic censorship of external authorities appealing to the wants of imaginary, abstracted "rational selves". One way of reading the tragic error of social theorists who have thought otherwise is to view such theorists as Faustian advocates who "want it all ways" or, more precisely, want more than philosophical argument can, in principle, deliver. In particular, they seek a system of social choice that will unite complete rationality with complete autonomy. But this can only be secured on condition that the authoritative and universal principles of reason can be exactly and *fully* internalized by the self-determination of the fallible and the particular – viz., by actual individual human beings. And this is a condition that is quixotic in the extreme. Moreover, even though we may accept that an individual would only achieve full personhood with full rationality, the resort to the *impersonation* of real subjects through an appeal to *abstract* rational selves has been a recipe for philosophical fraud and political tyranny.[43]

It is not to be assumed that our perspective ignores the fact that often the "education" of an agent's desires takes place through his interaction with other persons in his social environment or "moral community". However, insofar as such social interchange is responsible for the rectification of the wants and preference-structures of individuals, it should find its vehicle in an egalitarian public forum of free, open discourse, rather than in the coercive or manipulative modification of a subject's affects by degenerately paternalistic, external "oligarchs" – whether politicians or entrepreneurs.[44]

Chapter 14

From Normative Theory to Empirical Science

In the last five chapters, we have concentrated on an interpretation of the economic theory of choice, under conditions of certainty (CCT) or uncertainty (SET), as a normative theory of rational action.[1] However, we have emphasized that such an understanding is to be recognized as providing only the "conceptually prior" interpretation of such economic theory. In this context, an intriguing and fundamental issue remains. Is there a way in which an a priori and normatively construed theory, such as CCT,[2] could be *converted* into an empirical, descriptive theory of human behaviour? I believe so.

In part, and at a first level of causality, the materials and procedure for such a conversion have been introduced by our earlier discussion of reasons and causes in terms of the connection between norms and motivations. For instance, to the extent that an actual agent is suitably motivated to act in compliance with the rules espoused by *homo economicus*,[3] then, to that extent his behaviour will approximate the actions (necessarily) predicted for his perfectly rational counterpart. Whether or not, and the degree to which, any real-life consumer *is* so motivated by the appropriate structure of desires and beliefs is a contingent, empirical matter which provides an experientially falsifiable element for explanations utilizing ideal theories of rational behaviour such as CCT.

In other words, at any particular time, there is no a priori necessity that any set of real agents would be suitably motivated to follow the rules of rationality embedded in CCT, such that their actions would emulate those of rational economic man. Indeed, at this level of transforming a normative theory into a factually true one, it would appear that CCT has had uncertain success. In this regard, the charge of the "unrealism of the assumptions" directed towards neo-classical economics in general[4] suggests that, if not in principle, then at least in practice, the conversion of CCT, introduced as an a priori, normative system, into one which is descriptively true of real consumer behaviour, has proven elusive. More particularly, there is sufficient evidence of deviance by actual consumers from the behaviour of *homo economicus* described in CCT[5] to merit inquiry into the degree to which actual consumers are motivated to act in accordance with the rules of CCT defining the rationality of *homo economicus*.

But behind this empirical question lies a theoretical concern as to the existence and nature of a further mechanism, at a second level of causality, which would be ultimately reponsible for the *transition* of CCT from a normative system into an empirically true theory of actual behaviour. It seems evident to me that there is such a mechanism and to whose examination we shall now turn.

1. Converting Economic Norms into Economic Facts

In his *History of Economic Thought*, Eric Roll states that Adam Smith "was not content to state an abstract principle: his aim was to destroy the actual conditions which conflicted with the principle."[6] As I see it, Roll's comment accurately reports one instance of a factor that has implicitly or explicitly pervaded the activity of many notable economic theorists. I refer here to the fact that many economic scientists have, on the basis of value commitments, been concerned to actually *alter* the empirical phenomena by an appeal to which their explanatory hypotheses are confirmed. They have, moreover, frequently succeeded in their intentions. As the following discussion will reveal, there can be an important *pragmatic* difference in the confirmation procedures of economic theory as contrasted with those of physical theory – that is, not in the sense of the logic of validating economic hypotheses, but one which plays an actual causal role in the *generation* of economic phenomena.

In the first place, it is instructive to remember the familiar fact that one set of determinants of human behaviour is to be found in "objective" factors "external" to the agent's psychological make-up of beliefs and intentions. And one of the most important subsets of these environmental "causes" is provided by the rules of the social institutions within which such behaviour occurs. In a formal and official vein, such "social causation" operates through the enforcement of political and juridical legislation. The execution of such laws may function negatively as "limiting conditions" effectively preventing certain behaviour within a particular society, or may have the positive effect of coercing members of the society to behave in a specific way – as, for example, murder is legally deterred whereas paying taxes is positively enjoined. Less officially, institutional inducement of individual actions takes place through cultural or educational determinants such as media publicity, religious pressures, commercial advertisements, school curricula, etc. Generally, this type of social control functions informally, through the "influence" or "manipulation" of human behaviour.

246

Consider further that, outside of revolutionary situations, it is empirically true that most citizens are induced by legal commands or conventional influences to conform in their actions to the major prescriptions of their social institutions. Moreover, it is significant that the actual set of behavioural rules ordained in a particular society are, at least to a significant extent, a function of the value-judgments or ethical standards (especially those of the ruling classes) of that society. Injunctions against child labour and the institution of a graduated income tax furnish clear-cut illustrations of this relation.

In the light of these considerations, we may begin to elucidate a "mechanism" whereby CCT, insofar as it might originally be constituted by a priori norms of rational consumption, is converted into a factually true empirical theory. Suppose then, that at a given time in a certain society, the principles of an economic theory, understood in orthodox fashion as descriptive explanatory hypotheses are actually false. Consider, for instance, that a) consumers exhibit random variability rather than a consistent pattern in their purchasing behaviour. Or suppose that b) consumers are not buying more of available bundles of commodities, even though they can afford to do so. Well, if either behaviour a) or b) *were* occurring, it would, of course, disconfirm the empirical predictions of the neo-classical theory of choice (CCT), under its descriptive interpretation. In particular, behaviour a) would disconfirm consistency axiom A_3, while behaviour b) would disconfirm non-satiation axiom A_2.

But, suppose that CCT is originally proposed as a normative system defining and recommending a pattern of rational choice. In other words, the "axioms" of CCT are introduced as rules R_1-R_4 (and O) for maximizing material utility, rather than as empirical hypotheses A_1-A_4. In that case, one way of accounting for the fact that A_1-A_4 *would be* descriptively false of the consumer activity of a particular social system, S, if an attempt were made to apply A_1-A_4 to behaviour in S, is to claim that the agents within S do not follow R_1-R_4 with sufficient regularity. Thus, to take up the above illustration, agents displaying random variability in their consumer activity might be understood as failing to subscribe to consistency (transitivity) rule R_3, while those who do not purchase additional, obtainable commodities could be construed as not following R_2, recommending that a rational consumer ought to buy more of any available commodity.

Furthermore, it is especially critical to realize that the behaviour we have illustrated as refractory to CCT would be motivated by a different structure of desires than behaviour which does not conform to CCT. Thus, we might find that "random", erratic consumer choices were motivated by spontaneous, immediate types of desire rather than the deliberate, calculated, ordered desires determining choices in accord with the consistency rule R_3. Or, consumers exhibiting "sated" behaviour, in contravention of R_2, might, in Stoic fashion, be seeking an affective equilibrium by *contracting* their desires, and thereby diminishing the chances of frustration. Such an attitude would be in direct contrast to the "expansionist" motivational basis of action conforming to R_2 – of seeking to accommodate ever increasing desires for more material satisfaction, on the (dubious) assumption that preferring more of any available commodity necessarily enhances the prospects for securing greater utility.[7]

Consider, furthermore, our earlier discussion concerning the manner in which motivation provides the psychological sanction for obligation.[8] In this light, we might expect that the different psychological grounds or motives for the refractory behaviour would sanction, or be in support of, different moral standards than those implicit in CCT. Our expectation would not go unfulfilled.

Now, this "sanctioning" relation occurs within CCT at two levels. At the first level, psychological motivations overtly buttress or undermine submission to the explicit axioms of CCT, normatively construed (i.e., as rules R_1-R_4). Hence, as we have seen, deliberate, calculated desires would support following R_3, whereas immediate spontaneous ones would undercut following this rule. Likewise, an expansionist form of desire would vindicate R_2, whereas a Stoical, contractionist form would undermine such subscription. Moreover, and most significantly, such sanctioning occurs, albeit covertly, at a second level.

Second level sanctioning is due to the following consideration. If an agent follows the explicit norms of rationality (R_1-R_4) of CCT, then *ipso facto* he can be conceived as subscribing to more general *moral ideals* that are implicit within CCT, although their presence would no doubt be denied by neo-classical economists who seek to be methodologically respectable in denying that their theories are thus "value-laden". Take, for instance, the Stoical pattern of consumption which contravenes the "more is better" rule R_2. It is evident that the motivational basis, consisting of the "contraction of desires" predisposing such behaviour, would fail to sanction such an established moral ideal of economic liberalism, and implicit within CCT, as "the growth ethic", recommending that every individual ought to attempt to expand the possession of his material goods. For compliance with this ethical principle requires as its psychological ground what neo-classical economists have in fact postulated in CCT – a specific "maximizing" structure to motivation. And we have found that such maximizing takes a Benthamite Utilitarian form of an "expansionist" equilibrium, one which (allegedly) accommodates the satisfaction of as great a level of desire for the possession of material goods as is compatible with the purchasing power of the consumer's income.[9]

Or suppose that consumers display random variability in their purchasing pattern, in contravention of "consistency" rule R_3 of CCT. And consider that such behaviour is motivated by a psychological temperament disposing agents to the expression of spontaneity and immediacy of desire. In this case, we would find that such a motivational make-up would not offer a suitable psychological backing for subscribing to the normative requirements of the neo-classical liberalist's concept of the ideal state of moral character as represented by his ethical hero – *homo economicus* or rational economic man.[10] As described in Chapter 5, such an exemplary agent considers it incumbent upon himself to control any "impulsive" tendency towards the spontaneous satisfaction of immediate desire. For he realizes that only by the formation of a steadfast character, constituted by a general, virtuous disposition to act according to deliberate, systematic desires, would he be able to introduce that element of stability in his wants, which enables him to order his preferences in a complete, consistent fashion. And only by such an ordering can he attain (CCT's understanding of) the maximization of his utility. We find, in other words, that only that "orderly personality" or integrity of character as expressed by *homo economicus* provides for a pattern of motivation that would vindicate following rule R_3 of CCT.

Nevertheless, the neo-classical theorist need not consider himself stymied by the presence of *de facto* consumer behaviour he believes ought not to occur. For it is here that the aforementioned considerations concerning external, non-psychological conditions in the causation of human behaviour become relevant. Thus, if our neo-classical economist, wedded as he is to the liberalist ethos, were to gain political authority or significantly influence such authority and social institutions, he could apply his ethical standards by contributing to the enactment of legislation and the establishment of social conventions, compelling or encouraging motivations to engage in economic activity in conformity with his moral imperatives, while preventing or discouraging contrary inclinations. As a result, economic actions will come to exhibit adherence to the norms of rational consumption (R_1-R_4) prescribed in CCT under its normative reading.

But, in that case, he will acquire the grounds to reconstrue CCT as a descriptive, explanatory science wherein the observable facts of economic activity begin to conform to, and therefore confirm, the postulates of CCT understood as empirical hypotheses (A_1-A_4). But such a genesis will occur only by being (partially) caused to do so by the agency of the liberalist theorist himself *via* his influence on the construction of social constraints on economic motivations. In this way, then, the economic scientist can play a causal role in the conversion of his theory from its original form as a normative system prescribing rational conduct into a descriptively true empirical science explaining actual human behaviour. In a certain sense,[11] economic (and no doubt other social scientific) hypotheses can be "made true".

2. Methodological Implications

It will be useful to clarify certain methodological aspects of our account of the transition of CCT from a normative system into an empirical science.

On our interpretation of the conversion of normative theory into a descriptive counterpart, a pragmatic distinction is evident between the method of confirming the explanatory principles of economic science as compared with the method of natural science. Generally speaking, in the context of physical inquiry, the theorist must "wait upon observation" in order to ascertain whether actual physical phenomena exemplify the uniform patterns that his explanatory hypotheses imply, such that the phenomena confirm the hypotheses. On the other hand, since economic phenomena are themselves partially determined by contrivable social arrangements, the economic theorist is not constrained by such a passive, "wait and see" research procedure in seeking observable "data" that would confirm the predictions of his theoretical hypotheses. For he has the option, in the manner we have outlined, of actively assisting in the fashioning of institutional arrangements he believes would induce phenomena consistent with the implications of his proposed theory.

Our interpretation of the normative-descriptive conversion of CCT does not, however, lead us to conclude that, *within the final context of explanation*, the method of theoretical reasoning employed in neo-classical economics is essentially different from that used in natural science. More precisely, upon the transformation of CCT from an a priori normative theory into an empirical science of actual behaviour, the *logical structure* of economic explanation or confirmation does not differ from that of the hypothetico-deductive method employed in natural science. For, we shall see, that a) the theoretical explanation of *actual* economic phenomena still demands the subsumption of such phenomena under empirical hypotheses, and b) the confirmation of these "covering laws" still takes place by finding observational instances for them.

Consider first the case of explanations. Admittedly, we have argued that the choices of the ideally rational consumer postulated by CCT are explained by subsumption under generalizations (G" or H) which are necessarily true *a priori*. However, upon the normative-descriptive transformation of CCT, the methodological objective of this theory can change its focus to the explanation of the choices of *actual* consumers. And in order to account for the behaviour of such real-life agents, and at a sufficiently complete and fundamental level of explanation, we would find that CCT requires appeal to general empirical laws at two stages or levels. Let us see how.

In its initial normative construal, we have characterized CCT as advocating a set of rules for rational choice, R_1-R_4. Hence, in redeploying CCT for empirical explanatory purposes, the neo-classical theorist would seek to explain actual economic behaviour in terms of real agents following R_1-R_4. But, as we argued in Chapter 9, an agent follows a rule or norm only if he is subject to a motivational influence to do so. In this sense, we saw that an agent's assent to an ultimate norm either logically entails or pragmatically presupposes the presence of a psychological state which both vindicates subscription to the norm and causes the agent to perform the action recommended by it. Hence, an account of actual consumer choices would, at a deeper level of explanation, be constructed in terms of the subsumption of rule-governed behaviour under psychological laws reporting regularities of action following upon any consumer's susceptibility to certain kinds of motivation in specific circumstances.

But nor is this stratum of explanation the final one. For we have seen the neo-classical theorist must ensure that the socio-political arrangements provide adequate determinants of the relevant consumer motivations. But, again, therefore, at this most basic level, an adequate theoretical account of the presence of such motivations would take the form of the subsumption of economic motivations under socio-psychological generalizations linking initial conditions in the external social environment with consumer dispositions.

Let us call the general hypotheses adduced at these two basic levels of explanation the *foundational laws* of CCT.[12] But with respect to the confirmation of the second-level foundational laws it might seem, at first sight, that we do have a difference in the theoretical reasoning of neo-classical economics as compared with natural science. For have we not stressed the causal role which the economic theorist himself may play, through helping devise institutional constraints, of actually contriving the very phenomena which would validate such foundational laws? However, without undermining the theoretical importance of such practical measures, we should look more closely at their methodological import. And we may conclude that such practices do not issue in a disparity between the logical structure of the confirmation of these foundational laws of CCT and the empirical laws of natural science, but only in a pragmatic difference in their confirmatory procedures. For in order to *succeed* in "creating" the economic phenomena which will verify CCT as a descriptive science, the neo-classical economist must possess the requisite knowledge for such an undertaking. But such knowledge will be based on his theoretical beliefs concerning the connection between first, consumer behaviour and its motivation, and secondly, such motivation and its institutional causes. Such beliefs, we saw, can be expressed as contingent law-like statements. But such statements will supply the needed knowledge *only if they are true*, and the method of confirming/infirming their truth will consist, as with physical hypotheses, in the observation of positive/negative instances for them. Granted the intentions and actions of the economic theorist himself may be included in the antecedent conditions of the second-stage laws relating environmental causes with economic motivations; nevertheless, the logical structure of the observational validation of such laws will not thereby be altered.

Our conclusion here can be further supported and extended by clarifying its bearing on the question of the "a priori" dimension of CCT. We have seen that the neo-classical theory of rational choice, when it attempts to explain the actual behaviour of real consumers, must move from a normative theory to a descriptive science, and hence, must introduce a posteriori principles into an originally a priori theoretical system. But we might then ask what special contextual conditions in the original construction of CCT provides for the fact that this construction *can* be known a priori. And the answer, it seems to me, is implicit in the very consideration that neo-classical economics intends, as its conceptually prior object for CCT, the design of an essentially *normative* system prescribing rules for the rational behaviour of any consumer. For there is no epistemic barrier to prevent a designer from possessing a priori knowledge of the rules he *legislates* for activities within his design – such as that of an economic system. Put another way, since a system of normative principles does not *intend* to report facts, but to prescribe them, it is impervious to falsification by the facts. Moreover, our designer can even *conjecture*, independently of empirical observation, the descriptive laws governing the actual realization of his intended (social) artifact – in the case of CCT laws connecting real economic behaviour with consumer motivations, and those linking these motivations with institutional controls. Remembering that, for Kant, it is the capacity of reason to disclose a priori knowledge from within itself, it is in these ways that the designer exemplifies Kant's dictum that ... "Reason has insight only into that which it produces after a plan of its own."[13]

However, no human designer is cognitively equipped to have a priori knowledge of the *truth* of the empirical laws governing the operation of his design. Validation of such laws is inescapably a posteriori in social as well as physical science. Hence, the economic engineer, as much as the physicalist one, must "wait upon observations" to confirm whether or not the law-like hypotheses to which he must have recourse in *implementing* the intended object of his design, are, in fact, true – i.e., genuine laws. And, of course, if he employs false empirical hypotheses, he will *fail* to put his social plans into social practice. Although man can have a priori knowledge of what he intends to concoct, he can have only a posteriori knowledge of whether his concoctions will work. (Whether the available historical evidence indicates that the Divine Designer, if there be one, was similarly limited, I leave for the reader to decide.)[14]

3. The Regulative Primacy of Value-Judgments

The above defence of the continuity of the final structure of explanation and confirmation within natural and economic science should not, however, lead us to underrate or displace the crucial "regulative" function of pragmatic factors in the construction and testing of economic theory. In this context it is of the first importance to recognize the *primacy* of value-judgments in our conception of theory-construction in CCT. For we have argued that CCT can be rationally reconstructed, in a conceptually prior form, as a normative system recommending rules for rational consumer choice (R_1-R_4). Moreover, we have explicated the manner in which following R_1-R_4 would presuppose prior commitment to the moral values espoused by *homo economicus*, particularly those of individualistic acquisitiveness and self-restraint. Hence, normative considerations of an ethical kind function as final arbiters in the regulation of an economic "research programme"[15] – in this case, the programme underlying the formation of the neo-classical theory of consumer behaviour. For, on our interpretation, the theorist must first invoke a set of moral values as criteria for identifying the rules of rational behaviour which define the original normative system. In other words, an (unavowed) regulative aim of the research procedures of neo-classical theorists consists in the determination of those rules which prescribe such economic behaviour as gives expression to the moral ideals of *homo economicus*.

Nor would our reconstructed neo-classical economist be satisfied with the formation of an imaginary theoretical system representing economic activities directed towards ethically desirable ends. Rather, to the extent actual behaviour can be observed to be inconsistent with the implications of any theoretical principle, he would, in line with Roll's characterization of Adam Smith, aim "to destroy the actual conditions which conflicted with the principle."[16] And we have argued that his success in achieving such an aim would be in the degree to which, by deliberate participation in the formation of socio-political causes of economic motivations, he could help ensure the construction of an environmental framework motivating agents to submit to the norms of rational consumer choice. But compliance with such norms would empirically realize the ethical objectives which prompt the design of our neo-classicist's theory and guide his active "manipulation" of its verification.[17]

It is noteworthy, furthermore, that it is a feature of such normative primacy that the neo-classical theorist must apply social constraints that are themselves compatible with certain assumptions concerning the "moral geography" of his institutional environment. In this respect, it will be remembered that the subject to whom the axioms of CCT are applied is not only rational but free, in the sense that his choices are uncompelled – that is, he is acting under no external (or internal) constraint. Now, this assumption of consumer freedom is not introduced into CCT only in the context of CCT's status as a theoretical idealization. For the assumption also plays a theoretical role of embedding CCT within the social setting endorsed by neo-classical economics in general. Such a socio-economic environment is that defined by economic liberalism, a doctrine prescribing, as we have seen, the interrelated principles of unconstrained freedom of choice for the individual and laissez-faire political policy.[18] But, in consequence, any social controls which the neo-classical theorist recommends for motivating behaviour in accord with the rules of rational choice must be consistent with the individualistic freedom to which neo-classical economics is committed. In effect, it is our understanding that neo-classical economists responsible for the construction or use of CCT should re-conceive themselves as *political economists*.

These considerations enable us to be more specific about the *kinds* of social constraints the neo-classicist would deem both causally efficacious and ethically desirable for motivating consumers to subscribe to his norms of rationality. Given that CCT assumes individual freedom against a social background of political liberalism, we may conclude that only those measures of social control which are consistent with the "autonomous" decision-making of individual consumers are admissible. More precisely, planned controls must not constrain the individual agent against his desires; that is, they must not prevent him from choosing what he wants, or coerce him to choose as he does not want. In other words, our theorist may have recourse to controls which "influence" the motivations of consumers, rather than controls which directly coerce their behaviour. In general, then, such motivational influence would take place through the public media or education, although, in certain circumstances, it might also be exercised through the application of political legislation. In the latter case, however, it would be imperative that the aim, character and way of implementing the relevant laws have the voluntary approval of the maximum possible individual economic agents.

It is clear, moreover, that just such sorts of "manipulative" external constraints on consumer behaviour have been fashioned and activated in the tradition of neo-classical economics. Typically, such environmental influence has been exercised in the form of cultural publicity rather than formal legislation, although the informal nature of such control has not reduced its effectiveness. Hence, commercial advertisements, political propaganda, the teaching of the communal ideals incorporated in the "hidden curriculum" of formal education,[19] the social ethic embedded in the doctrines of religious denominations, etc., have concurred in producing the individualistic, acquisitive, and calculative patterns of motivation among individual con-sumers necessary to make them economic men – that is, to move them to follow the neo-classical rules of rational choice. Extensive documentation of this primarily empirical issue is beyond the scope of this philosophical inquiry. However, the evidence which Weber[20] invoked to establish a causal connection between the theological ethics of Calvinistic Protestantism and the "possessive individualism" required to motivate the choices of the rational agents represented in neo-classical economics provides some documentation of such an institutional-motivational nexus.

(Of course, none of the preceding considerations have displaced the all too familiar logical wedge – the neo-classical planner is not, *ex hypothesi*, precluded from devising measures of external control which would induce the desires themselves of the individual agents. Moreover, as we have argued in Chapter 13, sections 4 and 5, insofar as producers substantively engineer the pattern of consumer wants, the basic normative "frame" of neo-classical economics is put at risk. For the cardinal principle that competitive market processes are directed towards the optimal provision of individual consumer satisfaction is rendered problematic at best.)

We should observe that the harmonizing of theoretical analysis and political practice extends to other areas of neo-classical theory-construction than appears in our case-study of consumption. In general, whether theorizing about consumption, production or distribution, the neo-classical economist must devise measures of political control which are compatible with the moral ideals governing social relations in his institutional environment. But these controls and the economic actions he wishes to see included in social behaviour must be directed towards proposed goals that are consistent with the overarching ends of his society in general. But an incompatibility would ensue under those conditions wherein the moral criteria employed in the selection of economic goals diverged from the moral standards underpinning the basic ends of the actual social system. And this problem is compounded by the fact that such standards may be in contention or flux within the prevailing social order. Surely, for instance, the volatile conflict between those on the current scene who advocate an economic end consisting in a radical redistribution of wealth, and those who defend the *status quo* on this issue, bears ominous witness to an underlying conflict as to whether a more egalitarian form of distributive justice should displace individualistic liberty at the apex of the hierarchy of moral principles governing social relations in contemporary industrialized communities. In this context, neo-classical theory-construction should be placed in suspended animation. For the choice of economic goals must be predicated on a prior resolution of a classic ethical dilemma facing the general public – that of choosing between the moral principles themselves, with the ensuing requirement to *rank* the principles.

4. An Empiricist Rejoinder

We established in Chapter 5, section 4, that a prescriptive element recommending the moral excellence of a particular kind of rational agent underlay Alfred Marshall's approach to his classical construction of the theory of consumer behaviour. Marshall's work, then, provides perhaps the most telling substantiation of the regulative origin of CCT in normative theory-construction. Nevertheless, we may expect the short way with Marshall's way will appeal to proponents of the "official" methodology: Dismiss the ethical presuppositions of his economic theory as so much pseudo-scientific obfuscation of whatever sound "factual content" and, therefore, genuine scientific knowledge of economic behaviour Marshall's theory does offer.

However, it seems to me that this conventional empiricist response is an ill-advised one. For let us grant that Marshall's theorizing is informed and regulated by moral commitments. And we may further agree that his economic man is conceived independently of whether his postulated behaviour is also instantiated by that of actual agents. However, Marshall's theory is not thereby precluded from having "empirical import". For the procedure outlined above for converting normative theories into descriptively true ones could, in principle be applied to his theory. In this way, the statements of Marshall's economics concerning the behaviour of *homo economicus* would no longer be relegated to the status of ethical recommendation alone, but would also become empirically true of actual behaviour. Although remaining an ideal in a prescriptive sense, neo-classical economic man would lose his ideality in an ontological sense.[21] Moreover, as noted above,[22] it is my view that the neo-classical economists working within the tradition of Marshallian economics have already taken advantage of these measures in order to assist in the (approximate) social realization of the ideal system of behaviour represented by CCT.

5. Empiricism or Post-Empiricism?

In the preceding sections we have outlined what we may call a "liberalized" empiricism as characterizing the methodology of neo-classical choice theory. Although moral commitments do play a systemic, pragmatic role in the satisfaction of the truth-conditions for the theory, the ultimate structure of theoretical explanation and the confirmation of explanatory hypotheses can be accommodated within an empiricist methodology. From this perspective, however, we must part company with the work of writers on economic methodology who have aligned themselves with what has sometimes been called the "post-empiricist" theory of scientific method – the work of Hargreaves Heap provides a recent case in point.[23]

Building on the theses of such philosophers and historians of science as Quine, Feyerabend, Lakatos, and Kuhn,[24] the post-empiricist viewpoint challenges the claim of traditional empiricist methodology that one can choose between competing scientific theories on the basis of their comparative consistency with the empirical evidence of "theory-neutral", publicly observable "facts". In now familiar rebuttals, post-empiricists have argued against such a straightforward selection of theory *via* empirical test. In particular, two rival theories might each be consistent with the relevant sensory data (the "underdetermination of theories by data"), and scientists must use the logically primitive concepts of a theory to identify and describe the kinds of observations that are to count in testing the truth-claims of the theory (the "theory-ladenness of observations"). Accordingly, it is further argued that the prospects for any clear "objectivity" for scientific knowledge is put at risk: competing basic theories might simply be incommensurable with respect to their truth-value. Admittedly, economists are typically reluctant fellow travellers with post-empiricists. In appreciating that a wholesale acceptance of post-empiricist conclusions may lead to an arbitrary epistemic relativism where "anything goes" in the choice of scientific theories, Hargreaves Heap, for instance, wisely points out that empirical evidence can still count against those theories the application of which leads us to act upon a theory-independent world in ineffective ways. But such evidence need not prove uniquely decisive – it need not single out one theory as the sole effective master of nature in a particular domain.[25]

As we have been intent on developing our own general methodology for economics, it will serve the purposes of clarity to let it stand primarily on its own claims rather than engage in an elaborate response to the specific theses of Quine/Kuhn/Lakatos, *et al*. However, it will further elucidate our "liberalized empiricism" to take a specific explanatory context that is especially challenging for empiricist principles. Let us examine, then, an admittedly "hard case" for empiricist methodology: the important issue we introduced in Chapter 12, section 4, of the relation between "multiple selves", "pre-commitment" and intertemporal preference changes.

Now, on the basis of our own general perspective, we may agree with Hargreaves Heap that the underlying "conceptual scheme" of orthodox consumer theory restricts us to conceptualizing our observations of consumer behaviour as the maximization of the satisfaction of an ordered preference for goods by an individual who is himself conceived as merely an ordered set of preferences.[26] But, then, the behaviour of an individual who, in the expectation that his preference ordering will change from time t to t+n, "precommits" himself for t+n to the earlier ordering at t, provides a serious anomaly for CCT. In illustration, we may usefully modify and adapt our earlier examination on pages 215-17 above of the "incontinent" consumer who expects that he will impulsively expend his current income on commodities of immediate gratification. To simplify, let us suppose that he correctly expects at time t that his strongest preference, A, at time t+n will be to spend his disposable income on the "transient luxury" of an all-night "bender" with his buddies at the local pub, whereas his more considered preference at t is that his strongest preference at t+n be B – to allocate financial resources to home improvements. Accordingly, upon reasoned reflection at t, he precommits himself for t+n to his preference-ordering at t by an unbreakable arrangement with the pub bartender not to serve him at t+n.

Is, as Hargreaves Heap implies, an empiricist methodology incapable of providing an adequate explanation of such phenomena of "self-command" as pre-commitment?[27] Not in the final analysis. But conventional or received empiricist doctrine will certainly obstruct our understanding of such a conclusion. Let me elucidate a posture of "synthesis".

At first sight, it appears that even conventional empiricist methods of enquiry could resolve the explanatory problem – viz., that empirical predictions from a theory's hypotheses are falsified by observational evidence requiring a rejection or revision of the hypotheses. Hence, insofar as CCT identifies the consumer, S, with an ordered set of preferences, and his strongest preference at t+n is A, CCT's prediction of expenditure on A will be falsified by allocation of income to B. Moreover, the occurrence of the latter, but not the former, action at t+n is a publicly observable event that may, in standard empiricist fashion, lead the economist to consider a modification of CCT for the relevant circumstances.

On the other hand, other conventional empiricist principles would themselves frustrate the deployment of empiricist procedures of testing and revising the theory on the basis of observational findings. Most particularly, against received empiricist wisdom, the neo-classical theorist must come to recognize and accept that deeply entrenched "background assumptions" of a normative/ethical sort are internal to choice theory. To take up implications of our comments in Chapter 12, section 4, he must be prepared to acknowledge that an explanation/prediction of such phenomena as pre-commitment would require an inclusion of considerations of expressive rationality within CCT in rejecting a background assumption of exclusively instrumental rationality. And with such an inclusion would come a normatively richer conception of the individual agent as also comprising a reflective capacity capable of assessing the immediate preference orderings of his anticipated "selves" at different time periods. But with this fuller conception of human agency in economic affairs would also come a displacement of the hegemony of the Utilitarian moral calculus presupposed by CCT through the introduction of the explanatory relevance of moral autonomy for rational choice. Not only would a rational individual seek to maximize the satis-faction of his desires for materials goods in his consumer practices; he would also seek to be self-determining in his forms of choice, to undertake patterns of consumption that were expressive of the self he reflectively willed to be, not the lesser self moved impulsively by submission to external stimuli – such as by the attraction of a prolonged "bender".

On a related matter of methodology, the preceding practices of self-directed choice reveal the strain on the traditional empiricist perspective of the fact that the explananda for social scientists are provided by a world that social actors in part create. Such a perspective finds "natural objects" that are, in this view, encountered rather than constructed, more tractable to theoretical understanding. However, in being so disposed, it typically misses or under-plays the theory-practice nexus of economic science. And such an oversight arrests a full understanding of an important domain of social phenomena. For instance, the exhibition of the capability for reflective self-direction characteristic of expressive rationality is not guaranteed by innate dispositions of human beings. The shared conventions and institutions of a particular economic order will foster or suppress this dimension of humanity. And among the institutional determinants of the fruition or decay of this capability will be the social use of economic theories of rational choice. Customary empiricist inquiry that views social scientific theory-construction and observational validation as mutually exclusive enterprises will, no doubt, be inattentive to such a methodological symbiosis.

However, at the final level of the theoretical explanation of "self-binding" policies and expressive behaviour, basic empiricist canons reassert themselves. To begin with, it will be the impetus of "experimental control" itself that forces the attention of the conventional empiricist to address the reality and significance of the theory-practice link. For the predicted observations of his theories will often fail to materialize until the economist leaves room in the network of his theoretical hypotheses for reference to the manner in which the use of a theory itself can modify the behaviour of the subjects under investigation. Moreover, the explanatory model of such reference would also take an essentially empiricist form. More specifically, in order to account for economic behaviour that was induced or prevented through the application of, for example, neo-classical choice theory, an economist would need recourse to empirical laws connecting institutional causes to economic motivations – in this case, where the institutional determinants are, it must be granted, of an "incestuous" or self-referential character: i.e., the application of neo-classical theory itself to actual human affairs.

To summarize: By including normative assumptions of a moral kind within the corpus of the theory, and in invoking a theory-practice link in the explanation of social phenomena, our conception of the methodology of CCT would certainly disturb the complacency of a conventional empiricist. But we need not abandon salvageable and important traditions of empiricist epistemology by joining the rather fuzzy ranks of "post empiricists". Rather, we may recognize that, at the most fundamental level of the method of inquiry, neo-classical theory-construction still follows classical empiricist principles in ordering and understanding choice behaviour through subsumption under causal laws, and in insisting that all such understanding remain subject to "empiricist control" – i.e., the testimony of our shared experience. In short, neo-classical economists may remain consistent empiricists once they acknowledge a "liberalized" (or liberated?) version of traditional empiricist rules.

In a general vein, I suggest that our account in this chapter of the transition of economics conceived as a normative system into an empirical science is an illuminating way to read the historical development of most of economic theory, and to understand the relationship of such theory to concrete social practice or "forms of life". Moreover, an appreciation of certain structural features of economic theory at various "conceptual phases" of this development goes a long way, in my opinion, towards a final laying bare of the overall "logical structure" or method of enquiry of economic science in general. In the next chapter, I will attempt, therefore, to sketch a "rational reconstruction" of these phases.

Chapter 15

Neo-classical Economics and Scientific Utopias

Essentially, it seems to me that the main current in the method of construction of historically dominant economic theories or "paradigms"[1] is typified by the formulation of what might be called *scientific utopias*. Since the concept of utopia is held in general disrepute in both contemporary philosophical and scientific investigation, it will be necessary to carefully define the special meaning I am ascribing to "scientific utopia" in the hope of defusing whatever derogatory emotive force use of the concept might immediately arouse. It should be mentioned at the outset, furthermore, that I suspect that most orthodox economists would not agree to this characterization of the methodology of their inherited "paradigms". In exemplifying the construction of a scientific utopia we will again appeal to the theory of rational choice with respect to consumer behaviour (CCT), although I would suggest that the method of inquiry depicted would apply, *mutatis mutandis*, to the theory-construction undertaken for most overarching economic theories. But let me begin by clarifying in what sense I am claiming that the construction of CCT, at least initially[2] and primarily, was tantamount to the construction of a theory representing a "utopia".

1. Scientific Utopias and the Theory of Choice

As understood in ordinary language, a utopian item is characterized by two defining features both of which are, in *different* philosophical senses, "ideal". That is, the object or system so designated is:

a) ontologically ideal – it is imaginary or fictitious, existing only as a mental construct rather than literally in the spatio-temporal world, and

b) normatively ideal – it is a highly valuable or eminently good object of its kind, sometimes even a perfect such and such, exemplifying all the "good-making" characteristics of the particular class to which it belongs.

Given these defining features of our ordinary concept of utopia, it can be seen that, when taken in its original construction in the theoretical systems of Jevons and Marshall, CCT designates just such a utopia in those circumstances where the object called "utopian" is a proposed system of behaviour. In support of this conclusion, consider again axioms A_1-A_4 in the context of the (temporally) original construction of CCT which we shall label CCT_0.

Suppose further that we understand A_1-A_4 of CCT_0 under a descriptive interpretation as intending to report economic behaviour – that all consumers prefer more of any available commodity, that they uniformly order their preferences in a complete and transitive fashion, etc. Under this construal of the axioms it is clear that CCT_0 is at least utopian in sense a) above, since its primitive postulates are not literally true of the behaviour of actual consumers, but only of *homo economicus*, the ideally rational consumer, whose virtually omniscient cognitive abilities and complete affective consistency constitute extreme conditions which are beyond the capacity of real agents to fully exemplify. Of course, in this sense, we have seen that certain physical theories, such as those concerning ideal gases, could also be classified as utopian since they too include generalizations purporting to be true under conditions which are not realizable by actual phenomena. In other words, if sense a) were the sole criterion, any theoretical *idealization* of natural or social science would be correctly called utopian in that empirical situations only approximate, but never completely instantiate, the extreme conditions mentioned in the ideal theory.

Only by including the second criterion is it possible to demarcate genuine social scientific utopias from scientific idealizations generally. Such utopias, then, besides being ontologically ideal are also normatively so – they define a system of behaviour expressing a set of moral imperatives prescribing how agents acting within such a system ought to behave. However, there is typically a systemic connection between the two senses of ideality in constructed utopias. For frequently, one of the chief sources of the fictitious character of the construct is that real-life agents do not regularly behave as the utopia recommends they should.

Now, it can also be observed that CCT_0 satisfies this requirement of normative ideality for utopias. For CCT_0, in league with what we have claimed to be the case for its present-day successor – CCT – has an alternate normative construal wherein descriptive axioms A_1-A_4 are to be re-read as basic rules of rationality R_1-R_4 – that is, that the perfectly rational consumer *ought* to prefer more of any available commodity, *ought* to order his preferences in a complete and transitive fashion, etc. Moreover, it has been part of the burden of this study to reveal that R_1-R_4 do not, as might appear on the surface, *only* specify rules of instrumental value or hypothetical imperatives, and, in this way, preserve the scientific value-neutrality of CCT_0 (or CCT). On the contrary, we have argued that it has been and continues to be a misreading of the neo-classical theory of choice to interpret it as taking the maximization of utility as a *given* end which consumers invariably pursue, and merely delineating the means, articulated in rules R_1-R_4, which, if followed, will, as a matter of verifiable empirical fact, attain the desired end. Rather, we have established that R_1-R_4 presuppose *bona fide* moral imperatives.

To rehearse, we have shown in Chapter 5 that the neo-classical understanding of non-satiation rule R_2 testifies to the fact that the *form* of maximization expressed by this rule itself involves a moral choice of a Benthamite Utilitarian variety requiring an aggrandizing, "expansionist" pursuit of satisfaction prompted by ever increasing desires for material commodities. Such a choice is to be taken in lieu of a "contractionist" Stoic alternative directing one to curb such desires, with the aim of thus diminishing the likelihood of finding oneself thwarted or frustrated in the pursuit of one's material satisfaction. And in Chapter 5 we also elucidated the manner in which R_3 (or R_1 and R_4)[3] demand an ethical commitment to the (implied) family of virtues comprised of self-restraint, deliberativeness, etc. Indeed, we have suggested that the ultimate aim of the classical construction of the theory of choice (i.e., CCT_0) in the work of Marshall was to offer the abstract design of an ethical system whose concrete social realization would require just such excellence of moral character on the part of agents functioning successfully within it.

In sum, then, CCT_0 (and CCT) designates a system of behaviour that clearly exhibits the defining properties of a (social) utopia. Not only is the behaviour articulated in the theory – that of *homo economicus* – not precisely actualizable, but the actions ascribed to this rational agent express a systematic point of view of prudential and moral excellence.

2. An Objection: Reporting and Prescribing Values

At this point, it is imperative to focus more directly on a central question. Economic methodologists adhering to the "official view" might object to our account of the presupposition of ethical value-judgments in CCT on the grounds that we have confused two different kinds of value-judgment inclusion within economic science, one of which is methodologically legitimate, the other not. It is true, the objection might concede, that the propositions of the theory of consumer choice make at least implicit reference to valuations; but these references are nothing over and above reports or *descriptions* of the pattern and kind of valuations which actual consumers are observed to make as the basis for deciding on the comparative desirability of alternative action-choices.[4] Granted, it is of the essence of concrete consumer choices that they imply subscription to values, probably even moral ones, on the part of the agents making the choices. But these valuations belong to the category of reportable "facts", to be taken as "data" by the theorist, as much as any other element in the motivational make-up of the subjects being investigated. Consequently, to endorse *this* sort of incorporation of value-judgment in the construction of CCT is simply to endorse the construction of empirically true scientific theories – hardly an heretical stance. (Let us call the theorist's descriptions of the valuations of the subject under scrutiny *reportive* value-judgments.)

On the other hand, the objection continues, this methodologically impeccable position does not justify, and should not be confused with, the intrusion into the content of CCT of the economic scientist's *own* value-judgments concerning the intrinsic moral worth of alternative consumption patterns. Following pertinent canons of logical empiricism, it is maintained that the second kind of value-judgment inclusion is methodologically untenable. By incorporating the theorist's own ethical approval of certain kinds of consumer activity, it illicitly introduces a "subjective bias" into a form of inquiry which, in claiming scientific "objectivity", should keep to a dispassionate description and explanation of the kind of consumption which *does* occur. Only statements serving the latter function are empirically testable, and, therefore, admissible into the corpus of scientific theory. Moreover, the official view concludes, not only is it mandatory that CCT preserve its value-neutrality in this way, but, as a matter of fact, it *does* so – the propositions of CCT state *de facto* regularities in the motivations and behaviour of actual consumers and have not been formulated as expressions of the value attitudes of the economists constructing or accepting the theory.[5] (Let us call those value-judgments included in a social scientific theory as expressions of the moral beliefs of the theorist himself *prescriptive* value-judgments.)

Variants of the preceding objection are commonplace. In reply, it should first be agreed that the *distinction* between the two forms of value-judgment inclusion in social scientific theorizing is a sound and often extremely useful one. However, some economic methodologists supporting the official view argue as if the soundness of the distinction *alone guarantees* both a) the existence of value-neutrality, so understood, in the construction of CCT and b) the requirement of always keeping CCT, no matter what the theoretical aim, within the bounds of such value-neutrality.[6] But without the addition of further premises, the distinction itself entails neither a) or b). Moreover, as I see it, the kind of additional premises required to license the inference to a) or b) cannot themselves be justified with respect to the method of inquiry either actually employed (in the case of a) or demanded (in the case of b) for CCT.

Consider first the case of a). What further considerations might be invoked by the official view in order to provide reasons for believing the claim that only the value commitments of the subjects under study, not the neo-classical theorists conducting the study, are included with CCT? One kind of reason might be supplied by evidence revealing that the complex of moral values ascribed to economic agents in CCT were identified by inductive generalization from empirical surveys of the value-subscriptions of real consumers. Unfortunately two factors count decisively against the provision of such evidence.

To begin with, there is simply no documentation of any systematic observations of the value-commitments in the purchasing behaviour of consumers prior to the original formulation of the theory of choice (CCT_o) in the latter part of the nineteenth century. More importantly, the more recent surveys of consumer behaviour which *have* been undertaken do not offer an acceptable observational base from which to inductively infer the hypotheses of CCT construed as universal empirical laws reporting unexceptional uniformities in the behaviour of actual consumers;[7] and significantly, one of the main reasons for the recalcitrance of the observational data is that many consumers can be observed *not* to subscribe to the value commitments implied by CCT. For instance, some consumers exhibit "erratic" and inconsistent purchasing behaviour in terms of the empirical implications of CCT (that is their behaviour manifests contravention of transitivity axiom A_3). And further empirical inquiry reveals that such erratic consumption is often determined by subscription to a different set of values than those implicit in A_3; for they are found to prize an element of immediacy, spontaneity and random variability in human desires in rejection of the overriding worth of an all-pervasive, methodical calculatedness of motivation. Or again, "abstemious" consumer activity, manifesting inconsistency with non-satiation axiom A_2, does not go unobserved – some consumers, not preferring more of obtainable goods, forebear further purchases of available commodities, even when they can afford them. And sometimes it is found that the cause of such abstention resides in the positive valuation of an ascetic contraction of desires for material goods, in rejection of the "growth ethic"

266

underwriting behaviour in conformity with A_2 – that is, in refusing to endorse the desirability of constantly aggrandizing the possession of personal commodities.

Of course, it is open to proponents of the official view to retort that "inductivism" offers a misleading account of scientific method in the first place. They might argue that scientific laws are not validated through inductive generalization from the observation of individual instances. Rather, certain general hypotheses are first postulated and *then* subjected to observational test in the form of attempting to falsify the hypotheses on the basis of the perceivable evidence.[8] Hence, there was and is no methodological need to systematically survey the value attitudes of actual consumers before describing them in the hypotheses of CCT. One need only include such attitudes as part of the entire postulated empirical content of these hypotheses and then await the testimony of experiential findings.

However, even granting the validity of this criticism of inductivist methods, it is plain that orthodox methodologists cannot use it to salvage their argument that CCT only records the value-judgments of the consumers being investigated – i.e., only includes reportive value-judgments. For, as mentioned above, empirical evidence attests that actual consumers do not espouse the values, with the necessary regularity, which CCT implies they do. But in this case, the "postulational" method would also require that the hypotheses, A_1-A_4, (allegedly) reporting such valuations, be rejected or at least revised. However, neo-classical economists have preserved the standard formulation of the basic hypotheses of CCT, in the form of A_1-A_4, despite the apparently falsifying testimony of observational test.

We may conclude, then, that orthodox methodologists have not offered sufficient reason to justify their claim that neo-classical economists *qua* scientists have safeguarded their value-neutrality by not introducing their own value-judgments into the composition of CCT, but have merely made (implicit) reference to the value-judgments of actual consumers whose behaviour they are seeking to describe and explain. They have not, that is, justified a claim to the inclusion of reportive, but exclusion of prescriptive value-judgments. In other words, we have undermined their defence of a) above. And yet, their defence was, in any case, needless. For it seems to me that positive reasons can be provided to discredit b) – the indefeasible imperative of always preserving complete value-neutrality on the part of all economists responsible for the construction or use of CCT. Support for my view can be introduced by a further examination and legitimation of our conception of CCT as a scientific utopia.

3. Testing an Economic Utopia

We might begin, here, by removing the derogatory emotive connotation customarily surrounding the use of the term "utopia". The primary reason for the deprecatory reaction to suggested utopias is a widespread belief that, almost by definition, utopias are hopelessly impracticable proposals. Only day-dreamers, satisfied with the aesthetic elegance of the products of their all too fertile imaginations, would be concerned to construct (social) utopias. No social scientist, whose limited mandate *qua* scientist is to record and explain actual human affairs, however imperfect, or, at most, to advise social planners of the empirically possible alternative mechanisms for attaining social goals, has any business outlining utopias. For utopian designs i) display an incorrigible impracticality since they are empirically impossible to realise, and (ii) by incorporating ethical proposals of intrinsically worthwhile social ends, compromise the value-neutrality of the (social) scientist.

Let me, in the context of CCT, begin by dealing with charge i). *Prima facie* it is not without force. For, as a first approximation, it could be claimed that a requirement of what we might call the pragmatic legitimacy of a utopian (social) construct is that the system of behaviour it describes be empirically realizable, and we have already taken note of the fact that CCT fails this condition. But then, in concert with other utopian constructs, CCT formulates a theoretical idealization and, as we observed in our discussion of Simon's satisficing model, the requirement that idealized theories be amenable to (exact) empirical actualization is an excessive one. We may recognize this for the present context by translating the issue of the realizability of utopias into the explanatory status of idealized scientific theories, and reminding ourselves of certain conditions of adequacy for scientific explanation as adapted for the special case of theoretical idealizations.[9] Again, we need only insist that the extreme conditions reported by the statements of defensible scientific idealizations can be empirically approximated, and that whenever such approximation has actually occurred, the statements have been confirmed to the relevant extent.

But herein lies the crux of one difficulty for CCT *qua* social utopia. For it might be argued that the demands put on the reasoning ability and temperamental consistency of the agents who would act as CCT predicts are so severely impracticable as to make it empirically impossible for real consumers to even *approximate* the behaviour of their ideal counterparts in CCT. Consequently, the postulates of CCT would fail to satisfy even the modified R_4 criterion of "factual correctness" for the explanatory adequacy of scientific idealizations.[10] Or, removing the issue from the context of theoretical explanation and translating it back into terms of concrete social planning, since the system of behaviour or social utopia designated by CCT is so impracticable as to be not even approximately realizable, then CCT does not fulfill our requirement for the pragmatic legitimacy of utopian social constructions, even when the condition is liberalized to countenance approximative situations.

This argument cannot, however, be sustained. Let me defend my contention by drawing together some implications of our previous analyses, especially as they invoke the manner in which economists can acquire "verifications" for their value-laden theories by influencing the design of social policies. We might formulate the question of concern at this point as whether or not the social utopia represented by CCT can be elevated to the status of what we have called a *scientific* utopia, a system of behaviour that would not merit the dismissive attitude directed towards utopias in general. Our question resolves into ascertaining whether the system of behaviour represented by CCT can meet two individually necessary and jointly sufficient conditions or tests, U_1 and U_2, for any such system to be classified as a scientific utopia. In fact, we are already in the process of determining whether the utopian system formulated by CCT passes the first test, U_1 – namely, whether the empirical actualization of the utopian system can at least be approximated. The second, more intractable test, U_2, will be introduced and examined below.

As a prefatory note, it should be remarked that the problematic *ontological* ideality of CCT, the one which genuinely threatens the realization of the utopia the theory designates, is due more to the unbreachable affective *cum* moral consistency of *homo economicus*, than to his cognitive omniscience. For CCT can be modified further than (subjective) expective utility theory, SET, to formulate theories of rational choice for uncertain situations where not even significant probabilities can be assigned to the consequences of the available choices, which theories lessen the demands on the computational capacities of rational economic men to bring them more in line with the abilities of real-life agents.[11] It is rather the unfaltering acquisitiveness and "firmness of character" distinguishing *homo economicus* that, *prima facie*, appears to preclude the actualization of the utopia to which he belongs. For, it can justifiably be claimed, there is no universal prizing by actual consumers of the moral virtues expressed by such dispositions; but even if there were, it may be contended that such imperfect mortals would not be able to even approximate the perfect consistency with which *homo economicus* adheres to such ideals.

But such pessimism is premature. Consider again the normative rendering of the postulates of the original CCT_0 as R_1-R_4, and the moral imperatives concerning the "growth ethic" and impulse control underpinning these rules. Consider further that, within a concrete social system, a preponderant majority of economic agents do not follow these rules due to the fact that they do not subscribe to the ethical values presupposed by the rules, and where the endorsement of these values is alleged, within CCT_0, to be the ultimate justification for acting in accordance with R_1-R_4. Thus since R_1-R_4 are not generally followed, the postulates of CCT_0, under their factual interpretation as A_1-A_4, would be descriptively false. In other words, the system of behaviour represented by CCT_0 would constitute a utopia – an ideally moral, but fictional realm.

Given the preceding considerations, we may say that A_1-A_4 of CCT_0 report behaviour which *does* "occur" only in an imaginary "word" or system of economic behaviour, but they also prescribe behaviour *which ought to be occurring* in the actual world – that is, A_1-A_4 of CCT_0 presuppose a normative reading as rules R_1-R_4 for the behaviour of actual agents. Accordingly, if we were to put the analysis into hypothetical terms, we could say that if R_1-R_4 of CCT_0 *were* consistently followed by actual consumers, then A_1-A_4 of CCT *would be* descriptively true.

But the utopian world need not remain the final one. For a procedure for intentionally *altering* the *de facto* economic behaviour of actual society so that it begins to approach and finally approximate the system of actions defining the utopia is available. I refer again to the means, discussed in Chapter 14, which the economist has at his disposal for converting his theory, originally conceived as a normative system of behavioural rules, into a descriptively true representation of human behaviour. The basic intent of this mechanism, it will be recalled, is to induce agents to subscribe to the ethical values underwriting the rules. For submission to such values would *ipso facto* imply a disposition to follow the rules expressing the values. We noted, furthermore, that the medium of such inducement lay in the economic theorist's causal influence on the design and implementation of whatever institutional constraints on human behaviour would motivate an agent to act in accordance with these moral values. And, finally, to the extent that the economist was successful in thus transforming his a priori and ideally normative theory into social practice, we concluded that the basic rules defining the original normative system could be understood as being converted into the logically primitive and true hypotheses of a descriptive science.

In the case of CCT_0, the operation of the preceding mechanism would take the form of the conversion of the rules of consumer rationality R_1-R_4 into factually true hypotheses of consumer behaviour A_1-A_4. In this way, we might say that the reasons presupposed by the axioms of CCT_0 would become the causes of consumer behaviour. Of course, the application of the mechanism would, in all probability, never be completely successful. Consequently, A_1-A_4 would eventuate in an idealized theory wherein concrete economic phenomena approximated, but never fully exemplified, the extreme conditions of the theory. But if such a transformation of CCT_0 were possible, then the social system articulated by CCT would meet our first text U_1 for a (social) utopia to be classified as scientific. For the procedures for transforming a normative social theory into an empirically true social science has spelled out precisely the manner in which the realization of a utopian social system can be approximated.

But, as mentioned in Chapter 14,[12] there is evidence to confirm that the specific form of this mechanism which we have outlined for the case of CCT_0 *has already been in extensive and effective operation.* And there is no reason to believe that these conversion procedures could not continue to be successfully applied to CCT. *A fortiori,* real economic agents could act in accordance with R_1-R_4, *at least to an approximate degree.* In upshot, therefore, we may conclude that CCT does satisfy test U_1 for a scientific utopia.

Other aspects of our analysis of the philosophical foundations of CCT agree well with this conclusion. For instance, we have argued above[13] that value prescriptions or normative principles require an empirical sanction in terms of a motivational backing, or else they are unwarranted. In particular, thus, unless real-life consumers can be moved to follow rules R_1-R_4, then CCT, conceived as a normative system, would simply be *inapplicable* to actual behaviour. *A fortiori,* unless such agents can be provided with a motivating reason which justifies subscribing to the moral ideals presupposed by R_1-R_4, then CCT would not be vindicated as a normative system. Translated into the context of our present problem, the measures taken to empirically approximate CCT *qua* social utopia must affect the motivational structure of consumers to succeed in their intention.

However, it is to be remembered that an appeal to such motivational grounds *is* included in the assumptions of CCT. In an abstract, general vein it is found in the "maximization of utility" which the theory asserts rational consumers who submit to rules R_1-R_4 can expect. More concretely, it is found in the physical gratification, elevated self-image, social prestige, etc., such utility is anticipated by consumers to encompass. And economists themselves may promote the implementation of such motivational influences by participating in the creation of social conventions which predispose consumers to be moved by these very considerations of sensual pleasure, self-image, prestige, etc.

The fact that the social utopia represented by CCT is capable of empirical approximation may provide a rationale, furthermore, for the historical reluctance of economists to *abandon* CCT_o even though the value-judgments implicitly affirmed by the original theory did not correspond, with the requisite uniformity, to the value-judgments endorsed by actual consumers. For a divergence between the content of a defensible utopian theory and empirical phenomena need not be considered *as final*. By assisting in the societal management of the motivations of agents to subscribe to the value-system implicit in CCT_o, economists were equipped to help alter the *de facto* pattern of valuations of actual consumers to bring it into accord with that of CCT_o and thereby help *cause* economic phenomena to correspond to the implications of the theory's hypotheses.

Needless to say, contemporary economists who promote the "official view" of economic methodology would not admit to the preceding rationale for the retention of CCT_o in the face of such an incongruity between theory and observations, as the standard empiricist canons of scientific method to which such economists subscribe would preclude such an admission. On the contrary, since these very canons demand the rejection or revision of theories subject to such an incongruity, the continued retention of CCT_o despite a poor "theory-data" fit constitutes a theoretical anomaly for defenders of the official view, an anomaly which they have often camouflaged by illicit appeals to *ceteris paribus* clauses for idealized hypotheses.[14] Our investigation, however, enables us to see that the anomaly is only an apparent one. For we are now in a position to conclude that, with respect to the validation of utopian theories such as CCT, a suitable test is not to ascertain whether the theory is empirically true *tout court*; rather, the appropriate test is to determine whether or not such truth can be concretely *constructed* or (approximately) generated through socio-political practice.

This is not, however, the only test. For we have still to introduce the nature of the second necessary condition or test (U_2) towards legitimizing CCT as a scientific utopia. Such a test arises in response to another prevalent objection to allowing any utopian theory to be classified as scientific. And replying to this objection is a more perplexing task.

This charge is of the first importance. Science, it is often claimed, comprises a body of "objective" knowledge. But it is the hallmark of such objectivity

272

that there is a *rational* way for informed inquirers to reach agreement as to which propositions to admit into the scientific corpus – namely, those statements whose truth-claims adhere to the standard of logical consistency and/or can withstand the testimony of observational evidence. In the case of ethical judgments, the objection continues, there is no rational method, either by recourse to formal reasoning or factual observation, for securing general agreement as to which judgments can be deemed "true" or correct. Hence, moral judgments lack the necessary objectivity or "inter-subjective validity" to be included in the body of science. But utopian theories, by definition, incorporate just such moral judgments. Hence, such theories cannot be justifiably classified as scientific. Let it be granted, furthermore, that CCT belongs to the category of utopian theories. *A fortiori*, it is illegitimate to characterize CCT as formulating a *scientific* utopia.

The preceding argument penetrates to the heart of the problem of the final validation of CCT. But neither the proponents of the doctrine of the "value-neutrality" of economic science, or its critics, would want to challenge the premise demanding a rational decision-procedure for the acceptance of scientific propositions. The critical premise, rather, is the one which denies such rationality and, thus, objectivity to moral judgments. Understandably, it has been primarily the acceptance of this premise which has prompted "orthodox" economists to persistently argue that theories such as CCT are value-free. For along with the general scientific methodology formulated by logical empiricism, such economists have also endorsed the non-rational status of moral judgments promulgated by this philosophical school.[15] Accordingly, intent on justifying their belief that CCT belongs to objective science, supporters of the "official view" of economic methodology have felt it incumbent upon themselves to rebut an interpretation of CCT as presupposing ethical claims. (Of course, many of those who *have* argued that certain economic theories, like CCT, *are* (ethically) "value-laden" have done so with the express intention of discrediting the objectivity of economics. For they too have upheld the premise that, as moral judgments cannot be validated by rational procedures, they are wanting in objectivity.)

It is my belief, however, that even though CCT incorporates moral judgments, the question of its objectivity remains an open one. For it seems to me that the general thesis from which a denial of its objectivity is inferred – namely, the lack of a rational method for assessing the validity of competing moral claims – is an ill-founded one. Thus, two final problems, perhaps the most perplexing of all, remain for any complete investigation of the philosophical foundations of CCT:

a) the identification (if such can be found) of adequate grounds for maintaining that there exists a rational method of validating ethical value-judgments, and

b) assessing in the light of a) whether the ethical judgments presupposed by CCT *are* sound ones.

If these questions can be answered in the affirmative, we may conclude that CCT satisfies the final test, U_2, for the legitimation of a utopian theory as a scientific one – viz., that its moral presuppositions are rationally justified ones.

Before turning to these imposing questions an important related issue, concerning the *aims* of CCT as an instance of rational inquiry, needs to be elucidated.

It must be admitted that if the aims of CCT, or any social scientific theory, are *circumscribed* by those of natural science – i.e., the description, explanation and prediction of *de facto* phenomena – then only reportive, *not* prescriptive, value-judgments are admissible as part of the "cognitive content" of the theory. For, given these aims, it logically follows that only the values to which *actual* agents themselves subscribe function as elements in the motives or determinants of the behaviour of the subjects under study. Consequently, the inclusion of the theorist's own ethical commitments *would* introduce a subjective bias that could only impede the professed aims of explaining and predicting actual behaviour. Nor, therefore, would there be any *need* for the social scientist *qua* scientist to ascertain the possibility of a rational decision-procedure for prescriptive value-judgments, as the limits put on the objectives of a genuine science would render such a task irrelevant. Most importantly, it would follow that the construction of a utopian theory, with the theorist's aim to articulate a system of behaviour satisfying certain ideals of moral excellence, would be out of place in responsible scientific theorizing.

But an obvious question arises at this point – even though it is seldom asked. *Are* there compelling reasons for so limiting the aims of legitimate scientific inquiry? Why should the aims of social science *not* range beyond those of natural science? In particular, *why* must the scientist *qua* scientist eschew an objective of designing a utopian system of behaviour with its commitment to affirming standards of morally excellent conduct? No doubt, such a prohibition, under its many variants, is held to be a reasonable one by the consensus of contemporary methodologists as shown by their numerous disclaimers against extending the scope of the social sciences to encompass the espousal of "ultimate goals", "final ends", "intrinsic values", "ethical ideals", "categorical moral imperatives", and other members of the same family of value-judgments. Again, it is clear that the reasons for their reluctance to enlarge the objectives of social scientific inquiry to include the assertion of this type of normative claim centre around a suspicion or conviction that such claims are not decidable by rational means. Whether their reasons are convincing ones, whether, that is, there is no rational method available for investigators to justify fundamental moral judgments, is a question, therefore, to which we must seek a reply in the following chapter.

Chapter 16

Neo-classical Economics and the
Rational Justifiability of Moral Principles

The rational justifiability of basic ethical principles is a profoundly difficult problem and one that has been a perennial centre of philosophical controversy. A full-scale analysis of this issue would demand a discussion at least as long as this entire study. Accordingly, it will only be possible, in completing my examination of the theory of consumer choice (CCT), to provide some circumscribed and conditional comments about this vexed question, with particular concern for its bearing on the validation of neo-classical economics and this science's conception of human freedom.

1. Principles and Rational Decision-Procedures

In order to avoid misunderstanding, it should be stressed that the question at issue is that of the justifiability of *fundamental* moral judgments. More specifically, the category of judgment under investigation is not that of intermediate normative judgments such as "one ought to support one's children". Such a judgment, as we pointed out above,[1] can find justification or rational backing *via* deduction from a more general norm in conjunction with a factual premise – in the case of our example, perhaps from "one ought to preserve the social order" and "supporting one's children preserves the social order". But it is a familiar point that this kind of reasoning must, on pain of infinite regress, terminate in some basic, logically primitive ethical evaluation such as the Utilitarian principle that one ought to promote the general happiness. Thus, we might complete the preceding argument by adducing the major normative premise that one ought to perform actions conducive to general happiness and a minor factual premise claiming that preserving social order has general happiness as its causal consequence. Our concern, then, is to ascertain what kind of rational justification, if any, is available for such ultimate or basic moral evaluations, or what we might call *ethical principles*.

First of all, however, it is imperative that we more precisely explicate the meaning of "rational justification" for ethical principles. Given the main objective of this inquiry, that is, to ascertain the prospect of economics counting as a moral science, it will be appropriate to take the methods of empirical science as paradigmatic of a rational decision-procedure for demarcating warranted from unwarranted beliefs. In this context, it is evident that the essential aspect of the "rationality" or "objectivity" of such a procedure lies in its "intersubjective" or *impersonal authority*. In particular, thus, scientific methods do not leave it open for the individual investigator to accept or reject proposed hypotheses as *he* wills or chooses. With respect to formal matters, whether or not a set of hypotheses is mutually consistent, is not an issue to be resolved by invoking the variable attitudes of different individuals, but by a common appeal to *intersubjectively binding* inference rules. Similarly, the question of the empirical truth of candidate hypotheses is a matter to be settled by impersonal means, by the sense-perception of standard observers under normal conditions, and not by any arbitrary, subjective standard such as purely individual choice or preference. In this light, then, our question at hand concerns the possibility of specifying a defensible decision-procedure for demarcating warranted from unwarranted ethical principles in the form of a method that is:

a) *authoritative* – Its conclusions command (anyone's) assent; they are indefeasibly binding. In this sense the moral principles which are identified as warranted will exhibit the traditional mark of the "necessity" of such principles.

b) *impersonal* – Its conclusions are independent of the vagaries of purely private likings or choice, but apply to everyone impartially. In this sense, the moral principles which are validated by the procedure will bear the traditional mark of the "universality" of such principles.

2. Non-cognitivism and Moral Arguments

As recent meta-ethical analyses, particularly those expressed by "non-cognitivist" doctrines, have provided negative answers to our question, it will be useful to review and assess the grounds which a non-cognitivist account of moral judgments would claim precludes the provision of a rational way for deciding between competing moral principles. Perhaps the most influential of non-cognitivist theories have been the emotivism of A. J. Ayer[2] and C. L. Stevenson,[3] and the prescriptivism of R. M. Hare.[4] As Hare's views are the most sophisticated among these theories, and best exhibit a revealing connection with certain principles of neo-classical economics, we will concentrate on his prescriptivism as the most instructive representative of non-cognitivism.

As we have previously outlined the manner in which Hare resolves moral judgments into their descriptive and prescriptive meanings,[5] we need not again adumbrate Hare's understanding of the meaning of moral judgments. In any case, what is most germane for present purposes is Hare's treatment of *moral argumentation*.

In this context, we find that, *at least on the surface*, prescriptivism seeks, against the tendency of emotivism, to place moral arguments and discourse within the rational order. Thus, we observe Hare revitalizing the role of the practical syllogism in moral reasoning.[6] With the use of such a syllogism, we find the adducing of propositional reasons in support of propositional ethical conclusions and the deductive systematization of such argument. Such logical inference takes the form, mentioned above, of the entailment of an evaluative conclusion from the conjunction of an evaluative major premise and a factual minor one. But is there any kind of rational support the prescriptivist can offer for ultimate evaluative premises, those which, by definition, cannot be deduced from any logically prior evaluative premise – i.e., for our "first principles" of morals?

In reply to this question, prescriptivism is not completely silent. For Hare makes use of a variant of Kant's criterion of the universalizability of genuine moral principles.[7] If an agent is to rationally determine what fundamental moral principles should guide his actions he must a) choose which principles he can still commit himself to, after b) ascertaining the consequences of *anyone* acting according to these principles in similar circumstances, even if the agent himself should be on the receiving end of action he prescribes for everyone.

Nevertheless, it seems to me that prescriptivism, as with emotivist theories, can be understood as *denying* the possibility of attaining a rational justification for espousing particular ethical principles at the expense of others (in the sense of "rational" defined above). And, as I see it, the underlying reason for such impotence concerns the role, in the selection of ethical first principles, which the authors of these non-cognitivist theories ascribe to the category of what were historically called "passions". This category can be interpreted broadly to include any psychological state, occurrent or dispositional, that might function as an affective causal condition of human behaviour, or, in other words, a "spring of action". Hence, emotions, feelings, impulses, inclinations, desires, wants, attitudes, etc. would all count as "passions" as we are employing the term – as the

278

"moving forces" or motivating states of human behaviour. Most importantly, we find that in non-cognitivist meta-ethical theories it is such psychological states which must serve as the ultimate "reasons" for actions, capable of "justifying" logically primitive ethical principles. However, the use of the quotation marks here is to indicate the problematic status of these states in providing "reasons" or being "justificatory" in the context of such non-cognitivist analyses. Let me explain.

Suppose we were to ask an emotivist *why* an agent should perform the kinds of actions mentioned in a moral principle which the agent endorses – why, to take as an example the negative version of the Utilitarian principle, he should diminish the incidence of human suffering. Well, as far as the view expressed in Ayer's *Language, Truth and Logic* is concerned, the very question, if taken as a request for a logically cogent justification of the "truth" or "validity" of the principle, constitutes of kind of category mistake.[8] One can attempt to validate statements which express true or false propositions, such as factual and logical statements, but as ethical principles merely express feelings, not propositions, questions of truth or validity are inapplicable. The only "why question" that can be significantly asked is one seeking an *explanation*, rather than a justification, for the espousal of a moral principle. And the answer to this request belongs to empirical science, to a causal account comprising:

a)   the identification of the kind of feelings which operate as the immediate determinants of moral judgments, along with a description of the empirical relations between these feelings and the behaviour they excite, and

b)   a sociological investigation of the more remote causes, especially of the moral education or "social conditioning", which are mainly responsible for the formation of the agent's ethical feelings.

Stevenson's more sophisticated version of emotivism, moreover, does not substantially differ from Ayer's theory in precluding a rational justification for moral principles. It is true that Stevenson, in contrast to Ayer, stresses the fact that, in everyday discourse, reasons *are* given for ethical conclusions in an attempt to justify them. Thus, for example, we claim that *because* racial discrimination leads to human misery, we ought not to so discriminate. However, Stevenson analyzes moral "arguments" in such a way that their apparent rationality is rendered illusory. For the "inference" from a moral reason, consisting of a factual belief, to a moral conclusion, is a non-logical

279

one. Rather, it is simply a matter of psychological fact that certain empirical beliefs *causally* induce the expression of moral attitudes of approval or disapproval towards the type of actions mentioned in the conclusion.[9] The mark of an ultimate valuation lies in the fact that the "inference" between factual belief and moral attitude is not mediated by (i) further beliefs and (ii) more inclusive emotional attitudes articulated as more general evaluations. Rather, given the presence of certain beliefs – that action A, for example, produces general happiness, or protects human life, or is an outcome of individual freedom of choice – we simply find ourselves moved to express approval of A. In effect, a particular set of factual beliefs causally necessitate a particular set of basic or non-derivative attitudes, and this relation is not rationally criticizable. Abstracted from particular circumstances and generalized to cover the entire class of actions with that trait or that consequence, these non-derivative attitudes find linguistic formulation as our fundamental moral principles (e.g., "One ought to promote general happiness", "One ought to protect the life of innocent persons", "One ought to defend individual liberty", etc.).[10]

With respect to prescriptivism, we have mentioned that it is certainly Hare's intention to construct a meta-ethical theory that construes moral discourse as a rational activity. And, *to a degree*, it must be admitted that Hare succeeds. Thus, at the *intermediate* level of moral argument, by deductively systematizing the practical reasoning involved into the logical derivation of moral conclusions from factual propositions in accordance with more general moral statements, Hare, in diverging from emotivist accounts, re-affirms the rational structure of such reasoning, and, I think, advisedly. The scheme proposed for deductions is a licit one, and the concept of a justifying reason consisting of a proposition which (with the assistance of other propositions) *entails* the proposition to be deduced, is less problematic than the emotivist notion of practical "inference", wherein the assertion of factual beliefs counts as "reasons" even though they only bear a contingent, causal relation to the assertion of the evaluative "conclusions" they are alleged to justify. In other words, it seems to me that it is preferable, being less disruptive of the ordinary meaning of the concepts involved, to retain an interpretation of the structure of moral *argument* that preserves the logical meaning, that is, the "propositional entailment" sense of reasons and justifications.[11]

Moreover, when we move to the level of assessing our ultimate moral principles, Hare's appeal to the notion of the universalizability of defensible moral judgments does offer an authentic technique, of some force, in the rational criticism of such principles. If someone forms a moral judgment, on the grounds of certain descriptive criteria referring to empirical circumstances, then the demands of logical consistency require that, as a rational agent, he wills that anyone prescribe the same judgment for similar circumstances. If, therefore, an individual were to claim allegiance to an ultimate moral principle, even though he did not agree that others should apply the same principle to every instance of the kind of circumstances covered by the principle, especially when his own interests were at stake, then he could rightly be charged with irrationality. The factual circumstances which he offers as reasons for his moral judgments cannot, lacking the requisite generality, be considered *bona fide* reasons at all. In short, under such conditions, "universalizability" provides an effective instrument for the rational criticism of an opponent's adoption of moral principles which we find unacceptable.[12]

We may have recourse to the topical ethical dispute concerning the revival of capital punishment in illustration of this form of moral reasoning. Thus, Jones might profess adherence to the common moral principle, "One ought to protect the lives of human beings except as a means of self-defence". And it is in terms of this commitment that Jones expresses ethical disapproval of the reinstitution of capital punishment; most particularly, insofar as he does not believe that capital punishment deters murder, he does not believe that the empirical circumstances are such as to consider such punishment satisfying the exceptive condition of self-defence. However, upon the murder of someone close to him, Jones claims the murderer ought to be executed solely out of an interest of revenge, thus failing to prescribe his moral principle for everyone in the critical "test case" where he finds his own interests affected by the application of the principle. In such a situation, we can agree with Hare that Jones is correctly accused of inconsistent moral reasoning.

Nevertheless, although useful by way of negative criticism, or the logical subversion of an inconsistent ethical position, the criterion of universalizability offers no method for the *positive* justification of particular moral principles. That is, if an individual commits himself to a moral principle that is incompatible with one to which another subscribes, but both use their principles consistently, then any appeal to the fact that either principle passes the test of universalizability will be entirely unavailing in supporting one principle in preference to the other. Appeal to universalizability enables us, in effect, to rule out a certain sub-class of subscriptions to moral principles as logically deficient, but is impotent as far as providing a rational backing for *any* consistently held moral principle. To fulfill the latter task, we require some logically compelling justification of someone's commitment to specific moral principles themselves, not simply his acceptance of a logical rule requiring that the same principles be applied by anyone to all relevantly similar circumstances.

And yet, even though Hare does make exaggerated claims for the logical force of universalizability in ethical discourse, he does at least appreciate that universalizability is not logically complete as an argumentative technique. For he admits that it is logically possible that certain individuals whom he calls "fanatics" consistently prescribe a moral imperative, such as the destruction of a minority group, even when, upon the universalization of the prescription, they imagine those circumstances where they themselves would be the recipients of such treatment. Hare, not surprisingly, attempts to mollify the prospect of such an eventuality by maintaining that its empirical probability approaches zero. However, for our purposes, it is especially instructive to note Hare's reason for granting at least the logical propriety of holding a "fanatical" evaluation. As Hare comments:

> It is, indeed, in the logical possibility of wanting *anything* (neutrally described) that the "freedom" which is alluded to in my title essentially consists. And it is this which lets by the person whom I shall call the fanatic.[13]

Now, there are two important and, as we will observe later, systematically related elements in Hare's position here. On the one hand, the prescriptivity of moral judgments implies that those who sincerely assert that certain kind of actions ought to be performed, must have an inclination towards, a desire for, or, in general, a felt disposition towards the performance of the action.[14] And, it is this element which, as Hare understands it, licences the ethical beliefs of the consistent fanatic. For, no matter how eccentric, how "barbaric" the particular objects of one's inclinations may be, logical considerations put no closure on the variety of kinds of actions a person might be motivated to perform, and, therefore, to whose governing moral principle he can commit himself. The second element involves Hare's stress on the requirement of *individualistic freedom* in genuine moral reasoning. Echoing Kant, Hare claims that the authentic moral agent must himself decide on, must by his own choices, commit himself to his basic moral principles.[15]

But, if this is the case, then Hare's meta-ethical analysis faces an even worse dilemma with respect to the possibility of rational argument concerning ethical matters than we have observed emotivism to confront. In particular, the structure of prescriptivist reasoning lapses into incoherence through equivocation over the meaning of "a reason". For on the one hand, at the *intermediate* level of moral argument, Hare maintains that reasons justify a moral conclusion in the unproblematic sense, outlined above, wherein a set of propositions entails another proposition. But, on the other hand, the *ultimate* reason, which, furthermore, must carry the logical burden of warranting the intermediate reasons, belongs to a different, and, for Hare, questionable category of "reasons" – namely, the presence of a pro-attitude, a psychological motivation towards the performance of the kinds of action mentioned in the moral principle constituting the final major premise of the practical argument.[16]

Not that, as previous discussions of this inquiry attest,[17] there are not theoretical grounds for sympathizing with this dilemma of prescriptivism. Moral judgments (along with other evaluations) exhibit an essential *practicality*. Since it is a primary function of evaluative discourse to guide our conduct, to answer such questions as "What shall I do," then to say that something is good, or ought to be done, must provide a reason for seeking a certain kind of object or performing a particular kind of action. Indeed, it is a defining feature of moral concepts that moral value-judgments must offer reasons for *anyone* to seek or do something. But the provision of a sufficient reason for an agent *acting* in one way rather than another requires that a psychological disposition or motivating state to behave in that manner be ascribable to the agent. However, if "giving a reason" is construed only in its customary sense of one proposition being offered in justification of another one, then it would be impossible to satisfy this necessary condition of a reason being an adequate *reason for action*. For propositional contents, even someone's belief in them, do not, on their own, move anyone to action. As we observed in our presentation of the conceptual scheme for interpreting a certain class of events as human actions, such action-events are to be understood as caused by a *conjunction* of propositional beliefs and affective states (desires, inclinations, attitudes, etc.). It is understandable, then, that prescriptivism, in seeking to embed the rationality of ethical discourse within its dynamic role of guiding actions, would find itself equivocating with respect to the concept of a practical reason – on the one hand construing this concept to be instantiated by propositional entailment, on the other hand, by the expression of psychological attitudes.

Is there a *via media* through the horns of this dilemma? I think so. And in identifying such a resolution, it seems to me that the essential point lies in finding a rational basis for validating *emotive* states themselves – more particularly, for the basic set of such states variously referred to as ultimate attitudes, intrinsic desires, final ends, etc. Or we might specify our task as one of determining the conditions under which it would be intelligible to speak of an ultimate reason for an action as a certain type of "passion" – viz., a motivation which *both* justifies a moral principle prescribing the action, and "excites" or causes the agent to perform the action appropriate to complying with the principle.

3. An Historical Disclaimer: Hume

The preceding quest must, however, swim against the historical tide of British moral philosophy, particularly that stemming from Hume.[18] Within this tradition, it has been customary to draw a sharp contrast between reason and the emotions, or between cognitive and affective states, especially as these psychological processes constitute antecedent conditions of moral behaviour. Now Hume, in a similar vein to contemporary non-cognitivists, stressed the "dynamic" aspect of moral utterances, their use to evince attitudes and stimulate actions.[19] Reason, however, being "wholly inactive", comes up bankrupt in accounting for this conceptual connection of goodness with human conduct. Consequently, moral judgments, the determination of good and evil, cannot be "derived from reason":

> Morals excite passions, and produce or prevent actions. Reason of itself is utterly impotent in this particular. The rules of morality, therefore, are not the conclusions of reason.[20]

Rather, according to Hume, the distinction between vice and virtue is determined by a "moral sense" or internal feeling of approval or disapproval towards certain objects or actions when we are confronted by them. In effect, moral good and evil, rightness and wrongness, are not inherent qualities in objects or actions, but distinctions in the consequences of the operations of one's passions, in one's emotive reaction to those objects and actions.

This brief summary of Hume's ethical theory is familiar enough. But it is crucial, in the context of our present task, to grasp the implications of his analysis for the questions of the *relation* between reason and the emotions or passions in framing judgments of (ethical) value. If S pronounces that "One ought to do A", Hume would maintain that the essential element in the meaning of this utterance is the expression, or indeed "feeling", of the pleasing impression or peculiar "sentiment of approbation" engendered by S's contemplation of A. Indeed at one point, Hume goes so far as to say ... "The very feeling constitutes our praise or admiration."[21] Within Hume's general philosophy, this moral impression of "affection or disgust, esteem or contempt, approbation or blame" towards A can be classified as a secondary impression or passion ultimately dependent on original sensations of pleasure or pain associated with A. And it is this passion which motivates the will to seek or avoid the action praised or condemned. But what is critical for present purposes is that since this concrete passion or feeling of approbation or blame is the essential component of moral pronouncements, Hume contends that such utterances are not, in themselves, affirmations of which rational assessments or what we might call *epistemic appraisals* can be meaningfully predicated. That is, the family of questions concerning the truth or falsehood, correctness or incorrectness, reasonableness or unreasonableness, etc. of asserted statements is inapplicable to moral assertions. Hume's grounds for this conclusion merit review.

Generally speaking, Hume formulates a version of the correspondence theory of truth wherein truth consists, as he puts it, in the "proportions of ideas, considered as such, or in the conformity of our ideas of objects to their real existence."[22] For Hume, then, truth resides in an "agreement or disagreement" between what is asserted to be the case and what is "in reality" the case. Accordingly, the concept of truth necessarily implies an "other-directedness" or *representational* factor, a veridical correspondence between: a) at the formal level – one set of purportedly related ideas and the set of actually related ideas; or b) at the empirical level – an idea and the real object it allegedly represents.

Most importantly, it is on the basis of this representational property of items concerning which judgments of epistemic appraisal are appropriate, that Hume concludes that passions or affective states are not, in themselves, amenable to any such appraisal. For passions (along with volitions and actions) are not the sort of items which exhibit the required representational dimension; passions are, rather, concrete, integral units of immediate experience, in themselves "original existences", and hence, neither implying nor requiring any reference to further reality.[23] For Hume, such emotive states simply *are*; questions of their truth or rationality are irrelevant:

> When I am angry, I am angry, I am actually possessed with the passion and in that emotion have no more a reference to any other object, than when I am thirsty, or sick, or more than five foot high. 'Tis impossible, therefore, that this passion can be oppos'd by or contradictory to truth and reason.[24]

According to Hume, only ideas incorporate the representational element susceptible to judgments of truth or falsehood, and as ideas are the province of reason, reason alone is capable of forming such judgments. Admittedly, reason can discern the existence and properties of the objects of our emotions, or ascertain the most efficient means of securing such objects, and where judgments concerning these factors are under scrutiny we do, in a derivative sense, apply terms of epistemic appraisal to the passions, in, for instance, calling them unreasonable. However, in such situations, Hume argues that ... " 'tis not the passion, properly speaking, which is unreasonable, but the judgment".[25] Passions, *in themselves*, are not subject to epistemic appraisal. The presence of any sort of feeling, emotion, desire, attitude, etc. as a motivating force in an agent's psychological make-up is, therefore, neither rational nor irrational. Reason has no role in assessing or criticizing an agent's (non-derivative) motivations; they must simply be taken as given:

> Where a passion is neither founded on false suppositions, nor chooses means insufficient for the end, the understanding can neither justify nor condemn it. 'Tis not contrary to reason for me to prefer the destruction of a whole world to the scratching of my finger.[26]

Consequently, since the inclusion of "feelings of approbation or disapprobation" constitutes the distinguishing feature of ethical judgments, Hume believes that one is also in a position to conclude that inquiry regarding the truth or rationality of fundamental moral assertions is also misplaced. Where Ayer would maintain that moral judgments do not express propositions but feelings, and hence are neither true nor false, Hume would maintain that ethical utterances are the causal consequence of the occurrence of a particular class of feelings which, being passions, are not judgments period. As Hume comments ... "Morality is more properly felt than judged of."[27]

Hume's moral philosophy and its connection with his account of the passions has not been outlined as an exercise in historical exegesis. Rather, Hume's doctrines provide the classical and perhaps clearest formulation of the philosophical grounds of the still orthodox canon of (ethical) value-neutrality for social scientific method. As our study of non-cognitivist meta-ethics attested, an individual's choice of a basic moral principle is determined by an ultimate "passion" or pro-attitude he has towards some end of action. If then, with Hume, a scientist accepts the premise that such attitudes are not susceptible to rational assessment, he is only being consistent when he concludes that a social scientist *qua* scientist excludes prescriptive value-judgments from the body of his theories. For science intends to be a rational form of inquiry. But fundamental evaluations are amenable to rational justification only if the "passions" or psychological attitudes which motivate them are so amenable. And, not surprisingly, the preponderant majority of contemporary social scientists and methodologists *do* share the Humean (and recent non-cognitivist) view that this condition cannot be fulfilled. Or since final ends constitute the object of ultimate attitudes we could equivalently have phrased this view as the denial that final ends are accessible to a rational decision-procedure. Max Weber provided perhaps the classic case of the social scientists' acceptance of this position. As he contended:

> such questions as how conflicts between several concretely conflicting ends are to be arbitrated, are entirely matters of choice or compromise. There is no (rational or empirical) scientific procedure of any kind which can provide us with a decision here. The social sciences, which are strictly empirical sciences, are the least fitted to save the individual the difficulty of making a choice.[28]

4. Limiting Reason: The Link with Neo-classical Economics

Prior to challenging the preceding view, it is revealing to note that two important aspects of neo-classical economic theory are systematically connected with the traditional bar on the rational assessment of ultimate motivations or intrinsically desired ends. I refer to:

a)   the continuance in recent neo-classical analysis of the crudely mechanistic concept of human agency manifested by the conception of *homo economicus*, as, in Edgeworth's terms, a "pleasure machine", [29] which conception we introduced in Chapter 6, and

b)   the putative neo-classical justification of the free enterprise system provided by the doctrine of "consumer sovereignty" outlined in Chapter 5. It will be argued, furthermore, that a) and b) are mutually supportive in their backing of the Humean exclusion of affective states from the scope of rationality.

a) Consider first the persisting tendency of neo-classical economics to interpret economic behaviour in an overly simplified mechanistic fashion.[30] Again, without joining issue on the vexed question of whether the description of a teleological or goal-directed system of behaviour can be successfully "reduced to" or "translated into" a mechanistic one, it is, nevertheless, plainly true that the employment of any mechanistic theory, with only a rudimentary degree of sophistication of its theoretical constructs, will tend to remove its capacity to provide a complete explanation of subject matter involving mechanisms of a high level of complexity. But just such an incongruity occurs between the theoretical apparatus of the neo-classical account of consumer choice and certain types of actual consumer behaviour. Granted the "pleasure-machine" defining "rational" economic man within the neo-classical theory of choice (CCT) is, *on one level*, an eminently "intelligent" one. That is, given his "input" comprised by a set of desires of a certain form – i.e., taking the form of an aggrandizing or insatiable demand for the maximum satisfaction to be derived from such and such commodities – the pleasure-machine has an unlimited cognitive capacity to identify and order his wants such that he chooses to satisfy only that set which will bring him the greatest possible "pleasure". But concerning the substantive nature of the input itself, of the objects and form of his consumer "passions" or preferences, the pleasure-machine does not exercise intelligence. Rather, such anticipated pleasures are taken as given,[31] as raw material to be sub-mitted to the machine's instrumental calculations, and finally re-appearing, in refined form as the machine's "output", or processed product, as the maximal degree of economic man's actual, experienced pleasures. As the sadly neglected Veblen characterized this neo-classical conception of human agency, the economic subject is to be understood as ... "a lightning calculator of pleasures and pains, who oscillates like a homogeneous globule of desire for happiness under the impulse of stimuli that move him about the area, but leave him intact."[32]

It is significant that we can return to Hume's moral psychology for philosophical reinforcement of these limitations on the scope of economic man's rational powers. For Hume, all desires directed towards any object are generated by "the prospect of pleasure and pain" to be derived from securing that object.[33] The expected pleasures (or pains) induce the particular desires (or aversions), which motivating states the agent's reasoning powers must take as given and incorrigible. Not only is it impossible for reason to motivate action, but reason is further incapable of appraising and thereby inactivating hedonically induced motivations, or arbitrating between conflicting ones. An agent simply has whatever motivating states the hedonic mechanisms have causally necessitated for him, and he engages his rational capacity only to identify efficient means to attain the objects of his desires. Manifestly, Hume's view of the appropriate functions and relation of reason and desire in an agent's psychic economy is not far from supplying the historical roots of the neo-classical conception of economic agents as "rational" pleasure-machines.

b) The doctrine of consumer sovereignty has also tended to offer dubious and confused support for the preclusion of ultimate attitudes (or final ends) from rational decidability. To begin with, as we noted earlier,[34] the doctrine itself maintains that the entire competitive market system, denoted by the whole corpus of neo-classical economics (comprising production, exchange, consumption, and distribution theories) receives its normative justification from the purported fact that the processes of this system bring about the greatest possible satisfaction of the given desires of individual consumers when compared with any alternative system.[35] Now, we have mentioned that it is assumed within CCT that any individual consumer is free to choose whatever commodity-bundle he most prefers, where "freedom" is (implicitly) defined in the "soft determinist" sense of unconstrained action, of the agent being able to act according to his own strongest desire. And given their premise that the maximum satisfaction of individual consumer wants is the *summum bonum* of an economic system, we further observed[36] that neo-classical welfare economists, in an attempt to infer the normative conclusion that the operations of the free-market system are maximally conducive to attaining this *summum bonum*, introduced the critical additional premise that, as a general rule, the individual agent rather than external "authorities" is in a position of what we might call *epistemic privilege* – he himself knows best how to secure maximum well-being from the satisfaction of desire.[37] We may recall the way the economist Jerome Rothenberg put it:

> No concentrated group of outside evaluators can be found which comes anywhere near as close to expressing what is good for them as the individual members of the population themselves. Thus the set of individual preferences becomes accepted as the arbiter of their own welfare. Descriptive individualism in positive economics becomes transformed into normative individualism in welfare economics.[38]

Earlier,[39] in the light of certain practices of actual market economies, we raised some reservations concerning the presumed obviousness of the truth of the "epistemic privilege" premise and the adequacy of the concept of freedom in this neo-classical argument for consumer sovereignty. But the important point for our present discussion is the conceptual connection between the Humean doctrine of the non-rationality of ultimate wants and the doctrine of consumer sovereignty. For suppose that, contrary to the former doctrine, an individual's ultimate motivating states (or ends) *were* susceptible to rational appraisal. And recall our claim that any method which formulates a rational decision-procedure requires, by definition, that its criteria be impersonal (apply impartially to anyone) and authoritative (command assent). In that case, the force of the premise asserting an individual's epistemic privilege, so crucial to the argument for the principle of consumer sovereignty, is seriously weakened. For even if we *did* grant the claims (which can be challenged) that the individual agent has the most reliable perception of his wants, and can even identify the most efficient ways of attaining their objects, nevertheless, on the assumption of the rational decidability of such wants, the individual is *not* in an epistemically privileged position to determine whether his (basic) wants are rationally justified. External authorities would be no less (and perhaps more) competent than the agent himself to refer his set of desires to the legitimate, impersonal criteria of rationality for (ultimate) motivating states.

But, as we argued above, the application of such criteria would issue in the completion of the justificatory procedures of a chain of practical inferences in deciding which action an agent ought to perform. Hence, if such criteria were available, it would not be the case that the individual himself was necessarily the most qualified person to correctly determine what was "good for him" to do. His own preferences need not be taken as the sovereign arbiter of his own good. But we have seen that just such an assumption underlies the defence of the neo-classical principle of consumer sovereignty.

Clearly, the philosophic and economic issues converge on our central problem of the rational justifiability of ultimate attitudes. What, then, can be said in support of the view that such (non-derivative) psychological states *are* decidable by reason? In other words, in what way may we subject any agent's *motivations* to espouse basic ethical principles to rational criticism?

5. Rationality and Basic Motivating States

We might begin here by re-affirming, with Aristotle,[40] the necessary teleological dimension of moral judgments. Since appraising objects or actions as good or right has a distinctive use in guiding conduct, such judgments bear a conceptual rather than merely a contingent relation to the ends of human action. Or since being an end for someone entails being an object of his desire, we might put the same point in motivational terms by observing that judgments of moral goodness and rightness exhibit, on pain of losing their characteristic practicality, a conceptual connection with motivational states, with "springs of actions" – feelings, emotions, desires, etc.

It is significant that non-cognitivist meta-ethical theories would not want to deny this general feature of moral judgments (or value-judgments in general). Indeed, given Ayer and Stevenson's concentration on the emotive meaning of ethical terms and Hare's on their prescriptive role, it is clear that both emotivism and prescriptivism wish to emphasize the conceptually necessary relation between evaluations and human motivation, maintaining, respectively, that the main function of value-judgments is either to instigate actions or to command them.

However, these non-cognitive analyses are more restrictive than our view will be of the scope of rationality in moral discourse for the reason that, in concert with Hume, they exclude (ultimate) motivating states from rational assessment. Thus, we find Ayer[41] arguing that terms of epistemic appraisal are inapplicable to expressions of feeling; Stevenson[42] concluding that logical or scientific methods are not suitable for the resolution of ethical disagreement based on irreducible differences in the emotional make-up of the disputants; and Hare maintaining that as long as the fanatic's inclinations are such that he *desires* that anyone, himself included, should, in similar cases, be treated in the same horrendous way, then no method of argument, no "logical barrier" can be devised to show him the error of his ways.[43]

It seems to me, however, that the contention, implicit in Humean and non-cognitive analyses, that there is some insurmountable impasse to demarcating rational from irrational affective states is an ill-founded one. In the first place, both Hume and non-cogitivists illicitly stack the argument in their favour by failing to discriminate between diverse *kinds* of psychological "passions" or motivating states. We may concede that some subsets of the entire class of affective states are unquestionably not the sort of things which are accessible to rational (or irrational) assessment. Bodily sensations and momentary impulses are cases in point. Generally speaking, although such mental events are among the "moving forces" of human behaviour, they are too episodic and passive to be among those affects concerning which stable rational plans can be deliberately devised. But, as we shall argue below, it is not evident that the motivating states encompassed by *attitudes* are not susceptible to such cognitive, rational decision-processes. However, by not adequately distinguishing the properties and functions of different kinds of affective states, Hume and contemporary non-cognitivists have tended, in their explication of the manner in which "ethical feelings" motivate action, to employ a truncated model more suitable for analyzing the non-rational relation between bodily sensations and behaviour than the rational relation of full-fledged moral attitudes and human conduct. (Thus, in perhaps the clearest case of this conflation, we find Ayer claiming that moral judgments, being "pure expressions of feeling", are unverifiable on the same grounds as cries of pain are unverifiable.[44])

Before examining precisely *how* the expression of psychological attitudes can and does elicit rational criticism, it is important to notice an exceedingly significant (albeit wrong-headed) reason for at least the prescriptivist bar on the rational assessment of desires which bring about subscription to moral principles. To elucidate this reason, we might begin by turning again to Hare's tenet that the logical possibility of *wanting anything* supplies the essence of "human freedom."[45]

It will be remembered that Hare adheres to the Kantian doctrine of moral autonomy, that the "moral adult" is self-legislating, that he decides for himself which ethical principles to accept. But Hare realizes that any commitment to a moral principle, however autonomous, presupposes a motivation to follow the principle. However, contrary to Kant's insistence that moral motivation, being itself free, requires a transcendental or non-empirical determination of the will by reason alone,[46] Hare (less heroically but wisely) follows the tradition of British moral philosophy and locates such motivation in the normal channel of empirically determinable dispositions to action. Nevertheless, perhaps anticipating perennial objections questioning how "decisions of principle" can be "freely" made if their motivations are empirically necessitated, Hare claims that the fact that there are no *logical limits* to what an individual might desire does provide a place for his exercise of free choice in subscribing to moral principles. Why does Hare make this claim?

Although Hare himself does not explicitly deal with this question, it seems to me that an answer can be extrapolated from his work, and one which bears an intriguing and significant affinity with the rationale for the neo-classical defence of consumer sovereignty which we discussed above. In company with many philosophers who wish to preserve a substantial sense of freedom, while admitting causal determination, Hare, it seems to me, finds it in the individual's ability to act as he himself desires to act. Hence, in the realm of ethical decision, I freely commit myself to an ultimate moral principle if and only if my choice of the principle is a consequence of *my own* desire for a certain end to be attained by acting in accordance with the principle. However, rational considerations would undermine this type of freedom if, when matters of moral principle were at stake, there were logical limits to the kinds of end it were permissible for an agent to reasonably desire. Accordingly, in order to remove this threat, Hare argues that it "is the price we have to pay for our freedom"[47] that we recognize that it is not something that can be countered by rational manoeuvres, it is not an "offence against logic", for someone, in a morally significant context, to desire *any* end whatsoever, however bizarre, subject only to the condition that he wills that everyone have the same desire in similar circumstances.

Hare's position is not, however, convincing. Basically, by concentrating on one sense of "rational", at the expense of other genuine senses, his argument is guilty of an *ignoratio elenchi*. Thus, for Hare, rational methods cannot discredit any (universalized) desire underpinning a moral claim as long as the desire is *logically* impeccable, where, by a logical consideration, Hare understands one concerning the proper meaning or use of words.[48] And, with this sense of "logical" in mind, we can, for the sake of argument, agree with Hare that there is nothing *illogical*, there is no abuse of the meanings of the terms involved, for the fanatic, in prescribing that a certain race of people ought to be exterminated, to have a universalized desire that this be so, even if he were to become a member of that class.

But Hare's reasoning here is beside the point. For this meaning of "logical" need not exhaust the meaning of "rational"; hence, the fact that we have established that the ascription of some desire to an agent satisfies sound logical principles, does not *ipso facto* entail that it is rational for the agent to have such a desire. Even though it might make perfectly good linguistic sense to say of someone that he desires some final end, it remains an open question as to whether, in some "non-logical" sense, it is not irrational for him to seek such an end.

Hume, significantly, founders in a similar way, but with a different over-restriction of the concept of rationality.[49] In effect, Hume moves from correctly speaking of what is "contrary to truth" as what is "contrary to reason", to covertly misemploying "true" as a synonym for "reasonable". Hence, once he has argued that affective states or "passions" are neither true nor false, he immediately infers that they are neither reasonable nor unreasonable. But the inference begs the question until he has provided reasons for believing that what is "true or false" exhausts the meaning of what is "reasonable or unreasonable".

But, in what way, then, *are* ultimate attitudes amenable to rational criticism or validation? Essentially, the answer, historically indebted to the moral philosophies of Aristotle and Spinoza, is to be found in the manner in which it is possible for cognitive elements to interact with sensory-emotive processes in the determination of rational behaviour. It is significant that neo-classical economic theory, and Humean and non-cognitive meta-ethical doctrines, are basically at one in the manner in which they sell short the role of reason or cognitive elements in the causation of human conduct. Moreover, this mistake is in turn systematically responsible for a further confusion that unites these economists and moral philosophers – that concerning a tenable concept of individual freedom.

To see that the preceding charges can be sustained, and in order to begin elucidating the rational decidability of ultimate attitudes, let us first identify a candidate for a completely rational agent whose characteristics would satisfy the criteria of both neo-classical economics and non-cognitivist meta-ethics. It is evident that we need go no further than construct a "conceptual picture" of an updated version of the Edgeworthian "pleasure-machine" described above. It may be granted that proponents of the view we are criticizing might perhaps reject the sensationalist-hedonist psychology in which the notion of the pleasure-machine is embedded as scientifically discredited, and adopt some more recent empirical theory of motivation – say that of drive-reduction. Nevertheless, whatever the psychological theory to which these authors would appeal in order to explain the etiology of a subject's desires, it remains their view, as it did with Hume, that the subject's conscious cognitions, the source of his rational powers, must take *as given* whatever non-mediate emotive states he happens to have acquired through the contingencies of his sensory interaction with the external environment.[50] Given such incorrigible motivating states, the rational cognitive mechanisms of the human "system" may then, under propitious circumstances, be released in the selection of efficient pieces of behaviour towards the realization of the objects of such states. Objections that the subject's basic "passions" or motivating states might themselves be susceptible to rational appraisal would be met with a double-edged reply: Such a suggestion is inconsistent with the hypotheses of the psychological theory being employed, and, in any case, is incompatible with an eminently valuable norm of ethico-economic liberalism – that an individual be free to act as he desires.

However, the preceding conceptual picture of the rationally autonomous man, jointly conceived in neo-classical economics and non-cognitive ethics, amounts to a caricature of both the rational, deliberative capacities available for real-life agents, and the more complete kind of freedom such capacities permit. Let me explain.

We might first take cognizance of certain empirical facts. In contrast to "merely" physical or lower-level systems, the system of elements comprising the human agent, due to the inclusion of a cognitive consciousness, is not "dumb" to the origin of his emotions and desires, but can become aware of, can learn to identify the causes (or effects) of his motivating states.[51] Most importantly, to the extent to which the human subject[52] acquires such reflexive knowledge, i.e., self-knowledge, to that extent he develops his capacity for rationally controlling his (ultimate) wants, of criticizing and modifying his given passions. In this way, he is able to refashion the motivating states he happens to have and redirect them towards more inherently satisfying objects. Hence, in moving away from an excessively sensationalist model of motivation, with its overly "passive" concept of the subject as a receiver of motivating stimuli, we are in a position to see "reason" or reflective consciousness as, *pace* Hume, an "active" power *vis à vis* the passions which move us to action.

In this sense, the enlightened subject, whose cognitive processes are informed of the causes and structural properties of the desires he finds motivating him, acquires the capacity to be "self-determining" in his actions. No doubt, if antecedent conditions are not propitious, this level of rational capacity will remain inactivated. Accordingly, the subject's rational powers will not extend to the assessment of motivating states themselves, but will continue, in Hume's terms and *qua* neo-classical "pleasure-machine", to be the "slave of the passions," that is, merely the purveyor of optimal means towards given ends. Indeed, such an attenuation of human reason typifies the motivational structure of too many individuals within our present "consumer society" whose institutional conventions in turn reinforce and entrench the "mind set" defining and creating the economic men needed to perpetuate the society. But experiential findings are sufficient to refute economic and philosophical doctrines, or the implications of however fashionable psychological theories, which claim that the more restrictive view of the scope of reason is an inevitable and permanent feature of the logic of the human situation.

Perhaps in the light of this defence of an expanded scope for rational decision-making, an initially paradoxical summation of Spinoza concerning the role of reason in guiding moral behaviour is more understandable:

> A true knowledge of good and evil cannot restrain any emotion insofar as the knowledge is true, but only insofar as it is considered as an emotion.[53]

At least an important part of Spinoza's point might be put in the following way. It is true that, in everyday experience, many of our basic dispositions to actions are comprised of emotions or feelings which, because they have not been subjected to sufficient internal reflection and appraisal, are not expressedly rational (or irrational). But neither are they, like "pure sensations" or momentary impulses, *non*-rational states. For they are *virtually* rational. That is, if an agent submits these passions to the requisite deliberation, they can become constituents of rational (or irrational) desires, of considered policy. Put another way, through the medium of rational appraisal, the original emotions and feelings can be elevated to the level of full-fledged *attitudes*.

Nor need human subjects be peculiarly divested of their full rationality when engaging in economic behaviour; in particular, it is not at all evident that the deliberative capacities of actual economic agents are limited to those of an Edgeworthian "pleasure-machine". For instance, it is not the case that consumers need, or even uniformly do, stop short of rationally assessing the content and structure of their "passions" themselves, of their desires for material commodities. Consider, for example, our earlier discussion[54] of the Stoic "contractionist" alternative to the insatiable, "expansionist" form of consumer wants assumed in neo-classical theory; surely the former option can be (and is) employed by some agents upon a reasoned repudiation of the latter's unique worth. And yet, since such decisions demand an appraisal of the rationality of basic "passions" themselves, the theoretical apparatus of neo-classical economics is not equipped to accommodate them.[55] In short, the theoretical constructs of our neo-classical theory (CCT) are too rudimentary to provide an understanding of that range of actual economic behaviour which involves practical reasoning or deliberative mechanisms of the level of complexity wherein the agent directs his rational choices towards the selection or revision of ultimate consumer *attitudes* themselves. (Nor can the neo-classical economist adequately defend CCT from this charge by appealing to CCT's status as a (descriptive) idealization. For it is of the nature of the theoretical principles of CCT to preclude acknowledgement of the consumer's own rational remoulding of his wants, not merely to articulate an ideal "limiting" case of rational activity that actual consumer behaviour can only approximate.)

In sum, we may conclude that, contrary to the assumptions common to Hume, non-cognitivist ethics, and neo-classical economics, an agent's basic motivations, his non-derivative desires (or ends), *are* amenable to rational assessment.

The procedure for ascertaining the rationality of ultimate motivating states reveals, furthermore, the confusion and inadequacy in the concept of freedom jointly avowed in neo-classical economics and non-cognitivist ethics – viz., wherein the generic sense of freedom is that of being able to act as one desires, subject only to the qualification, in prescriptivism, that freedom concerning moral decisions requires universalized desires. For, even if an agent is acting on the basis of a universalized desire, ignorance of the causal and structural properties of this motivating state can be as real a constraint on his action-capabilities as a physical impediment or the external coercion of another agent. Contrariwise, if he becomes conscious of these properties he increases his power of action. For instance, in the unenlightened situation, he might be following desires which are mutually frustrating, or whose activation issues in inherently unsatisfying end-states.[56]

But if he had knowledge of these properties, including knowledge of the causal antecedents generating his desires, by manipulating the antecedents he could ameliorate his situation in remoulding the debilitating desires he happens to find as present constituents of his psychological make-up. Hence, by becoming aware of the determinants of his given dispositions to actions, he can pursue strategies that will produce dispositions more in accord with his "true good". Without this capacity to assess the rationality of our given desires, we could not avoid being the passive victims of disadvantageous motivations, rather than active designers of the kind of motivations we would want to be motivated by.[57] In short, such self-knowledge, in emancipating us from an (often pernicious) *ignorance* of the causal processes responsible for our motivations, and thereby extending the range of actions we are able, to our advantage, to perform or avoid, is the source of an important element of free choice that is absent from the truncated notion of freedom embedded in neo-classical economy theory and non-cognitivist moral philosophy.[58]

(It should be mentioned, however, that the freedom or "self-determination" made possible by this knowledge is not logically incompatible with scientific determinism. For there is no convincing reason to believe that the development and implementation of the requisite cognitive processes are not themselves susceptible to a causal or law-governed explanation.)

Again, instead of speaking of ultimate attitudes, we could equivalently speak of the final ends constituting the objects of such attitudes. And having established that there are cognitive processes accessible for determining the rationality of such attitudes or ends, we might profitably return to the point made previously concerning the action-guiding role of moral judgments, which role implied an "internal" or conceptual connection with the motives or ends of action. And we might ask what *kind* of properties those attitudes or ends, which furnish the motivational backing for the acceptance of fundamental moral principles, must exhibit in order that such attitudes or ends be considered rationally justified?

6. Rational Ends and Moral Science

As Aristotle long ago argued,[59] the concept of a final end entails certain criteria that any object of desire must meet if it is to be correctly classified as an entirely *final* end, that is, something which is desired solely for itself and not as a means to some further end. In particular, thus, a final end must, in Aristotle's terms, be "self-sufficient", a term denoting a complex property comprising two characteristics:

a) the end sought must be capable of being desired in separation from other aims, and

b) it must be fully satisfying or "lacking in nothing" – that is, having attained such an end, we would not be yet disposed to replace it through some other pursuit.

It seems to me that Aristotle's insights concerning ultimate ends are basically sound. This judgment can be supported by noting the properties of pursued ends which *fail* to meet the criteria Aristotle proposes. In essence, if an object cannot meet criteria a) or b), then it *cannot*, logically cannot, function as a genuinely final end – i.e., as one only desired for its own sake. For, if it cannot be desired in isolation from other ends, then it is never desired for itself alone, but only in conjunction with some other goal, and more importantly, if its attainment is not fully satisfying, then it could cease to be an object of desire at all.

Moreover, by exercising the freedom, described above, to become conscious of the inherent properties and causal processes connected with his desires, it is possible for the human agent to review his *de facto* motivating states for the purpose of determining whether they fulfill those conceptual requirements for ultimate attitudes or final ends which Aristotle identifies. And, most importantly, in the light of such self-knowledge, insofar as he identifies that his ends deviate from those criteria, he will, by gaining control of the causes of this deviance, be equipped to bring his motivations into closer accord with the criteria. He will, that is, become able to ascertain if his given ends-in-view, the objects of his actual basic wants, are separable, and more germane to our present argument, whether they are inherently fulfilling – and, if not, to revise them accordingly.

But what the capacity to activate such self-determination or autonomy is tantamount to is nothing less than the ability to assess the rationality of one's ultimate attitudes or ends, to submit one's motivational structure to specific rational norms. And we argued earlier that if we could provide just such a method for determining the rationality of ultimate attitudes, then the problem of finding a way to rationally justify our fundamental moral principles would be resolved, commitment to these principles being an outcome of having such attitudes. In other words, the chain of reasons for espousing any particular ethical judgment could be successfully terminated and, thus, rationally decidable argument would be possible concerning ethical issues. Moreover, the primary rationale for demanding that social science be "value-free" – the lack of such decidability – would, therefore, be removed. Accordingly, the construction of CCT *qua* scientific utopia could be legitimately deemed a rational enterprise. Are we not, in short, home-free?

The answer – perhaps. But before turning to the main reason for this guarded reply, it will be useful to deflect an impending objection to the line of argument we have pursued. Have we not, it might be charged, simply embraced a version of the "naturalistic fallacy" concerning the analysis of value-judgments? More specifically, have we not defined moral value in terms of a certain kind of empirical property – roughly, that an end is intrinsically good if and only if its realization is fully satisfying to any agent who is informed as to the structural and causal properties of his motivations; or, alternatively, that an action is morally right if and only if its performance is conducive to the attainment of such an end? But, so the argument continues, such definitions are open to well-known and conclusive objections such as the fact that it is not self-contradictory to suppose that an end or action has moral value but lacks the property mentioned in the definiens.

Without challenging non-naturalist analyses of the meaning of moral judgments directly, we can, nevertheless, establish that our account of the rational *justification* of moral judgments is impervious to such charges of naturalistic fallacy. Indeed, in defending our case we can make use of precisely that tactic which non-cognitivists have employed to attack ethical naturalism – i.e., the appeal to the action-guiding *purpose* of moral discourse. For, in effect, our account did not *intend* to provide a *definition* of moral concepts in terms of empirical properties. Our account has sought, rather, to identify those very conditions which any system of moral principles must fulfill if it is to adequately serve its own unique end of guiding our conduct.

But we do claim that it *is* self-contradictory to argue, as non-cognitivists in the tradition of Hume implicitly do, that a system of ethical principles is impervious to further rational criticism, even though acting on the motivations underpinning the principles brings about the realization of ends-in-view that are *not* fully satisfying. For, in this case, an ethical system would be considered rationally secure even though it did *not* successfully fulfill its *accepted* purpose of guiding our conduct. Put another way, we have seen[60] that naturalists and non-naturalists are agreed that "functional" entities or "artifacts" do have empirical criteria for the ascription of evaluative properties to them – in particular, an individual artifact is a good specimen of its kind if and only if it serves its distinctive end or function well. But a system comprised of a set of moral principles is as much an artifact as any other product of human design; consequently, it is subject to rational assessment on the grounds of whether or not it efficiently fulfills the end (i.e., guiding action) for which it was designed. To refuse to apply such grounds to the justifiability of an ethical system would be as irrational as refusing to accept or reject a scientific theory on the basis of whether it served its function well – that of explaining and predicting empirical phenomena.

There is, however, a well-founded reason for the *guardedness* of our final reply to the question of the rational decidability of moral principles. What concerns us here are the reasons for my reservation at the introduction of this chapter, cautioning that we might have to rest content with a *conditional* answer to this question. The crucial point is that sufficient grounds are not yet available to warrant the conclusion that some particular set of moral principles could satisfy the criterion of the *universality* or *impersonal* character of rationally justifiable principles. But neither are there adequate grounds, at present, for *denying* that some moral system could fulfill this criterion. Or, given our account of the structure of the chain of justification for value-judgments, our reservation reduces to the problem of the present absence of sufficient evidence to categorically affirm or deny that the motivations for agents to commit themselves to moral principles permit these principles to exhibit the necessary universality.

Basically, the difficulty arises because there is no a priori guarantee that different agents, who nevertheless share knowledge as to the appropriate properties of their motivations, will find the *same* final ends fully satisfying. But if there should not be such a concurrence, then it remains possible that the diverse ultimate attitudes of different agents, which "passions" both cause and provide the terminating justification for the espousal of moral judgments, would take objects that satisfied the criteria for final ends, and yet be mutually conflicting – that is, yield commitments to logically incompatible systems of moral principles. Or, in a logically weaker case, diverse attitudes would issue in compatible but distinct set of moral principles. At any rate, in either case, "enlightened" moral attitudes would still not provide for satisfaction of the impersonal dimension required of a procedure for rational or "objective" decisions on moral questions. For informed inquirers would

300

not be able to reach agreement as to which system of moral principles to accept as "true", or which system displayed "warranted assertability". Under these circumstances, therefore, an "objective" social science should eschew the inclusion of (prescriptive) moral judgments.

Nevertheless, it is just as critical to realize that neither is there any a priori guarantee that different agents, similarly informed as to the properties of their motivations, will *not* find the same final ends fully satisfying.[61] And if they should so happen to concur, then an argument, parallel in structure to the preceding one, but reaching precisely the opposite conclusion would be forthcoming. In particular, thus, we could warrantedly conclude that "enlightened" moral attitudes permitted the fulfilment of the condition of impersonal authority demanded of a method governing a rational choice among competing systems of moral principles. And, under these new conditions, we could, therefore, further conclude that there is no compelling reason why an "objective" social science *must* exclude ethical evaluations from the corpus of its theories. In effect, we have developed a Kantian "conditions of the possibility" argument for the rational decidability of moral principles and the objectivity of a value-laden social science. But we have concluded that the satisfaction of these conditions remains undecided.

Indeed, the truth-value of the main premises of both arguments denying (in the first) and affirming (in the second) the agreement of enlightened agents as to ultimate attitudes or ends, remains at the present state of scientific inquiry, an *open empirical* question. Hence, with the evidence *now* available, the appropriate epistemic response is to suspend judgment with respect to the truth-value of these premises and the conclusions concerning (i) the rationality/non-rationality of moral principles and (ii) the legitimacy/illegitimacy of a value-impregnated social science to which the premises lead. In returning to the Aristotelian tradition of teleological ethics we can, nevertheless, shed further light on the issues upon which a grounded acceptance or rejection of these premises is conditional.

It is well-known that in Aristotelian moral philosophy the standard for ethical judgments is provided by the *telos* or end which is purported to be the defining characteristic of the species man.[62] The important point, for our purposes, is that the concept of the Aristotelian telos combines two features, the first empirical, the second, normative:

(i) an observable end-state towards which all men, for the very reason that they belong to the class of entities called men, have an innate tendency, and

(ii) an evaluative ideal for man as a species permitting either the comparative appraisal of individual men on the basis of the degree to which each approximates to the species ideal, or the appraisal of alternative activities or "styles of life" on the basis of the degree to which each is conducive to the realization of man's end *qua* man.

Now, we need not endorse the questionable doctrines of essentialism, final causality in nature, and a view of man as himself some sort of divinely conceived artifact, with which Aristotelian and kindred teleological ethical theories have, with some justice, been charged, in order to elicit from the Aristotelian fusion of the empirical and normative a hypothetical principle that is especially germane to our present problem. Put in its original essentialist and teleological framework, we can formulate the principle as follows:

A: If the class of men, insofar as they are men, have a tendency towards the same final end (or ends), then moral principles are rationally decidable.

Of course, in the Aristotelian framework, the defining property of the class, "mankind" is the unique capacity of members of this class to engage in activity "according to a rational principle".[63] In other words, man *qua* man is *ipso facto* a rational agent. With this point in mind, then, we may remove the essentialism implicit in the antecedent of A, and by further translating out the teleological element in this antecedent, we can reformulate A in less problematic, more straightforwardly empirical terms as:

A': If all men, in those circumstances in which their cognitive capacities are fully operative,[64] move towards the same end-state(s), then moral principles are rationally decidable.

More precisely, only the antecedent of A' is empirical, A' itself being an analytically true unpacking of the conditions sufficient for rational decidability. Nevertheless, given A', and confirmation of the truth of its antecedent, we could then detach the truth of its consequent, and thus be in a position to justifiably reject the doctrine that value-neutrality is, under all circumstances, mandatory for social science.[65]

To a degree, this analysis resembles the claims of those non-cognitivists, such as C. L. Stevenson,[66] who argue that a rational solution of ethical disagreements presupposes a "common human nature", in the sense that all human beings share the motivations required to approve or disapprove of the same kinds of conduct, or that they have final ends in common. However, their position differs significantly from ours in that, in their view, ends are understood as the objects of the *de facto* desires or motivating states which human beings just happen to have. Moreover, given wide variances in non-cognitive sources of attitudes (e.g., innate temperament and early upbringing) across different individuals, social strata and cultures, scepticism concerning the truth of the presupposed communality of "human nature" is only too supportable. On our account, however, it is only those ethical motivations which have undergone the cognitive or rational review outlined above that we must presuppose all human beings as having in common, to be justified in concluding that it is always, in principle, possible for reasonable men to reach agreement on their choice of moral principles.

As this presupposition (call it M) amounts to an empirical conjecture, it is, presumably, to the investigations of scientific psychology that we must turn for its confirmation or falsification. It will, however, be a special type of empirical psychology to which we must appeal. That is, it will not be sufficient to have recourse to standard psychological theories that seek to account for human behaviour by subsumption under laws referring to uniform relations between *given* motivations and subsequent behaviour. Rather, the appropriate science must be one which formulates law-like hypotheses representing uniform relations between *appraised* motivations or *rational* attitudes and the actions they cause. We might, therefore, characterize the relevant scientific theory as an *empirical cum rational* psychology.[67]

Now consider that a suitable theory of this sort has been developed, and that its well-attested hypotheses *do* imply M. In that case, CCT would be halfway to meeting our final condition U_2 for classification as a scientific utopia. In other words, we would then be able to conclude that the moral presuppositions of the utopian theoretical system articulated by CCT were amenable to rational validation. But, of course, our task would still be only half completed. For it would remain to actually submit CCT to test U_2. And this involves determining whether the moral principles governing the system of behaviour represented by CCT *are* rationally justified.

Assuming these principles are rationally justifi*able*, we still await a sustained effort to justify them. Nevertheless, although I believe such a project to be a pressing one, I do not find its prospects encouraging. But it is not that I repudiate the inclusion of ethical ideals in the construction of some social scientific theories, or deny that the vindication of such values is by way of motivational factors. It is rather that I believe that the principles of psychological motivation appealed to in the framework of the neo-classical theory of consumer choice (CCT) must be capable of providing the foundations for a sound moral science. For I would argue that what is good for man is to be motivated by desires which actually *will* satisfy his needs as a rational organism. However, I doubt that the motives affirmed and prescribed in CCT, like those requiring the continual suppression of spontaneous impulse and the expression of interminable acquisitiveness, as a matter of fact, *do*. But reasoned support for my suspicion demands further inquiry into moral psychology itself, which investigation must be deferred until a future occasion.

Chapter 17

Conclusion

It will be useful to close these investigations of the philosophical foundations of the neo-classical theory of individual choice (CCT) by drawing together the major theoretical views that I have promulgated.

Our understanding of CCT began against the background of the "orthodox" conception of scientific theories endorsed by the "mainstream" neo-classical economists responsible for the construction and employment of CCT. This "official view" of theory-construction and validation followed in the traditions of classical empiricism. Within such a context, as we remarked in the Introduction, two related doctrines of scientific method are paramount:

1. the explanatory generalizations of scientific theories are comprised of contingent hypotheses that are falsifiable by observational evidence.

2. scientist *qua* scientist subscribes to a standard of "ethical neutrality". He does not countenance the inclusion of moral value-judgments prescribing how agents ought to act in the corpus of his scientific theories.

In this light, however, at a first level of analysis, our interpretation of CCT broke decisively with the orthodox conception and its empiricist under-pinning. Let us rehearse how.

To begin with, we argued that the basic explanatory generalizations of CCT (G" or H) expressed necessary, a priori truths that were not amenable to empirical falsification. If the antecedent conditions of these hypotheses were met, it was logically impossible that the consumer choice mentioned in the consequent not be enacted. In the case of G", this necessity was parasitic upon that of explanatory principle G' of general action-theory, as explanations of consumer choices were found to be special cases of explanations of human actions. And the logical necessity or "conceptual truth" of G' lay in its use as a (corrigible) principle for interpreting phenomena as action, in particular in its (implicit) *definition* of actions as events caused by some set of occurrent wants and beliefs. H, furthermore, only augmented the claim to non-contingency of G". For H amounted to a reformulation of G" in order to capture the fact that the explanatory system of

CONCLUSION

CCT directly applied to *ideally rational agents*. And, so construed, it was evident that the antecedent conditions of H, explicating the meaning of any ideally rational consumer, logically entailed the kind of action such a rational economic man (*homo economicus*) would perform.

Of course, *homo economicus* is not your average man. He is endowed with certain superior cognitive and affective capacities that cannot be precisely exemplified, but only approximated, by real agents. For instance, as the subject to whom CCT applies, he was provided with the virtual omniscience of being able to infallibly ascertain the utility-incomes of all possible consumption choices. In short we observed that CCT formulates a *theoretical idealization*.

But what kind of idealization is CCT? Appreciation of the fact that CCT assumed the *rationality* of the subject under study offered the essential clue. Given this aspect, we concluded that CCT, in its conceptually prior form, gave expression to a *normative* theory of rational behaviour. Under this interpretation, the maximization assumption of CCT no longer intends to *report* a factual, psychological truth but *recommends* a classical Utilitarian standard as defining the ultimate end of *homo economicus* – namely, that he ought to maximize his utility or the subjective satisfaction he derives from the use of material commodities. Accordingly, descriptive axioms A_1-A_4 of CCT were reinterpreted as instrumental rules R_1-R_4, understood as *prescribing* the practices which the ideally rational consumer would follow in order to most efficiently attain his final end of maximum utility.

But does a normative reading of CCT support a claim that the theory presupposes moral values? Or, put another way, do we have grounds for contending that the neo-classical theorists employing CCT have not practised their avowed policy of ethical neutrality? We have argued that the answer to these critical questions is affirmative. Two considerations were especially germane to this conclusion.

In the first place, we have observed that subscribing to non-satiation rule R_2 implies a commitment to the questionable moral imperative of economic liberalism known as the "growth ethic". *Homo economicus* displays the moral attitude of "possessive individualism" – the disposition to incessantly aggrandize the accumulation of personal material goods. We have found, moreover, that such an attitude is not logically or empirically inevitable. For there are open ethical alternatives to this expansionist form of utility maximization fostered by such Benthamite Utilitarianism. We encountered such an option, for example, in the Stoic directive to increase satisfaction by contracting certain desires, rather than uniformly following a policy of "more is better".

Secondly, we have noted that following transitivity rule R_3 demanded a "consistency" in the consumer's preferences which, in turn, required a stable, enduring pattern in his material wants. And such stability, we claimed, presupposed a commitment to an ideal evolution of human nature summarized by the virtue of "calculatedness" in the character of *homo economicus*, as expressed by his vigilant restraint of immediate impulse in favour of a methodical, well-ordered pattern of wants. Indeed, in returning to the historical roots of neo-classical economics in the work of Marshall, we explicated the manner in which the degree of moral excellence alleged to reside in the character of *homo economicus* was employed as the ultimate justification of the free-market system his real-life imitators populated.

Nor did our theses concerning the logical structure and moral dimension of CCT require substantial revisions for situations where the deliberation of economic men faced uncertain evidential support. Indeed, our analysis of the extension of CCT within the standard model of (subjective) expected utility theory, SET, only ramified our conclusions that neo-classical choice theory took a priori truth conditions for the behaviour of ideally rational men. In moving to uncertain situations, moreover, the moral import of conventional choice theory was also augmented, most particularly for the theory's political "frame". For, upon the subsumption of CCT within a theory of social choice in general equilibrium theory *cum* welfare economics, neo-classical economics was seen as continuing the "system of natural liberty" underwriting the classical tradition. However, once individuals undertook choice under conditions of uncertainty, we found that certain actual market practices threatened both the "sovereignty" or moral autonomy of the individual consumer and the "social optimality" or common good traditionally promised for a competitive economic order comprised of self-interested, but free, individuals engaged in voluntary exchange.

In sum, we were presented with an initial analysis of CCT as an a priori-*cum*-normative-*cum* idealized theory that was not value-free. Moreover, none of the basic axioms of CCT, i.e., A_1-A_4, could be displaced without frustrating both the explanatory and normative roles of the overarching system of natural liberty in which these particular assumptions played their essential part. At first sight, then, it might have appeared that we were faced with a methodological dilemma – either CCT had no scientific utility or the traditional empiricist theory of science should be abandoned. But the dilemma was not compelling. For, *at a final level of analysis*, we argued, in effect, that an interpretation of CCT could remain within the rules of a "liberalized" empiricist method, and yet the theory adequately serve scientific aims such as the explanation and prediction of actual economic behaviour. There were two parts or phases to this deeper understanding.

It was first necessary to provide a link between normative and factual reasoning in the context of *individual* decision-making. And such a connection was found in the fact that normative principles, including those expressing moral values, require a type of pragmatic justification or psychological vindication in the form of motivations to follow such norms. Otherwise, normative systems would be simply inapplicable to concrete behaviour. In the case of CCT, such motivations are exemplified in the pattern of personal acquisitiveness and impulse-control disposing individual agents to follow the rules of rationality (R_1-R_4) recommended by the theory.

But, therefore, we found ourselves in a position to conclude that explanation of actual rule-governed behaviour could meet empiricist precepts. For such explanations subsume an instance of such behaviour under empirical laws relating specific sorts of individual behaviour with particular kinds of motivation.

However, such motivations are not, as neo-classical economists have often assumed, universal, innate dispositions of human nature. This became clear at the second phase of our "empiricist" level of analysis. For here, in placing individual economic men in a social setting, we took note of the form in which external, institutional constraints induced the motivations of the "micro-units". And we saw that the methodological implications of such a nexus were of the first importance. By assisting in the construction of the social constraints determining economic motivations in conformity with the principles of his normative system, the economic theorist was furnished with a mechanism whereby he could help *convert* his originally a priori and normative theory, such as CCT, into a descriptively true science of human action. Again, however, the logical structure of the resulting explanations of actual (consumer) behaviour was seen to be essentially empiricist. For, at the most general level, consumer choices were derived from socio-economic laws connecting the appropriate motivations with institutional determinants.

There was, however, a significant pragmatic caveat to such an empiricist understanding. In contrast to the practices of the physical theorist, the economist can intentionally promote the validation of his general hypotheses by placing his influence on social controls among the institutional causes of the data which confirm the hypotheses.

CONCLUSION

Not surprisingly, in moving to the wider social context, the normative dimension of economic methodology again became decisive. For we observed that the institutional determinants of individual motivations were constituted by *contrivable* social arrangements that are alterable by conscious human decision. And such decisions may be based on moral ideals deemed worthy of guiding social relations in a particular society. At the most profound plane of inquiry, Economics must make a theoretical transition to Political Economy. For the theorist must ascertain whether the operative criteria for selecting economic goals are consistent with the moral standards defining the more general ends of his society.

In other words, economic science must merge with moral science. But, in the light of this consideration, we came to a final conception of CCT as attempting to give expression to a "scientific utopia", an ethically ideal, but imaginary system of behaviour. Nevertheless, in the application of the procedures for converting a normative theory into empirical science, we were given reason to believe that the social utopia designated by CCT could at least be moved from the neo-classical theorist's imagination to approximate instantiation in the real world.

But would such a shift issue in the realization of a morally justified social order? Unfortunately we found no direct answer to this crucial question. For we were compelled to seek a preliminary answer to the more basic question of whether moral principles themselves were rationally decidable. And we reached the conclusion that, given the available scientific knowledge, it remains an *open empirical question* whether this classic problem can be resolved affirmatively or negatively.

However, we did establish that non-cognitivist moral philosophy and neo-classical economics have been at one in declining to endorse the main presupposition of the rational justifiability of moral principles – the amenability of ultimate attitudes to cognitive appraisal. But in so refusing, they have united in error. The scope of human rationality *does* extend to the cognitive assessment of fundamental motivating states. Clearly, the neo-classicist's concept of the human subject or person as a "pleasure-machine" has truncated that theorist's vision of man's rational powers. And his recourse to behaviourist and crude functionalist interpretations of rational choice has been observed to only exacerbate this defect. In so confining rationality, moreover, we have noted that neo-classical theory has obstructed recognition of a substantial sense of human freedom that comes with man's distinctive ability to subject the forces which move him to rational review.

309

CONCLUSION

Nevertheless, in the final analysis, rational economic man is only an atrophied image of man in reality. No doubt the use of the economic theory of his behaviour has been among the cultural determinants reducing the reality to the image. But, again, man has the freedom, in exercising the full range of his reason, to remove himself from the "moving force" of errors he has brought to consciousness.

Notes

Chapter 2

[1] See, in this respect, J. Buchanan, "Is Economics the Science of Choice?" in J. Buchanan, *What Should Economists Do?* (Indianapolis, Ind.: Liberty Press, 1970), pp. 39-63, L. Robbins, *An Essay on the Nature and Significance of Economic Sciences*, 2nd edn. (London: Macmillan, 1935), pp. 73-75, and V. Walsh and H. Gram, *Classical and Neo-Classical Theories of General Equilibrium: Historical Origins and Mathematical Structure*, (Oxford: Oxford University Press, 1980), pp. 264-65.

[2] See, for example, W. Baumol, *Economic Theory and Operations Analysis*, 4th edn. (Englewood Cliffs, N.J.: Prentice-Hall, 1977), Chap. 9, secs. 6-11, for a lucid presentation of this form of the theory of choice.

[3] In the standard mathematical modelling of consumer choice theory, a further axiom asserting the "continuity" of the preference relation is included. Formally, for any bundle X, if we define $A(x)$ as the least as good as X set and $B(x)$ as the no better than X set, then $A(x)$ and $B(x)$ are closed. In verbal terms, for any two goods x, y in a bundle, X, by reducing x incrementally and increasing y in similar fashion, we can identify another bundle Y, which is indifferent to X. Such continuity of preferences is necessary in order to mathematically represent a preference ordering by an adequate utility function. However, as the continuity assumption is primarily of formal technical significance, rather than of fundamental empirical or normative importance, we shall not further address its content or implications in this study. (Similar comments apply to the frequent assertion of a "reflexiveness" axiom – i.e., for any commodity-bundle, X, X is indifferent to itself, X.)

[4] See C. G. Hempel, *Aspects of Scientific Explanation* (New York: Free Press, 1966), esp. Ch. 12, pp. 333-76, for a canonical analysis of deductive-nomological models of explanation.

[5] See W. Baumol, *Economic Theory and Operations Analysis*, Ch. 9, sec. 7, for an explanation of the derivation of consumer equilibrium within CCT.

[6] In chapters 11, 12 and 13, we shall also examine certain implications of CCT's inclusion within general equilibrium theory and its extension to a theory of choice under conditions of uncertainty.

NOTES

[7] R. Rudner, *Philosophy of Social Science* (Englewood Cliffs, N.J.: Prentice-Hall, 1966), p. 59.

[8] For general critiques of the empirical adequacy and normative force of the transitivity or consistency axiom see P. Anand, "Are the Preference Axioms Really Rational", *Theory and Decision*, Vol. 23, 1987, pp. 189-214, sec. 3, and R. Sugden, "Why be Consistent? A Critical Analysis of Consistency Requirements in Choice Theory", *Economica*, Vol. 52, 1985, pp. 167-84.

[9] See D. Davidson, J. C. C. McKinsey and P. Suppes, "Outline of a Formal Theory of Value", *Philosophy of Science*, Vol. 22, 1955, pp. 140f.

[10] P. Anand, "Are the Preference Axioms Really Rational?" secs. 3.4, 3.5 and 3.6.

[11] See W. Baumol, *Economic Theory and Operations Analysis*, p. 189, for the explanation behind this conclusion.

[12] See F. Machlup, "Equilibrium and Disequilibrium", for a general review of the use of the concept of equilibrium in economic theory in his *Essays in Economic Semantics* (Englewood Cliffs, N.J.: Prentice-Hall, 1963), pp. 43-72. And see F. Hahn, *On the Notion of Equilibrium in Economics* (Cambridge: Cambridge University, 1973).

[13] It should not be assumed here that we are agreeing with the neo-classicist choice of a simple, precise concept of equilibrium in preference to factual accuracy, nor with the uses to which this concept is put in CCT, including its normative deployment. Indeed, we will take serious issue with this concept below, especially in Chapter 7.

[14] See, for example, R. Rudner, *Philosophy of Social Science*, pp. 59-63. For a moderate view of the limited explanatory power of an important idealized theory, see D. M. Hausman "Are general equilibrium theories explanatory?" in D. M. Hausman (ed.), *The Philosophy of Economics: An Anthology* (Cambridge: Cambridge University Press, 1984), pp. 344-59. Hausman's general methodological perspective is more fully elucidated in his recent book, *The Inexact and Separate Science of Economics* (Cambridge: Cambridge University Press, 1992).

[15] See C. G. Hempel, *Aspects of Scientific Explanation*, p. 248, who labels this criterion his R3 condition of adequacy for the components of a scientific explanation.

[16] S is indifferent between A and B = df. not (S prefers A to B) and not (S prefers B to A).

[17] Presentation of a dispositional analysis of wanting and believing would take us somewhat afield. For such an analysis of the former concept see the illuminating discussion by R. Brandt and J. Kim, "Wants as Explanations of Actions", *Journal*

of Philosophy, Vol. LX, 1963, pp. 425-35. For an investigation of a dispositional construal of belief, along with the attendant difficulties involved, see, for example, J. J. Leach, "Explanation and Value Neutrality", *British Journal for the Philosophy of Science*, Vol. 19, 1968, pp. 93-108, sec. 4. The concept of knowledge in CCT, it should be noted, is to be defined in terms of belief.

[18] R. Carnap, "Testability and Meaning", *Philosophy of Science*, Vol. 3, 1936, pp. 419-71, secs. 8-10.

[19] It is imperative to notice that (neo-classical) economists explicitly define the choice of X in terms of, or identify the choice of X with the actual observable purchasing of X. In other words, economists deal with what one might call *external* choice rather than with the more traditional philosophical construal of choice as an internal, mental event which functions as an antecedent condition to overt action. This point will be further discussed in Chap. 4.

[20] Rudner, *Philosophy of Social Science*, p. 58.

[21] Hutchison, *The Significance and Basic Postulates of Economic Theory*, p. 41.

[22] Of course, the option remains for economic theorists to forego the attempts, *via* idealizing assumptions, to formulate completely universal laws, by adopting the methodological alternative of employing statistical-probabilistic generalizations as explanatory principles. In that event, an inductive-statistical model of economic explanation might be attempted wherein the explanans, in virtue of its probabilistic laws, provides good, inductive support for the explanandum. However, neo-classical economists, at least in the construction of theories of choice, have generally demurred from presenting their explanatory laws in probabilistic form, preferring, as we have seen, when confronted with recalcitrant empirical evidence, to construct universal generalizations for empirically unactualizable "ideal cases", which hypotheses usually incorporate "ceteris paribus" clauses in their formulations. Neo-classical theorists have defended this strategy by claiming a preference for the superior simplicity of generalizations of universal form rather than for the increase in descriptive truth that would accrue if such generalizations were stated in probabilistic form. One should observe here that even the von Neumann-Morgenstern theory of choice under conditions of risk (J. von Neumann and O. Morgenstern, *Theories of Games and Economic Behaviour*, 2nd edn. (Princeton, N.J.: Princeton University Press, 1947), employ strictly universal generalizations. Consider, for instance, the rationality principle of this theory asserting roughly that all rational consumers choose that course of action which maximizes their expected utility. It is clear that the probability factor in such an hypothesis is located in the meaning of the term "expected utility" (utility of the outcome weighted by its probability), not in the form of the principle, which remains universal. For a general discussion of logical features of expected utility theory, see chapter 12 below.

[23] In this case, G would violate Hempel's R4 criterion of "factual correctness" for the constituents of a scientific explanation. See his *Aspects of Scientific Explanation*, pp. 248-49.

[24] Antecedent condition (5), requiring that an agent be psychologically *and* physically capable of performing a certain action, plays a central explanatory role. This condition is especially crucial in securing a universal form for the statement of G'; for the comprehensiveness of (5) enables it to render innocuous numerous putative counter-examples to the truth of G'. One should emphasize, in particular, that (5) includes the factor that action A be *physically* possible for S to perform. In other words, such external, non-subjective factors of an agent's situation as the interference of other agents and the obstructions of the physical environment are prevented by condition (5) from furnishing counter-examples to G'.

[25] I realize that the meaning and tenability of the analytic-synthetic distinction has been subjected to considerable controversy, especially since the work of W. V. O. Quine (see "Two Dogmas of Empiricism", in his *From a Logical Point of View*, 2nd edn. (Cambridge, Mass.: Harvard University Press, 1961), Chap. 2, pp. 20-46.) The assumption of such a distinction will, however, facilitate our philosophical analysis of CCT and it is hoped that the meaning of the concepts "analytic" and "synthetic" in our investigation will be clear from the context in which they appear.

[26] For a different analysis of the "analyticity" or empirical testability of economic theories, reaching the conclusion that neo-classical economics should be classified as an unfalsifiable division of applied mathematics, see Alexander Rosenberg, "If Economics is not a Science, what is it?" *Philosophical Forum*, Vol. 14, Summer, 1983, pp. 296-314. Rosenberg returns to this topic in Chapter 8 of *Economics – Mathematical Politics or Science of Diminishing Returns* (Chicago: University of Chicago Press, 1992), pp. 228-54.

[27] See p. 14 and note 19 above.

[28] "Equivalent counterpart" in the sense that the content of the axiom implies that it is functioning as a particular application of condition (1) of G' to economic phenomena. Hence we are not using "equivalence" in the logical sense of mutual implication.

[29] I say "completes" rather than constitutes a counterpart condition for we might alternatively construe the knowledge constraint of CCT as being a component of an ability condition. Lack of such knowledge would, as it were, function as a psychological impediment to choice, thus failing to satisfy the consumer freedom condition. One might also want to incorporate the condition of adequate income under the umbrella of consumer freedom as lack of sufficient financial resources would obviously function as an external, objective obstacle to choice. In sum, the

presence of consumer freedom comprehensively entails that the action (particular purchase) is both psychologically *and* physically possible for the agent to perform. Nevertheless, I have sometimes presented the knowledge and income constraints as though they were distinct to that of freedom for the reason that such a division is usually employed by economists in formulating CCT, although, strictly speaking, they can be included within a comprehensive definition of consumer freedom.

[30] L. von Mises, *Human Action: A Treatise on Economics*, (New Haven: Yale University Press, 1949), p. 858.

[31] For this interpretation, see especially L. von Mises, *The Epistemological Problems of Economics* (Princeton, N.J.: Van Nostrand, 1960), Ch. 1.

[32] Hutchison, *The Significance and Basic Postulates of Economic Theory*, p. 27.

[33] *Ibid.*, Chap. 2, sec. 3.

[34] L. Robbins, *An Essay on the Nature and Significance of Economic Science*, pp. 78-79.

[35] *Ibid.*, pp. 86-87, these "inner experiences" being, for Robbins, the "valuations of the individual".

[36] O. Lange, "The Scope and Method of Economics", in *The Review of Economic Studies*, Vol. XIII, 1945-46, pp. 20ff.

[37] For Rosenberg's original empiricist perspective see his *Microeconomic Laws: A Philosophical Analysis* (Pittsburg, University of Pittsburg Press, 1976); for his later view of neo-classical theory as applied mathematics see his "If Economics is not a Science, what is it?" *Philosophical Forum*, Vol. 14, Summer, 1983, pp. 296-314, and his *Economics − Mathematical Politics or Science of Diminishing Returns*, (Chicago: University of Chicago Press, 1992), Chap. 8, pp. 228-54.

[38] See M. Friedman, "The Methodology of Positive Economics", in his *Essays in Positive Economics*, (Chicago, Ill.: University of Chicago Press, 1953), pp. 3-43. The critical literature on the position expressed in Friedman's article is now voluminous. Rather than adding to this volume with a direct appraisal of my own, I have preferred to let the development of my own views on the methodology of economics stand in contrast to those of Friedman. In this context, Chapters 2, 10, 11 and 12 of this study are especially relevant. And for a perceptive assessment of recent views on the general issue of "realism", in
economics, see D. M. Hausman, "Problems with Realism in Economics," *Economics and Philosophy*, Vol. 14, No. 2, 1998, pp. 185-213.

[39] A place for contingency in the actual existence of particular states-of-affairs within a theoretical framework whose basic explanatory principles are necessarily true a

priori is a theme stressed even by classical rationalist philosophers. See, for example, G. W. Leibniz, "Letters to Queen Charlotte of Prussia" (1702), in *Leibniz Selections*, ed. P. P. Weiner (New York: Charles Scribner's Sons, 1951), pp. 363-64.

[40] Hutchison, *The Significance and Basic Postulates of Economic Theory*, p. 34.

[41] *Ibid.*, p. 162.

[42] See especially W.V.O. Quine, "Two Dogmas of Empiricism".

[43] The epistemological roots of this sort of a priori principle can be found in the neo-Kantian pragmatism of philosophers such as C. I. Lewis. See, for example, his *Mind and the World Order* (New York: Dover, 1929), Chap. 8. For a more recent and precise explication see the work of W. Sellars, for example, "Is there a Synthetic a Priori?", in his *Science, Perception and Reality* (New York: Humanities Press, 1963), pp. 298-320, or, *Science and Metaphysics* (London: Routledge and Kegan Paul, 1968), Chap. IV, pp. 91-115.

[44] Admittedly, the meaning of the notion expressed by such phrases as "conceptual scheme", "conceptual structure", etc. has remained notoriously vague in recent philosophical literature. However, it is intended that the illustrations examined herein, for instance, the action-theoretic framework for interpreting human behaviour, and Newtonian mechanics as a scheme for conceptualizing the motion of material bodies, will furnish sufficient indication of the meaning of "conceptual scheme", etc.

[45] "Conceptual truths" should be distinguished from "logical truths" or even "strictly analytic truths". For logical truths are better confined to substitution instances of the axioms and theorems of formal logic, while strictly or "merely analytic" statements are those which can be translated into such substitution instances with the help of appropriate definitions. Rather, our conceptual truths G' and G" are cases of what we have called *relativized* synthetic a priori principles. See R. Brandt and J. Kim, "Wants as Explanations of Actions" for a related notion of what these authors call a synthetic, but quasi-analytic principle. To quote one of their examples (p. 427), "If daydreaming about P is pleasant to X, then X wants P".

[46] Some, like Gilbert Ryle of course, *The Concept of Mind* (London: Hutchison, 1949), would deny that there really is an ontological commitment to "inner events" even in our "action-theoretic" discourse, as a perspicacious analysis of ordinary action-talk would show. I disagree with Ryle's view, but a presentation of my reasons for doing so is beyond the scope of this inquiry.

[47] See, for example, W. Sellars, "Philosophy and the Scientific Image of Man" in his *Science, Perception and Reality*, Chap. 1, pp. 1-40, J. Margolis, *Philosophy of*

Psychology (Englewood Cliffs, N.J.: Prentice-Hall, 1984), Chap. 2, pp. 8-33, and Paul M. Churchland, "Eliminative Materialism and the Propositional Attitudes", in his *A Neurocomputational Perspective: The Nature of Mind and the Structure of Science*, (Cambridge, Mass.: MIT Press, 1995) Chap. 1, pp. 1-22.

[48] I. Newton, *Mathematical Principles of Natural Philosophy and His System of the World* (1687), trans. by A. Motte, ed., F. Cajori (ed.), (Berkeley, California: University of California Press, 1960), p. 13.

[49] For instance, as E. Nagel observes in *The Structure of Science* (New York: Harcourt, Brace and World, 1961), p. 181, "... we might now adopt the first axiom as the *criterion* for the equality of temporal periods – two times being *defined* as equal if during them a body moving under the action of no forces covers equal distances along a straight line".

Chapter 3

[1] Mark Blaug, in his *The Methodology of Economics* (Cambridge: Cambridge University Press, 1980), esp. Chap. 15, subjects this methodological tendency of contemporary economists to critical scrutiny.

[2] O. Lange, "The Scope and Method of Economics", p. 30.

[3] This point of view will be further clarified and criticized in the next chapter.

[4] Again, an optimal action-choice (means) is one that could not be bettered (although it might be equalled) under the circumstances (information, constraints, etc.) towards the realization of an objective.

[5] We shall argue below (esp. Chap. 16), against neo-classical orthodoxy, that criteria of rationality can be extended to the assessment of (final) ends, not just means.

[6] Baumol, *Economic Theory and Operations Analysis*, p. 204.

[7] For a conventional account of the irrationality of intransitivities see D. Davidson, J.C.C. McKinsey and P. Suppes, "Outline of a Formal Theory of Value", p. 145. Or see G. Tullock, "The Irrationality of Intransitivity", *Oxford Economic Papers*, Vol. 16, 1964, pp. 401-06. Critical response by economists themselves to this orthodox view can be found in Paul Anand, "Are the Preference Axioms Really Rational?" sec. 3, and R. Sugden, "Why be Consistent? A Critical Analysis of Consistency Requirements in Choice Theory".

[8] M. Friedman and L. J. Savage, "The Expected Utility Hypothesis and the Measurability of Utility", *Journal of Political Economy*, Vol. LX, Dec. 1952, pp.

463-72. In the theory of choice under conditions of risk the consumer attempts to maximize the value of expected utility (the utility of an outcome weighted by its probability) rather than utility *simpliciter*. We shall focus on this version of choice theory in Chapter 12.

[9] For confirmation of the "orthodox view" see, for example, K. Klappholz, "Value Judgments and Economics", *The British Journal for the Philosophy of Science*, Vol. 15, 1964, pp. 97-114, and S. Roy, *Philosophy of Economics: On the Scope of Reason in Economic Inquiry* (London: Routledge, 1989), esp. Chap. 2. For a useful survey of the history of the "fact-value" controversy in economics, see T. W. Hutchison, *"Positive" Economics and Policy Objectives* (London: Allen and Unwin, 1964). For the historical context, see also G. Myrdal, *The Political Element in the Development of Economic Theory*, trans. by P. Streeten (London: Routledge and Kegan Paul, 1953). More recent developments are reviewed in M. Blaug, *The Methodology of Economics*, Chap. 5, and in D. M. Hausman and M. S. McPherson, "Taking Ethics Seriously: Economics and Contemporary Moral Philosophy", *Journal of Economic Literature*, Vol. XXXI, June, 1993, pp. Chaps. 3-4.

[10] See, for example, N. Rescher, *Introduction to Value Theory* (Englewood Cliffs, N.J.: Prentice-Hall, 1969), Chaps. 1-3, or C. W. Churchman, *Prediction and Optimal Decision* (Englewood Cliffs, N.J.: Prentice-Hall, 1961), for a clear account of the general meaning of value-ascriptions.

[11] It is imperative to note that the antecedent condition of "freedom" in D represents a very comprehensive class of cirumstances, including as suggested in note 29 of Chapter 2, the consumer's possession of sufficient income, but also such factors as the availability of the desired commodities and lack of interference from other consumers. In general, if a consumer is acting under the idealized condition of freedom, then there are, to speak roughly, neither subjective, psychological, nor objective, environmental barriers to his purchasing a preferred commodity.

Chapter 4

[1] Representatives of such a reinterpretation are, for instance, J. Rothenberg, "Values and Value Theory in Economics", in S. R. Krupp (ed.), *The Structure of Economic Science* (Englewood Cliffs, N.J.: Prentice-Hall, 1966), pp. 221-42; I. D. M. Little, *A Critique of Welfare Economics*, 2nd edn. (Oxford: Oxford University Press, 1957), Chap. 2, and J. Hirshleifer, *Price Theory and Applications* (Englewood Cliffs: Prentice-Hall, 1976), p. 85.

NOTES

[2] D. Braybrooke, "Economics and Rational Choice", in P. Edwards (ed.), *The Encyclopedia of Philosophy* (New York: Macmillan and Free Press, 1967), Vol. 2, p. 455.

[3] J. Hirshleifer, *Price Theory and Applications*, p. 85.

[4] Thus I. D. M. Little, *A Critique of Welfare Economics*, 2nd edn., (Oxford: Oxford University Press, 1957), p. 25, interprets the principle that "a consumer acts in order to maximize his utility" as meaning "the man must behave in the way he said he would behave."

[5] J. Rothenberg, "Values and Value Theory in Economics", pp. 227-37.

[6] P. Samuelson, "A Note on the Pure Theory of Consumer's Behaviour", *Economica*, Vol. 5, February 1938, pp. 61-71.

[7] *Ibid.*, p. 71.

[8] S. Wong, *The Foundations of Samuelson's Revealed Preference Theory* (London: Routledge and Kegan Paul, 1978), p. 6.

[9] P. Samuelson, *Foundations of Economic Analysis* (Cambridge, Mass.: Harvard University Press, 1947), p. 22.

[10] See Wong, *The Foundations of Samuelson's Revealed Preference Theory*, Chap. 5, for a lucid explanation of the operationalist methodology underlying Samuelson's revealed preference theory, in particular.

[11] See A. C. Michalos, *Foundations of Decision-Making* (Ottawa: Canadian Library of Philosophy, 1978), Chap. 4, sec 3, for a systematic analysis of the meaning of choice.

[12] Nor are we here ruling out the possibility that there may be other, more general grounds why behaviourist *cum* neutralist theory-constructions fail to have explanatory power for even simple choice situations. Indeed, I think there are such grounds, some of which will be pursued in Chapters 6 and 7.

[13] See, for example, M. Blaug, *Economic Theory in Retrospect*, 3rd edn. (Cambridge: Cambridge University Press, 1978), pp. 372-74, or see B. Caldwell, *Beyond Positivism: Economic Methodology in the Twentieth Century* (London: Allen and Unwin, 1982), Chap. 7, pp. 147-58, for a useful general scrutiny of the employment of the stability assumption in the theory of consumer behaviour.

[14] J. Rothenberg, "Values and Value Theory in Economics", pp. 233-35.

[15] Again, in Chapter 16, we shall argue, against the prevailing view in economics, that final ends are also amenable to rational appraisal.

[16] See G.E.M. Anscombe, *Intention* (Ithaca, N.Y.: Cornell University Press, 1957), p. 66.

319

NOTES

[17] See p. 32. But also see note 7 to Chap. 3.

[18] See I. Kant, *Foundations of the Metaphysics of Morals* (1785), trans. by L. W. Beck (Indianapolis, Ind.: Bobbs-Merrill, 1959), pp. 46ff.

[19] See p. 33 above.

[20] K. Lancaster, "Welfare Propositions in terms of Consistency and Expanded Choice", in *The Economic Journal*, Sept. 1958, pp. 464-79.

[21] *Ibid.*, p. 465. I. D. M. Little, *A Critique of Welfare Economics*, Chap. 2, proposes a similar normative criterion to Lancaster.

[22] Lancaster's own "good-characteristics" analysis of consumer behaviour, where the immediate objects of desire and preference are not individual commodities themselves but the characteristics of such commodities as, for instance, the elegance and durability of our automobiles, is a step in the right direction in providing a theoretical framework for a choice theory with normative applicability. Ironically, however, Lancaster claims that the term "characteristics" was chosen for its "normative neutrality", thus consciously rejecting what could be the most promising theoretical virtue of his "new approach" to the theory of consumer choice. (See K. Lancaster, "Change and Innovation in the Technology of Consumption", *American Economic Review*, Vol. 56, no. 2, 1966, pp. 74-123, and "A New Approach to Consumer Theory", *Journal of Political Economy*, Vol. 74, no. 2, 1968, pp. 132-57.)

[23] See M. Hollis and E. Nell, *Rational Economic Man: A Philosophical Critique of Neo-Classical Economics* (Cambridge: Cambridge University Press, 1975), for an extended study of the link between neo-classical economics and the epistemology of logical positivism.

Recently, however, there have been some welcome indications by economists, fully conversant with the "mainstream" tradition, of dissatisfaction with the persistence of a predominantly positivist understanding of economic method. Particularly welcome are the recommendations of "methodological pluralism" or a "problem-dependent" method of enquiry to be found in the works of Bruce Caldwell, *Beyond Positivism: Economic Methodology in the Twentieth Century*, esp. Chap. 13, and Laurence Boland, *The Foundations of Economic Method* (London: Allen and Unwin, 1982), esp. Chap. 12. Philosophers themselves writing on economic methodology have begun to part company with positivist conceptions. Two important contributions in this direction are D. Hausman, *The Inexact and Separate Science of Economics* (Cambridge: Cambridge University Press, 1992) and A. Rosenberg, *Economics – Mathematical Politics or Science of Diminishing Returns* (Chicago: University of Chicago Press, 1992). The arguments of Rosenberg's book provide instructive contrast with his earlier empiricist views in his *Microeconomic Laws: A Philosophical Analysis*

(Pittsburg, University of Pittsburg Press, 1976). See also C. Dyke, *The Philosophy of Economics* (Englewood Cliffs, N.J.: Prentice-Hall, 1981).

On the other hand, drawing on "postmodernist" thought, the economist Donald McCloskey raises severely sceptical questions concerning the very significance of epistemology and methodology for economics. See his "The Rhetoric of Economics", *Journal of Economic Literature*, Vol. 21, No. 2, June 1983, pp. 481-517. For a philosopher's response to McCloskey, see M. Hollis, "The Emperor's Newest Clothes", *Economics and Philosophy*, Vol. 1, April, 1985, pp. 128-33.

[24] For a good discussion on the issues involved here see, I. Scheffler, *The Anatomy of Inquiry: Philosophical Studies in the Theory of Science* (New York: Alfred A. Knopf, 1967) pp. 127-222.

[25] See esp. Chaps. 8 and 9 below.

[26] For another philosophical critique of this sort of programme in economics, see. C. Dyke, "The Question of Interpretation in Economics", *Ratio*, Vol. XXV, 1983, pp. 15-29.

Chapter 5

[1] Again, see K. Klappholz, "Value Judgments and Economics", for a succinct presentation of this orthodox view. Or see his "Economics and Ethical Neutrality", in the *Encyclopedia of Philosophy*, Paul Edwards (ed.), (New York: Macmillan and Free Press, 1967), Vol. 2, pp. 451-54. For confirmation that the espousal of ethical neutrality among economists is based on agreement with principles of logical positivism, or at least Humean empiricism, see S. Roy, *The Philosophy of Economics: On the Scope of Reason in Economic Inquiry* (London: Routledge, 1989), Chap. 2.

[2] A. R. Louch has gone so far as to offer such an (extreme) interpretation of economic theory in general, claiming that "shorn of its alleged descriptive character classical economics becomes a moral theory", advocating that economics laws and formulae be construed as policy statements, and that we picture economics as a game defining the economic system which is "something of our own contrivance made of rules which have our blessing" (*Explanation and Human Understanding*, Oxford: Oxford University Press, 1966), pp. 74; 197.

[3] For an illuminating critique of the moral presuppositions of mainstream economics see the following articles by A. K. Sen: "Rational Fools: A Critique of the Behavioral Foundations of Economic Theory", *Philosophy and Public Affairs*, Vol. 6, Summer 1977, pp. 317-44; "Choice, Orderings and Morality", in S. Korner, (ed.), *Practical Reason* (Oxford: Oxford University Press, 1974), pp. 54-67; "Descriptions as Choice", *Oxford Economic Papers*, Vol. 32, 1980, pp. 353-

69; "The Moral Standing of the Market", in E. F. Paul, F. D. Miller Jr. and J. Paul (eds.) *Ethics and Economics*, (Oxford: Basil Blackwell, 1985), pp. 1-19; and *On Ethics and Economics* (Oxford: Basil Blackwell, 1987). Further dissent from the "orthodox" view can be found in Michael S. McPherson, "Want Formation, Morality and Some Interpretive Aspects of Economic Inquiry", in Norma Hahn, R. H. Bellah, P. Rabinow and W. M. Sullivan (eds.), *Social Science as Moral Inquiry* (New York: Columbia University Press, 1983) pp. 96-124; M. Hollis, "Rational Preferences", *Philosophical Forum*, Vol. 14, 1983, pp. 246-62; S. Hargreaves Heap, *Rationality in Economics*, (Oxford: Basil Blackwell, 1989); S. Roy, *The Philosophy of Economics: On the Scope of Reason in Economic Inquiry*, (London: Routledge, 1989); A. Etzioni, *The Moral Dimension: Towards a New Economics*, (New York: Macmillan, 1988); D. M. Hausman and M. S. McPherson, who themselves claim that "positive and normative economics are frequently intermingled", provide a lucid, insightful survey of the present state of the issue in "Taking Ethics Seriously: Economics and Contemporary Moral Philosophy", *Journal of Economic Literature*, Vol. XXXI, June, 1993), pp. 671-731; see also their "Economics, Rationality and Ethics", in D. M. Hausman (ed.), *The Philosophy of Economics*, 2nd edn. (Cambridge: Cambridge University Press, 1994), pp. 252-77. Hausman's and McPherson's views are more fully elaborated in their *Economic Analysis and Moral Philosophy* (Cambridge: Cambridge University Press, 1996).

[4] We are making no claim here that the "self-understanding" of their methodological practice indicates that neo-classical economists have deliberately, let alone deviously, introduced value-judgments masquerading as factual ones into their theories. But we shall be claiming that an unavowed presupposition of (moral) values does characterize CCT, whether or not economists constructing or using the theory are aware of this situation.

[5] For the exact specification of a structural interpretation of CCT see pp. 38 f. above.

[6] K. Boulding, "Economics as a Moral Science", *American Economic Review*, Vol. 59, 1969, p. 6.

[7] See J. Bentham, *An Introduction to the Principles of Morals and Legislation* (1789) (reprint, London: University of London, 1970), pp. 17f.

[8] It should be cautioned here that the content of A_2 does not imply that a consumer will necessarily purchase more of any particular commodity, x, when more of x becomes obtainable or affordable. To begin with, x has to be a commodity that is at least on his "preference map" – that is, for which he has some desire. Moreover, assuming x is among his material wants, purchasing more x may require him to reduce his purchase of some other commodity, y, for which he has a relatively higher level of desire than x. Or if x is what economists call an "inferior good" (of very low quality – say, second hand clothing), an increase in

the consumer's real income or purchasing power will induce him to decrease his purchase of x by replacing x with more desirable goods. Nevertheless, none of these conditions gainsays the basic truth-claim of A_2 – that, other things (e.g., prices and income) remaining equal, a rational consumer prefers to possess more of what he already wants.

The axiom of non-satiety, furthermore, plays a critical analytical role within CCT. In particular, it is an assumption that is integral to the demonstration that indifference curves have the "normal" properties of a negative slope and non-intersectability. And the violation of A_2 no longer guarantees that indifference curves have the normal characteristics of being convex to the origin. But if any of these properties does not obtain, there can be no determination of a utility maximizing point of equilibrium as the point of tangency of the consumer's budget line with his highest attainable indifference curve (see Baumol, *Economic Theory and Operations Analysis*, 4th edn., pp. 197-206). Moreover, as we shall argue in Chap. 11, secs. 2-4, a version of A_2 is essential to the subsumption of CCT within the important explanatory and normative framework of general equilibrium theory.

[9] Of course, J. S. Mill, in distinguishing between higher and lower quality pleasures, or differences in kind as well as degree of pleasure (utility), may have proposed a way for Utilitarianism to part company with the "expansionist" principle (see Mill's *Utilitarianism* (1861), (New York: Bobbs-Merrill, 1957), pp. 11ff. However, neo-classical economics has followed Bentham, not Mill, on this matter.

[10] See especially, Epictetus, *Moral Discourses and Fragments* (London: Dent, 1910).

[11] Similar considerations would apply to a "revealed preference" approach to choice behaviour.

[12] Epictetus, *Moral Discourses and Fragments*, p. 10.

[13] The phrase is that of C. B. MacPherson. See his *The Political Theory of Possessive Individualism* (Oxford: Oxford University Press, 1962).

[14] See E. J. Mishan, *The Costs of Economic Growth* (London: Staples Press, 1967), especially part III, pp. 109-66, and his "The Growth of Affluence and the Decline of Welfare", in H. E. Daley (ed.), *Economics, Ecology, Ethics: Essays Towards a Steady-State Economy* (San Francisco: W. H. Freeman, 1980), pp. 267-81.

[15] The *locus classicus* is to be found in J. S. Mill, *On Liberty* (1859), (Indianapolis, Ind: Hackett, 1978), chap. 1.

[16] E. J. Mishan, *The Costs of Economic Growth*, part III, and "The Growth of Affluence and the Decline of Welfare", p. 268.

NOTES

[17] As referenced earlier, (note 7, ch. 3), however, the exceptionless binding force of the transitivity axiom has recently been challenged by some economists themselves.

[18] Especially in contexts of the multi-dimensionality of utility (see pp. 18f. above). And see Bruce Caldwell, *Beyond Positivism*, Chap. 7, pp. 150-58 for a discussion of experimental research on intransitive choice patterns. Or see Alex C. Michalos, *Foundations of Decision Making* (Ottawa: Canadian Library of Philosophy, 1978), pp. 28-29; Paul Anand, "Are the Preference Axioms Really Rational", sec. 3; and R. Sugden, "Why be Consistent? A Critical Analysis of Consistency Requirements in Choice Theory".

[19] See note 13 to Chapter 4 above for references to discussions of the stability or constancy of tastes assumption.

[20] See M. Blaug, *Economic Theory in Retrospect*, 3rd edn., p. 373.

[21] See, for instance, E. Mandel, *Marxist Economic Theory*, 2 vols. trans. by B. Pearce (New York: Monthly Review Press, 1968), Vol. 1, Chap. 5, and W. Dugger, "Methodological Differences between Institutional and Neoclassical Economics", *Journal of Economic Issues*, vol. 12 (1979), pp.899-909.

[22] The terms "rational economic man" and "*homo economicus*" will be used interchangeably in this study.

[23] J. S. Mill anticipated this neo-classical conception of the attitudes of *homo economicus* when he wrote that "the desire for the present enjoyment of costly indulgence" was antithetical to the "economic motive" of the desire for wealth. See his *Essays on Some Unsettled Questions of Political Economy* (1844), Reprint (London: London School of Economics, 1948), pp. 137-38.

[24] L. Robbins, *An Essay on the Nature and Significance of Economic Science*, p. 157.

[25] A. Marshall, *Principles of Economics*, 9th Variorum edn. (1st edn. 1890), (London: Macmillan, 1961), Vol. 1, pp. 20-21. We are not, in examining the classical formulation of CCT in Marshall's work, interested in a merely historical exercise. Rather, to my mind, Marshall's *Principles* exhibits the tensions of the normative *versus* descriptive dimensions of CCT in a strikingly clear way. Although more recent formulations of the theory are equally susceptible to the same fact-value conundrums, such a liability tends to be camouflaged by the technical refinements of the basic theoretical system.

[26] *Ibid.*, p. 120. See especially Book I, Chap. II, Book II, Chap. III; Book III, Chap. II and V; and Book VI, Chap. XIII for Marshall's characterization of rational economic man in his consumer behaviour.

[27] *Ibid.*, pp. 120ff.

NOTES

[28] *Ibid.*, p. 66, note 1.

[29] *Ibid.*, p. 6.

[30] See M. Weber, *The Protestant Ethic and the Spirit of Capitalism*, trans. by T. Parsons (New York: Charles Scribner's Sons, 1958), pt. 1, Chap. II and his *General Economic History* (New York: Collier Books, 1961), Chap. 30.

[31] M. Weber, *General Economic History*, p. 260.

[32] M. Weber, *The Protestant Ethic and the Spirit of Capitalism*, p. 53.

[33] J. Schumpeter, *Ten Great Economists: From Marx to Keynes* (London: George Allen and Unwin, 1952), p. 104.

[34] W. A. Weisskopf, *Economics and Alienation* (New York: Dutton, 1971), Chap. III, pp. 78ff.

[35] See, e.g., H. Marcuse, *One-Dimensional Man* (Boston: Beacon Press, 1964). Compare also, T. Scitovsky, *The Joyless Economy: An Inquiry into Human Satisfaction and Consumer Dissatisfaction* (Oxford: Oxford University Press, 1976).

[36] See, e.g., A. H. Maslow, *Motivation and Personality*, 2nd edn. (New York: Harper and Row, 1970).

[37] This point will be developed in the next chapter. See also our discussion in the present chapter of CCT's use of a Benthamite conception of utility maximization.

[38] A. Marshall, *Principles of Economics*, p. 119.

[39] *Ibid.*, p. 120.

[40] *Ibid.*, p. 66.

[41] *Ibid.*, p. 66. It would be of no avail attempting to defend Marshall here by arguing that he is concentrating on the macro level of national planning rather than the micro level of individual decisions, and that a policy of calculatedness, impulse-control, etc. *is* uniformly appropriate in the macro context. In the first place, the passages from Marshall are taken from his analysis of individual consumer demand. But, more importantly, neo-classicists are systematically precluded from analyzing macro demand in separation from the micro context. For it is a standard doctrine of neo-classical economics that the macro demand for consumer products is the *aggregated* result of the autonomous decisions of the individual consumers – the "micro-units". Hence, from the point of view of neo-classical theory, if an economist is to recommend a social or macro policy of deliberate, planned consumption, the success of this policy would have to be viewed as the outcome of such calculatedness on the part of the micro-units.

NOTES

[42] This point of view will be examined more fully in chapters 11, 12 and 13.

[43] A. Marshall, *Principles of Economics*, p. 67.

[44] *Ibid.*, p. 66.

[45] See especially Adam Smith, *An Inquiry into the Nature and Cause of the Wealth of Nations* (1776), E. Cannan (ed.), (New York: The Modern Library, 1937), Book II, Chap. III.

[46] A. Marshall, *The Principles of Economics*, p. 67.

[47] *Ibid.*, p. 70.

[48] *Ibid.*, p. 65.

[49] *Ibid.*, p. 69.

[50] For insightful comment on the irrationality of letting a general disposition to be "calculating" in one's decision-making usurp one's spontaneity of character see J. Elster, *Ulysses and the Sirens: Studies in Rationality and Irrationality* (Cambridge: Cambridge University Press, 1979), pp. 40-41.

[51] See Marshall, *Principles of Economics*, Book III, Chap. II and also Book VI, Chap. XIII.

[52] *Ibid.*, p. 90.

[53] For an instructive discussion of issues bearing on the distinction between instrumental and expressive rationality see, for example, M. Hollis, "Rational Man and Social Science", in Ross Harrison (ed.), *Rational Action: Studies in Philosophy and Social Science* (Cambridge: Cambridge University Press, 1979), pp. 1-15. Hollis's perspective is extensively developed in his *The Cunning of Reason* (Cambridge: Cambridge University Press, 1987). For an economist's critique of the lack of an adequate concept of expressive rationality in economic theory, see S. Hargreaves Heap, *Rationality in Economics*, Chap. 8.

[54] I. Lakatos, "History of Science and its Rational Reconstruction" in R. C. Buck and R. S. Cohen (eds.), *Boston Studies in The Philosophy of Science*, Vol. VIII (Dordrecht, Holland: D. Reidl, 1971), p. 91. Lakatos' comment, of course, plays upon Kant's dictum that "thoughts without content are empty, and intuitions without concepts are blind" (I. Kant, *Critique of Pure Reason* (1787) trans. by N. K. Smith (London: Macmillan, 1929), p. 93.

[55] As anticipated by J. S. Mill (see note 23 to this chapter).

[56] Once again, the normative requirement of the transitivity or "consistency" axiom, has been contested. See Chap. 3, note 7 above.

NOTES

[57] Marshall, *Principles of Economics*, p. 89.

[58] *Ibid.*, p. 90.

[59] *Ibid.*, p. 89.

[60] *Ibid.*, p. 90.

[61] *Ibid.*, p. 88 note.

[62] *Ibid.*, pp. 86-89.

[63] *Ibid.*, p. 689.

[64] In support see *Ibid.*, Book III, Chap. I, sec. 2, p. 85; Book III, Chap. II, sec. 4; and Book VI, Chap. XIII, sec. 1.

[65] *Ibid.*, p. 89.

[66] No doubt there are echoes in Marshall's distinction between higher and lower wants of J. S. Mill's distinction between higher and lower quality pleasures (see *Utilitarianism*, pp. 11ff). As Mill finds preferable moral value in higher *kinds* of pleasure, so Marshall finds it in higher *kinds* of desires or wants.

Chapter 6

[1] G. L. S. Shackle, *A Scheme of Economic Theory* (Cambridge: Cambridge University Press, 1965), p. ix.

[2] The *locus classicus* is M. Friedman, "The Methodology of Positive Economics". For a "textbook" explication of such methodological unity, see R. G. Lipsey, *An Introduction to Positive Economics*, 4th edn., (London: Weidenfeld and Nicholson, 1975), Part I, pp. 3-59.

[3] W. W. Jevons, *Theory of Political Economy*, 4th edn. (London: Macmillan, 1924 [1st edn. 1871], p. 21.

[4] Some representatives of this view are A. R. Louch, *Explantion and Human Action* (Oxford: Oxford University Press, 1966); P. Winch, *The Idea of a Social Science and its Relation to Philosophy* (London: Routledge and Kegan Paul, 1958); W. H. Dray, *Laws and Explanation in History* (Oxford: Oxford University Press, 1957); R. S. Peters, *The Concept of Motivation*, 2nd edn. (London: Routledge and Kegan Paul, 1960); G. H. von Wright, *Explanation and Understanding* (Ithaca, N.Y.: Cornell University Press, 1971). D. Braybrooke, *Philosophy of Social Science* (Englewood Cliffs, N.J.: Prentice-Hall, 1987) Chap. 3.

[5] See W. S. Jevons, *Theory of Political Economy*, 4th edn. (London: Macmillan, 1924 [1st ed. 1871]) and F. Y. Edgeworth, *Mathematical Psychics* (1881), (reprint, London: London School of Economics and Political Science, 1932).

[6] J. Bentham, *Introduction to the Principles of Morals and Legislation*, p. 11.

[7] For recent discussions of the link between utilitarianism and economic theory see J. A. Mirrlees, "The economic uses of utilitarianism", and Frank Hahn, "On some difficulties of the utilitarian economist", and A. Sen and B. Williams, "Introduction" in A. Sen and B. Williams (eds.), *Utilitarianism and Beyond* (Cambridge: Cambridge University Press, 1982), pp. 63-84; pp. 187-98; pp. 1-21.

[8] For an economist's confirmation of the continuance of "invisible hand" principles in contemporary economics, see L. A. Boland, *The Foundations of Economic Method*, Chap. 3, especially pp. 54ff.

[9] Neo-classicists propose a "Pareto-optimum" measure of a Utilitarian standard of the common good aligned with their doctrine of consumer sovereignty (see p. 67 above). More precisely, "common good" is defined as the "Pareto optimal" maximization of the satisfaction of the totality of given consumer desires – viz., any movement from such a Pareto optimal state will make some consumer worse off in terms of the satisfaction of his *de facto* wants.

[10] See J. S. Mill, *Utilitarianism*, p. 10.

[11] In this regard, see the illuminating historical studies of Philip Mirowski in his *More Heat than Light: Economics as Social Physics, Physics as Nature's Economics* (Cambridge: Cambridge University Press, 1989). Or see the earlier investigation of A. G. Pikler, "Utility Theories in Field Physics and Mathematical Economics", I and II, *British Journal for the Philosophy of Science*, Vol. 5, 1954 and 1955, pp. 47-58; 303-18.

[12] A. G. Pikler, "Utility Theories in Field Physics and Mathematical Economics", pp. 303ff. This is a view which has also been extensively examined, endorsed and further explained by Mirowski (see reference in preceding note).

[13] Edgeworth, *Mathematical Physics*, p. 15.

[14] For the general claim that contemporary economics conceives human behaviour in mechanistic terms see N. Georgescu-Roegen, "The Entropy Law and the Economic Problem" in H. E. Daly (ed.), *Economics, Ecology, Ethics: Essays Towards a Steady-State Economy* (San Francisco: W. H. Freeman, 1980), pp. 49-59, and his *The Entropy Law and the Economic Process* (Cambridge, Mass.: Harvard University Press, 1971), esp. the "Introduction" and Chap. 2, sec. 1. See also, P. Mirowski, *Against Mechanism: Protecting Economics From Science* (Totawa, N.J.: Rowan and Littlefield, 1988), and F. H. Knight, *On the History*

and Method of Economics (Chicago: University of Chicago Press, 1956), Chap. VIII, pp. 179-201.

[15] See especially Chap. 8, secs. 3-4 and Chap. 13, secs. 4-5.

[16] J. S. Mill, *Utilitarianism*, Chap. 4.

[17] A. R. Louch has gone so far as to offer such an (extreme) interpretation of economic theory in general. As confirmation, see his claim referred to in note 2 to chapter 5 above.

[18] C. D. Broad, *Five Types of Ethical Theory* (London: Routledge and Kegan Paul, 1930), pp. 189-90.

[19] C. Taylor, *The Explanation of Behaviour* (London: Routledge and Kegan Paul, 1964), p. 220.

[20] B. F. Skinner, *Science and Human Behaviour* (New York: Macmillan, 1953), p. 87.

[21] "Equilibrating" behaviour would now be interpreted behaviouristically as equating marginal rates of substitution of one commodity for another with the ratio of their respective prices. (Rather than defining equilibrating behaviour in terms of ratios of marginal utilities.)

[22] Similarly to the case of pleasure, in a consistently behaviourist framework, insofar as the concept of a "rewarding" state connotes an inner mental state (e.g., something consciously satisfying to a subject), it too would require translation into "physicalist" language – i.e., a publicly observable consequence of behaviour which increased the probability of such behaviour occurring under similar stimulus conditions in the future.

[23] R. S. Peters, *The Concept of Motivation*, pp. 14ff.

[24] For general criticism by an economist of a lack of sufficient scope in neo-classical theory for an adequate inclusion of the varieties of empirical motivations for choice, especially those which incorporate moral motivation, see the following by A. K. Sen, "Rational Fools: A Critique of the Behavioral Foundations of Economic Theory", sec. VII; "Choice, Orderings, and Morality"; "Utilitarianism and Welfarism", *Journal of Philosophy*, Vol. 76, 1979, pp. 463-89, and *On Ethics and Economics*, Chap. 7.

Chapter 7

[1] See, for instance, P. Geach, "Good and Evil", in *Analysis*, Vol. 17 (1956), pp. 33-42.

NOTES

[2] See e.g., R. M. Hare, "Geach: Good and Evil", *Analysis*, Vol. 18 (1957), pp. 102-12.

[3] See C. G. Hempel, "The Logic of Functional Analysis", in his *Aspects of Scientific Explanation*, pp. 297-330 for a useful general survey of the concepts and structure of functionalist theories.

[4] For the classic source of systems theory see L. von Bertalanffy, *General Systems Theory* (New York: G. Braziller, 1968). A recent overview is provided in George J. Klir, *Facets of Systems Science* (New York: Plenum Press, 1994). For a philosopher's perspective, see C. W. Churchman, *The Systems Approach and its Enemies* (New York: Basic Books, 1978). For an example of a mechanistic approach to systems see James G. Miller, "Introduction" in *Chicago Behavioural Sciences Publications No.1: Profits and Problems of Homeostatic Models in the Behavioural Sciences* (Chicago: University of Chicago Press, 1954). For an affirmation that mechanistic structures are inappropriate to explain the behaviour of "higher level" systems such as individual agents and social groups, see E. Laszlo, *System, Structure and Experience* (New York: Gordon and Beach Science Publishers, 1969), Chap. 1.

[5] For the claim that system approaches to economic theory are based primarily on an analogy with mechanistic systems, see P. Mirowski, *More Heat than Light: Economics as Social Physics, Physics as Nature's Economics*, and see the articles by A. J. Cohen, D. W. Hands, B. Barnes, M. N. Wise, "Review Symposium" on Mirowski's book in *Philosophy of the Social Sciences*, Vol. 22, No. 1, March 1992, pp. 78-141. See also, G. Pikler, "Utility, Theories in Field Physics and Mathematical Economics, II and II", K. Boulding, "General Systems Theory – The Skeleton of a Science" in his *Beyond Economics* (Ann Arbour: University of Michigan Press, 1968), especially pp. 95-97, and F. H. Knight, *On the History and Method of Economics*, Chap. VIII.

[6] L. von Bertalanffy, *General Systems Theory*, p. 55.

[7] See note 4 to Chapter 4 above.

[8] Again, see F. Machlup, "Equilibrium and Disequilibrium" for a discussion of the concept of equilibrium in economic theory.

[9] *Ibid.*, p. 54.

[10] See Gilbert Ryle, *The Concept of Mind*, Chap. IV, sec. 6 for an analysis of this difficulty for hedonistic explanations generally.

[11] See for example, R. Leftwich, *The Price System and Resource Allocation*, 3rd edn., (New York: Holt, Rinehart and Winston, 1966), p. 67.

[12] As suggested, for instance, by J. Rothenberg, "Values and Value Theory in Economics", pp. 227f and p. 237; or by the philosopher D. Braybrooke, "Economics and Rational Choice", p. 455.

[13] An influential case in point is I. D. M. Little, *A Critique of Welfare Economics*, Chaps. 1 and 2.

[14] W. J. Baumol, *Economic Theory and Operations Analysis*, pp. 204-05.

[15] *Ibid.*, p. 205.

[16] Such as Little, *A Critique of Welfare Economics*, Chap. 2.

[17] See Mark Blaug, *Economic Theory in Retrospect*, p. 356.

[18] Again, Little, *A Critique of Welfare Economics*, Chap. 2, will be taken as a representative case of such economic behaviourism.

[19] *Ibid.*, p. 25.

[20] See p. 44 above.

[21] Little, *A Critique of Welfare Economics*, p. 29.

[22] See K. Boulding, "Some Contributions of Economics to the General Theory of Value", *Philosophy of Science*, Vol. 23, no. 1, 1956, p. 6.

[23] Little, *A Critique of Welfare Economics*, p. 35.

[24] *Ibid.*, p. 42ff.

[25] In economic language, such a situation is known as the problem of "interdependent utility functions". See L. D. Schally "Interdependent Utility Functions and Pareto Optimality", *Quarterly Journal of Economics*, Vol. 86, 1972, pp. 19-24.

[26] Little, *A Critique of Welfare Economics*, p. 44.

[27] See, on this issue, the classic discussion of emulative consumption in J. S. Duesenberry, *Income, Saving and the Theory of Consumer Behaviour* (Cambridge, Mass.: Harvard University Press, 1949), Chap. 3, sec. 5, pp. 28-32. And see E. J. Mishan, "The Growth of Affluence and the Decline of Welfare", p. 271.

[28] See pp. 46f. above.

Chapter 8

[1] See R. Macklin, pp. 403ff of "Explanation and Action: Recent Issues and Controversies", *Synthese*, Vol. 20, 1964, pp. 388-415 for a useful review of the

positions of different philosophers on whether or not reasons can be causes. An emphatically sceptical view of such a possibility serving as an explanatory framework for economics is expounded in Chapter 5 of A. Rosenberg, *Economics-Mathematical Politics or Science of Diminishing Returns* (Chicago: University of Chicago Press, 1992), pp. 112-51.

[2] For an endorsement of such a view, along with the claim that explanation by reasons (beliefs and desires) should be replaced by a causal framework drawn from a sociobiological model in the construction of a scientific theory of human behaviour, see A. Rosenberg, *Sociobiology and the Preemption of Social Science* (Oxford: Basil Blackwell, 1980).

[3] See Chap. 2, sec. 2.

[4] A. I. Melden, *Free Action* (London: Routledge and Kegan Paul, 1961), p. 52.

[5] See Chap. 2, sec. 2.

[6] D. Davidson, "Action, Reasons, and Causes", in his *Actions and Events* (Oxford: Oxford University Press, 1980), essay 1.

[7] *Ibid.*, p. 14.

[8] *Ibid.*, p. 14.

[9] See Macklin, "Explanation and Action: Recent Issues and Controversies", pp. 403ff, for a categorization of the views of philosophers on the question of whether or not there is a necessary connection between reasons and action. And see A. Rosenberg "Obstacles to Nomological Connection of Reasons and Actions", *Philosophy of Science*, Vol. 10, 1980, pp. 79-91.

[10] See pp. 25ff. above.

[11] In this context see A. Downs, *An Economic Theory of Democracy* (New York: Harper and Row, 1957), pp. 27-30.

[12] Since G', although "analytically true", is revisable, we might characterize it as (only) "pragmatically analytic".

[13] On a traditional empiricist analysis of basic physical laws. For a contrasting view applied to Newton's theory of motion see pp. 27-29 and p. 130f. above.

[14] For a representative discussion of these issues, see C. V. Borst (ed.), *The Mind-Brain Identity Theory* (London: Macmillan, 1970), J. Searle, *The Rediscovery of the Mind* (Cambridge, Mass.: MIT Press, 1992), Chaps. 1-2, and P. Churchland, *The Engine of Reason, The Seat of the Soul: A Philosophical Journey into the Brain* (Cambridge, Mass.: MIT Press, 1995).

[15] These comments apply *a fortiori* to a behaviourist model of economic behaviour; for we have already seen in Chapter 4 how a behaviourist construction of CCT *precludes its normative applicability*.

[16] As, for instance, by D. Easton, "Limits of the Equilibrium Model in Social Research", in *Chicago Behavioural Publications No. 1: Profits and Problems of Homeostatic Models in the Behavioural Sciences*, p. 31.

[17] At least to an approximate degree, as the behaviour represented by CCT *qua* idealization constitutes a limiting case that can rarely, if ever, be completely exhibited by actual agents.

[18] But, again, such necessity as claimed by CCT has not gone without challenge – see Chap. 3, note 7 above.

[19] This crucial point will be more fully elaborated in Chapter 16.

[20] We are speaking here of metaphysical libertarianism (free human actions are uncaused), not the political variety.

[21] See S. Roy, *Philosophy of Economics*, Chap. 2. But see p. 49, and note 3 to Chapter 5 above.

[22] In Chapter 16.

[23] M. Blaug, *Economic Theory in Retrospect*, 3rd edn., p. 59.

[24] See p. 81 above, note 8 to Chapter 6, and Chapter 11, sec. 3.

[25] Pareto, in his theory of income distribution provides an early and emphatic example of such neo-classical moral conservatism. In his *Cours d'Economie Politique*, 2 Vols., (Lausanne:Rouge, 1896-97), Book III, Chap. 1, he formulated what he took to be an empirical law expressing a regularity in the distribution of personal income, for any country, in any historical period, thus: $N=Ax^{-B}$ where N is the number of persons receiving income x or more, and A and B are constants. Moreover, Pareto was, at that time, an ardent advocate of both (i) value-free social science and (ii) the moral worth of classical liberalism, affirming the incontrovertible right of freedom of choice for individual economic agents, along with its implied doctrine of laissez-faire government policy. Applied to questions of economic distribution such liberalism (now called neo-conservativism!) proscribed political intervention to remove the *de facto* inequalities of income that had resulted from the operation of "natural market mechanisms". Most importantly, Pareto saw no inconsistency in such a moral commitment and his value neutrality as a scientist. For he believed, in virtue of the empirical necessity asserted by his positive income law, that such intervention would, in any case, be futile in the long run; *a fortiori* such an outcome was empirically inevitable independently of his personal

moral views – even though, by an allegedly unplanned concurrence, they did happen to be of the laissez-faire variety.

[26] The practical deliberations here might be those of a public or political body, rather than an individual agent. For the antecedent conditions of a social scientific law, whose satisfaction is required for the applicability of such laws, often include reference to human intentions. And generally the realization of such intentions can be thwarted (or facilitated) by the operation of external constraints, such as the enforcement of political legislation. Hence, a recognition of the truth of social scientific laws does not provide an adequate apologia for political quietism.

[27] J. S. Mill, *Principles of Political Economy*, 2 vols., 1st edn. (London: J. W. Parker, 1848), Vol. 1, pp. 239-40, my italics.

[28] K. Marx, *Grundrisse: Foundations of the Critique of Political Economy*, trans. by M. Nicolaus (Harmondsworth, Middlesex: Penguin Books, 1973), p. 87.

[29] *Ibid.*, p. 87.

[30] Eric Roll, *A History of Economic Thought*, 4th edn. (London: Faber and Faber, 1973), p. 150.

[31] *Ibid.*, p. 149.

Chapter 9

[1] In Chapter 12 below.

[2] Recognition of G" as a rationalization of course requires that one note the failings of certain behaviourist and mechanistic "reductions" of the conceptual system of CCT.

[3] See S. Toulmin, "Reasons and Causes", in R. Border and F. Cioffi (eds.), *Explanation in the Behavioural Sciences* (Cambridge: Cambridge University Press, 1970), pp. 1-26 for a succinct discussion of this claim.

[4] See C. G. Hempel, "Explanation in Science and History", in W. Dray (ed.), *Philosophical Analysis and History* (New York: Harper and Row, 1966), p. 118, or A. J. Ayer, *Man as a Subject for Science* (London: University of London, Athlone Press, 1964), pp. 13ff.

[5] R. M. Hare, *The Language of Morals* (Oxford: Oxford University Press, 1952), *Freedom and Reason* (Oxford: Oxford University Press, 1963) and *Moral Thinking* (Oxford: Oxford University Press, 1981).

[6] R. M. Hare, *Descriptivism* (London: Oxford University Press, 1963), p. 126.

⁷ For an instructive discussion of this relationship, see. W. D. Falk, "Ought and Motivation", in his *Ought, Reasons and Morality* (Ithaca, N.Y.: Cornell University Press, 1986), pp. 21-41; T. Nagel, *The Possibility of Altruism* (Oxford: Oxford University Press, 1970), Chaps. 1-2; and W. Frankenna, "Obligation and Motivation in Recent Moral Philosophy", in A. J. Melden (ed.), *Essays in Moral Philosophy* (Seattle: University of Washington Press, 1958), pp. 40-81.

⁸ See W. D. Falk, "Ought and Motivation", for the original distinction. Or see Thomas Nagel, *The Possibility of Altruism*, Chap. 2, for a classification of philosophers in terms of whether they defend internalist or externalist positions.

⁹ See, e.g., C. G. Hempel, *Aspects of Scientific Explanation*, pp. 469ff.

¹⁰ As, for example, in the emotivism of A. J. Ayer, *Language, Truth and Logic*, 2nd edn., (New York: Dover Publications, 1952), Chap. 6, and C. L. Stevenson *Ethics and Language* (New Haven: Yale University Press, 1944), or the prescriptivism of R. M. Hare (see note 5 to this chapter).

¹¹ The points of this paragraph will be further developed in Chapter 16.

¹² K. Klappholz, "Value Judgments and Economics", pp. 98-99. The view expressed in this quotation is also found in Klapphlz's "Economics and Ethical Neutrality", in P. Edwards (ed.), *Encyclopedia of Philosophy* (New York: Macmillan, 1967), p. 451.

¹³ See K. Klappholz, "Value Judgments and Economics", pp. 104, 105, and "Economics and Ethical Neutrality", p. 453.

¹⁴ See p. 81 above, note 9 to Chap. 6, and the extended discussion of the "social frame" of neo-classical utility theory in Chap. 11, secs. 3-6 and Chap. 13, sec. 1.

¹⁵ The qualifier "blunt" is important here; for there are significant contexts in which a continuance of a distinction between what a consumer actually does and what he ought to do is methodologically useful. It is just that an uncritical and doctrinaire adherence to "Hume's Law" has often blinded economic methodologists to the fruitfulness in theory construction of recognizing the systemic *connection* between economic facts and values. This connection will be more fully developed in Chapters 14 and 15 when we discuss the ethico-political conversion of behavioural rules into descriptive laws.

¹⁶ Mill, *Utilitarianism*, p. 7.

¹⁷ G. E. Moore, *Principia Ethica* (Cambridge: Cambridge University Press, 1903), sec. 10; sec. 40.

¹⁸ Mill, *Utilitarianism*, p. 48f.

¹⁹ See pp. 94f. above.

[20] See, for example, H. J. Paton, "The Alleged Independence of Goodness", in P. A. Schlipp (ed.), *The Philosophy of G. E. Moore* (Lasalle, Illinois: Open Court, 1942), pp. 113-34.

[21] See Baumol, *Economic Theory and Operations Analysis*, p. 191; and p. 111 above.

[22] As often in Chapter 15 below.

Chapter 10

[1] See H. A. Simon, "A Behavioural Model of Rational Choice" in his *Models of Man: Social and Rational*, (New York: John Riley and Sons, 1957), Chap. 14, pp. 241-60, or his "From Substantive to Procedural Rationality", in F. Hahn and M. Hollis (eds.), *Philosophy and Economic Theory*, (Oxford: Oxford University Press, 1979), pp. 65-86; Simon's "satisficing" theory of rational choice proposes an alternative to both the neo-classical maximizing principle and its idealized informational base. In this context, see also J. G. March, "Bonded Rationality, Ambiguity, and the Engineering of Choice", in J. Elster (ed.), *Rational Choice* (New York: New York University Press, 1986), pp. 142-70. But compare, I. Levi, "Rationality Unbound", in W. Sieg (ed.), *Acting and Reflecting:The Interdisciplinary Turn in Philosophy* (Dordrecht, Holland: Kluwer Academic Publishers, 1990), pp. 211-221. We shall examine Simon's theory in some detail in Chap. 12, sec. 3.

[2] Even if the demand is weakened to require probable knowledge of consequences in order to maximize "expected utility", we shall explain in chapter 12 that the cognitive requirements for rational agents remain severely idealized.

[3] See Robbins, *An Essay on the Nature and Significance of Economic Science*, pp. 156-58.

[4] See, for instance, R. E. Bales, "Act-utilitarianism: account of right-making characteristics or decision-making procedure?" *American Philosophical Quarterly*, Vol. 8, 1971, pp. 257-65.

[5] "Direct" in the sense that these axioms are only true of the behaviour of the ideally rational consumer. Nevertheless, they are indirectly applicable to the behaviour of actual consumers insofar as such consumers can approximate the behavioural implications of the axioms.

[6] See, for example, Baumol, *Economic Theory and Operations Analysis*, pp. 197-98.

[7] G", we observed in chapter 2, shares the basis of its "analyticity" with G' – in the special case of G" as a principle for categorizing all *economic* actions as events caused by some set of mentalistic wants and beliefs.

NOTES

[8] Again, along the same line as our comment on G' and G" on pp. 24-25, we should stress that *instances* of H are not empirically falsifiable either. Rather H permits the formulation of explanations or *explanatory arguments* for (economic) actions that are empirically testable.

[9] Rudner, *Philosophy of Social Science*, pp. 58-59.

[10] In Chapters 15 and 16.

[11] Myrdal, *The Political Element in the Development of Economic Theory*, Chap. 4.

[12] For a generalization of such a claim to economic behaviour in general see G. Stigler, "Economics or Ethics?" in S. McMurrin (ed.), *Tanner Lectures on Human Values* (Cambridge: Cambridge University Press, 1981), pp.143-91.

[13] Myrdal, *The Political Element in the Development of Economic Theory*, p. 93.

[14] *Ibid.*, p. 95.

[15] But see note 4 of Chapter 5.

[16] Myrdal, *The Political Element in the Development of Economic Theory*, p. 92.

[17] Such grounds are in accord with Hempel's R3 and R4 criteria for the acceptability of scientific explanations (see *Aspects of Scientific Explanation*, pp. 248-49).

[18] Although the majority of neo-classical economists themselves do (mistakenly) make this claim.

[19] The manner in which originally normative a priori theories such as CCT are indirectly or pragmatically applicable to actual subjects by means of their transformation into descriptive, a posteriori theories will be elucidated in Chapter 14.

[20] See Friedman, "The Methodology of Positive Economics", pp. 8-9, where the opposed claim is made that "the only relevant test of the *validity* of a hypothesis is comparison of its predictions with experience. The hypothesis is rejected if its predictions are contradicted ... "

[21] As understood in neo-classical theory.

[22] See Chapter 2, sec. 1 above.

Chapter 11

[1] See especially our original discussion of idealizations in Chap. 2 sec. 1 above.

[2] Here I follow the analysis in P. J. Simmons, *Choice and Demand* (London: Macmillan, 1974), pp. 39ff.

[3] For both the mathematical and behavioral properties of "convexity" in consumer preferences see K. Arrow, "Economic Equilibrium" in K. Arrow, *General Equilibrium: Collected Papers*, Vol. 2 (Oxford: Blackwell, 1983), p. 119.

[4] Adapted from H. A. J. Green, *Consumer Theory*, rev. edn. (London: Macmillan, 1976), pp. 49ff.

[5] *Ibid.*, p. 50. Strict convexity implies that indifference curves have no straight sides or faces; if there were such features, then again there would be indeterminacy of choice with respect to points within the straight side – see Green, *Consumer Theory*, pp. 40 and 50.

[6] For recent confirmation from an economist see S. Hargreaves Heap, *Rationality in Economics,* Chap. 3, sec. 2; Chap. 6, sec. 4 and Chap. 9, sec. 5.

[7] K. Arrow, "An Extension of the Basic Theorems of Classical Welfare Economics" in K. Arrow, *General Equilibrium*, p. 41.

[8] D. Gauthier, *Morals by Agreement* (Oxford: Oxford University Press, 1986), p. 318. See also D. Hausman, "What are General Equilibrium Theories" in W. Sieg (ed.), *Acting and Reflecting: The Interdisciplinary Turn in Philosophy*, pp. 108f.

[9] Lucid, classic discussions of general equilibrium theory can be found in the collected articles in K. J. Arrow, *General Equilibrium*; T. J. Koopmans, *Three Essays on the State of Economic Science* (New York: McGraw-Hill, 1957), Chap. 1; G. Debreu, *Theory of Value: An Axiomatic Analysis of Economic Equilibrium* (New Haven, Conn.: Yale University Press, 1959); K. J. Arrow and F. H. Hahn, *General Competitive Analysis* (Edinburgh: Oliver and Boyd, 1971). For a more recent discussion see E. R. Weintraub, *General Equilibrium Analysis: Studies in Appraisal* (Cambridge: Cambridge University Press, 1985), and his "Appraising Equilibrium Analysis", in *Economics and Philosophy*, Vol. 1, No. 1, 1985, pp. 23-37.

[10] See K. Arrow, "Economic Equilibrium", p. 118.

[11] In technical terms, at such a point of optimum production, the "marginal rate of transformation" for each pair of commodities must be equal for all firms (the marginal rate of transformation between commodities x and y [MRTxy] measures the amount by which the output of y must be decreased to produce one more unit of x with all other outputs remaining constant).

[12] See K. Arrow, "Economic Equilibrium", p. 120ff. For a rigorous mathematical demonstration see G. Debreu, *Theory of Value*, Chap. 6.

[13] Smith's own formulation of the "invisible hand" theme is to be found in A. Smith, *An Enquiry into the Nature and Causes of the Wealth of Nations*, Bk. IV, Chap. II, p. 423.

[14] T. Koopmans, *Three Essays on the State of Economic Science*, p. 41.

[15] See K. Arrow, "An Extension of the Basic Theorems of Classical Welfare Economics", p. 40.

[16] For the claim that a non-satiation assumption is required to ensure the satisfaction of this principle see K. Arrow and F. Hahn, *General Competitive Analysis*, p. 21. A_2' is logically weaker than the original A_2 in that A_2', unlike A_2, does not require that the rational consumer be unsated with respect to *any* purchasable commodity. This is discussed further in the text below.

[17] See K. Arrow, "Economic Equilibrium", p. 110.

[18] T. C. Koopmans, *Three Essays on the State of Economic Science*, p. 45f.

[19] See K. Arrow, "An Extension of the Basic Theorems of Welfare Economics", p. 37.

[20] See H. Gravelle and R. Rees, *Microeconomics* (London: Longman, 1981), pp. 426-27.

[21] For a clear, succinct exposition of the relevance of non-satiation in the indirect proof of the first part of the Fundamental Theorem see the "Introduction" by the editors of F. Hahn and M. Hollis (eds.), *Philosophy and Economic Theory* (Oxford: Oxford University Press, 1979), pp. 5ff.

[22] See K. Arrow, "Economic Equilibrium", p. 121.

[23] The primary reason for nonconvexities in production which would frustrate the existence of a general equilibrium is provided by increasing returns to scale – i.e., for a particular production process, increasing all inputs in a certain proportion would increase outputs by a higher proportion.

[24] A clear explanation of why nonconvexities in production or consumption issue in such a violation of the second part of the Fundamental Theorem is given in R. Boadway and H. Bruce, *Welfare Economics* (Oxford: Basil Blackwell, 1984), pp. 104ff.

[25] T. C. Koopmans, *Three Essays on the State of Economic Science*, p. 35.

[26] Mathematically, (strict) increasing monotonicity is such that: If $x > y$, then $f(x) > f(y)$. Hence the non-satiation expressed by axiom A_2 indicates the monotonicity of the utility function; for if there is at least one more unit of some good in commodity-bundle x than bundle y (and no less of any other), then, for any consumer, the satisfaction or utility derived from x is greater than that derived from y (i.e., $f(x) > f(y)$).

[27] T. C. Koopmans, *Three Essays on the State of Economic Science*, p. 35.

339

[28] Technically speaking, a "continuity" axiom is also required for the mathematical construction of this utility function. (See note 3 to chapter 2 above.) It is worth observing, as the referenced note implies, that in contrast to the non-satiation and convexity axioms (A_2 and A_4), we would agree that the continuity axiom *is* a subsidiary technical assumption introduced in order to make the theory of choice mathematically tractable. (On this conception of continuity, see D. M. Hausman, *The Inexact and Separate Science of Economics*, p. 17f.)

[29] A good general discussion of this thesis can be found in M. Hesse, "Duhem, Quine and a New Empiricism" in H. Morick (ed.) *Challenges to Empiricism,* (Belmont, Cal: Wadsworth, 1972), pp. 208-28.

[30] W. V. O. Quine, "Two Dogmas of Empiricism", p. 41.

[31] See e.g., A. Grunbaum, "The falsifiability of a component of a theoretical system" in P. K. Feyerabend and G. Maxwell (eds.), *Mind, Matter and Method,* (Minneapolis: University of Minnesota Press, 1966), pp. 273-305.

[32] W.V.O. Quine, "Two Dogmas of Empiricism", p. 44.

[33] K. J. Arrow and F. H. Hahn, *General Competitive Analysis*, p. vii.

Chapter 12

[1] R. Sugden, "Rational Choice: A Survey of Contributions from Economics and Philosophy", *The Economic Journal*, Vol. 101 (July 1991) p. 757.

[2] L. J. Savage, *The Foundations of Statistics,* 2nd edn. (New York: Dover, 1972).

[3] A lucid exposition of these features of subjective probability can be found in M. D. Resnick, *Choices: An Introduction to Decision Theory,* (Minneapolis: University of Minnesota Press, 1987), ch. 3, pp. 68-80. I follow Resnick (pp. 13-14 and 68-80) in classifying action-choices in situations wherein only subjective, not objective, probabilities can be assigned to possible consequences of alternatives as genuine cases of decision under risk. Some decision-theorists would prefer to reserve risk situations to those wherein objective probabilities can be assigned, and classify cases where subjective estimates are made as those of decision under uncertainty (*simpliciter*).

[4] L. J. Savage, *The Foundations of Statistics*, p. 19.

[5] L. J. Savage, M. Bartlett, *et al. The Foundations of Statistical Inference: A Discussion* (London: Methuen, 1962), p. 11. Or as de Finnetti clearly states ... "in order to avoid frequent misunderstanding it is essential to point out that [subjective] probability theory is not an attempt to describe actual behaviour; its subject is coherent behaviour, and the fact that people are only more or less

coherent is unessential". (B. de Finnetti, "Foresight: Its Logical Laws; Its Subjective Sources", in H. E. Kyburg, Jr. and H. E. Smokler (eds.), *Studies in Subjective Probability*, 2nd edn. (Huntington, N.Y.: Krieger, 1980), p. 71, note e.

[6] Originally in J. von Neumann and O. Morgenstern, *Theory of Games and Economic Behaviour*. On its use in economics see J. C. Harsanyi, "Morality and the Theory of Rational Behaviour", in A. Sen and B. Williams (eds.), *Utilitariansim and Beyond* (Cambridge: Cambridge University Press, 1982), pp. 52ff. A clear explanation of von Neumann-Morgenstern utility theory can be found in M. D. Resnick, *Choices*, Chap 4, sec. 3.

[7] G. H. von Wright, *Norms and Obligation* (New York: The Humanities Press, 1963), p. 111.

[8] H. A. Simon, "A Behavioral Model of Rational Choice" in his *Models of Man: Social and Rational*, p. 241.

[9] H. A. Simon, "A Behavioral Model of Rational Choice", or "Rationality and Administrative Decision Making", in his *Models of Man*, p. 246; p. 203.

[10] H. A. Simon, "Progress in Philosophy", in W. Sieg (ed.), *Acting and Reflecting: the Interdisciplinary Turn in Philosophy*, p. 61.

[11] H. A. Simon, "Rationality and Administrative Decision Making", p. 202.

[12] For the contrast between substantive and procedural rationality, see esp. H. Simon, "From Substantive to Procedural Rationality" in F. Hahn and M. Hollis (eds.), *Philosophy and Economic Theory*, pp. 67f.

[13] H. A. Simon, "Rationality and Administrative Decision Making", pp. 204-05.

[14] Others have reached a similar conclusion for their own reasons. See, for instance, W. Riker and P. C. Ordeshook, *An Introduction to Positive Political Theory* (Englewood Cliffs, N.J.: Prentice-Hall, 1973), pp. 21-23.

[15] H. A. Simon, "A Behavioral Model of Rational Choice", pp. 246ff.

[16] *Ibid.*, p. 247.

[17] See, e.g., A. C. Michalos, "Rationality Between the Maximizers and the Satisfiers", *Policy Sciences*, Vol. 4 (1973), p. 237.

[18] I. Levi, "Rationality Unbound" in W. Sieg (ed.), *The Interdisciplinary Turn in Philosophy*, p. 213.

[19] R. E. Bales, "Act-utilitarianism: Account of Right-Making Characteristics or Decision-Making Procedure?", *American Philosophical Quarterly*, Vol. 8, No. 3, July 1971, pp. 257-65.

NOTES

[20] A. Michalos, "Rationality Between the Maximizers and the Satisfiers", p. 232.

[21] *Ibid.*, p. 232.

[22] R. E. Bales, "Act-utilitarianism: Account of Right-Making Characteristics or Decision-Making Procedure?", esp. pp. 260ff.

[23] A. Michalos, "Rationality Between the Maximizers and the Satisfiers", p. 233.

[24] *Ibid.*, p. 232; H. A. Simon ,"Rationality and Administrative Decision Making", p. 202.

[25] C. G. Hempel, "Typological Methods in the Natural and Social Sciences" in *Aspects of Scientific Explanation*, p. 168.

[26] C. G. Hempel, "Studies in the Logic of Explanation" in *Aspects of Scientific Explanation*, p. 248.

[27] G. Loomes and R. Sugden, "Regret Theory: An Alternative Theory of Rational Choice Under Uncertainty", *Economic Journal*, Vol. 92, 1982, pp. 805-24. See also R. Sugden, "Rational Choice: A Survey of Contributions From Economics and Philosophy", pp. 761ff. and D. Bell, "Regret in Decision Making Under Uncertainty", *Operations Research*, Vol. 30, 1982, pp. 961-81.

[28] G. Loomes and R. Sugden, "Regret Theory: An Alternative Theory of Rational Choice Under Uncertainty", p. 820.

[29] R. Sugden, "Rational Choice: A Survey of Contributions from Economics and Philosophy", p. 762.

[30] G. Loomes and R. Sugden, "Regret Theory: An Alternative Theory of Rational Choice Under Uncertainty", p. 809.

[31] See the Aristotelian principle described in the last section, p. 204.

[32] G. Loomes and R. Sugden, "Regret Theory: An Alternative Theory of Rational Choice Under Uncertainty", sec. iv.

[33] *Ibid.*, sec. v.

[34] *Ibid.*, p. 809.

[35] See esp. p. 46f. above.

[36] G. Loomes and R. Sugden, "Regret Theory: An Alternative Theory of Rational Choice Under Uncertainty", see esp. pp. 808-09 and p. 820.

[37] *Ibid.*, p. 820.

[38] R. Sugden, "Rational Choice: A Survey of Contributions from Economics and Philosophy", p. 763.

NOTES

[39] This theme will be more extensively discussed in Chapter 16.

[40] See J. Elster, *Ulysses and the Sirens: Studies in Rationality and Irrationality*, especially Chap. II, for an extended discussion of the meaning and rationality of "self-binding" policies.

[41] See p. 72 above.

[42] For an economist's appreciation of the significance of this phenomenon see S. Hargreaves Heap, *Rationality in Economics*, Chap. 6, sec. 3 and Chap. 8, sec. 4.

[43] See, e.g., J. Mackie, *Ethics:Inventing Right and Wrong* (Harmondsworth, Eng.: Penguin Books, 1977), Chap. 7, sec. 6.

[44] See note 38 to this chapter.

Chapter 13

[1] The marginal rate of technical substitution of input A for input B ($MRTS_{AB}$) refers to the amount of B that a firm can give up by increasing the use of A by one unit and still produce the same quantity of output.

[2] Hayek's writings on this topic are to be found especially in his classic articles "Economics and Knowledge" and "The Use of Knowledge in Society", collected in F. A. Hayek *Individualism and Economic Order* (Chicago: University of Chicago Press, 1948), Chaps. II and V, respectively. For pertinent later writings see, for instance, "The Results of Human Action but not of Human Design" in F. A. Hayek, *Studies in Philosophy, Politics and Economics*, (London: Routledge and Kegan Paul, 1967), Chap. 6, or "The Errors of Constructivism" and "The Pretence of Knowledge" in F. A. Hayek, *New Studies in Philosophy, Politics, Economics and the History of Ideas* (Chicago: University of Chicago Press, 1978) Chaps. 1 and 2, respectively.

[3] See, e.g., D. Lavoie, "The Knowledge Problem", Chap. 3 of his *National Economic Planning: What's Left* (Cambridge, Mass: Ballinger, 1985). And see J. Birner and R. van Zijp (eds.), *Hayek, Co-ordination and Evolution: His legacy in philosophy, politics, economics and the history of ideas* (London: Routlege, 1994) for a critical overview of Hayek's work.

[4] See "Economics and Knowledge", sec. 1.

[5] See "Economics and Knowledge", sec. 9, and "The Use of Knowledge in Society", sec. 6.

[6] F. A. Hayek, "Economics and Knowledge", p. 50.

[7] *Ibid.*, p. 42.

NOTES

[8] *Ibid.*, p. 54 and "The Use of Knowledge in Society", sec. 6.

[9] F. A. Hayek, "The Use of Knowledge in Society", pp. 77f; pp. 80f; and "Economics and Knowledge", sec. 9.

[10] *Ibid.*, p. 89.

[11] V. Walsh and H. Gram, *Classical and Neoclassical Theories of General Equilibrium: Historical Origins and Mathematical Structure* (New York: Oxford University Press, 1980), pp. 264-65.

[12] Of course, it is a critical point that the level of satisfaction for any particular individual in a general equilibrium state will depend on his share of the "original endowments", i.e., his share of ownership of the prevailing factors of production. And there will be distinct general equilibria for different distributions of these initial resources across individuals. We will return to some comments on the normative significance of this point in sec. 7 of this chapter.

[13] We should point out here that in the last two decades there has been an increasing concentration by mainstream economists on the construction of theories under conditions of uncertainty or imperfect information. Of special concern in this work has been the analysis of situations of "asymmetric information", wherein one agent to an economic transaction has knowledge which a participating agent lacks. Although the focus of such analysis is rather different than the one we are pursuing in this chapter, it is a significant finding for us that, under conditions of asymmetric information in a competitive economy, market distortions may result: either no equilibrium exists for a certain market, or, most importantly for our concerns, one that is not socially desirable. Consider, for instance, the pervasive phenomenon of signalling, where a signal is something an agent may acquire to make himself appear more valuable. For example, in the labour market, let us take the case where prospective employees know their real abilities, whereas employers do not. But let us assume that those of higher ability invest in advanced education to signal that ability and in this way secure an increased wage. However, on the further assumption that such education does not increase the marginal productivity of those who obtain it, it would follow that the equilibrium for this labour market is socially wasteful; here, the private gain from investment in educational signals is not socially desirable. (For an early review of problems of imperfect information in competitive markets see M. Rothschild, "Models of Market Organization with Imperfect Information: A Survey", *Journal of Political Economy*, Vol. 81, 1973, pp. 1283-1308. For a later survey concentrating on problems of asymmetric information, including signalling, see H. Varian *Microeconomic Analysis*, 3rd edn. (New York: W. W. Norton, 1992), Chap. 25.

NOTES

[14] J. Rothenberg, "Values and Value Theory in Economics", pp. 240-41 (my italics). Variants of our principle of epistemic individualism have been a philosophical mainstay of the liberalist political tradition of classical and neo-classical economic thought. See, for instance, Adam Smith, *An Inquiry into the Nature and Causes of the Wealth of Nations*, Bk. IV, Chap. II, p. 423; J. S. Mill, *Principles of Political Economy*, Bk. V, Chap. XI, sec. 2; J. A. Broome, "Choice and Value in Economics", *Oxford Economic Papers*, Vol. 30, 1978, pp. 313-33.

[15] See T. Scitovsky, *The Joyless Economy: An Inquiry into Human Satisfaction and Consumer Dissatisfaction* (Oxford: Oxford University Press, 1976), Chaps. 12-13.

[16] See J. K. Galbraith, *The New Industrial State,* 3rd edn. (Boston: Houghton Mifflin, 1978), Chap. XIX; or his discussion of the "dependence effect" in his *The Affluent Society*, 4th edn., (Boston: Houghton Mifflin, 1984), Chap. XI, pp. 126-33.

[17] T. Scitovsky, *The Joyless Economy*, p. 273.

[18] *Ibid.*, p. 273.

[19] Put thus strongly, this philosophical principle has itself been the source of intense controversy in recent years. See, for instance, W. Sellars, "Empiricism and the Philosophy of Mind" in his *Science, Perception and Reality*, pp. 127-96.

[20] See, e.g., J. K. Galbraith, *The Affluent Society*, ch. XI, pp. 126-33, and "A Review of a Review" (Reply to Solow), *The Public Interest*, No. 12, 1967, pp. 109-18 and T. Koopmans, *Three Essays on the State of Economic Science*, pp. 165-66.

[21] J. Baudrillard, *For a Critique of the Political Economy of the Sign*, trans. by C. Levin (St. Louis: Telos Press, 1981), p. 82.

[22] For a recent discussion of the moral and political significance of such a "private zone", see J. S. Fishkin, *The Limits of Obligation*, (New Haven: Yale University Press, 1982), Chap. 4, pp. 20-24.

[23] A useful explanation along these lines is supplied by R. M. Hare, *Freedom and Reason*, Chap. 5, pp. 67-85.

[24] Perceptive examinations of self-deception can be found in D. Davidson, "Deception and Division"; D. Pears, "The Goals and Strategies of Self-Deception"; both in J. Elster (ed.), *The Multiple Self,* (Cambridge: Cambridge University Press, 1985), pp. 59-77, and pp. 79-92, respectively; and J. Elster, *Sour Grapes: Studies in the Subversion of Rationality* (Cambridge: Cambridge University Press, 1983), Chap. 4, sec. 3, pp. 148-57.

[25] B. Spinoza, *Ethics* (1677), Part IV, Preface, in B. Spinoza, *Ethics, Treatise on the Emendation of the Intellect and Selected Letters*, trans. by S. Shirley, ed. by S. Feldman (Indianapolis, Ind.: Hackett, 1992), p. 152.

[26] See D. M. Winch, *Analytical Welfare Economics* (Middlesex: Penguin, 1971), pp. 34ff; pp. 95ff; R. Boadway and N. Bruce, *Welfare Economics* (Oxford: Basil Blackwell, 1984), Chaps. 1 and 6.

[27] J. Elster, *Sour Grapes*, Chap. 3.

[28] A. Sen, *On Ethics and Economics*, p. 46.

[29] Elster, *Sour Grapes*, Chap. 3, esp. p. 117.

[30] See Chap. 5, sec. 1 above.

[31] D. Davidson, "How is Weakness of the Will Possible?" in D. Davidson, *Essays on Actions and Events* (Oxford: Oxford University Press, 1980), p. 42.

[32] As explained in section 5 above, however, when subject to akrasia, an agent's actual preferences are not manifested or revealed in his overt choices.

[33] Instructive elucidations of this problem can be found in J. Harsanyi, "Morality and the theory of rational behaviour", sec. 7; B. Williams, *Ethics and the Limits of Philosophy* (London: Williams and Collins, 1985), pp. 40ff; R. E. Goodin, "Laundering Preferences" and A. Gibbard, "Interpersonal comparisons: preference, good, and the intrinsic reward of a life", both in J. Elster and A. Hylland (eds.), *Foundations of Social Choice Theory* (Cambridge: Cambridge University Press, 1986), pp. 75-101, and pp. 165-93, respectively; R. B. Brandt, "Two Concepts of Utility" in H. B. Miller and W. H. Williams (eds.), *The Limits of Utilitarianism* (Minneapolis: University of Minnesota Press, 1982), pp. 169-85; R. C. Jeffrey, "Preference among Preferences", *Journal of Philosophy*, Vol. 71, 1974, pp. 377-91.

[34] See A. K. Sen, "Choice, Orderings, and Morality", secs. 3 and 4; "Rational Fools: A Critique of the Behavioral Foundations of Economic Theory", pp. 15ff.

[35] On such informational paucity in conventional economic theory see A. K. Sen, "Rational Fools: A Critique of the Behavioral Foundations of Economic Theory", sec. VII, and his *On Ethics and Economics*, Chap. 2.

[36] J. C. Harsanyi, "Morality and the Theory of Rational Behaviour", pp. 55f.

[37] *Ibid.*, p. 56.

[38] *Ibid.*, p. 56.

[39] For a useful review of the issues involved see the articles in M. Hollis and S. Lukes (eds.), *Rationality and Relativism* (Oxford: Basil Blackwell, 1982).

[40] See I. Berlin, *Two Concepts of Liberty* (Oxford: Oxford University Press, 1958).

[41] Cited in Berlin, *Two Concepts of Liberty*, p. 36.

[42] For this restriction and its rationale see I. M. Copi, *Symbolic Logic*, 5th edn., (New York: Macmillan, 1979), p. 72.

[43] Of course the social choice procedures recommended in this paragraph would still have to come to terms with Arrow's "impossibility" theorem – that under certain apparently desirable conditions, it is logically impossible to devise a choice method that provides a social ordering or consistent preference ranking for a group by aggregating the consistent preference rankings of the individuals constituting the group. (See K. Arrow, *Social Choice and Individual Values,* 2nd edn. (New York: Wiley, 1963); and his "Values and Collective Decision Making" in F. Hahn and M. Hollis (eds.), *Philosophy and Economic Theory*, pp. 110-26.)

[44] Our comments in this paragraph have an affinity with the notion of an "ideal speech situation" specified by J. Habermas. See, for instance, his "Towards a Theory of Communicative Competence", *Inquiry*, vol. 13, 1970, pp. 360-75.

Chapter 14

[1] For specific arguments on this interpretation concerning CCT see Chap. 9, sec. 1, and Chap. 10, sec. 2; for SET, see Chap. 12, secs. 1 and 2.

[2] For the sake of simplicity of exposition, we shall concentrate in the next three chapters on the theory of choice under conditions of certainty (CCT). In any case, as none of the arguments of these chapters turns on the level of evidential support for an agent's deliberation and choice, any conclusion reached in them can be applied, *mutatis mutandis*, to the theory of choice under conditions of uncertainty – our SET.

[3] Such compliance does not require that we be consciously and explicitly formulating such rules.

[4] See M. Friedman, "The Methodology of Positive Economics" and T. C. Koopmans, "The Construction of Economic Knowledge" for a discussion of this charge and their radically different responses to it.

[5] For confirmation of such deviance see, for example, H. H. Kassarjian and T. S. Robertson (eds.), *Perspectives in Consumer Behaviour* (Glenview, Ill.: Scott, Foresman, 1968), especially Chaps. 1, 2, 3. For reports of the violation of the principles of choice in the model for uncertainty (SET), see P. J. H. Shoemaker, "The expected utility model: its variants, purposes, evidence and limitations", *Journal of Economic Literature*, Vol. 20, 1982, pp.529-63; D. Kahneman and A. Tverksy, "Prospect Theory: an analysis of decision under risk", *Econometrica*,

Vol. 47, 1979, pp. 263-91; P. Anand, "Are the Preference Axioms Really Rational?" Some of Anand's comments also apply to economic choice under certainty.

[6] E. Roll, *A History of Economic Thought*, 4th edn. (London: Faber and Faber, 1973), p. 149.

[7] Compare our previous examination of such spontaneous and stoical motivation (pp. 59ff. and pp. 52ff. respectively).

[8] See Chap. 9 above.

[9] See Chap. 5, sec. 1 above, and the critical role of "wanting more" in our discussion of general equilibrium *cum* welfare economics in Chap. 11, sec. 4.

[10] That the character traits specified for *homo economicus* have involved a commitment to moral virtues was argued in Chapter 5, sec. 4.

[11] A sense which is not to be confused with logically bogus senses. For instance, I am not concerned here to (wrongly) argue that the existence of so-called "self-fulfilling predictions" in social scientific procedures entails a methodological distinction between natural and social science.

[12] Of course, such psychological and socio-psychological laws have not yet been avowed within neo-classical economics itself.

[13] I. Kant, *Critique of Pure Reason*, trans. by N. K. Smith, B xiii, p. 20.

[14] In the light of this paragraph, we might put Kant's quotation in more perspicacious form as "Reason has insight only into that which it *intends to* produce after a plan of its own". (Italicized words added.)

[15] The fertile concept of a "research programme" and its bearing on the methodology of science was introduced by I. Lakatos. See, for instance, his "History of Science and its Rational Reconstruction". And see the attempts of several authors to apply Lakatos' methodology to economics in S. Lastis (ed.), *Methods and Appraisal in Economics* (Cambridge: Cambridge University Press, 1976). See also R. E. Backhouse, "The Lakatosian Legacy in Economic Methodology" in R. E. Backhouse (ed.), *New Directions in Economic Methodology* (London: Routledge, 1994), pp. 173-91.

[16] See note 6 of this chapter.

[17] Once again, in concert with note 4 to Chap. 5, we need not assume that the neo-classical theorist is explicitly aware of, or consciously intends, such ethical objectives.

[18] It should be cautioned, that by a certain cunning of history (not reason), such economic liberalism is now called neo-conservatism.

[19] See I. Illich, *Deschooling Society* (New York: Harper and Row, 1971).

[20] See especially M. Weber, *General Economic History*, Chap. 20 and his *The Protestant Ethic and the Spirit of Capitalism*, Part 1, Chap. 11.

[21] Again, it seems to me that the most fertile questions concern the *relation* between normative and descriptive theoretical systems, not, as has seemed to dominate recent meta-ethical inquiry, the question of whether or not normative discourse is "reducible" to factual discourse. Indeed, a persistent preoccupation with the latter question has led scientific methodologists to lose sight of the former.

[22] See p. 255 above.

[23] See S. Hargreaves Heap, *Rationality in Economics*, esp. Part I.

[24] Basic sources from these authors would be W. V. O. Quine, "Two Dogmas of Empiricism", secs. 5 and 6; and *Theories and Things* (Cambridge, Mass.: Harvard University Press, 1981); P. Feyerabend, "How to be a Good Empiricist – a Plea for Tolerance in Matters Epistemological" in H. Morick (ed.), *Challenges to Empiricism*, pp. 164-93, and *Against Method* (London: New Left Books, 1975); I. Lakatos, "History of Science and its Rational Reconstruction" in R. C. Buck and R. S. Cohen (eds.), *Boston Studies in the Philosophy of Science*, Vol. VIII (Dordrech, Holland: D. Reidel, 1971), pp. 91-136; and "Falsification and the Methodology of Scientific Research Programmes", in I. Lakatos and S. Musgrave (eds.), *Criticism and the Growth of Knowledge* (Cambridge: Cambridge University Press, 1970), pp. 91-196; T. S. Kuhn, *The Structure of Scientific Revolutions*, 2nd edn. (Chicago: University of Chicago Press, 1970).

[25] See S. Hargreaves Heap, *Rationality in Economics*, pp. 32ff.

[26] See note 6 to Chap. 11 above.

[27] See S. Hargreaves Heap, *Rationality in Economics*, Chap. 6, sec. 4.

Chapter 15

[1] See T. S. Kuhn, *The Structure of Scientific Revolutions*, 2nd edn. (Chicago: University of Chicago Press, 1970), for the introduction of this concept which is quickly, and unfortunately, becoming a household term.

[2] In this chapter, the terms "initially", "originally", "in the first instance", etc. are used in both a temporal and conceptual sense.

NOTES

[3] R_1 requires that the rational consumer be able to compare any two combinations of commodities in terms of relative preference. And R_4 requires that he ascertain marginal rates of substitution (or marginal utilities) and take care that, as a rule, scarce goods are not relinquished for relatively plentiful ones. Hence, both R_1 and R_4 also demand the family of virtues found in the "calculatedness" of *homo economicus*. However, as these character traits have already been required by R_3, I have dealt with them under the analysis of this principle.

[4] Barring, of course, "behaviourist" reconstructions of CCT which, as we observed in Chapter 4, seek to eschew reference to the "mentalistic" valuations of even the subjects under study.

[5] Samuelson's comment mentioned in Chapter 4 that the "maximizing" principle of CCT "does not imply that consumers behave rationally in any normative sense" is indicative of this view (Samuelson, *Foundations of Economic Analysis*, p. 22).

[6] In this respect, see T. W. Hutchison, *"Positive" Economics and Policy Objectives*, p. 10.

[7] Again, see H. H. Kassaryian and T. S. Robertson (eds.), *Perspectives in Consumer Behaviour*, especially Chaps. 1-3.

[8] The *locus classicus* of this position is to be found in K. R. Popper, *The Logic of Scientific Discovery* (New York: Basic Books, 1979).

[9] See the original specification of such conditions on p. 209.

[10] It should be observed here that we are adapting rather than simply following Hempel on the application of the R_4 criterion. For as analyzed above (in Chapter 2, sec. 2 and Chapter 8, sec. 2), the basic explanatory generalizations of CCT (G" or H) are logically necessary statements, not the contingent empirical laws of Hempel's deductive-nomological model of explanation. (We have, nevertheless, explicated (pp. 37ff.) the empirical testability of the *explanatory arguments* provided by CCT, and identified [Chapter 14, sec. 2] the levels of explanation at which empirical laws bear on the applicability of the rules of rationality of CCT.) In our case, it would be approximation to empirical truth of the individual "axioms" (A_1-A_4) and the ability conditions (complete information and freedom) that would be subject to Hempel's (modified) R_4 criterion for an acceptable explanans.

[11] For a useful review of the decision rules formulated for such situations, see N. Resnick, *Choices*, Chap. 2.

[12] See p. 255.

[13] See Chapter 9, sec. 1.

NOTES

[14] "*Ceteris paribus*" clauses for idealized general laws refer to actualizable "interfering conditions" that are claimed to remain equal (i.e., constant) in confirming the truth of such laws. For instance, the "law of demand" is frequently stated as "whenever the price of a commodity rises, then *ceteris paribus*, less units are purchased at successively higher prices". Thus understood, economic generalizations only claim to predict, and thus be confirmed by, the occurrence of actual economic behaviour which is not preceded by the "disturbing factors" which the "ceteris paribus" clause intends to rule out. However, it has been a notorious complaint against economic methodology that mainstream economists have often invoked tacit *ceteris paribus* conditions in order to insulate a favoured hypothesis from all possible falsifying evidence – against the rules of an empiricist epistemology they profess to endorse. Hence, confronted with empirical data apparently inconsistent with the predictions of a prized hypothesis, the disputed stratagem is to contend that "other conditions" have not remained equal or constant and that such obtruding conditions have led to the maverick results – but without even clearly specifying what such interfering factors may be. For a classic criticism by an economist of such a *ceteris paribus* dodge, see T. W. Hutchison, *The Significance and Basic Postulates of Economic Theory*, pp. 40ff. And see D. Hausman, *The Inexact and Separate Science of Economics*, pp. 133-42 for a perceptive analysis by a philosopher of the use of *ceteris paribus* clauses in economic laws.

[15] See Klappholz, "Value Judgments and Economics", pp. 98-99, where the non-rationality of moral statements is implied by the claim that they lack "truth-value". See also L. Roy, *The Philosophy of Economics*, Chap. 2

Chapter 16

[1] See pp. 144f.

[2] A. J. Ayer, *Language, Truth and Logic*, especially Chap. VI, and "On the Analysis of Moral Judgments," in A. J. Ayer, *Philosophical Papers* (London: Macmillan, 1954), pp. 231-49.

[3] C. L. Stevenson, *Ethics and Langauge*, especially Chap. VII; "The Nature of Ethical Disagreement", *Sigma*, 1948; and "Relativism and Non-relativism in the Theory of Value", *Proceedings of the American Philosophical Association*, 1961-62. The articles are reprinted in P. W. Taylor (ed.), *The Problems of Moral Philosophy*, 2nd edn. (Enrico, California: Dickenson, 1972), pp. 370-75; 375-82.

[4] R. M. Hare, *The Language of Morals; Freedom and Reason; Descriptivism; Moral Thinking.*

[5] See p. 143f. above.

351

[6] See Hare, *The Language of Morals*, Part I.

[7] Hare, *Freedom and Reason*, Ch. 2, especially secs. 2-3, and *Moral Thinking*, Chap. 6.

[8] Ayer, *Language, Truth and Logic*, pp. 111-13.

[9] See Stevenson, *Ethics and Language*, Chap. 7, or "The Nature of Ethical Disagreement", in P. W. Taylor (ed.), *The Problems of Moral Philosophy*, pp. 373-74.

[10] In the remainder of this chapter, we shall use the phrase "non-derivative (or non-mediate, or basic, or ultimate) attitude" in the sense of this paragraph. That is to say, a non-derivative attitude is one which is not parasitic on, or a special case of, a more general attitude. For instance, in the context of Stevenson's emotivism, S would express an attitude of approval towards, say, capital punishment in commending it as a morally good institution. And let us assume that this attitude is caused by his belief that capital punishment deters murder. However, such an attitude is not an ultimate or non-derivative one as it itself is mediated by a more inclusive attitude (and further belief) – i.e., S's pro-attitude towards actions that promote social happiness (and his belief that deterring murder has this effect).

[11] Although, outside of the context of argument, we have argued above (Chap. 9, sec. 1) that there is a pragmatic or motivational sense of justification and "reason for action".

[12] The comments of this paragraph may be understood as augmenting, in the context of moral reasoning, our brief remarks on the "impersonal authority" of reason on p. 277 above.

[13] Hare, *Freedom and Reason*, p. 110.

[14] *Ibid.*, p. 170.

[15] See especially Hare, *The Language of Morals*, pp. 77-78.

[16] In effect, at the final level of justifying moral principles, as long as any agent is employing his principles consistently, the "argumentative techniques" of prescriptivism collapse into other forms of noncognitivism, such as emotivism. In particular, let us assume that the consistency condition is met, and that an ethical dispute concerning principles is rooted in an irreducible disagreement in attitude, that is, one that remains even though all parties to the controversy hold all relevant factual beliefs in common; in such cases, only non-rational, "persuasive" techniques such as oratory and propaganda would be capable of securing agreement.

NOTES

[17] See our interrelated examinations of the relation between obligation and motivation (Chapter 9), and between reasons and causes (Chapter 8).

[18] See D. Hume, *A Treatise of Human Nature* (1739-40), L. A. Selby-Bigge (ed.), (Oxford: Oxford University Press, 1888), Book II, Part III, sec. 111.

[19] *Ibid.*, Book III, Part I.

[20] *Ibid.*, p. 457.

[21] *Ibid.*, p. 471.

[22] *Ibid.*, p. 448.

[23] The intentionality or "aboutness" of such passions (angry at, fear of, etc.), being mental events, should not be confused with their (absence of a) representational aspect.

[24] Hume, *A Treatise of Human Nature*, p. 415.

[25] *Ibid.*, p. 416.

[26] *Ibid.*, p. 416.

[27] *Ibid.*, p. 470.

[28] M. Weber, *The Methodology of the Social Sciences*, edited and trans. by E. A. Shills and F. A. Finch (New York: The Free Press, 1949), pp. 18-19. For an economist's agreement see K. Klappholz, "Economics and Ethical Neutrality", pp. 452-53. Or see S. Roy's survey of the acceptance of "Hume's Law" by leading contemporary economists (in his *Philosophy and Economics*, Chap. 2).

[29] Such a reductive understanding of human agency is, as the economist Hargreaves-Heap well argues, still current in the neo-classical conception of the economic subject as a "set of well-behaved preferences". (see S. Hargreaves-Heap, *Rationality in Economics*, Chap. 3, sec. 2; Chap. 6, sec. 3 and Chap. 9, sec. 5).

[30] As we argued in Chapters 6, 7 and 8.

[31] On this point, see G. Stigler and G. Becker, "De gustibus non est disputandum", *American Economic Review*, Vol. 67, 1977, pp. 76f., and A. Rosenberg, "Prospects for the Elimination of Tastes from Economics and Ethics", in E. F. Paul, F. D. Miller, Jr. and J. Paul (eds.), *Ethics and Economics*, pp. 48f.

[32] T. Veblen, "Why is Economics not an Evolutionary Science?" (1898) in his *The Place of Science in Modern Civilization and Other Essays* (New York: Russell and Russell, 1961), p. 73.

[33] Hume, *A Treatise of Human Nature*, p. 414.

[34] See Chapter 5, p. 67, and Chapter 13, sec. 2.

[35] Again, it is claimed that value-neutrality would be preserved in that the relevant justification would be that of a *hypothetical* imperative (i.e., if actual consumers desire such and such, the processes of the neo-classical system will be maximally conducive to the satisfaction of these given desires in the "Pareto optimal" sense explained in Chap. 11, sec. 3).

[36] See the discussion in Chap. 13, sec. 2 above.

[37] The position of epistemic privilege may be seen as a corollary of, or simply another way of putting, the principle of epistemic individualism which we examined in Chap. 13, sec. 2.

[38] Rothenberg, "Values and Value Theory in Economics", p. 241; first quoted on pp. 388-89 above.

[39] See Chap. 13, especially secs. 3, 4, 5 and 7.

[40] Aristotle, *Nichomachean Ethics*, Book I, Chap. 1, in R. M. McKeon, ed., *Basic Works of Aristotle* (New York: Random House, 1941).

[41] Ayer, *Language, Truth and Logic*, p. 108.

[42] Stevenson, "The Nature of Ethical Disagreement", in P. Taylor (ed.), *The Problems of Moral Philosophy*, p. 370.

[43] Hare, *Freedom and Reason*, pp. 110-11; 170.

[44] Ayer, *Language, Truth and Logic*, pp. 108-09.

[45] Hare, *Freedom and Reason*, p. 110.

[46] See Kant, *Foundations of the Metaphysics of Morals*, especially section 3.

[47] Hare, *Freedom and Reason*, p. 111. See also his *Moral Thinking*, Chap. 10, sec. 5, and Chap. 12, secs. 8 and 9.

[48] Hare, *Freedom and Reason*, p. 110.

[49] Hume, *A Treatise of Human Nature*, pp. 415-16.

[50] In Hume's terms "Reason is and ought only to be the slave of the passions." with the implication mentioned in the text above that "...tis not contrary to reason to prefer the destruction of the whole world to the scratching of my finger." (*Ibid.*, pp. 415-16).

[51] Humeans, of course, would not deny this fact; nevertheless, they fail to trace out its full consequence for the rational assessment of affective states.

NOTES

[52] It should be noted that all of what follows can remain neutral on the *ontological* question concerning mind-body materialism or dualism – that is, whether conscious mental states are identical with brain processes. In particular, the operations of "reflective consciousness" do not presuppose the acts of some immaterial substance. An identification of these operations with material brain processes would be consistent with the thesis we are arguing.

[53] B. Spinoza, *Ethics* (1677), Part IV, proposition xiv, in B. Spinoza, *Ethics, Treatise on the Emendation of the Intellect and Selected Letters*, trans. by S. Shirley, ed. by S. Feldman, p. 161.

[54] See Chapter 5, sec. 1 above.

[55] To be fair, not all economists have been insensitive to the need to assess the rationality of an agent's wants themselves. See, for instance, J. C. Harsanyi's distinction between an individual's "manifest" and "true" preferences in his "Morality and the theory of rational behaviour", which type of distinction we discussed in Chap. 13, sec. 6.

[56] For further illustration of the kind of rational considerations to be employed in the assessment of affective motivational states, it is instructive to review the empirical studies of cognitive psychologists in the domain of abnormal psychology. See, for example, A. Ellis, "Rational-emotive therapy", in R. J. Corsini (ed.), *Current Psychotherapies*, 3rd edn. (Itasa, Ill.: Peacock Press, 1984), pp. 196-238, and A. T. Beck, *Cognitive Therapy and the Emotional Disorders* (New York: International Universities Press, 1976).

[57] We may remind ourselves here of Spinoza's explanation of "bondage" on page 236 above.

[58] Whether, in a Marxist vein, non-cognitivist ethics or meta-ethics are mere epiphenomena of the economic processes of an underlying free enterprise "mode of production" is a tantalizing question, that is, however, beyond the scope of this enquiry.

[59] Aristotle, *Nichomachean Ethics*, in R. M. McKeon (ed.), *Basic Works of Aristotle* (New York: Random House, 1941), Book I, Chap. 7, p. 942.

[60] See pp. 97f. above.

[61] Compare the discussion of the "convergence" of scientific beliefs on the one hand, and ethical beliefs on the other, in B. Williams, *Ethics and the Limits of Philosophy* (London: Williams and Collins, 1985), Chap. 5.

[62] Aristotle, *Nichomachean Ethics*, Book I, Chap. 7.

[63] *Ibid.*, p. 493.

NOTES

[64] And, therefore, would be informed of the causes and properties of their motivating states.

[65] Of course, for certain methodological aims, value-neutrality would still be mandatory. In particular, if the social scientist intends to explain or predict *de facto* behaviour, he should restrict himself to reportive value-judgments, even if moral principles are rationally decidable. On the other hand, if these principles are so decidable, there is no compelling reason to believe that social scientific theory construction should be *limited* to such aims.

[66] See C. L. Stevenson, "The Nature of Ethical Disagreement", in P. W. Taylor (ed.), *The Problems of Moral Philosophy*, especially pp. 374-75.

[67] Such a theory should not be confused with the "rational psychology" pursued in mediaeval philosophy of mind, as the latter discipline was constituted by a purely a priori form of inquiry.

References

Anand, P. "Are the Preference Axioms Really Rational", *Theory and Decision*, Vol. 23, 1987, pp. 189-214.

Anscombe, G. E. M. *Intention*. Ithaca, N.Y.: Cornell University Press, 1957.

Aristotle, *Nichomachean Ethics*, in R. M. McKeon (edn.), *Basic Works of Aristotle*. New York: Random House, 1941.

Arrow, K. *Social Choice and Individual Values*. 2nd edn., New York: Wiley, 1963.

Arrow, K. "Values and Collective Decision Making", in F. Hahn and M. Hollis (eds.), *Philosophy and Economic Theory*. Oxford: Oxford University Press, 1979.

Arrow, K. *General Equilibrium: Collected Papers*, Vol. 2, Oxford: Blackwell, 1983.

Arrow, K. "Economic Equilibrium", in K. Arrow, *General Equilibrium: Collected Papers*, Vol. 2, Oxford: Blackwell, 1983.

Arrow, K. "An Extension of the Basic Theorems of Classical Welfare Economics", in K. Arrow, *General Equilibrium: Collected Papers*, Vol. 2, Oxford: Blackwell, 1983, pp. 13-45.

Arrow, K. J. and Hahn, F. H. *General Competitive Analysis*. Edinburgh: Oliver and Boyd, 1971.

Ayer, A. J. *Language, Truth and Logic*, 2nd edn. New York: Dover Publication, 1946.

Ayer, A. J. "On the Analysis of Moral Judgments", in A. J. Ayer, *Philosophical Papers*. London: Macmillan, 1954, pp. 231-49.

Ayer, A. J. *Man as a Subject for Science*. London: University of London, Athlone Press, 1964.

Backhouse, R. E. "The Lakatosian Legacy in Economic Methodology", in R. E. Backhouse (ed.). *New Directions in Economic Methodology*. London: Routledge, 1994.

Bales, R. E. "Act-utilitarianism: account of right-making characteristics or decision-making procedure?" in *American Philosophical Quarterly*, Vol. 8, 1971, pp. 257-65.

Baudrillard, J. *For a Critique of the Political Economy of the Sign*, trans. by C. Levin. St. Louis: Telos Press, 1981.

REFERENCES

Baumol, W. *Economic Theory and Operations Analysis*, 4th edn. Englewood Cliffs, N.J.: Prentice-Hall, 1977.

Beck, A. T. *Cognitive Therapy and the Emotional Disorders*. New York: International Universities Press, 1976.

Bell, D. "Regret in Decision Making Under Uncertainty", in *Operations Research*, Vol. 30, 1982, pp. 961-81.

Bentham, J. *An Introduction to the Principles of Morals and Legislation* (1789). Reprint. London: University of London, 1970.

Berlin, I. *Two Concepts of Liberty*. Oxford: Oxford University Press, 1958.

Bertalanffy, L. von. *General Systems Theory*. New York: G. Braziller, 1968.

Birner, J. and van Zijp, R. (eds.). *Hayek, Co-ordination and Evolution: His legacy in philosophy, politics, economics and the history of ideas*. London: Routledge, 1994.

Blaug, M. *Economic Theory in Retrospect*, 3rd edn. Cambridge: Cambridge University Press, 1980.

Blaug, M. *The Methodology of Economics*. Cambridge: Cambridge University Press, 1980.

Boadway, R. and Bruce, N. *Welfare Economics*. Oxford: Basil Blackwell, 1984.

Boland, L. *The Foundations of Economic Method*. London: Allen and Unwin, 1982.

Borger, R. and Cioffi, F. (eds.), *Explanation in the Behavioral Sciences*. Cambridge: Cambridge University Press, 1970.

Borst, C. V. (ed.). *The Mind-Brain Identity Theory*. London: Macmillan, 1970.

Boulding, K. "Some Contributions of Economics to the General Theory of Value", *Philosophy of Science*, Vol. 23, no. 1, 1956, pp. 1-14.

Boulding, K. *Beyond Economics*. Ann Arbour: University of Michigan Press, 1968.

Boulding, K. "Economics as a Moral Science", *American Economic Review*, Vol. 59, 1969, pp. 1-12.

Brandt, R. and Kim J. "Wants as Explanations of Actions", *Journal of Philosophy*, Vol. LX, 1963, pp. 425-35.

Brandt, R. B. "Two Concepts of Utility", in H. B. Miller and W. H. Williams, *The Limits of Utilitarianism*. Minneapolis: University of Minnesota Press, 1982.

REFERENCES

Braybrooke, D. "Economics and Rational Choice", in P. Edwards (ed.), *The Encyclopedia of Philosophy*. New York: Macmillan and Free Press, 1967, Vol. 2, pp. 454-58.

Braybrooke, D. *The Philosophy of Social Science*. Englewood Cliffs, N.J.: Prentice Hall, 1987.

Broad, C. D. *Five Types of Ethical Theory*. London: Routledge and Kegan Paul, 1930.

Broome, J. A. "Choice and Value in Economics", *Oxford Economic Papers*, Vol. 30, 1978, pp. 313-33.

Buchanan, J. "Is Economics the Science of Choice?" in J. Buchanan, *What Should Economists Do*? Indianapolis, Ind.: Liberty Press, 1970, pp. 39-63.

Caldwell, B. *Beyond Positivism: Economic Methodology in the Twentieth Century*. London: Allen and Unwin, 1982.

Carnap, R. "Testability and Meaning", *Philosophy of Science*, Vol. 3, 1936, pp. 419-71 and Vol. 4, 1937, pp. 2-40.

Churchland, P. M. *A Neurocomputational Perspective: The Nature of Mind and the Structure of Science*. Cambridge, Mass.: MIT Press, 1989.

Churchland, P. M. *The Engine of Reason, the Seat of the Soul: A Philosophical Journey into the Brain*. Cambridge, Mass.: MIT Press, 1995.

Cohen, A. J.; Hands, D. W.; Barnes, B.; Wise, M. N. "Review Symposium on Philip Mirowski's *More Heat than Light: Economics as Social Physics, Physics as Nature's Economics*", in *Philosophy of the Social Sciences*, Vol. 22, No. 1, March 1992, pp. 78-141.

Copi, I. M. *Symbolic Logic*, 5th edn. New York: Macmillan, 1979.

Daley, H. E. (ed.). *Economics, Ecology, Ethics:Essays Towards a Steady-State Economy*. San Francisco: W. H. Freeman, 1980.

Davidson, D., "Essays in Actions and Events" Oxford: Oxford University Press, 1980.

Davidson, D., "Actions, Reasons and Causes" in D. Davidson, *Essays on Actions and Events*. Oxford: Oxford University Press, 1980.

Davidson, D. "How is Weakness of the Will Possible?" in D. Davidson, *Essays on Actions and Events*. Oxford: Oxford University Press, 1980.

Davidson, D. "Deception and Division" in J. Elster (ed.). *The Multiple Self*. Cambridge: Cambridge University Press, 1985.

REFERENCES

Davidson, D., McKinsey, J.C.C. and P. Suppes. "Outline of a Formal Theory of Value", *Philosophy of Science*, Vol. 22, 1955, pp. 140-60.

de Finnetti, B. "Foresight: Its Logical Laws; Its Subjective Sources", in H. E. Kyburg, Jr. and H. E. Smokler, (eds.). *Studies in Subjective Probability*, 2nd edn. Huntington, N. J.: Krieger, 1980, pp. 53-118.

Debreu, G. *Theory of Value: An Axiomatic Analysis of Economic Equilibrium.* New Haven, Conn.: Yale University Press, 1959.

Downs, A. *An Economic Theory of Democracy.* New York: Harper and Row, 1957.

Dray, W. H. *Laws and Explanation in History.* Oxford: Oxford University Press, 1957.

Dugger,W. "Methodological Differences between Institutional and Neo-classical Economics", in *Journal of Economic Issues*, Vol. 12, 1979, pp. 899-909.

Duesenberry, J. S. *Income, Saving and the Theory of Consumer Behaviour.* Cambridge, Mass.: Harvard University Press, 1949.

Dyke, C. *The Philosophy of Economics.* Englewood Cliffs, N.J.: Prentice-Hall, 1981.

Dyke, C. "The Question of Interpretation in Economics", *Ratio*, Vol. XXV, 1983, pp. 15-29.

Easton, D. "Limits of the Equilibrium Model in Social Research", in *Chicago Behavioural Sciences Publications No. 1: Profits and Problems of Homeostatic Models in the Behavioural Sciences.* Chicago: University of Chicago Press, 1954.

Edgeworth, F. Y. *Mathematical Psychics* (1881). Reprint. London: London School of Economics and Political Science, 1932.

Ellis, A. "Rational-emotive therapy", in R. J. Corsini (ed.), *Current Psychotherapies*, 3rd edn. Itasa, Ill: Peacock Press, 1984, pp. 196-238.

Elster, J. *Ulysses and the Sirens: Studies in Rationality and Irrationality.* Cambridge: Cambridge University Press, 1979.

Elster, J. *Sour Grapes: Studies in the Subversion of Rationality.* Cambridge: Cambridge University Press, 1983.

Elster, J. (ed.). *The Multiple Self.* Cambridge: Cambridge University Press, 1985.

Elster, J. (ed.). *Rational Choice.* New York: New York University Press, 1986.

Elster, J. and Hylland, A. (eds.). *Foundations of Social Choice Theory.* Cambridge: Cambridge University Press, 1986.

Epictetus. *Moral Discourses and Fragments.* London: Dent, 1910.

REFERENCES

Etzioni, A. *The Moral Dimension: Towards a New Economics*. New York: Macmillan, 1988.

Falk, W. D. "Ought and Motivation", in W. D. Falk, *Ought, Reasons and Motivation*. Ithaca, N.Y.: Cornell University Press, 1986, pp. 21-41.

Feyerabend, P. "How to Be a Good Empiricist – a Plea for Tolerance in Matters Epistemological", in H. Morick (ed.), *Challenges to Empiricism*. Belmont, Cal.: Wadsworth, 1972.

Feyerabend, P. *Against Method*. London: New Left Books, 1975.

Fishkin, J. S. *The Limits of Obligation*. New Haven: Yale University Press, 1982.

Frankenna, W. "Obligation and Motivation in Recent Moral Philosophy", in A. I. Melden (ed.), *Essays in Moral Philosophy*. Seattle: University of Washington Press, 1958, pp. 40-81.

Friedman, M. "The Methodology of Positive Economics", in M. Friedman, *Essays in Positive Economics*. Chicago: University of Chicago Press, 1953, pp. 3-43.

Friedman, M. and Savage, L. J. "The Expected Utility Hypothesis and the Measurability of Utility", *Journal of Political Economy*, Vol. LX, Dec. 1952, pp. 463-72.

Galbraith, J. K. "A Review of a Review", *The Public Interest*, No. 12, 1967, pp. 109-18.

Galbraith, J. K. *The New Industrial State*, 3rd edn. Boston: Houghton Mifflin, 1978.

Galbraith, J. K. *The Affluent Society*, 4th edn. Boston: Houghton Mifflin, 1984.

Gauthier, D. *Moral Agreement*. Oxford: Oxford University Press, 1986.

Geach, P. "Good and Evil", *Analysis*, Vol. 17, 1956, pp. 33-42.

Georgescu-Roegen, N. *The Entropy Law and the Economic Process*. Cambridge, Mass.: Harvard University Press, 1971.

Georgescu-Roegen, N. "The Entropy Law and the Economic Problem", in H. E. Daly (ed.), *Economics, Ecology, Ethics: Essays Towards a Steady-State Economy*. San Francisco: W. H. Freeman, 1980, pp. 48-59.

Gibbard, A. "Interpersonal Comparison: preference, good, and the intrinsic reward of a life" in J. Elster and A. Hylland (eds.), *Foundations of Social Choice Theory*. Cambridge: Cambridge University Press, 1986, pp. 165-193.

Goodin, R. E. "Laundering Preferences" in J. Elster and A. Hylland (eds.), *Foundations of Social Choice Theory*. Cambridge: Cambridge University Press, 1986, pp. 75-101.

Gravelle, H. and R. Rees. *Microeconomics*. London: Longman, 1981.

REFERENCES

Green, H. A. J. *Consumer Theory*, rev. edn. London: Macmillan, 1976.

Grunbaum, A. "The falsifiability of a component of a theoretical system", in P. K. Feyerabend and G. Maxwell (eds.), *Mind, Matter and Method*. Minneapolis: University of Minnesota Press, 1966, pp. 273-305.

Habermas, J. "Towards a Theory of Communicative Competence", *Inquiry*, Vol. 13, 1970, pp. 360-75.

Hahn, F. "On some difficulties of the utilitarian economist", in A. Sen and B. Williams (eds.), *Utilitarianism and Beyond*. Cambridge: Cambridge University Press, 1982, pp. 187-98.

Hahn, F. *On the Notion of Equilibrium in Economics*. Cambridge: Cambridge University Press, 1973.

Hahn, F. and Hollis, M. (eds.). *Philosophy and Economic Theory*. Oxford: Oxford University Press, 1979.

Hare, R. M. *The Language of Morals*. Oxford: Oxford University Press, 1952.

Hare, R. M. "Geach: Good and Evil", *Analysis*, Vol. 18, 1957, pp. 102-12.

Hare, R. M. *Descriptivism*. London: Oxford University Press, 1963.

Hare, R. M. *Freedom and Reason*. Oxford: Oxford University Press, 1963.

Hare, R. M. *Moral Thinking: Its Levels Method, and Point*. Oxford: Oxford University Press, 1981.

Hargreaves Heap, S. *Rationality in Economics*. Oxford: Basil Blackwell, 1989.

Harsanyi, J. C. "Morality and the theory of rational behaviour", in A. K. Sen and B. Williams (eds.), *Utilitarianism and Beyond*. Cambridge: Cambridge University Press, 1982, pp. 39-62.

Hausman, D. M. (ed.). *The Philosophy of Economics: An Anthology*. Cambridge: Cambridge University Press, 1984.

Hausman, D. M. "Are general equilibrium theories explanatory?" in D. Hausman (ed.), *The Philosophy of Economics*. Cambridge: Cambridge University Press, 1984, pp. 344-59.

Hausman, D. M. "What are General Equilibrium Theories" in W. Sieg *Acting and Reflecting: The Interdisciplinary Turn in Philosophy*. Dordrecht: Kluwer, 1990, pp. 107-14.

Hausman, D. M. *The Inexact and Separate Science of Economics*. Cambridge: Cambridge University Press, 1992.

362

REFERENCES

Hausman, D. M. (ed.). *The Philosophy of Economics*, 2nd edn. Cambridge: Cambridge University Press, 1994.

Hausman, D. M. "Problems with Realism in Economics", *Economics & Philosophy*, Vol. 14, No. 2, 1998. pp. 185-213.

Hausman, D. M. and McPherson, M. S. "Taking Ethics Seriously: Economics and Contemporary Moral Philosophy", *Journal of Economic Literature*, Vol. XXXI, June, 1993, pp. 671-731.

Hausman, D. M. and McPherson, M. S. "Economics, Rationality, and Ethics". in Hausman, D. M. (ed.) *The Philosophy of Economics,* 2nd edn. Cambridge: Cambridge University Press, 1994, pp. 252-77.

Hausman, D. M. and McPherson, M. S. *Economic Analysis and Moral Philosophy.* Cambridge: Cambridge University Press, 1996.

Hayek, F. A. von *Individualism and Economic Order*. Chicago: University of Chicago Press, 1948.

Hayek, F. A. von *Studies in Philosophy, Politics and Economics.* London: Routledge and Kegan Paul, 1967.

Hayek, F. A. von *New Studies in Philosophy, Politics and the History of Ideas.* Chicago: University of Chicago Press, 1978.

Hempel, C. G. *Aspects of Scientific Explanation.* New York: Free Press, 1966.

Hempel, C. G. "Explanation in Science and History", in W. Dray, (ed.), *Philosophical Analysis and History.* New York: Harper and Row, 1966, pp. 95-126.

Hempel, C. G. "Typological Methods in the Natural and Social Sciences", in C. G. Hempel, *Aspects of Scientific Explanation*, pp. 155-71.

Hempel, C. G. "The Logic of Functional Analysis", in C. G.Hempel, *Aspects of Scientific Explanation*, pp. 297-330.

Hempel, C. G. "Studies in the Logic of Explanation" in *Aspects of Scientific Explanation,* pp. 245-90.

Hesse, M. "Duhem, Quine and a New Empiricism", in H. Morick, (ed.), *Challenges to Empiricism.* Belmont, Cal.: Wadsworth, 1972, pp. 208-28.

Hirshleifer, J. *Price Theory and Applications*. Englewood Cliffs, N.J.: Prentice-Hall, 1976.

Hollis, M. "Rational Man and Social Science", in R. Harrison (ed.), *Rational Action: Studies in Philosophy and Social Science.* Cambridge: Cambridge University Press, 1979, pp. 1-16.

REFERENCES

Hollis, M. "Rational Preferences", *Philosophical Forum*, Vol. 14, 1983, pp. 246-62.

Hollis, M. "The Emperor's Newest Clothes", in *Economics and Philosophy*, Vol. 1, April, 1985, pp. 128-33.

Hollis, M. *The Cunning of Reason*. Cambridge: Cambridge University Press, 1987.

Hollis, M. amd Nell, E. *Rational Economic Man: A Philosophical Critique of Neo-Classical Economics*. Cambridge: Cambridge University Press, 1975.

Hollis, M. and Lukes, S. (eds.). *Rationality and Relativism*. Oxford: Basil Blackwell, 1982.

Hume, D. *A Treatise of Human Nature* (1739-40), L. A. Selby-Briggs (ed.). Oxford: Oxford University Press, 1888.

Hutchison, T. W. *The Significance and Basic Postulates of Economic Theory* (1938). Reprint. New York: A. M. Kelley, 1960.

Hutchison, T. W. *Positive Economics and Policy Objectives*. London: Allen and Unwin, 1964.

Illich, Ivan. *Deschooling Society*. New York: Harper and Row, 1971.

Jeffrey, R. C. "Preferences among Preferences", *Journal of Philosophy*, Vol. 71, 1974, pp. 377-91.

Jevons, W. S. *Theory of Political Economy*, 4th edn. London: Macmillan, 1924 (1st edn. 1871).

Kahneman, D. and Tverksy, A. "Prospect Theory: an analysis of decisions under risk", *Econometrica*, Vol. 47, 1979, pp. 263-91.

Kant, I. *Critique of Pure Reason* (1787), trans. by N. K. Smith, London: Macmillan, 1929.

Kant, I. *Foundations of the Metaphysics of Morals* (1785), trans. by L. W. Beck. Indianapolis, Ind.: Bobbs-Merrill, 1959.

Kassaryian, H. H. and Robertson, T. S. (eds.). *Perspectives in Consumer Behaviour*. Glenview, Ill.: Scott, Foresman, 1968.

Klappholz, K. "Value Judgments and Economics*", The British Journal for the Philosophy of Science*, Vol. 15, 1964, pp. 97-114.

Klappholz, K. "Economics and Ethical Neutrality", in P. Edwards (ed.), *Encyclopedia of Philosophy*. New York: Macmillan, 1967, Vol. 2, pp. 451-54.

Klir, George J. *Facets of Systems Science*. New York: Plenum Press, 1991.

REFERENCES

Knight, F. H. *On the History and Method of Economics*. Chicago: University of Chicago Press, 1956.

Koopmans, T. J. *Three Essays on the State of Economic Knowledge*. New York: McGraw-Hill, 1957.

Korner, S. (ed.). *Practical Reason*. Oxford: Oxford University Press, 1974.

Kuhn, T. S. *The Structure of Scientific Revolutions*, 2nd edn. Chicago: University of Chicago Press, 1970.

Kyburg, H. E. and Smokler, H. J. (eds.). *Studies in Subjective Probability*, 2nd edn. Huntington, N.Y.: Krieger, 1980.

Lakatos, I. "Falsification and the Methodology of Scientific Research Programmes" in I. Lakatos and S. Musgrave (eds.), *Criticism and the Growth of Knowledge*. Cambridge: Cambridge University Press, 1970, pp. 91-196.

Lakatos, I. "History of Science and its Rational Reconstruction", in R. C. Buck and R. S. Cohen (eds.), *Boston Studies in the Philosophy of Science*, Vol. VIII. Dordrecht, Holland: D. Reidel, 1971, pp. 91-136.

Lancaster, K. "Welfare Propositions in Terms of Consistency and Expanded Choice", *The Economic Journal*, Vol. 68, Sept. 1958, pp. 464-79.

Lancaster, K. "Change and Innovation in the Technology of Consumption", *American Economic Review*, Vol. 56, No. 2, 1966, pp. 74-123.

Lancaster, K. "A New Approach to Consumer Theory", *Journal of Political Economy*, Vol. 74, no. 2, 1968, pp. 132-57.

Lange, O. "The Scope and Method of Economics", *Review of Economic Studies*, Vol. 13, 1945-46, pp. 19-32.

Lastis, S. (ed.). *Method and Appraisal in Economics*. Cambridge: Cambridge University Press, 1976.

Laszlo, E. *System, Structure and Experience*. New York: Gordon and Beach Science Publishers, 1969.

Lavoie, D. *National Economic Planning: What's left?* Cambridge, Mass.: Ballinger, 1985.

Leach, J. J. "Explanations and Value Neutrality", *British Journal for the Philosophy of Science*, Vol. 19, 1968, pp. 93-108.

Leftwich, R. *The Price System and Resource Allocation*, 3rd edn. New York: Holt, Rinehart and Winston, 1966.

REFERENCES

Leibniz, G. W. "Letter to Queen Charlotte of Prussia" (1702), in *Leibniz Selections*, P. P. Weiner (ed.). New York: Charles Scribner's Sons, 1951, pp. 355-67.

Levi, I. "Rationality Unbound", in W. Sieg (ed.), *Acting and Reflecting: The Interdisciplinary Turn in Philosophy*. Dordrect, The Netherlands: Kluwer Academic Publishers, 1990, pp. 211-221.

Lewis, C. I. *Mind and the World Order*. New York: Dover, 1929.

Lipsey, R. G. *An Introduction to Positive Economics*, 4th edn. London: Weidenfield and Nicholson, 1975.

Little, I. D. M. *A Critique of Welfare Economics*, 2nd edn. Oxford: Oxford University Press, 1957.

Loomes, G. and Sugden, R. "Regret Theory: An Alternative Theory of Rational Choice Under Uncertainty", *Economic Journal*, Vol. 92, 1982, pp. 805-24.

Louch, A. R. *Explanation and Human Understanding*. Oxford: Oxford University Press, 1966.

Machlup, F. "Equilibrium and Disequilibrium", in Machlup, F., *Essays in Economic Semantics*. Englewood Cliffs, N.J.: Prentice-Hall, 1963, pp. 43-72.

Mackie, J. *Ethics: Inventing Right and Wrong*. Harmondsworth, Eng.: Penguin Books, 1977.

Macklin, R. "Explanation and Action: Recent Issues and Controversies", *Synthese*, Vol. 20, 1969, pp. 388-415.

MacPherson, C. B. *The Political Theory of Possessive Individualism*. Oxford: Oxford University Press, 1962.

Mandel, E. *Marxist Economic Theory*, 2 vols., trans. by B. Pearce. New York: Monthly Review Press, 1968.

March, J. G. "Bounded Rationality, Ambiguity and The Engineering of Choice", in J. Elster (ed.), *Rational Choice*. New York: New York University Press, 1986, pp. 142-70.

Marcuse, H. *One Dimensional Man*. Boston: Beacon Press, 1964.

Margolis, J. *Philosophy of Psychology*. Englewood Cliffs, N.J.: Prentice-Hall, 1984.

Marshall, A. *Principles of Economics*, 9th Variorum edn. (1st edn. 1890), Vol. I. London: Macmillan, 1961.

Marx, K. *Grundrisse: Foundations of the Critique of Political Economy*, trans. by M. Nicolaus. Harmondsworth, Middlesex: Penguin Books, 1973.

REFERENCES

Maslow, A. H. *Motivation and Personality*, 2nd edn. New York: Harper and Row, 1970.

McCloskey, D. "The Rhetoric of Economics", *Journal of Economic Literature*, Vol. 21, No. 2, June, 1983, pp. 481-517.

McMurrin, S. (ed.). *Tanner Lectures on Human Values*. Cambridge: Cambridge University Press, 1981.

McPherson, M. S. "Want Formation, Morality and Some Interpretive Aspects of Economic Inquiry", in N. Hahn. R. H. Bellah, P. Rabinow and W. M. Sullivan (eds.), *Social Science as Moral Inquiry*. New York: Columbia University Press, 1983, pp. 96-124.

Melden, A. I. *Free Action*. London: Routledge and Kegan Paul, 1961.

Michalos, A. C. "Rationality Between the Maximizers and the Satisfiers", *Policy Sciences*, Vol. 4, 1973, pp. 229-44.

Michalos, A. C. *Foundations of Decision Making*. Ottawa: Canadian Library of Philosophy, 1978.

Mill, J. S. *Essays on Some Unsettled Questions of Political Economy* (1844). Reprint. London: London School of Economics, 1948.

Mill, J. S. *Principles of Political Economy*, 2 vols. 1st edn. London: J. W. Parker, 1848.

Mill, J. S. *On Liberty* (1859), Indianapolis, Ind: Hocketh, 1978.

Mill, J. S. *Utilitarianism* (1861). New York: Bobbs-Merrill, 1957.

Miller, H. B. and Williams, W. H. *The Limits of Utilitarianism*. Minneapolis: University of Minnesota Press, 1982.

Miller, J. G. "Introduction", in *Chicago Behavioural Sciences Publications No. 1: Profits and Problems of Homeostatic Models in the Behavioural Sciences*. Chicago: University of Chicago Press, 1954.

Mirowski, P. *Against Mechanism: Protecting Economics From Science*. Totawa, N.J.: Rowan and Littlefield, 1988.

Mirowski, P. *More Heat than Light: Economics as Social Physics, Physics as Nature's Economics*. Cambridge: Cambridge University Press, 1989.

Mirrlees, J. "The economic uses of utilitarianism", in A. Sen and B. Williams (eds.), *Utilitarianism and Beyond*. Cambridge: Cambridge University Press, 1982, pp. 63-84.

Mises, L. von. *Human Action: A Treatise on Economics*. New Haven: Yale University Press, 1949.

367

REFERENCES

Mises, L. von. *The Epistemological Problems of Economics*. Princeton, N.J.: Van Nostrand, 1960.

Mishan, E. J. *The Costs of Economic Growth*. London: Staples Press, 1967.

Mishan, E. J. "The Growth of Affluence and the Decline of Welfare", in H. E. Daley (ed.), *Economics, Ecology, Ethics: Essays Towards a Steady-State Economy*. San Francisco: W. H. Freeman, 1980, pp. 267-81.

Moore, G. E. *Principia Ethica*. Cambridge: Cambridge University Press, 1903.

Morick, H. (ed.). *Challenges to Empiricism*. Belmont, Cal.: Wadsworth, 1972.

Myrdal, G. *The Political Element in the Development of Economic Theory*, trans. by P. Streeten. London: Routledge and Kegan Paul, 1953.

Nagel, E. *The Structure of Science*. New York: Harcourt, Brace and World, 1961.

Nagel, T. *The Possibility of Altruism*. Oxford: Oxford University Press, 1970.

Neumann, J. von and Morgenstern, O. *Theories of Games and Economic Behaviour*, 2nd edn. Princeton, N.J.: Princeton University Press, 1947.

Newton, I. *Mathematical Principles of Natural Philosophy and His System of the World*, (1687), trans. by A. Motte; F. Cajori (ed.). Berkeley, California: University of California Press, 1960.

Pareto, V. *Cours d'Economie Politique*, 2 Vols. Lausanne: Rouge, 1896-97.

Paton, H. J. "The Alleged Independence of Goodness", in P. A. Schlipp (ed.), *The Philosophy of G. E. Moore*. La Salle, Ill.: Open Court, 1942, pp. 113-34.

Paul, E. F., Miller, F. D. Jr., and Paul, J. (eds.). *Ethics and Economics*. Oxford: Basil Blackwell, 1985.

Pears, D. "The Goals and Strategies of Self-Deception", in J. Elster (ed.), *The Multiple Self*. Cambridge: Cambridge University Press, 1985.

Peters, R. S. *The Concept of Motivation*, 2nd edn. London: Routledge and Kegan Paul, 1960.

Pikler, A. G. "Utility Theories in Field Physics and Mathematical Economics", I and II, *British Journal for the Philosophy of Science*, Vol. 5, 1954-55, pp. 47-58; 303-18

Popper, K. R. *The Logic of Scientific Discovery*. New York: Basic Books, 1959.

Quine, W. V. O. "Two Dogmas of Empiricism", in W. V. O. Quine, *From a Logical Point of View*, 2nd edn. Cambridge, Mass.: Harvard University Press, 1961, Ch. 2, pp. 20-46.

REFERENCES

Quine, W.V.O.. *Theories and Things*. Cambridge, Mass.: Harvard University Press, 1981.

Rescher, N. *Introduction to Value Theory*. Englewood Cliffs, N.J.: Prentice-Hall, 1969.

Resnick, M. D. *Choices: An Introduction to Decision Theory*. Minneapolis: University of Minnesota Press, 1987.

Riker, W. and Ordeshook, P.D. *An Introduction to Positive Political Theory*. Englewood Cliffs, N.J.: Prentice-Hall, 1973.

Robbins, L. *An Essay on the Nature and Significance of Economic Science*, 2nd edn. London: Macmillan, 1935.

Robbins, L. *The Evolution of Modern Economic Theory*. London: Macmillan, 1953.

Roll, E. *A History of Economic Thought*, 4th edn. London: Faber and Faber, 1973.

Rosenberg, A. *Microeconomic Laws: A Philosophical Analysis*. Pittsburgh: University of Pittsburgh Press, 1976.

Rosenberg, A. "Obstacles to Normological Connection of Reasons and Action", *Philosophy of Science*, Vol. 10, 1980, pp. 79-91.

Rosenberg, A. *Sociobiology and the Preemption of Social Science*. Oxford: Basil Blackwell, 1980.

Rosenberg, A. "If Economics is not a Science, What is it?" *Philosophical Forum*, Vol. 14, Summer 1983, pp. 296-314.

Rosenberg, A. "Prospects for the Elimination of Tastes from Economics and Ethics", in E. F. Paul, F. D. Miller and J. Paul (eds.), *Ethics and Economics*. Oxford: Basil Blackwell, 1985, pp. 48-68.

Rosenberg, A. *Economics–Mathematical Politics or Science of Diminishing Returns*. Chicago: University of Chicago Press, 1992.

Rothenberg, J. "Values and Value Theory in Economics", in S. R. Krupp (ed.), *The Structure of Economic Science*. Englewood Cliffs, N.J.: Prentice-Hall, 1966, pp. 221-42.

Rothschild, M. "Models of Market Organization with Imperfect Information: A Survey", *Journal of Political Economy*, Vol. 81, 1973, pp. 1283-308.

Roy, S. *The Philosophy of Economics: On the Scope of Reason in Economic Inquiry*. London: Routledge, 1989.

Rudner, R. *Philosophy of Social Science*. Englewood Cliffs, N.J.: Prentice-Hall, 1966.

Ryle, G. *The Concept of Mind*. London: Hutchison, 1949.

369

REFERENCES

Samuelson, P. "A Note of the Pure Theory of Consumer's Behaviour", *Economica*, Vol. 5, Feb. 1938, pp. 61-71.

Samuelson, P. *Foundations of Economic Analysis.* Cambridge, Mass.: Harvard University Press, 1947.

Savage, L. J. *The Foundations of Statistics* 2nd edn. New York: Dover, 1972.

Savage, L. J., Bartlett, M. *et al. The Foundations of Statistical Inference: A Discussion.* London: Methuen, 1962.

Schally, L. D. "Interdependent Utility Functions and Pareto Optimality", *Quarterly Journal of Economics*, Vol. 86, 1972, pp. 19-24.

Scheffler, I. *The Anatomy of Inquiry: Philosophical Studies in the Theory of Science.* New York: Alfred A. Knopf, 1967.

Schumpeter, J. *Ten Great Economists: From Marx to Keynes,* London: George Allen and Unwin, 1952.

Scitovsky, T. *The Joyless Economy.* Oxford: Oxford University Press, 1976.

Searle, J. *The Rediscovery of the Mind.* Cambridge, Mass: MIT Press, 1992.

Sellars, W. *Science, Perception and Reality.* London: Routledge and Keagan Paul, 1963.

Sellars, W. "Is there a Synthetic A Priori?" in W. Sellars, *Science, Perception and Reality.* London: Routledge and Kegan Paul, 1963, pp. 298-320.

Sellars, W. "Philosophy and the Scientific Image of Man", in W. Sellars, *Science, Perception and Reality.* London: Routledge and Kegan Paul, 1963, pp. 1-40.

Sellars, W. "Empiricism and the Philosophy of Mind" in W. Sellars, *Science, Perception and Reality.* London: Routledge and Kegan Paul, 1963.

Sellars, W. *Science and Metaphysics.* London: Routlege and Kegan Paul, 1968.

Sen, A. K. "Choice, Orderings and Morality", in S. Korner (ed.), *Practical Reason.* Oxford: Oxford University Press, 1974, pp. 54-67.

Sen, A. K. "Rational Fools: A Critique of the Behavioral Foundations of Economic Theory", *Philosophy and Public Affairs*, Vol. 6, Summer 1977, pp. 317-44.

Sen, A. K. "Utilitarianism and Welfarism", *Journal of Philosophy*, Vol. 76, 1979, pp. 463-89.

Sen, A. K. "Description as Choice", *Oxford Economic Papers*, Vol. 32, 1980, pp. 353-64.

Sen, A. K. "The Moral Standing of the Market", in E. F. Paul, F. D. Miller Jr. and J. Paul (eds.), *Ethics and Economics.* Oxford: Basil Blackwell, 1985, pp. 1-19.

REFERENCES

Sen, A. K. *On Ethics and Economics*. Oxford: Basil Blackwell, 1987.

Shackle, G. L. S. *A Scheme of Economic Theory*. Cambridge: Cambridge University Press, 1965.

Shoemaker, P. J. H. "The expected utility model: its variants, purposes, evidence, and limitations", *Journal of Economic Literature*, Vol. 20, 1982, pp. 529-63.

Sieg, W. (ed.). *Acting and Reflecting: The Interdisciplinary Turn in Philosophy*. Dordrecht, Holland: Kluwer Academic Publishers, 1990.

Simon, H. A. *Models of Man: Social and Rational*. New York: John Wiley and Sons, 1957.

Simon, H. A. "A Behavioural Model of Rational Choice", in H. A. Simon, *Models of Man: Social and Rational*. New York: John Wiley and Sons, 1957, Chap. 14, pp. 241-60.

Simon, H. A. "Rationality and Administrative Decision Making", in H. A. Simon, *Models of Man: Social and Rational*. New York: John Wiley and Sons, 1957, pp. 196-206.

Simon, H. A. "From Substantive to Procedural Rationality", in F. Hahn and M. Hollis (eds.), *Philosophy and Economic Theory*. Oxford: Oxford University Press, 1979, pp. 65-86.

Simon, H. A. "Progress in Philosophy", in W. Sieg (ed.), *Acting and Reflecting: the Interdisciplinary Turn in Philosophy*. Dordrect: Kluwer, 1990, pp. 57-62.

Simmons, P. J. *Choice and Demand*. London: Macmillan, 1974.

Skinner, B. F. *Science and Human Behaviour*. New York: Macmillan, 1953.

Smith, A. *An Inquiry into the Nature and Causes of the Wealth of Nations* (1776). New York: The Modern Library, 1937.

Spinoza, B. *Ethics* (1677), in B. Spinoza, *Ethics, Treatise on the Amendation of the Intellect and Selected Letters*, trans. by S. Shirley, ed. by S. Feldman. Indianapolis, Ind.: Hackett, 1992.

Stevenson, C. L. *Ethics and Language*. New Haven: Yale University Press, 1944.

Stevenson, C. L. "The Nature of Ethical Disagreement", *Sigma*, 1948, reprinted in P. W. Taylor (ed.), *The Problem of Moral Philosophy*, 2nd edn. Enrico, California: Dickenson, 1972, pp. 370-75.

Stevenson, C. L. "Relativism and Non-relativism in the Theory of Value", *Proceedings of the American Philosophical Association*, 1961-62, reprinted in P. W. Taylor

REFERENCES

(ed.), *The Problems of Moral Philosophy*, 2nd edn. Enrico, California: Dickenson, 1972, pp. 375-82.

Stigler, G. and Becker, G. "De gustibus non est disputandum", *American Economic Review*, Vol. 67, 1977, pp. 76-90.

Stigler, G. "Economics or Ethics?" in S. McMurrin, *Tanner Lectures on Human Values.* Cambridge: Cambridge University Press, 1981, pp. 143-91.

Sugden, R. "Why be Consistent? A Critical Analysis of Consistency Requirements in Choice Theory", *Economica*, Vol. 52, 1985, pp. 167-84.

Sugden, R. "Rational Choice: A Survey of Contributions from Economics and Philosophy", *The Economic Journal*, Vol. 101, July, 1991, pp. 751-85.

Taylor, C. *The Explanation of Behaviour.* London: Routledge and Kegan Paul, 1964.

Taylor, P. W. (ed.). *The Problems of Moral Philosophy*, 2nd edn. Enrico, California: Dickenson, 1972.

Toulmin, S. "Reasons and Causes", in R. Borger and F. Cioffi (eds.), *Explanation in the Behavioral Sciences.* Cambridge: Cambridge University Press, 1970, pp. 1-26.

Varian, H. *Microeconomic Analysis*, 3rd edn. New York: W. W. Norton, 1992.

Veblen, T. "Why is Economics not an Evolutionary Science?" (1898), in T. Veblen, *The Place of Science in Modern Civilization and Other Essays.* New York: Russell and Russell, 1961, pp. 56-81.

Walsh, V. and Gram, H. *Classical and Neo-Classical Theories of General Equilibrium: Historical Origins and Mathematical Structure.* Oxford: Oxford University Press, 1980.

Ward B. *What's Wrong with Economics?* New York: Basic Books, 1972.

Weber, M. *The Methodology of the Social Sciences*, ed. and trans. by E. A. Shills and H. A. Finch. New York: The Free Press, 1949.

Weber, M. *The Protestant Ethic and the Spirit of Capitalism*, trans. by T. Parsons. New York: Charles Scribner's Sons, 1958.

Weber, M. *General Economic History*, trans. by F. H. Knight. New York: Collier Books, 1961.

Weintraub, E. R. *General Equilibrium Analysis.* Cambridge: Cambridge University Press, 1985.

Weintraub, E. R. "Appraising Equilibrium Analysis", in *Economics and Philosophy*, Vol. l, No. l, 1985, pp. 23-37.

REFERENCES

Weisskopf, W. A. *Economics and Alienation*. New York: Dutton, 1971.

Williams, B. *Ethics and the Limits of Philosophy*. London: Williams and Collins, 1985.

Winch, P. *The Idea of a Social Science*. London: Routledge and Kegan Paul, 1958.

Winch, D. M. *Analytical Welfare Economics*. Middlesex: Penguin, 1971.

Wong, S. *The Foundations of Samuelson's Revealed Preference Theory*. London: Routledge and Kegan Paul, 1978.

Wright, G. H. von. *Norm and Obligation*. New York: The Humanities Press, 1963.

Wright, G. H. von. *Explanation and Understanding*. Ithaca, N.Y.: Cornell University Press, 1971.

INDEX

Action
  meaning, 27, 79-80, 126-27, 163
  action theory and economic theory, 17-25
  and reasons/causes, 119-31
Advertising, 56, 229-36
Akrasia, 233-34
Analyticity
  and causality, 120-31
  and explanatory arguments, 23-25, 164
  and explanatory laws, 15-25, 160-69, 197-99
Anand, P., 12, 312, 317, 324, 348, 357
Aristotle, 290, 293, 298, 354-55, 357
Arrow, K., 176, 190, 338, 339-40, 347, 357
Autonomy
  meaning, 224, 230-31, 259-60, 290-97
  and paternalism, 238-44
  and preferences, 231-44
Axioms
  as descriptive statements, 7-8, 11-12
  as not obtaining, 172-75
  as rules, 150-52
  of consumer choice theory, 7-8
Ayer, A.J., 279, 286, 290-91, 335, 351-52, 354, 357

Bales, R.E., 205-6, 336, 342, 357
Baudrillard, J., 231, 345, 357
Baumol, W.J., 31, 111-12, 155, 311-12, 317, 323, 331, 336, 358
Behaviourism
  ends and stimulus-response theory, 90-96
  explanatory limitations, 41-44

interpretation of economic terms, 38-40, 105-6, 109-11
  normative inadequacy, 44-48, 113-18
Belief
  and action explanation, 17-21, 198
  and akrasia, 235-36
  and probability judgments, 192-94
Bentham, J., 51, 81, 322, 325, 328, 358
Berlin, I., 240, 347, 358
Bertalanffy, L. von, 103, 330, 358
Blaug, M., 136, 317-19, 324, 331, 333, 358
Boulding, K., 51, 116, 322, 330-31, 358
Broad, C.D., 89, 90-91, 94, 329, 359

Calculatedness
  and transitivity, 59-63
  as moral ideal, 68-78, 266
Carnap, R., 14, 313, 359
Causes
  meaning, 122-23, 142
  and action, 122-31
  and empirical laws, 120, 142
  and explanation, 119-22
  and reasons, 89, 119-35
Ceteris Paribus Conditions, 35, 123, 163, 272
Choice
  meaning, 38, 41-42, 46, 99
  consumer choice theory:
    under certainty conditions, 6-9
    under uncertainty conditions, 32, 191-99
Comparability (Completeness)
  axiom of, 7, 150, 172, 187
Competition. See Market
Completeness. See Comparability

INDEX

Friedman, M., 22, 32, 169, 315, 317, 327, 337, 347, 361

Functionalism
and value-judgments, 97-102
interpretation of choice theory, 102-3
see also Explanation; Systems Theory

Galbraith, J.K., 229, 345, 361
Gauthier, D., 177, 338, 361
Growth
-ethic, 54-56, 248-49, 266-67
in production, 56, 181, 183, 227, 229, 231

Hahn, F., 190, 312, 328, 336, 338-41, 347, 357, 362, 371
Hare, R.M., 143-44, 277-78, 280-82, 290-93, 330, 334, 345, 352, 354, 362
Hargreaves Heap, S., 257-59, 322, 326, 338, 343, 349, 353, 362
Harsanyi, J.C., 239-40, 341, 346, 355, 362
Hausman, D., 312, 315, 318, 320, 322, 338, 340, 351, 362-63
Hayek, F.A. von, 219-23, 228, 232, 343-44, 358, 363
Hedonism
ethical, 47, 87-90
psychological, 47, 87-96, 112-13, 154
Hempel, C.G., 209, 311-12, 314, 330, 335, 337, 342, 350, 363
Historical
background to utility theory, 80-90, 153-56
conditions for scientific laws, 138-40
Holism
of scientific theory, 187-90

Hollis, M., 320-22, 326, 336, 339, 341, 346-47, 357, 362-64
Hume, D., 125, 129, 143, 146, 149, 154, 215, 284-86, 288, 291, 293-96, 299, 353-54, 364
Hutchison, T.W., 16, 22, 25, 313, 315-16, 318, 350-51, 364

Idealization
affective, 158-60
and satisficing, 199-210
and scientific utopias, 262-64, 268-72
and verification, 9-15
cognitive, 10, 157-60, 218-19
in choice theory, 10, 11, 35-36
in natural science, 10, 11
normative, 160-65, 169-71, 262-63
under uncertainty, 191-96, 198-99
Imperatives
categorical (moral), 3, 49, 53-54, 71-78, 151-56, 264
hypothetical (prudential,instrumental), 1, 49, 60-69, 70, 151-52, 263-64
see also Norms
Individualism
epistemic, 4, 226, 228-30, 232-33, 235-36, 238, 289-90
normative, 54, 225-26, 231-33, 238, 255, 289
possessive, 54, 78
Information
and product complexity, 227-31
direction, 223, 228-30
disemination in price system, 219-22
distorted, 234-36
Institutions
and moral ends, 254-56

INDEX

Studies in Economic Ethics and Philosophy

Studies in Economic Ethics and Philosophy

J. Kuçuradi (Ed.)
The Ethics of the Professions:
Medicine, Business, Media, Law
X, 172 pages. 1999
ISBN 3-540-65726-6

S. K. Chakraborty and S. R. Chatterjee
(Eds.)
Applied Ethics in Management
Towards New Perspectives
X, 298 pages. 1999
ISBN 3-540-65726-6

P. Koslowski (Ed.)
The Theory of Capitalism in the Ger-
man
Economic Tradition Historism, Ordo-
Liberalism, Critical Theory,
Solidarism
XII, 577 pages. 2000
ISBN 3-540-66674-5

P. Koslowski (Ed.)
Contemporary Economic Ethics
and Business Ethics
IX, 265 pages. 2000
ISBN 3-540-66665-6

L. Sacconi
The Social Contract of the Firm
Economics, Ethics and Organisation
XV, 229 pages. 2000
ISBN 3-540-67219-2

M. Casson and A. Godley (Eds.)
Cultural Factors in Economic Growth
VIII, 244 pages. 2001
ISBN 3-540-66293-6

Y. Shionoya and K. Yagi (Eds.)
Competition, Trust, and Cooperation
IX, 252 pages. 2001
ISBN 3-540-67870-0